REVELATION;

ITS NATURE AND RECORD.

BY

HEINRICH EWALD,

LATE PROFESSOR IN THE UNIVERSITY OF GÖTTINGEN; AUTHOR OF "THE HISTORY OF ISRAEL," "PROPHETS OF THE OLD TESTAMENT," ETC.

Translated from the German

BY THE

REV. THOMAS GOADBY, B.A.,

PRESIDENT OF THE BAPTIST COLLEGE, NOTTINGHAM.

Wipf & Stock
PUBLISHERS
Eugene, Oregon

Wipf and Stock Publishers
199 West 8th Avenue, Suite 3
Eugene, Oregon 97401

Revelation
Its Nature and Record
By Ewald, Heinrich
ISBN: 1-59244-694-9
Publication date 5/19/2004
Previously published by T&T Clark, 1884

TRANSLATOR'S PREFACE.

THIS first volume of Ewald's great and important work, *Die Lehre der Bibel von Gott*, is offered to the English public as an attempt to read Revelation, Religion, and Scripture in the light of universal history and the common experience of man, and with constant reference to all the great religious systems of the world. The task is as bold and arduous as it is timely and necessary, and Ewald was well fitted to accomplish it. Oriental literature, the Biblical languages, the history of Israel and its relation to contemporary history, the exegesis of the prophetic, evangelical, and apostolic records of Scripture were the study and occupation of his long and laborious life. His mind, of singular penetration and grasp, and of wonderful breadth and spiritual insight, never lost its vigour even in his old age. If, in his spirit and temper, Ewald had more of the fervour of the prophet than of the calmness of the philosopher, and in his style less of lucid brevity than of diffuse though magnificent eloquence, his fault is more than condoned by the lofty moral earnestness of his faith and the poetic glow of his massive periods.

In the present state of religious thought in England and America, the conceptions of a powerful, independent, and original mind, whose reverent study of Holy Scripture has greatly advanced the science of Biblical criticism, cannot but be regarded as of unusual importance. The more complete the freedom from the traditions of the Church, the more likely will it be that truth will be seen in some new fresh light, and the more valuable will be the contribution afforded to the readjustment of our beliefs. This is exactly the position and this is exactly the merit of Ewald's work. Its author stood almost alone among those who, on the one hand, were guided mainly by Ecclesiastical Confessions, and who, on the other, followed the changing light of an inadequate and frigid Rationalism. He adhered to the conceptions of Revelation and Holy Scripture, but he placed both upon a scientific basis; he opposed Rationalism, but he gave to his opposition a validity and strength which even Rationalists cannot refuse to respect. His doctrinal system is imperfect, and falls short of the fulness devout faith demands, but it harmonizes with the philosophical and scientific tendencies of our time, and saves some of the main positions of Evangelicalism which the experience of centuries has verified. Conscientious conviction, especially on such subjects as the doctrine of the Holy Spirit, may carry us to conclusions beyond those which Ewald states; but it will be a great gain to modern religious thought if, working upon the lines which Ewald lays down, it is carried by the methods of historical and critical inquiry as far as Ewald ventures. The principles which run through this work are precisely similar to the principles which modern science accepts. Everything rests upon the basis of fact, and is ultimately subjected to the test of experience. Revelation is treated as a great historical process, a development, an evolution, and the consummation which Christ brings is shown to be the result and issue of all that had previously arisen. The history of Israel is regarded as informed by one predominant purpose, working out one great issue; and its culmination in Christianity is for the enrichment and salvation of the world. The work has therefore not simply a theological, but a high and significant apologetic value, which those who are called upon to deal with the various forms of modern scepticism will not be slow to recognise. The age that is disposed to accept the "Origin of Species," as if not the last word of physical science, at least the new starting-point to its ultimate consummation, may well be asked to ponder with thought and care the principles of historic evolution, of unconscious spiritual selection, of survival of the fittest, conspicuously illustrated and exemplified in Ewald's discussion of the nature and progress, the conflicts and triumphs of Revelation, Religion, and Scripture.

It is needless perhaps to add that, while commending this volume to the notice of all students of theology and Holy Scripture, neither the publishers nor the translator wish to be identified with the peculiar doctrinal views of our author. In a subsequent volume, consisting of selected chapters from the theology of Ewald, which it is proposed to publish as soon as practicable, some of these peculiar views may be presented and explained more at large. Meanwhile, the present volume is issued as another proof, as Professor Dillmann says, of Ewald's profound, original, and penetrating mind, reverent and childlike spirit, nervous thought, eloquent inspired style, and unsurpassed masterly skill in disclosing the innermost thoughts and feelings of antiquity.

The translator gratefully acknowledges the ready kindness and courtesy of the widow of the late learned Professor, in placing at his disposal pamphlets and manuscripts helpful in the better understanding of Ewald's theological position; and also the generous and friendly aid of the Rev. J. F. Smith in interpreting this confessedly difficult author.

NOTTINGHAM, 1884.

CONTENTS.

---o---

	PAGE
INTRODUCTORY. THE DOCTRINE OF THE WORD OF GOD,	1

PART I.

THE NATURE OF THE REVELATION OF THE WORD OF GOD.

	PAGE
I. Revelation and Religion,	7
1. Revelation,	7
2. The Fear of God, or Religion,	29
3. Reciprocal Influence of Religion and Revelation,	37
II. The Stages of Revelation,	42
1. The Revelation of the Individual,	42
2. The Revelation of the Prophets,	47
3. The Revelation of Moses,	77
4. The Revelation of Christ,	106
5. The Consummation of all Revelation,	118
Special Characteristics of the Consummation of all Revelation,	136
III. The Results of Revelation,	139
1. The Higher Community among Men,	140
2. The Priesthood,	148
3. The Spiritualization of Humanity and its Aims,	150

PART II.

REVELATION IN HEATHENISM AND IN ISRAEL.

	PAGE
I. The Founding of a True Community of God,	155
1. The Origin and changing Feeling of its Need,	157
2. The Imperfect Satisfaction of the Need,	165
3. Its Perfect Satisfaction,	182
II. The Conflict against all Degeneracy of Revelation,	193
The Opposition of Heathenism and True Religion,	193
1. In General,	193
2. Specially,	210
In the First Period,	215
In the Second Period,	223
In the Third Period,	240
3. The Final Victory in this Conflict,	251
Special Characteristics of the Opposition to Heathenism,	265

x   CONTENTS.

		PAGE
III.	The Rise of the Power of the Holy Spirit,	270
	1. Its Significance and Possibility,	270
	2. Its Realization,	276
	3. The Holy Nation,	283

PART III.

REVELATION IN THE BIBLE.

			PAGE
I.	1.	What preceded all Holy Scripture,	303
	2.	The General Relation of Literature to the National Life,	306
	3.	Natural Simplicity and Artificiality in Literature,	318
	4.	The Advantages and Deficiencies of all Literature,	330
II.	5.	The Rise of Holy Scripture,	339
	6.	The Settlement and Limitation of the Canon,	352
	7.	The Ante-Canonical and Post-Canonical Position of the Sacred Books,	367
	8.	The Sacredness of the Bible neither arbitrarily determined nor arbitrarily determinable,	375
III.	9.	The Nature of the actual Sacredness of the Bible,	390
	10.	The further Significance of the Bible and its Sacredness,	399
	11.	The Sacredness of the Bible in its Manifoldness and its Unity,	420
	12.	Conclusion. Comparison with other Sacred Books,	432
IV.	13.	Consequences. Growing Value of the Bible,	436
	14.	The proper Use of the Bible,	443
V.	15.	The Way through the Bible to Revelation and Religion,	464

Index of Subjects, ... 467
Index of Scripture References, ... 479

REVELATION; ITS NATURE AND RECORD.

INTRODUCTORY.

THE DOCTRINE OF THE WORD OF GOD.

§ 8. IT is not the Bible only and the true religion taught by it that knows something of a revelation of divine words for man; all historical religions without exception proceed from such a basis. Islamism, as a perverse mixture of Christianity and Judaism, may be omitted; but all the rest, whether fully or as good as fully independent of the Bible, have sought superhuman words or in their place divine hints and tokens, and have estimated above everything, where it was thought they were possessed, divine words, commands, and laws.

It is not then the word of God in itself, or even the fulness of such words, nor their being revealed, by which true religion, as the Bible requires it, is distinguished. Comparison of everything of a similar nature outside the Bible with what is contained in it is however essential; (*a*) to assure us from every kind of religion, even the lowest, how necessary the revealing of divine words is for man; (*b*) to enable us the more surely to understand the biblical revelation, from the nature of all others; (*c*) to show whether and how far the word of God as the Bible presents it, as well in its first activity and manifestation as in its distinct revelations and their subsequent issues, itself actually excels all others in its ways of procedure and results.

The Bible speaks throughout of two high divine powers which mediate between God and the universe, and especially humanity, viz. the Spirit of God and the Word of God. They are equal, harmonious, lead the one to the other, or wait the favourable moment when they can both work together. The Spirit vivifies, energizes; the word determines and decides; the Spirit gives the possibility of life to creation, the word determines how the same is to shape itself in detail from first to last; the Spirit empowers to right conduct and action, the word brings definite divine thoughts and determinations of will; the Spirit underlies life, the word directs it.

Hence the Spirit of God is not said to reveal or manifest itself; it is recognizable only by its effects. The word is, however, itself the revelation of the hidden thought. But God, with His thought, mind, and will, is especially hidden and deep for man. The word of God must be revealed to man if he is to perceive and know it. With creation the thought of God comes into the light of day. The Bible, after mentioning the preparatory work of the Spirit of God, begins with "God said," and in the course of human events often repeats it. To know the divine thought, *i.e.* the divine truth of anything, is to know the word of God concerning it. In this widest and deepest sense the Bible everywhere teaches that the word of God can be known.

But the word of God has a special signification for man; it reveals that will of God in conformity with which man is to live and act. The knowledge of God's nature and why He reveals His will to man in this or that way is given along with the revelation of the word of God in this special sense. Two things are presupposed;—the existence and efficient working of a true God; and the capacity in man to ascertain whether a revelation of divine words is actually from God or not. These will be subsequently discussed; our only presupposition here is, according to the feeling and faith of antiquity in which the conception of the word of God firmly developed itself, the following:—

§ 9. " God stands over against man invisible and obscure, inarticulate and mute ; only in moments of terrible danger and with fear and trembling may He with difficulty be beheld or heard, found or felt. To perceive a clear voice from Him, a direction for the life, is the purest happiness and good fortune. The darkness, the silence, the remoteness from God become the greater and the more cheerless, the longer man remains confronting Him without beholding a light or hearing a voice." Such feelings and experiences peculiar to antiquity have not yet wholly passed away.

In contradistinction to this the Bible is full of the word of God, shows it not as a possibility but a realized fact, publishes it, rejoices in its truth. In the Old Testament we see the pure Divine Ego face to face with man, revealing who it is who speaks and what He commands. In the New, Christ appears as Himself the Word of God, in human form bringing that word as near as possible to man, but without contradicting, rather presupposing the truth of the word of the Old Testament.

§ 10. But difficulties meet us on the threshold of our inquiry. Since we ever think of human word and speech under the terms word and speech, and we know that God is not man—

(*a*) How can the word of God, in the biblical sense of the term, be revealed, and how has it in reality been revealed ?

(*b*) Why in antiquity and perfected in the highest conceivable form only in one nation, Israel ?

(*c*) Wherefore handed down in Holy Scripture and to be derived only from it ?

(*d*) Withdrawn as it is from all our present conditions, feelings, and knowledge in its rise and development, how is it by us to be found again, and how applied for our salvation, in the restricted and limited form of a dead multitude of books of a foreign tongue ?

These difficulties tower on high and bar the way to the sanctuary where lies the costly treasure of living eternal truths. But they admit of solution; the remote, the unintelligible and strange may become near, familiar and loved, so that we would not wish it otherwise than it is. If dust and ashes are thrown upon these questions, and if some in our day will not hear of divine revelations and doctrines, the more ready must we be to elucidate them in their high importance and for us fully indispensable truth. And since the matter concerns obscure and strange phenomena, we must not proceed as in a short course from above downwards, but rather approach our subject step by step.

PART I.

THE NATURE OF THE REVELATION OF THE WORD OF GOD.

§ 11. THERE is an immediate and a mediate revelation of God corresponding to the broader or narrower sense of the term, Word of God. The immedate revelation is without a perfectly clear and sufficiently sure word. It may become a full living word, for a determinate thought and truth of God is in it, but it lacks expression by the clear light of discourse. It is of three kinds :—

1. The original revelation of God given with the human spirit in creation. This involves the close connection and reciprocity of the divine and human spirit, and nothing can compare with it in glory and wondrousness. It is a faculty or inner power of man; it has creative force, and a special history. It is called "the Spirit of God in man," "spirit," "the inner light," "the lamp" in the dark depths of man, "which God Himself holds in His hand," and in the later parts of the Bible, "conscience." But however glorious it is, and however wonderful its influence, and whatever variety of strength, clearness, efficiency it shows in different men, it is not one and the same with the word of God of which we specially speak. It is the indispensable beginning for revelation, a laboratory in which the divine word prepares and makes effective its utterance, a haven in which it collects itself, a light by which it is recognised and attested, but not the word of revelation itself, and sharply to be distinguished from it.

2. The creation itself as it stands in its eternal glory and perfection before the gaze of man's spirit. The more God is otherwise known, the more this whole infinite visible creation

declares His invisible glory and reveals His hidden nature and will (Ps. xix.).

3. The whole history of the human race. To the mind prepared for divine instruction, the painful or joyous experiences of men in the world's great history, teach divine truths of eternal significance and perpetual freshness and force. Israel was to remember, and was often reminded, of its past history, revealing as it did God's saving grace: by types of the old covenant our Lord showed the meaning of His sufferings and death; and youthful Christianity beheld in Christ the fulfilment and realization of all that earlier generations anticipated and desired. But human history with its mighty pulsations revealing God's will to the mind prepared to receive it, is not expressed in words, and is wholly dark or dumb the less is known otherwise of the true God.

§ 12. These forms of immediate revelation are taken up and perfected in the mediate revelation, the word of God; for all revelation, so far as it is genuine and necessary, is ultimately in agreement with itself. But mediate revelation is that alone which deserves the name "Revelation" in the fullest sense, and is so designated in the Bible.[1] Mediate revelation expresses itself in intelligible and distinct words. Since word and speech presuppose thoughts and propositions, and these are intelligible to man only by human language, the word of God, as the Bible contains it, is understood to be such sentences and discourse as express indeed what God demands of man, and how He reveals Himself to us in His true nature, but all mediated through human language. That the word of God comes to us through human discourse is assumed in the Bible as self-evident, and is characteristic of revelation. Hence it is seen, revelation is an historical incident or has come to man only in the course of human history. And just this is its purest and eternal excellence,

---

[1] 1 Sam. iii. 7; Isa. xxii. 4; Dan. x. 1. In New Testament often with ἀποκαλύπτεσθαι.

viz. that it presents to men clear thoughts, words, and sentences that have already passed through the mind and been articulated in the language of its human mediators, expressing and explaining both how man should act in harmony with God's will, and the ultimate ground of it—who the true God in His essential being is.

But revelation mediated by human words is to be distinguished also from that given on rare occasions, and represented as coming from heaven in spoken words. The ten commandments were so pronounced; heavenly voices attended the most conspicuous events of Christ's earthly history; these are exceptional. Moreover voices from below or from the mouth of a beast are known, but epistles or manuscripts falling from heaven are extravagant suppositions foreign to the whole of the Bible.

Revelation mediated through clear human discourse is the revelation of the word of God we are now to consider, and upon the path of revelation true religion follows and then inseparably attends it.

I.—REVELATION AND RELIGION.

1. *Revelation.*

§ 13. Revelation has its peculiar contents; in other words, its own proper subject and province. It expresses what is the will of God to men, whether in a given case or in general; how in conformity with true godliness human conduct is to shape itself; and if it speaks of the nature of God and His relation to men, it is only to declare the more convincingly how men should live and act in accordance therewith.

Within this special province of religious life and conduct, revelation supplies what is not otherwise known nor derived from another source. It is original, creative, flowing freshly as living water from a spring.

It differs from *poetry*, which it resembles as a seizure

by an overmastering thought with which it remains in its immediateness, in that poetry as a mood of mind yields to and obeys every subject of thought, but revelation concerns only a limited province of thought and a special feeling of need. It differs from *science* which investigates, and demonstrates from their own peculiar nature, the reasons, the connection, the worth and uses of all things, in that it has a definite domain, a limited content and an immediateness in its thought coming from above as command for man and maintaining itself in this higher tendency. It differs from *doctrine*, which it may nevertheless become, in that it does not arrange a content already given or established, reproduce it correctly and elucidate it, but produces what is original and creative.

§ 14. As with everything creative, revelation has an activity wholly peculiar to itself, and a corresponding active facultative cause from which it flows as from a living spring. Misunderstandings and errors as to whence revelation originates arise from not going far enough to the source of its activity, or from going beyond it.

1. The well-spring of revelation is not the original faculty in man whereby he knows God, which we designate the original revelation given in the spirit of man in creation. This faculty is a gift of God in all men equally and something quiescent; it is not yet activity, least of all that activity of which we are in quest; it is as mere spirit not word as yet; and historically it may fall into error in its outlook toward God and even raise itself proudly against Him; can it, then, be one and the same with the revelation of the word of God, or itself this word of God? Nevertheless this original faculty, the highest immediate revelation, is the ground and basis without which and apart from which mediate revelation cannot occur.

The active facultative cause of mediate revelation may be designated one of the many capacities of the human spirit, but it is not to be confounded with any other of them. For mediate revelation excites to activity the whole mind of man as nothing else does, but has its own peculiar contents. It is not to be traced back to reason or put on a level with it. Reason perceives and knows thoughts and things, suffers them not to be unobserved in their own nature, surveys and masters them intellectually; just as understanding apprehends them not incorrectly in detail; and reason may err in details, especially when understanding is wanting to it, and may become vain and suppose it gains the mastery of what is yet beyond its power of adjustment.

2. Conscience is not the invisible ground and flowing spring of revelation. To seek the faculty of mediate revelation here is not as in the former case to seek it where it is not found at all, but to seek it where only its after-effects are active. Conscience is the power of the aroused moral self-consciousness; it is one of the original powers of the human spirit, but it is not like reason and understanding, a way-breaking faculty; nor is it creative like the capacity of which we are in quest; it is rather a preserving and restraining, not a producing activity, and in connection with revelation it is a subordinate or by-faculty, not the chief faculty itself. It needs, as determinate contents and material, the certain and undeniable, by which it is moved to stand firm, and according to which its judgment is given. It varies in its activity with the clearness of insight and the nobleness of motive. It wins the greatest significance where revelation has replenished the mind with truths dearer than all outward good. It is most sensitive and tender, most enlightened, most powerfully resistent, and most victorious in conflict where it has appropriated most completely the highest truths revelation furnishes.[1]

§ 15. To find the true and proper activity and faculty of

[1] It is thus not accidental that the word "conscience" does not occur in the Old Testament earlier than Eccles. x. 20; in the Apocrypha nowhere but in Wisd. of Sol. xvii. 11, and 2 and 3 Macc.; in the New Testament is found only in Paul's Epistles; not at all in the Gospels, John viii. 9 not being the Evangelist's. But in Hebrew the simple word לֵב was used with the same meaning as "heart".

the human spirit, of which we are in search, that we may understand in what way it must be moved in order to attain to revelation, the following preliminary considerations may be best:—

In the human mind, of wonderful nature, there lie, as if compactly enfolded within it, all the hardly numerable special capacities which, on closer contemplation of the apparent infinitude of the impulses, movements, and acts of the intellectual life of mankind, we distinguish from each other. Not one of them in reality can be fully separated from all the others, the whole mind being in high efforts and struggles, put in requisition; only inasmuch as in accordance with the limitation and divisibility of all human endeavours and works, every intellectual movement of man shapes itself differently as to time and person, the different capacities always become conspicuous as the mind is in such or such a mood, and turned in this or that direction. With these possible diversities clearly in view, we must distinguish further—

1. There are capacities of the human mind which, with respect to all intellectual action, we may designate way-making capacities, such as understanding, reason, judgment, and the yet obscure feeling preceding their exercise or still remaining when they are insufficient. Nothing affects the human mind but these spontaneously appear.—Other capacities, like memory and conscience, if they are to become active and fruitful, require a greater fulness of contents which must be previously given to them, and also, as applied with perseverance and discipline to wholly special human needs and endeavours, unite one with another or with several others, and so become wholly new capacities, which again arise only historically and are not to be confounded with the purely original. Thus, no man could become a poet if there

---

is in modern languages; although Hebrew was furnished early with expressions for intellectual and spiritual phenomena. [Ewald further says that *das Gewissen* needs *das gewisse;* and מַדָּע in Eccles. x. 20, LXX. συνίδησις is only equivalent to "consciousness."]

did not lie in the human mind a poetic capacity; this too is not possible without the original faculty of imagination, and moreover it does not arise from this alone, but is formed only by closest union and co-operation with other similar original faculties of the human mind, and only in a special mood and excitement of the mind. So indeed the possibility of science presupposes in him who seeks to work in it creatively a corresponding scientific capacity, which however does not consist merely in understanding, reason, and judgment. And as neither the scientific nor the poetic are simple faculties of the human mind, so they appear at least in any deeper activity only as genuine historical powers, the scientific later than the poetic; thence also, in individuals differently developed at different times and places, as everything historical at once enters into the infinitude of individual phenomena and culture.

2. These capacities that arise only with history show great diversity in their activity when they once develop, or indeed have already in many ways further developed, their active energies. The simple capacities work in all times and in all men so uniformly that nothing but the rare exception is matter of surprise; but here, as with everything historical, enters almost unlimited manifoldness and diversity. This special conjoint working of two or three of the human capacities, so different in themselves, may occur in some particular men in a higher degree than in others; through special incitements it may, in some particular periods of time, be more strongly aroused than in others, and be more steadily maintained at a fixed high pressure; and in happy moments it may pass from the mind of the one or the few in whom it has been strongly called into action, and stir and influence the minds of many others with increased fervour and force. All this lies from the first in the alternatives of historic possibilities. We know, for example, that the poetic art is active at all times among all nations; but how rare are the occasions when really great poets arise, and how little is it the case that

their most splendid creations are uniformly valued and esteemed at all times and among all nations!

3. Two consequences of the most weighty significance follow. The first is that (*a*) each of such special historic capacities may furnish as its fruits truths and doctrines of its kind which may serve, when once they have entered into the day and the light of human history, for light and leading to innumerable other minds. What a great poet or scientific thinker or artist has created with more or less of perfection, may be a joy and satisfaction, or a model and inspiration to the end of time. The intellectual fellowship which for ever exists among men, makes such fruits of genius, even amid all the changes of human destiny and all the desolations of time, with difficulty or not at all destructible. The other consequence is that (*b*) each of such capacities may for its special activity make a corresponding way or create an impetus which shall enable others to repeat this activity continually for similar ends; and whilst this living repetition becomes even easier, the first effort and labour, of enormous difficulty, through which only the way became possible, may gradually pass into oblivion. The beautiful forms which poetry has created for its own purposes remain for endless repetition, even if their first creators with their creative pains have long since passed away; and the paths by which new scientific truths and doctrines are discovered, when once made, stand open to the easier steps of subsequent times. Indeed, it may ultimately be found that the later workers scarcely comprehend at all by what pains and under what actual circumstances the way was broken at first, and they may even use ungratefully what they ought to feel lays them under continual and most thankful obligation.

§ 16. Revelation belonging, then, in its activity to this last-named circle of human capacities, it must have a historical basis. The same conclusion has already been reached from very evident premises involving its mediation by human language. But to discover this historical basis, to trace the way in which revelation became a historical power and arrived at its highest development, is far more difficult than to trace back poetry and science to their source, because revelation goes back to the very earliest ages of the world. Indeed, the period of the first origin of revelation presupposes other periods and conditions of the human race as such, which must have preceded. Who can to-day, or could in the remotest antiquity known to us, definitely determine when revelation arose and became a historical power? In the scattered reminiscences of its oldest history every nation knows something of presages and the power of divine oracles. All antiquity known to us by literature, lived under the influence of the feeling that mankind without the knowledge of God and His word is inconceivable. It is of consequence, therefore, that we inquire into periods and conditions of human development which can now be recognised more particularly by the few great indestructible results and products of spiritual endeavour, and on the other hand by the ever similar nature of every human and of the divine mind. The inquiry may be difficult, but it is necessary, since for many reasons it is urgently desirable to find the true beginning and ultimate impelling force of a movement so incomparably unique, in order then to follow it upon the perhaps long way in which only everything historical becomes rightly productive of result.

1. It must in the outset be noted that the human mind in its very creation is imprisoned as in a darkness out of which only by efforts and endeavour it raises itself. Imprisoned in the sensuous body, stretching forth the senses as feelers, it does not yet KNOW, which alone distinguishes man from beast, but in FEELING it finds an obscure and easily misleading beginning and incitement to knowledge. Buried in the feeble, limited individual body, essentially the same in all men, yet exposed to the accidents that beset the individual, it is easily excited and aroused, and must indeed be first instigated from without in order to acquire more definite direction of its

activity, and to develop all its powers. Incited by impressions, desires, and inclinations, it struggles with great force outwards, and cannot succeed to its own true satisfaction with proper enjoyment and gain if it does not learn at the same time constantly and calmly to gather itself up into itself with all its different capacities and endeavours. So is it still with the child; so is it to some extent even with the full-grown and highly cultured man; so must it have been, only with an incomparably more protracted unreadiness, yet even purer susceptibility, with the man of primeval times.

Every more violent incitement from without must have been to the primitive man an advantage, even a beneficence, for it summoned from their depths the hidden capacities of his mind and set them at work. But all the experiences and incitements of the mind from without were the more powerful and impressive, the more freshly and susceptibly man stood face to face with the varied changing universe around him, and the less he knew of the deeper laws of creation. Every severely-felt bodily want, every newly-experienced need of life, roused most powerfully his slumbering capacities that it might be supplied; but he would soon feel that he had not with this supply attained everything he desired. The misfortunes, defects, and terrors of human life, with difficulty or not at all mastered, of which there are always enough, were the more numerous and burdensome in primitive times, the less man had learned either to conquer or to endure the ills and perils of nature; but only the more profoundly must he be stirred to realize the limits and weakness of his position, as well as to struggle in his soul for new means to obviate such dark evils. Every unforeseen occurrence, whether painful or pleasant, forced the mind out of its obscure repose, and compelled it the more irresistibly to look out beyond itself.

2. As soon as the human mind through such incitements from without had become sufficiently active and awake, its feelings more tender and plastic, and its whole youth raised

to a double youth of buoyant energy, there would be developed within it two opposite activities which indeed distinguish it from the first and in all ages, but would then be capable of such specially youthful quickening. On the one side it would begin to project itself upon the whole universe visible and invisible, in order, as its impressions were felt, the more surely and perfectly to take it into itself; to picture everything visible or conceivable as like itself, living, that is, after its own nature, and to express the diversities of individual things by the gradations of life itself. Human speech, the ultimately fixed expression of human thought, is the standing memorial of this tendency; some of its ramifications retaining indelible traces of it to this day. To the primitive mind everything lived and moved even as itself, no matter how unlike it might be to perception. On the other hand, over against this tendency of the human spirit to measure everything in accordance with itself, was developed the wholly other power of comparing all the infinitely manifold objects of its knowledge, of thinking the actual or possible contrary of everything that once became a distinct object of thought, in order to perceive the first the more clearly by its counterpart, the second, and by the "No" here to recognise the more surely the "Yea" yonder. For as this latter power of the human mind meets the former as equal with equal, or as the necessary complement of it, man is competent to perceive the one object just as vividly, and trace it just as accurately, as the other, its direct opposite, and thereby to know both alternately with the greater precision and certainty: and this apart from all subsequent development of individual human languages has remained for mankind a fundamental law of thought.

In accordance with this law the primeval man, as soon as he had recognised his own power as insufficient in all the most important wants and needs of life, would perceive over against it a wholly other power, the opposite of his own, as standing over him; and if he could conceive the contrary of many things as merely possible without knowing or maintaining it to be anything more than a mere thought, here had he at last found the truest of all and the most real, of whose existence he could be just as certain as of his own, whose higher life indeed he had borne in his own without knowing it—God. He finds Him who is most deeply hidden in his own spirit, and therefore hides Himself also most readily from him, who nevertheless may ultimately be less and less disregarded and a thousand times ignored, stirs Himself at length the more vigorously and irrepressibly; and in Him alone he finds actually the inexhaustible help and power he seeks, the infinite Spirit in which alone his own spirit can attain rest and peace.

But his whole thinking now moved with logical consistency in the antithesis of the Divine and Human. Conscious of the Divine as the higher spiritual power behind himself, he must feel the same Spirit as just as certainly existent behind everything outside himself. Moreover, with equal certainty must he feel that this *Divine*, standing behind all visible things, is to no other creature so near as to himself; and only with this feeling and the knowledge developing itself out of it can the circle of all these movements or thoughts of the human spirit be perfectly rounded and complete, and the basis of a creaturely life be won which is found in no other earthly creature but man alone.[1]

It is only the way just indicated which from the first beginning of his creation led man to God, and leads him similarly to-day. The beginning of this way points us indeed far beyond all definitely-known history into those primitive times the nature of which we can only infer from

---

[1] The correctness of this whole view is shown in that the oldest Semitic tongues endeavour to give as strikingly as possible the distinction as well as the mutual relation of the ideas, God and man; אֱלוֹהַּ and אֱנוֹשׁ correspond in formation as correlates, but the former signifies "strength," the latter "weakness." Only the oldest Semitic tongue, and no other tongue but the Semitic, has such correlates expressing this double idea: God, the strong; Man, the weak.

the traces that remain. As the Bible from its very first narrative presupposes the existence of God as known to men, so there is no single human language, from the earliest moment when we can historically follow it, which does not possess, as long since given in it, a word for God. In this the Bible coincides with the oldest portions of the Veda and the Avesta which equal it in age, and with Egyptian literary memorials which surpass it, going back as they do to the third and fourth millenniums before Christ. That the Chinese language has no word for God is only a mistake of some missionaries; its oldest expressions for this idea suffered, it is true, a violent shock after the labours of Confucius, but this statesman himself falls in an age corresponding somewhat to that of a Kant among ourselves, or to our own modern German period. Moreover, if a single existent language in a wholly decayed tribe of the great island-world should actually possess no word for God, as some missionaries assert, this would only be one of the many proofs how deeply such a tribe had declined from its earlier and better times. Rather may we maintain with certainty that human speech, as without the antithesis of God and man so without a word for God, is not thinkable and never actually existent; but just for this reason we can ascend neither by language, the oldest memorial of all human culture, nor by any other historical proof, higher than to the above indicated beginning of the way in which the thought of God occurred to man.

If, however, man felt thus, not only the complete insufficiency of his own power, but also in the midst of this and because of it felt the more certainly and clearly that there is a power standing over him and everything human, and yet so near and so akin to him, and among all creatures only to him, it is readily understood how he learned to direct his own spirit to that spirit; how he accustomed himself in every more vigorous excitation of his spirit to think the more vigorously of Him; how especially he sought to draw from this higher power confronting him counsel and help in every deeper life-need and despondency. Thus, in the twilight and dawn of his youth, man found the infinite spirit in whom alone his own spirit has rest and peace.

3. This first knowing, however, this continual seeking anew of the already known God, is not the goal of all activity thus aroused in the human mind. To the importunate quest of the human spirit every other object that confronts it, at first inflexible and dumb, or dark and terrible, may, the more it is vigorously and unweariedly contemplated, questioned, scrutinized, and not suffered to rest, disclose itself, reveal its meaning and its nature, and as if echoing back the right words make reply. Just this is the intellectual point of connection which unites the whole creation on the one side and the special spirituality of man on the other, viz. that to his questioning mind everything in creation may become vocal, that nothing need remain to him without meaning, and therefore without words and thoughts, but rather the more vigorous and directly penetrating his question is, the more loudly the right answer appears to sound back to him, and only the word that echoes back as if irresistibly from the object appears to be that which is elevated about his mere questioning and thought; and how animated this questioning and answering could be right in the primitive times is clear from what has already been said (p. 15). How then should not He answer the earnestly perseveringly questioning spirit of man—He of whose spirit man's is but a luminous reflection and an enkindled spark, and to Whom in his searching and questioning he can draw near quite otherwise than to the visible things of creation? If these answer him as he questions and inquires with intelligence and urgency, there come indeed words in which he hears something of the import and nature of things, but nothing which corresponds to his own intellectual elevation and glory or to his own nature; in the other case, however, are words given which not merely correspond to all this, but at once infinitely transcend it, which once heard benefit and delight him as his own clearer light and his own

purer power, the like of which he ever seeks anew in new needs without any failure of the supply.

§ 17. And yet many sceptics of our day would be able to object here that all this may well have been only a fancy of men of whom the Bible or antiquity speaks, who supposed that in this or a similar way they heard divine words, did there not come to us from the other side something just as certain which may serve for further confirmation, and is not less spoken of in the Bible. He who, for instance, will not deny all truth of things and all firm persistence, that is, all law of the universe, must concede that, supporting and sustaining all visible things, there are invisible forces which stand over man and exist independently of him, and which he can know perchance only gradually, yet with more and more completeness. The Bible everywhere presupposes this, and sums up all these separate forces in living comprehensiveness under the higher name of the Spirit of God. Now if man had not in himself a capacity to know such forces (and we may designate this capacity of his briefly, according to the Bible, as his spirit), he would never know them, still less would he be able as he does to employ and use them consciously at his own pleasure. But contemplating and investigating the visible things of the universe and their different properties, he learns to distinguish the forces of the things of creation; affected by the characteristics and changes of human history, and applying his mind to their examination and scrutiny, he learns to distinguish the forces at work therein. All this happens to him more or less perfectly; hardly only in the outset does it happen, or even in further usage and facility, at all events not accidentally as if it might have been altogether omitted, but as may be said briefly, according to the Bible, because God Himself as creator so wills it. God's Spirit in this way, notwithstanding its infinitude, stoops to man's when man's raises itself to it in the proper manner, so that gradually and progressively he may know those infinite and in this union at least eternal divine forces as they are in truth. If, now, man uplifts his spirit in the right way to God as to Him who stands over all creation and all history, and in whose mind alone they find their harmony, the same result may happen as in the previous case; the Divine Spirit may actually so stoop to man's and meet it in all its verity that the words and thoughts which in this communion live and move, and come forth to man in their own power, form at once words of command for him, because here, as he feels and knows, it is not the universe and history that interpret to him portions of their phenomena, but it is the voice of his own true Ruler and Lord that speaks to him. The Bible often expressly says and everywhere indicates that God continually waits, that with His Spirit he may meet that of man even of the feeblest and most solitary; it expresses, however, essentially the same truth under the image of the friend who is properly nearest to all men if also in himself the most wondrous. Thus we see the possibility of the working together of the divine and the human spirit, and the still further possibility also that the divine may overpower the human, and even wholly absorb it into itself. That this possibility if realized might shape itself in a hundred directions with the greatest diversity lies in the nature of everything human and historical. But a mere commencement and of inconsiderable extent may bear imperishable fruit.

If the sceptic is unwise in denying God, just as unwise should we be to deny all truth to such conceptions as Divine Word or word of God, or to seek to banish them from the speech of "cultured" men. He who to-day denies God occupies professedly a position which strict logic compels him to take; but he who supposes, as the Bible does, that the denial of God is folly itself, will not be unwise in his handling of these conceptions and terms. The concession that the word of God in its highest and purest sense comes to us not without human mediation, and therefore is limited, as man is, in place and time, involves also the concession that every living man is justified, and, if he desires to appropriate it to himself, obligated carefully to mark in what way this word is always true. But with the earliest and just on this account least perfect beginnings of revelation something of divine truth is mingled; and without such beginnings all further progress would have been impossible. The deterioration of an impulse and precedent given by divine determination is in this case, as in similar cases in human history, a later occurrence; how this prevailed will presently be discussed; but here it concerns us rightly to recognise with respect to revelation that which is original and results from the pure divine necessity, and is not yet influenced by human vanity and weakness.

To man in that primitive age what a moment it must have been when, from that Being who, he felt, was at once the mightiest and most mysterious, from whom he sought in his anguish and need to elicit speech and response, counsel and help, and who remained nevertheless so long before him in silence and reserve, he for the first time distinguished a clear word sounding toward him, a short sentence, it may be, but of luminous import and beneficent effect! The thought of hearing such a response in all clearness from above was now changed to actual realization; that Ego, whom he was sensible of not simply as his own better Ego, but as standing infinitely above his mere puny self, and whose clear decision he had so deeply yearned to hear, now became vocal before him with word and encouragement. When once he had thus heard words which, as if from the mouth of the otherwise so silent Deity, sounded suddenly towards him, laid hold upon him wonderfully, delivered him from his unrest and helplessness, why should he not again in similar circumstances hope for similar aid?

§ 18. But this is not all. It was not really with his sense of hearing alone that man in his profoundest wrestling for his whole life and existence sought to enter the immediate presence of God as the Being he had once known as invisible yet actually present; for properly speaking it is ever the whole man that stands face to face with God. Struggling therefore with all the deepest faculties of his mind for the revelation of the unseen God, it was possible that there should arise actually before the eye of his spirit a living image of that God whose gracious presence and help he so eagerly sought; that a luminous splendour should flash suddenly before his vision, and God Himself appear to move vividly towards him. In point of fact, the whole incident attains its higher living reality and revelation, in the truest sense of remote antiquity reaches its highest stage only in this vision of God. Here also presents itself what appears to us to-day probably singular and strange—the same phenomenon as in the previous case of hearing a voice from God; although it is true that many things not yet clearly thought and known before press, in certain moments, upon the mind as if in solid palpable form before the sight, and every thought becomes quite clear to us only as it occurs to the soul in bright intuitiveness, or what is essentially the same thing, is illustrated by some kind of sensuous image. To primeval man, therefore, in moments of highest tension and excitement of mind, why should it not be that in full living reality, and thence seen as with the bodily eye, He should appear whom it was the deepest longing of all the best part of antiquity to behold shining forth out of His darkness, and whose livingness and reality are without doubt ultimately and alone the highest? Man desires not simply to hear, but also to behold; and only that which is clearly beheld is for him the most certain and memorable.[1] And because with all this there happens only what in its last possibility God Himself as Creator wills, so the Bible often speaks of God as not only opening the ear, but also in higher vividness the eye of man,[2] so that he may behold Him near, and hear the word from Him in such clear personal directness as never before. But however much this vision of

---

[1] Job xlii. 4, 5.
[2] 2 Sam. vii. 27; Job xxxiii. 16; Ps. xl. 7, cf. with Isa. l. 5. Num. xxii. 31, cf. with Ps. cxix. 18. N. T. ἀποκαλύπτειν.

God may be the highest revelation, nevertheless revelation itself is concerned with the hearing of clear words, as even the oldest representations of such rare historical moments give us clearly to understand.[1]

The peculiarity, however, of everything that can be regarded as the word of God given in revelation is that it sounds forth simply from above, and strikes man as inevitable command, or otherwise as a sure saying and self-evident truth. God speaks to man as He must speak to him, being his self-potent Lord and self-confident God; and unmistakeably there is a truth to which man must submit, and to which he cannot too readily adapt himself. In this way undoubtedly in the highest antiquity, but at first only here and there, the feeling of man in his direct relation to God was developed; and happy the place where this childlike sentiment, this beginning of all piety, was early developed with the greater firmness! But as certainly as this sun-clear transparency, this confident rock-like assurance, marks emphatically the phenomena of the word of revelation, and the simple elevation of the whole incident rests in it, so no genuine revelation can overstep the limit prescribed for it in its very origin. Revelation must necessarily be mediated by human language as man hears the divine truth from above, and a man also may become the feeble instrument for manifesting a lofty truth standing over him and over all other men; but it is just this becoming manifest, yea the irresistible and violent pressing through of the divine truth itself, which steps into history in this whole transaction. And so far as it is only the peculiar force of the truth itself, and above all of the divine truth, that breaks the way for it, there cleaves to it always something of mysterious obscurity which has no place in the truth itself; for the hearer, however, and for the man by whom it is made known, something of mystery remains. "The silent God becomes vocal; His inner purpose, till then hidden to man, becomes

---

[1] Gen. xvi. 14, cf. with 7-13. Num. xxii. 31-33; Job xlii. 2-6; Jer. xxiii. 18.

manifest; His secret is discovered, and He discovers it to whom He will;"[1] these are the old expressions which describe this incident on its inner side. That there are indeed good, necessary and permanently valid reasons for these inner characteristics of this whole event, but that these as certainly do but mark and distinguish in revelation the phenomenon of its first and earliest occurrence, which, because it is first and earliest, is creatively most violent, will be further evident as we proceed.

§ 19. But, at all events, here what may be rightly called revelation is an accomplished fact; a very short, perhaps, but yet a full and clear word coming directly from God, revealing to man in his perplexity and helplessness the mind and will of God, and suddenly enlightening and irradiating his own spirit. Earlier than at this stage it does not exist; but here it is certainly found. It is thus something historical, and yet reaches away up to the remotest primitive times, as may also be seen to-day from human language. For as the words for the idea of God are conspicuous beyond all history more definitely known to us, so all the names for what we designate God's saying (Lat. *oracular*) belong to the oldest of all lingual possessions we are acquainted with. The best proof of this is that in the oldest languages there are words which give this idea of divine oracle in all brevity, although the idea itself is by no means so very simple, and must therefore have been originally expressed with much more definiteness. But the infinite frequency of the occurrence, as it obtained acceptance, created ultimately, even in those primitive times, such abbreviated expressions as served exclusively to designate it.[2] How correctly up to this point the origin of revelation has been

---

[1] Amos iii. 7; Jer. xxiii. 18. סוֹד indicates that which is in itself dark, mysterious, then "secret counsel;" then by a new derivative נוֹסַד, to "advise with any one secretly."

[2] As *oraculum*, λόγιον. If the Hebrew, on the other hand, just as little as the German, has such words, this is explained by the early loss of the oldest expressions for these ideas, since in both a wholly new age began early when a more definite expression was requisite. The English "gospel" is nevertheless still short enough.

discussed in detail, the Bible shows us clearly enough in its narratives of those remotest primitive times. For according to these a very long time passes away before men hear such a word from God as could in the sense of antiquity be held as revelation. What God says to the different creatures at their creation, according to the Book of Origins, is only the eternal will of the Creator; to man when just created He speaks more definitely than to the rest of the creatures,[1] only because man stands nearer to Him spiritually than they, and there never was a time when, according to his natural endowments, man could not have understood the will of the Creator. Similarly the later narrator,[2] only in more vivid representation, depicts the development of the peaceful primitive age of man, so far as there was in it something corresponding to the pure divine will. But according to the same narrator, a revelation of God very deeply affecting men in actual opposition to God occurs as early as the time of Paradise;[3] and going forth as it does out of the midst of the confusion of human affairs in order to publish to man, surprised and alarmed, the will of God, it gives in the transition to the common history of the world the typical example of the exigency and distress of life in which most revelations happen to man. Since then, however, according to this and subsequent narrators, revelation is never discontinued in human history.[4]

But in order to understand more completely the eager search after revelation on the part of man, and the very violent and stormy way in which it readily surprised him (§ 40 ff.), it may not be overlooked here that everything wanting to man, the urgent need of which he deeply feels, if long missed, is at length sought and even demanded with the more uneasiness and violence. To-day all the truths here in question have been long since given, are universally recognised, and are so little denied by sensible people, that, strictly speaking, our concern is rather about their proper application. Yet

[1] Gen. i. 28-30. Cf. with ver. 22.   [2] Gen. ii. 5-25.
[3] Gen. iii.   [4] Gen. iv. 6 ff., vi. 4 ff., and so on.

what a world was that upon which either not at all or scarcely more than at a distance the light of truth had yet risen, which gradually felt the urgent need of it in this darkness with ever deeper pain, yearned for it more and more eagerly, but only with such difficulty could win it! And yet must man learn to win this, as every other boon, by his own proper toil, and upon the right way, or it remains to him something distant and strange; but here the question concerned truths without which, as man felt his darkness, neither the individual nor society can attain a peaceful condition and find happiness in work and repose. Where an oppressive want prevails, the search for the means of removing it may be all the more active, and the endeavour to remove it as far as possible only may when once excited become the more uneasy and violent; whilst every truth much sought when it breaks upon men with its first force may seize him with deeper grasp. But here the question concerns not merely truths which most powerfully touch and most deeply move the spirit of man, but the question is also and at last exclusively whether man will or will not hold fast these truths when they are once known. So that, since the whole incident as to its possibility rests ultimately in the will of the Creator alone, all this cannot be better expressed than by the word of God in the mouth of the old prophet, "in their distress will they seek me."[1] But as certainly as such words of the best old prophets suggest it, the whole incident of revelation in its most original form, as more particularly described above, occurs as part of the divine will and purpose.

§ 20. Revelation, therefore, is a spiritual incident in human history. In its origin it goes back to the very dawn of human history, yet it was possible only at a certain stage of that history. Having once taken place, as with every other mental activity, it may readily be repeated, and from inconsiderable beginnings may be carried forward infinitely whether for good

---

[1] Hos. v. 15; cf. Amos viii. 11 f.; Isa. xxx. 21, and indeed Christ's last public word to Jerusalem, Matt. xxiii. 28 f.

or ill. As an incident of mental experience it goes back to the mystery of all origination of thought and clear views of things. What man can command the desired appropriate thought to arise at his caprice or summons? Every truly new thought, much more every clear view of things, although never so eagerly sought, comes only as if uncalled, involuntarily surprising and overmastering man, falling as a spark in the prepared tinder, and in an instant seizing and illuminating the whole mind. But revelation is distinguished from all other thoughts and intuitions, in that it flashes in upon the mind of man the conviction how the will of God calls upon him to act, or also who God Himself is who impels him to act thus. If the light of any other thought as it rises upon man may lay hold of his whole mind, such a thought as this must seize it with incomparably deeper grasp, and influence it more powerfully, because it strikes the whole spirit of man as the voice of the Lord from above; and man, too, on his part feels indeed when he can walk in such a light and word of his God that now he stands and acts in living connection with Him who alone can supplement his limited power, and lead his steps aright.

Furthermore, it does not admit of doubt that as man has been placed in creation from the beginning, divine thoughts and truths could flash forth upon him, and he could learn to follow them, only in this way. The whole question respecting the necessity and truth of revelation resolves itself in the last issue into a question concerning the existence and truth of God Himself. He who does not acknowledge God in His full verity and His distinctness from man, cannot believe in a divine revelation; but he who acknowledges Him can understand that the process described above is the only true way in which revelation can come to man. For if man really has from the beginning by the will of the Creator the capacity to know God and His will, this original revelation is yet only as a tinder waiting for the spark which shall fall upon it and kindle it; the falling and kindling of the spark could only be by the movement and activity above described. And just as little does it admit of doubt that the thought of God and His will coming to man in this way as a wholly new force, overmastering and yet brightly luminous, could be of striking truth and correctness; otherwise it must be denied altogether that man is so created that he can know what is true and do what is right. But if up to the occurrence of this wholly new and wonderful movement and activity man had found his way in the world, even only in small matters; if he had learned to distinguish that which is beneficial from that which is hurtful to him, that which fills him with unanticipated joy and satisfaction from that which occasions gloom and sadness; then, supposing an enlightening thought occurred to his mind and a clearly heard word was given from Him who alone is the highest and purest thought, and therefore the truest and most necessary, he could also find his way in the sphere of divine truth thus opened to him. Truth is for man what he has verified, what he knows with his best knowledge as corresponding in all its parts with actual fact, and, so far as it is supersensuous, with the higher necessity; and if on this account there is here a shorter there a longer way for man until he in his doubt finds truth wholly, yet it is not a boon denied to him from the beginning.

Moreover, it is for this reason not necessary that the activity of revelation, as soon as it is aroused, should furnish man forthwith with the whole fulness and highest purity of truth concerning God and His will. Rather is it of immeasurable importance that it should begin among mankind at all, and that with this beginning there should arise an impulse, a task, a toil to attempt everything on the once-opened way, and, as far as possible, to attain upon it what can be attempted, and may perhaps at last be perfectly attained. Only in an isolated and sporadic activity, as the pressure of life's need occasioned, did originally all revelation arise; and only from a coincidence and higher harmony of many such single oracular fragments could a higher whole of divine truths be formed.

But if in a deeper need and perplexity of human affairs God had once stepped forth perceptibly out of His darkness to the spirit of man, if He had revealed Himself as if visible to the clearest eye and audible to the most attentive ear, why now should not man in new and ever more severe complications and despondencies, yearn again and again for the same incident to occur, and, as far as he could contribute to it, endeavour with all his might to reproduce it in his experience? Thus this special activity of the human spirit could be exercised and developed with unwearied sedulity, with growing experience and wisdom, with larger aptitude and fruitfulness; similarly, notwithstanding all diversity, as the poetic, or artistic, or scientific, or any other even more special activity of the human mind may, from the smallest beginnings if only they are sound, be raised to power and elevation by no means measurable beforehand. Errors and serious mistakes, too, possible upon this as upon every other not merely divine but human path, might always be retrieved by retracing the steps and starting anew in better form. And so could the darkness and the alienation between man and God arising out of it, and readily growing more and more mischievous, be fully and happily cleared up and removed, as far as this was possible, upon the way here opening itself.

2. *The Fear of God, or Religion.*

§ 21. As soon, however, as man, to whom such a revelation has occurred, resolves to follow loyally the clear word of God he has thus received, and actually lives in accordance with it, there arises further the wholly new relation of man to God, which we rightly designate, according to the Bible, the fear of God or religion. It does not arise earlier than at this stage of the development of man's spiritual being, but here it not only can, but must arise as the true aim of revelation. For why should the divine fire fill the human spirit with the light of insight into the divine will, and with its own impelling glow, unless for the purpose of constraining to action in harmony with the clearly-heard word of God? And it will certainly lead the more irresistibly to such conduct the more clearly it shines as a new light of the inner life, and the less, where it arises, obduracy and numbness of spirit resist its impulse and fervour. But he who attempts to follow the divine light of truth which has dawned upon the mind, will do it because he is afraid of violating the clearly perceived will of his God; in point of fact, therefore, from fear of God as his highest Lord, and fear of violating His word. The importance of this biblical fear of God as an experience in this case already of the highest and most comprehensive kind, makes it necessary to consider it more particularly in all its elements.

1. It is certain that fear must actually move man if, not in one single act only, but in the whole of his earthly life, the will of God is to be obeyed. Fear is given to all creatures as a means of self-preservation; and in man it is not originally the low and unworthy thing it may become through his guilt. As an original power of the human mind, fear may be exalted and ennobled by its object; and here that object is the highest and the holiest conceivable, God. As all dangers culminate for man in this one, that of disobedience to the clearly-known will of God,[1] it is self-evident that fear directed in all purity and vividness to its highest object, God and His will, so far from being without value for man, can never be sufficiently watchful and strong. It is necessary to make this conspicuous, because our subject requires it, and the whole Bible, as well the Old Testament as the New, takes this view. Moreover, it is asked, is the fear of God, or in Latin garb, religion, needful for the men of to-day as it was for those of old times, after it has once historically developed itself, as it has, to its high significance and importance?

---

[1] Christ expresses this very strikingly, Matt. x. 28; Isaiah, too, long before, says essentially the same thing, with strong emphasis, viii. 11-13; and the Deuteronomist enforces it, xiii. 5.

Now it is certain that the fear man may have may be incomparably greater and more alarming than mere animal fear. In all his growing efforts and enterprises he feels himself surrounded by infinite dangers; his spirit, too, sensible to all fear, readily, as we have seen, beholds God over against itself, and face to face with Him is most profoundly sensible of its own impotence, or even of its own guilt and sin, and alarmed for the future. "God has so done it," says the Bible itself, "that men should fear before Him;"[1] and what limit is there to this fear? But we must remember that in fear, as a capability of the power of the spirit of man, lies the possibility of the most beneficent and salutary as well as of the most pernicious effects. By uniting all the rest of the capabilities of the human spirit upon one single aim, fear can give the most wonderful power to man, not merely in avoiding threatening ill, but also by virtue of the necessary antithesis in seeking and attaining salvation. It is thence nearly akin to the sacred power of conscience, as is evident from what has already been said. But, on the other hand, imagination can fill the mind with so many groundless fears that it may be depressed and darkened thereby infinitely more than is possible to beasts; and indeed close by the side of fear is found the blood-curdling of a boundless superstition. In this case, should it be directed towards a person, not a thing, the feeling of timid shrinking back, common to all fear, is turned into terror and slavish dread, or becomes absolute estrangement and hate.

The more closely and intimately true religion brought together, as person and person, man and God, the more it became conscious that in the long run not fear but love formed the strongest bond of union, that, indeed, all darkness and dread lying in mere fear must be dissolved in the higher serenity and joy of unconstrained love. Nor does the New Covenant first teach this; Moses himself, as we know with historical certainty, already placed the love of God higher than

[1] Eccles. iii. 14.

mere fear, and expected from it the best observance of the divine commands.[1] In a different connection Christ reproduced this truth;[2] but His favourite disciple, John, at a time when the love of God to man had at length manifested itself most intimately and perfectly, set the requirement of love in sharp distinctness, and added without hesitation, "perfect love," where it rules, "casteth out fear."[3] So that from its first beginning to its lofty close the revelation of the true religion requires of man rather love to God than fear of Him. Yet not even John could maintain, in contradiction to all the well-known expressions of the Old Testament, that the fear of God is something superfluous, or even pernicious; he seeks only to remove from it all that may be obscure, gloomy, and dull, with which he saw it so conspicuously overburdened at that time amongst the Jews. So far as man must ever fear to violate the clearly-known will of the Lord his God, fear must ever remain; yet love, in its pure and genuine sway, counteracts all doubtful hesitation and active misgiving, and fear returns, indeed, but now purified, transfigured, restraining itself to its proper function.

It may be noted further, however, that the Bible nowhere commends "fear" in a wide and general sense; but it depicts frequently enough the salutary effect of religious fear in man's indurated or careless estrangement from God.[4] Moreover, it shows, less frequently perhaps, but not with less truth, how the unanticipated experience of the divine help and near-

---

[1] The historical memorial (Exod. xx. 6; Deut. v. 10) is secure against all doubt. The Deuteronomist (vi. 5, x. 13, xi. 1) simply introduces afresh with new emphasis what had already been given by Moses in the early time of the community.

[2] Matt. xxii. 37. "Fear not!" is a word Christ often and emphatically utters (Matt. x. 26, 31, xiv. 27, xvii. 7, xxviii. 5, 10; Mark v. 36). And yet He speaks also as in Mark x. 28.

[3] 1 John iv. 18. Here, however, the discourse is specially of the personal relation of the Christian to God in prayer and desire. In his Gospel John uses the word "fear," "to fear," only where it is necessary; so free is his relation to the thought itself. And yet he would certainly not disapprove what Paul says appropriately in 2 Cor. vii. 15; Phil. ii. 12.

[4] Ps. lxxvi. 8-12; John i. 5-16; cf. Jer. iii. 8.

ness,[1] or the marked presence, in the person or character of another, of the divine strength and power,[2] may overpower or overawe the spirit, but only so as to replenish it possibly with a fulness of divine thoughts, and give to it an impulse to higher and holier life. To this end simply does the Bible touch upon such moments in the lot of man. Nor is it to be overlooked that what we should speak of as "reverence" is often called "fear" in the simple language of the Bible, although in the oldest Hebrew what is to be revered or venerated on account of its high character is not unrecognised.[3]

§ 22. 2. But fear in itself, however necessary, is insufficient as the first element of true religion. To stop with it and be content with it, although its object be a mysterious Being high above man and far from him, a God known but dimly or in a mistaken and perverse way, this is not the biblical idea of religion, it is rather the mark and characteristic of heathenism. The Bible regards it as of first importance what man fears as the mysterious power above him, associates the knowledge of God with all true fear of God, makes such fear proceed from knowledge as the very beginning and necessary condition of its existence.

Already it is apparent that strictly speaking the Bible has no word for the idea under consideration, so short and indeed so indeterminate as the Latin *religio*. Now *religio* is undoubtedly more suitable than *metus* or *timor*, because it does not indicate fear or dread generally, but only fear of that which lays a man under obligation, and thence is akin to "conscience;" and further, it expresses, what was peculiar to the ancient Romans, the deeper awe before all mystery, and especially before that which is divine and cannot be disregarded with impunity. A similar word is scarcely found in

[1] As related with such striking truth and from primitive times, Gen. xvi. 13, xxviii. 16 f.

[2] As in the case of Abraham, Gen. xx. 8; Moses, Ex. xxxiv. 29 f.; Christ, Mark iv. 41; Luke v. 8-10; and the first Christians, Acts ii. 43, v. 5, 11.

[3] By נוֹרָא in the old song, Ex. xv. 11; later in the Pentateuch and elsewhere repeated often with the greatest emphasis.

any other purely heathen language. The Greek has no such short word with the same distinct idea. Islamism, too, leaves so little to moral freedom and spontaneity that it calls religion "guidance." Notwithstanding, it is to be regretted that the word *religio* has become naturalized in the languages of Christian nations, for it does not express the relation of man to the true God. As with the "true oracle," so with the "true religion," no single word satisfactorily describes it, for it arose in a historical time far back in the primitive ages. The Hebrew expressed it by the phrase "fear of Jahveh,"[1] not Elôhim; the name that gives the most determinate idea of the true God appearing most suitable. Later poets (chiefly Job, and in the mouth of Eliphaz) employ, for the sake of brevity, and in a connection where the sense cannot be doubtful, the single word "fear," to which Hebrew usage nevertheless shrank from giving the general sense of *religio*.

The phrases "knowledge of Jahveh,"[2] or more fully, "knowledge and fear of Jahveh,"[3] are also employed by the prophets to indicate true religion; calling needful attention to the fact of the actual existence of such knowledge, since the hope is that by its own vital power it will spontaneously bring forth fruit. But what this knowledge is, whether scanty or abundant, whether more or less clear and reliable, much depends, according to biblical teaching, upon obedience in the fear of God to what is known as God's will. Indeed, all true religion essentially consists in continual and anxious attention to all real knowledge of God's will, with a view to ordering the life more perfectly and happily in conformity with it. Abraham is the highest example of this in the Old Testament.[4] Job thinks he possesses the sound knowledge of a long godly life, yet it is not till his eye is opened to truths before unknown in their completeness that he comes to do right in the fear of

---

[1] LXX. θεοσέβεια. The phrase in Gen. xxxv. 5 is no exception, because it signifies "divine alarm;" and Gen. xx. 11 comes from an older usage of speech.

[2] Hos. iv. 1; Jer. xxxi. 34; cf. Isa. liv. 13.

[3] Isa. xi. 2; cf. Handbook, § 339*b*.   [4] Gen. xxii. 1-18.

God.[1] The disciples of Christ are animated by this fear, but its salutary effect becomes most conspicuous after their eyes are opened to many an enigma whose burden before oppressed them.[2] Not only in these cases of rare elevation, but everywhere in the Bible, it is seen that our knowledge of divine things can never be sufficiently rich and clear and certain. Moreover, whatever it is, it gives simply the rules and measure of human conduct, and prepares the mind to act in accordance therewith; the power to act comes with the uplifting of the heart to God and the fear of His holy name.

§ 23. 3. In the midst of the earnest realities of life, fidelity to the known will of God is preserved whether in the peaceful flow of events or in never-failing dangers, only as the knowledge already possessed is not suffered to lie idle or slumber in inactivity. Here again the fear of God is the motive power; and even if fear is transfigured to the purest love, that love itself will not forget that it must not violate God's will and offend God Himself, and cannot but fear lest it should, so that the fear of God ever remains the impulse to right conduct. Furthermore, in the experience of life, knowledge grows in certainty and clearness by means of right action; new complications and conflicts show, too, the deficiencies of existing knowledge; and if in these high struggles the mind is to be intent and ready for new knowledge, as well as kept from abandoning the certainty of that already possessed, it must still, in the fear of God, and in childlike docility, listen anew to His voice, and obey it in the same fear, raised, it may be, to a higher and purer fervour. For in the relation of man to God, as everything proceeds from continual intentness and turning of the mind to Him, resting upon the immutable and therefore calm and deep foundations of the knowledge and fear of God, so everything must come back to it, and thus the relation becomes vital and fruitful.

§ 24. But everything spiritual is mysterious,—spiritual life

---

[1] Job xxxviii. 1–xlii. 6.
[2] In Luke xxiv. 13–32 graphically and truly depicted.

and its action, mystery itself. Nowhere is this recognised more strikingly, and with more universal validity, than in the apothegm, "God's secret counsel," *i.e.* His word and His counsel, above all, the possibility that He should, as friend to friend, disclose His secret mind, "have they who fear Him."[1] The true and necessary fear of God will always carry in itself something of mystery. The knowledge it presupposes springs from the deepest and most mysterious impulse of human experience and thought, and extends to the loftiest points of human conception and inquiry, and is never perfected, because it touches all the ultimate questions concerning God, the universe, and man. Yet the mystery is not in this knowledge, for the knowledge proceeds from revelation, *i.e.* the dispersion of the original dark mystery. Nor does it lie in the fact that the fear of God primarily makes itself felt as indispensable in the restless yearnings of the most troubled periods of human history, and finds its origin and the days of its mightiest progress in the deeper sources and incitements of human effort;[2] but rather in this, that it places the historical man, independently of his will, in some living relation to God, unites the deepest experiences and endeavours of the individual man with the divine will,—valid for all men and the whole universe, and so for him,—and thus touches all the eternal secrets of the divine nature and of human destiny. As the converse with God of the hidden thought and endeavour of man, as a continuous reciprocal relation between the individual and his God, it is in vain and even mischievous to seek with rude hand to disturb, or with violent hand to strip off this living mystery.

But it is not on this account a mere sentiment, nor to be derived from the obscure source of mere sentiment or disposi-

[1] Ps. xxv. 14; very similarly Job xxix. 4; Prov. iii. 32; cf. Job xv. 8; Jer. xxiii. 18 ff.; also already Amos iii. 7; cf. p. 24, note. The older parts of the Book of Proverbs do not employ the word סוֹד in this sense (Prov. xi. 13, xx. 19, xv. 22, xxv. 9).

[2] Strikingly depicted in its first sources, Isa. xxx. 19-21; cf. Ex. vi. 29-xv. 21, according to old reminiscence; Acts ii.-v., according to newer.

tion, as if, like joy or pain or desire, it were a mood of mind casually coming and going. From its peculiar knowledge, and as a wholly special kind of fear, it is rather a special faculty of the spirit, just as powerful as any other, within its own province mightier than all others, and being unique in itself, not to be replaced or interchanged. Its characteristic is this, it knows a will which all spiritual beings, the most isolated and the strongest as well as the feeblest, must equally follow; it is itself resolved to follow it, and by nothing in all the universe can it be deterred from following it, because this fear is so great and so unparalleled that it conquers every other. Its activity, like that of all self-dependent energies, is seen in the two directions which are historically possible; it throws off what is foreign to it, and appropriates what corresponds to its own nature, and aids in accomplishing its ever greater and more manifold tasks that reach away to the infinite. Its victorious power of resistance is shown in the lives of many biblical heroes, pre-eminently in Joseph's, with its brilliant deed and luminous word, and Joseph was neither a patriarch nor a prophet, but a man as others, a possible example for even common men. Once exercised and proved in its defensive energy, this power grows wonderfully in its own creative enterprise and endeavour. Where, indeed, in the Bible or out of it, is any divine service for man, whether apparently small or conspicuously great, accomplished without it? or where has it not been proved that human work is abiding and useful in its issues only in proportion as it is done in the fear of God?

3. *Reciprocal Influence of Religion and Revelation.*

§ 25. One of the first splendid results of the more energetic activity of the fear of God is its purifying and fostering reaction upon revelation. Itself a consequence of the still imperfect stirrings of revelation, no sooner does it develop its peculiar power but it influences revelation, its ultimate result;

so inseparably are both united by a higher law superior to both.

The reason is this: Revelation throws out to man brief thoughts of God and sharply-imperative expressions concerning His will. In these thoughts and expressions, mixed up with what is true and salutary, may be found that which is only half-true and obscure, or even erroneous. This is possible, because revelation occurs only through the co-operation of the human and divine spirit, and the contents of revelation depend, therefore, upon special momentary moods of mind in the individual man. But if the possible imperfection of revelation in the beginning is not to be avoided, it may be removed when the fear of God for which it is destined appropriates the contents of revelation and seeks to follow them as God's will. For in this attempt the whole man must act, the new knowledge which lies behind the contents of the revelation must adjust itself with all earlier established knowledge, and the final result must show whether the hoped-for salvation is here found or not. Indeed, the more frequently, the more eagerly and thoroughly the contents of revelation are tested, the more certainly must appear how much therein is true and salutary; and thus the active fear of God will refine or verify, or even discredit these contents. If now a revelation, coming to the individual man as long since otherwise given or in new and creative form, consisting of a single sentence, or of a number of previously received analogous sentences, whether it be clearer in its setting or only simply verifying itself,—if such revelation on its part ultimately reacts upon the man by virtue of such active fear of God, there begins an ever-repeating circle of reciprocal influence which, as it repeats itself, may immeasurably increase on the one hand the truth and certainty of the manifold contents of revelation, on the other the power and salvation of the fear of God. That is to say, revelation awakens active religious life, which in its turn verifies or sifts revelation, and this again, with purified or authenticated force, may replenish or quicken anew the practical religious life.

In fact, the Old Testament sets before us in the most graphic way in the Book of Job how fruitful and conducive to salvation this round of movement may become. Job enters into a circle of divine truths and precepts long since revealed; his fear of God leads him to order his life uprightly in accordance with them; but in the subsequent high conflict of experience this fear of God, never wholly lost, constantly renewing itself in its unwearied activity, enables him to see, as never before, some of the old revealed sentences in their imperfection and obscurity; others, on the contrary, in their firm, rock-like unchangeableness and luminous clearness; then comes for him the time when, casting off the imperfect, at length with growing courage he wins in the more perfect a most wonderful new certainty of his whole spiritual life, and becomes thereby rightly prepared to receive, in other and yet higher conflicts, the light and salvation of a revelation incomparably surpassing all he had previously known and believed.[1] Just at the close of its whole contents the Bible shows us, in its lucid history of the most powerful of the apostles, the same round of influences. For it is nothing but the old inherited fear of God itself, specially quickened in him, that leads Paul to see aright the whole compass and range of the old revelations as well as the true nature and demands of the new; and hardly has he done this in all thoroughness and sincerity when the new revelation throws back its incomparably higher light upon his mind, and invests his old fear of God with an energy, confidence, and joy wholly new and sufficiently potent to transform his whole spiritual life.

In this way revelation, as soon as it arose in its first least perfect beginnings, had in its own active movement and the primary issue of it, the best means of developing and perfecting itself; and nowhere can be seen so clearly as here how in antiquity it was certainly one of the many possible capacities and exercises of the human mind. Poetry or science takes

---

[1] Cf. the chief passage, Job xxvii. 3, and the incidental but not on that account unimportant expression, xiii. 23, with the whole grand close, xlii.

its rise from its peculiar inner necessity, in the great development of humanity; but once arisen, its special contents and artistic charm induce numberless subsequent attempts and trials; in like manner, the activity and art of revelation, once begun, its own products led it ever forward until it had accomplished the utmost that was possible in antiquity. If a wholly special elevation of the human mind was needed to call forth revelation and make a way for it, yet the way, when made, would itself, with its special art and facility, like the charm of the poet's numbers, or the convincing method of proof in science, allure to endless repetition. Moreover, new needs form always the strongest incentive to the production of new poems, or the pursuit of new scientific investigations when the way lies open; similarly, the living experience of the first less perfect utterances and claims of revelation, *i.e.* the active fear of God, impelled the mind powerfully forward, and made it possible that revelation should rise to ever new and ever higher efforts.

But—to continue this example—poetry, when it has once become an art, connects itself with every subject of thought, and may be reproduced everywhere and at all times as fresh needs arise, and with fresh grace; revelation, however, has a very determinate content of thoughts and truths, viz. such as concern the right relation between God and man, and the duties this involves, if man is to follow the will of God. That these thoughts and truths thus limited and defined should admit of final completeness is at least fairly conceivable. For they do not touch the realm of all possible inquiry, experience, and knowledge; and if they did, science itself, which seeks to take possession of this realm wholly and fully, may perhaps anticipate an end, when all its material shall be exhausted, even if this exhaustion lies to-day at an invisible distance from us; but revelation has only a limited domain. Moreover, these thoughts and truths thus circumscribed must have sought their earliest possible perfecting, because they are indispensable for progress in all higher human life and endeavour. The inner possibility for the attainment of such perfection is given in just this wonderful reciprocal action between the fear of God once practically awakened, and its unfathomably deep original impulse, revelation; a reciprocal action so necessary, and once properly set in motion so unceasing, that it could not come to repose again until revelation brought the last word of God to light which it could express, and published the purest and highest will of the true God which it could reveal and declare. But in point of fact this reciprocal action, although the only true and inexhaustible agency which could in this case lead to consummation, did not suffice for the outward perfecting; whilst here, as everywhere in historical human affairs, everything must equally coincide from without and from within, if a true perfection is to be attained.

Rightly to apprehend this, we must consider further that the contents of revelation are completed only when they give what they should give as equally valid and equally perfected for all men without exception. For the question is concerning truths that are not simply to serve for special aims of life, and perhaps special men, but which shall have authority for all men equally as the necessary ground of all human life and effort; truths which may establish the same salvation for the most isolated man as for every other, in which all meet as spiritually equal, and without which no bond of common salvation and beneficent effort is possible, uniting the whole of humanity of all lands and all ages. However much of wealth of enduring truth a revelation may contain, however many portions of revelation of analogous contents may contribute to form what is a noble whole, so long as these can appear as a genuine ground for the active fear of God only to the individual, or can have authority as such ground only to a limited circle of men, they do not afford what is here required. For this, more particularly regarded, two things are requisite: (1) that the contents of the revelation in all the subjects here essential can be esteemed as actually complete, therefore that no single, important, and necessary truth belonging to this province is wanting; and (2) that, since everything depends upon the use of revelation and upon life in conformity with its type, it shall admit of equal and easy application for all men without exception. Only where both these coincide can we speak of a true perfecting of revelation. If it is considered, however, from what limited, scattered, and imperfect beginnings all revelation proceeds, it will readily be felt that a further and more difficult[1] way was to be made if revelation should be truly perfected. And yet, according to the testimony of the Bible and all historical experience continued till to-day, such perfection has been attained; it must be ours then to note here more exactly in what historical stages, upon the basis of the reciprocal action between revelation and the fear of God, the consummation has been won.

II.—THE STAGES OF REVELATION.

1. *The Revelation of the Individual.*

§ 26. As with everything resulting from a deeper struggle of the spirit, so with the seeking and finding of revelation, it is pre-eminently an affair of the individual man. Only the individual felt originally in the exigency of life this urgent need to hear the voice of his God: it was assuredly the extremest struggle of prayer which alone seemed capable of drawing forth such a voice, and which for many actually drew it forth; but this prayer, when it comes from its earliest impulse and with original force, breaks forth from the profoundest depths of the soul.

But whether this or another cause be active, even in later times, not at all rarely, we meet with a revelation an individual experiences of which he remains conscious subsequently, and incidentally mentions as expressly received by himself. We do not mean revelations arising artificially, and on this

[1] *I.e.* ampler, and more difficult to make.—Tr.

account often obscure and erroneous, of which also mention is made in the Bible; nor indeed such revelations as are spoken of by the patriarchs and other men of primitive times; nor those introduced by artistic poets, like the writer of the Book of Job;[1] although all these bear witness that in the conception of the Bible all revelation is originally the affair of the individual, and needs not the mediation of a prophet. But when a poet, who nowhere gives himself out as a prophet, but everywhere pours forth the deepest thoughts of his heart in the simplest strains, speaks of a revelation happening to him;[2] or when Paul, before he was an apostle at all, or even a Christian, had experience purely for himself of a revelation of whose wonderful power the New Testament cannot say enough:[3] in such cases we readily understand how, according to the Bible, the ear of the man who is most solitary, and perhaps but little prepared beforehand, may stand open to the divine voice.

Speaking generally, it is a matter of little consequence, as against the contents of a truth of revelation itself, through whom it is revealed. Paul tells his Philippians[4] that if in anything they are of another mind than he, God will reveal to them in His own time where the truth lies. That is to say, Paul intimates that they may follow his instructions in full confidence with the reservation that they may in time to come receive from above a still better enlightenment; through whom, he leaves undetermined, since nothing depends upon it. An extremely striking narrative in the Old Testament shows also that even a hired prophet like Balaam must in a particular affair become a true prophet. Moreover, it is not necessary that the content of a revelation be in itself something entirely new; only to the individual whom it surprises perhaps in a moment of severest spiritual conflict is it so new and so transcendent that in his innermost spirit he can exult greatly in having received it directly from God. It was thus that the poet

---

[1] Job iv. 12–17, xv. 8, xxxviii.–xlii. 6.   [2] Ps. xl. 7, E. V. 6.
[3] Gal. i. 15 f.; Acts ix. 1–19, xxii. 5 ff., xxvi. 12 ff.   [4] Phil. iii. 15.

exulted as he felt himself overpowered by an impression of the divine truth that the outward offering was not indispensable,[1] although one or another great prophet, without this poet being aware of it, might have already expressed the same truth; and Paul, too, by one of the most potent of revelations, was first convinced of a truth which hundreds of Christians had fully accepted long before, though the greater part of his own race obstinately rejected it as altogether impious and profane.

§ 27. The peculiar energy with which each revelation may be charged may here be very clearly recognised. Bringing to the spirit of man suddenly from above a new thought, and claiming for it as divine his whole will, it readily drives out all other free thoughts, and fixes attention exclusively upon this: at least such is the case when revelation is as pure and energetic as is possible to it. If now the new thought comes at a time when the strength of the individual as against all other men is profoundly needed and urgently claimed, the effect may be conspicuously great. The spirit of the individual can never be invested with mightier energy than when one new thought wholly fills it, whose truth is known to be firmly grounded in the divine mind, and which contains at the same time God's special will for him; the whole uncertainty of changing timid thoughts, dividing and deadening the hearts of men, vanishes before that one thought which alone is certain, overpowering, and dominant. Should it relate not to the soul's salvation of this individual or of the few standing near to him, but to the eternal weal of the whole community in which he lives, then, the more difficult it is to execute it, the more powerfully will it impel him, if only he seeks to hold it fast. But if the times when the individual feels himself so impelled are times of dissolution and universal decay, in which, if he seeks to follow the divine call, too clearly and too surely received, he has all men against him, then the divine energy of revelation must make itself so tense in him, and so mightily

[1] Ps. xl. 7 (6).

increase and renew its own power, that in the fragile human instrument its extremest effort is sustained. And since every new thought touching the deepest mysteries of which we here speak may not necessarily first flash up in its fullest clearness and certainty only in one man, but assuredly only by the firm, constrained, and concentrated power of the spirit of one man can be successfully carried out; we see that the energy of revelation in the individual, and in the individual only, can accomplish the highest task which is possible upon a determinate stage of the general development of the spirit of man. In Moses, as in Christ absolutely, though in a wholly different form, the power of revelation was active as the concentrated energy of the individual; the time in which each arose was a time of general dissolution, and from first to last neither the one nor the other was simply and only a prophet in the customary sense of the term.

But as the revelation of the individual can thus accomplish the highest possible task, and includes in itself that which is earliest and latest in the course of this whole development, so also may it most readily degenerate, as indeed in human affairs everything may, which does not rest upon the common practice of the many, but upon the exceptional capacities and special efforts of the few. The individual man who, possessed by a thought that elevates him wonderfully, fights single-handed against a whole world, breaks up with high victorious power old and pernicious corruption, and effectually lays the foundation of a new and better condition of things, we may designate, in the ancient sense of the term, a hero, and the special spirit which must be pre-eminently active in revelation (§ 16-18), the heroic spirit. But every spirit that uplifts itself mightily in the world by work among men and becomes victorious, finds its human imitators; even Moses had his, in the centuries immediately succeeding, when the growing disorganization of the community he founded called forth anew with extraordinary power the energy and efforts of the individual. The spirit of Jahveh came upon this or that valiant hero of these centuries;[1] or, as is well said, it "sprang upon him,"[2] since every new spiritual movement comes with a bound, especially where it surprises men most with its wonderful force, and hurries them along irresistibly; or even more strongly it is said, it "clothed him,"[3] as if one could see by the whole external aspect of the hero how the new spirit which had seized him from within maintained itself permanently in his whole appearance, adorning him resplendently, or being, so to speak, suffused around him like the splendour of a new robe. These are the brief phrases by which posterity sought to preserve the remembrance of the heroic spirit in such men; and memorable heroes as they were in the best sense of the word in the judgment of posterity, that there actually came upon them something of the heroic spirit of Moses, is not in the least to be doubted. If Moses, once seized by the genuine spirit of revelation, worked on uniformly through his whole life under its influence, this was not the case with these successors of his, who in other respects resembled him. Revelation may indeed at first very distinctly enlighten and uphold the individual man, so long at least as he suffers himself to be seized and sustained solely by its energy; but just because he stands alone, his moods and resolves are prone to change; and if by the utmost strain of the energy of the heroic spirit then aroused the one thing which first urged him forward is attained, there comes back upon him, because he is alone, increasing lassitude, or perhaps a carelessness unknown before, and culpable infirmity. In addition to this, the individual just as such supposes he has no need always and perfectly to maintain his standing on the same elevation of life as the great predecessor he imitates. And history teaches that, in the course of those centuries, not

---

[1] As Judg. iii. 10, xi. 29, cf. iii. 15, and many similar passages.

[2] This is the signification of צָלַח, Judg. xiv. 6, 19, xv. 14; 1 Sam. x. 6, 10, xvi. 16, xviii. 10; since it is related to סָלַד, זָנַק; but צָלֵחַ, "to be fit," is wholly different.

[3] Judg. vi. 34; otherwise employed, 1 Chron. xii. 18; 2 Chron. xxiv. 20.

one of the heroes of the Spirit, nobly as they struggled at times, and unlike as they were to each other, ever became equal to Moses. The transition from the highest and mightiest of its kind to the deepest degeneracy is easy; it is only a very gradual process, it is true, but in the example of Samson it is already seen to be complete.[1]

2. *The Revelation of the Prophets.*

§ 28. Above the initial stage of revelation, which, although it is essential in itself, is exposed to all human alternations, there arises another, not the highest, yet conditioning the necessary progress to every higher. This is the revelation of the prophets. Here is presupposed a distinct Deity, with His peculiar characteristics, whose revelation is already the means of salvation to many, and whose word is sought through the mediation of one who is capable of eliciting it. The first simplicity and immediateness of the search for revelation and the experience of it now cease, and it will be shown as we proceed how readily also in this case, as in every case of complicated relations, the first purity might more and more disappear. But nevertheless a great step forward was here possible, and, moreover, the only step which could now be taken.

For this species of revelation must, before all things, raise itself above the mere accidents of the revelation of the individual, which, as we have seen, is capable of accomplishing the highest tasks, yet may also too easily sink down lowest of all. The man who is here the instrument of revelation must in his inquiry direct his mind to a definite Deity, acknowledged not merely by himself, but also by others; and only what is in conformity with the nature of Him whom already others know and fear can he hear and announce as the right

---

[1] The phrase "the Spirit of God began to pierce him," Judg. xiii. 25, indicates sarcastically how little this Spirit was supposed to dwell in him peacefully and uniformly.

word of revelation.[1] Not what the prophet, as the casual individual man, knows and counsels, but only the knowledge and counsel of the Deity standing as well over the prophet as over the person for whom he acts, does this latter seek to learn; it is held then as a supreme law that the prophet shall not speak that which pleases himself, but only that which pleases his God; and what a significance this principle may have as soon as it is vivified in the light of the fear of God! For the revelations sought for others, though in the highest degree different in occasion and character, yet proceeding from the same well-known Deity, a like spirit must penetrate them all. Thus in the outset is given, besides elevation above the caprice and arbitrariness of the individual, besides consistency and higher uniformity, the possibility also of a more and more refined practice and culture of revelation.

Moreover, to the men who seek it, revelation may also become in this case more perfect. He who speaks for others must be able to elevate his mind freely above itself; how much more must he do this who desires to be capable of communicating to others the clear divine sentences and words he has heard, and to communicate them as clearly as he has heard them, and penetrated with the same fear of God with which he himself would execute them. The certainty and distinctness of all knowledge grow when there is the capability to impart it to another with the like certainty and distinctness, especially of knowledge which enters into the world with new and creative force, and is to serve at the same time as another's rule of action. But here are sentences whose contents are to impel him who hears them as divine to carry them out in the fear of God; he therefore who will communicate to others, that they may act in conformity with it, a word of God he thinks he has received, must communicate it to them in such a way that he does not fail to awaken with respect to its observance the same fear of God with which he himself would carry it out.

[1] Num. xxii.–xxiv.; Jer. xxiii. 16, 21, 32; Ezek. xiii. 2 ff. Cf. *Jahrb. der Bibl. Wiss.* ix. p. 15 ff.

But still another thing is to be added which, especially in its consequences, is very important. For in verifying all that may be held as the word of God, it is of service that not merely the individual can follow it, but every one who is in like position as to the knowledge or also as to the practical need of it. And this general validity of a truth of religion grows the more he in whom the light of a revelation shines can secure the communication of it in the same divine light to as many others as possible, or can induce them to act as far as may be in accordance with it. For the highest result here attainable is that revelation, taken as a mere capability, should, though not all at once, yet progressively in successive stages, more and more publish such truths as may be of universal validity and thence of eternal duration,—such as are calculated to promote the soul's salvation of all men without exception. Moreover, it is a great step if, beyond the individual man in whom it first strongly moves, it even attempts only to work upon others, and to accustom them to its voice and the importance of it. All the energy which dwells in revelation, and which, as we have seen (§ 27), is so intrinsically great, must thus be doubled, and can grow from stage to stage still higher. For this reason it is the oracle that first lays the foundation of what in human affairs the farther they are developed is the more indispensable, viz. a community of men, growing ever larger and more compact, and based upon similarity of spirit and of spiritual endeavours.

At first this would naturally be attended with uncertainty. The impulse of revelation must have moved powerfully in individuals until some one of them was emboldened, in answer to the request of another or several others, to draw forth for them also in their need a voice of God; but how much would be requisite besides to give to such a mediator an enduring confidence among others! And yet this higher cultivation of what belongs to the essential nature of revelation must already have taken place in prehistoric times, since the words for the idea of the prophet or foreteller go back in all languages to those primitive times which we can only approximately estimate aright by their abiding results. Only the first movements of poetry are to all appearance earlier, for the oldest portions of revelation known to us always flow in the same lofty speech that befits the higher excitement of the human mind and the impulse to illustrate it by a corresponding elevation of discourse.[1] As this tendency of revelation became more completely developed and strengthened there grew up, without doubt, a peculiar language as the constant uniform vehicle of all divine words or oracles, the language which, varying according to its special subject, elevates itself to the sweep of the poet's lines. Through such an utterance there sounds conspicuously the sublime ego of the Deity in whose spirit the human voice of the prophet spoke; and this short but mighty word, with the corresponding elevation of all the thoughts and words that found expression, was the characteristic mark of the divine discourse.[2] What at first involuntarily, simply from the inner pressure of the man as he struggled for a divine word, resounded towards him in surprising tones, might, if the oracle became farther developed, easily become a mere standing custom of prophetic speech; but it served at all events to maintain for a long time the universal mysterious style of this high discourse.

§ 29. That among the people of Israel prophets were sought out in the most ancient times, and that Moses was not chronologically the first of them, admits of no doubt.[3] What Moses was is clear enough. He was the greatest prophet, not merely of Israel, but of all antiquity, and his life-work having essentially a prophetic character, yet at the

---

[1] What is said in the *Proph. des Alt. Bundes*, i. p. 51 f. with respect to Hebrew, applies just as well to the oldest prophet-like pieces of the Egyptians and Greeks and other old nations, and is repeated in the Koran.

[2] As may be seen now very clearly in the sacred speech of the Egyptian hieroglyphics.

[3] Hos. xii. 13, Moses is called quite indefinitely a prophet, as if he were only one of the many prophets mentioned in ver. 10. The meaning is, one who was a mere prophet once sufficed to lead Israel so nobly. That there were prophets in pre-Mosaic times, Gen. xx. 7, xxv. 22 clearly express.

same time transcends it as a new creation. After he became the founder of a community of the true religion in which everything spiritual, and so the working of the prophetic spirit, took its true course and aim, and with this for the first time obtained its full freedom, all prophecy, as was possible in antiquity, became more and more transformed in freer and higher exercise. The prophet of the true God did not merely wait for those who sought him out and wished through him to hear the voice and receive the counsel of God. Moses did not wait thus, but rather, as the spokesman and servant of God, worked freely in relation to all men, and his word became the freest expositor and defender of the mind and being of God to the world. Accordingly each member of this community has the unimpeachable right to step forth as a prophet of the true God, and attempt what may be possible to him as such; and while it was admitted that there can never be too many genuine prophets in Israel, it was held to be Israel's peculiar glory that it had had an abundance of them from the earliest times.[1] If, now, the highest freedom which prophetic action could win for itself in antiquity was thus given, this freedom had yet its proper limits, since the prophet, standing in this great compact community of the true God, and conscious that his freedom was preserved only through its continuance, was under restraint to the main characteristics and unalterable laws of the true religion, which had authoritative sway only in that community. The co-operation of these two apparently opposite yet mutually necessary powers that conditioned and ennobled everything, viz. freedom and its proper limitation, must have become most active and fruitful after the time of David and Solomon, when the very existence of this community of the true religion was imperilled as it had never been before. It is from the prophets of these centuries, whose works, moreover, have been most completely preserved,

[1] Cf. Hos. xii. 10 and the proverb explained in the *Lehrbuch*, etc., p. 680; but also all we know of the schools of the prophets (*Hist.* ii. 599 f.). Such extremely free prophetic schools, with the freedom of prophecy itself, we find nowhere else in antiquity.

that we shall show upon what a new and elevated stage revelation can be placed by the labours of prophets, if only they truly strive after and more and more perfectly accomplish what lies in their destiny. And collating with care all that is known to us from authentic and trustworthy sources, we can sketch so clear a picture of the actual work of the men of the Divine Spirit, that we may in brief refer its five principal features to the five principal but different names by which the old language designates the genuine prophet in the manifoldness of his vocation.

1. Nothing is more noteworthy, in the outset, than that everything attests how vigorous the reciprocal action between genuine religion and revelation was among the prophets. This fear of God, according to the fundamental law of the community of the Old Covenant, was to animate every member of it, and must constantly dwell in the prophet in the most active and the purest form; this is regarded as so very self-evident that only one of the latest prophets, at a time when it was of moment once more to reawaken in Israel the undiminished ardour and the thorough integrity of the old lofty prophets, designedly places before our eyes [1] a vivid ideal description of it to arouse emulation where he could, and first of all to stimulate and admonish his own spirit. It is the most animating and inspiring description possible, and might be applicable equally to every member of the community of the genuine fear of God, did not one see that pre-eminently and necessarily the prophet himself is meant. The older prophets did not deem it essential to draw such ideal pictures of the life and aims of the genuine prophet, but so much the more clearly in the case of every one of them does his own actual life speak, as all the strictly historical traces show.[2] Of Amos,

---

[1] Isa. l. 4-9; a universal application actually follows, ver. 10. The better life of the godly is sketched, l. 10, cf. xli. 5, lix. 19. The great Unnamed repeats in all his discourses his great word, "Fear not!" (similarly to Christ), but still in the proper place lays stress upon the right fear, so confirming our previous remarks, p. 29 f.

[2] Such traces are given in the *Proph. des Alt. Bundes*, and in the History.

THE STAGES OF REVELATION. 53

Hosea, Isaiah, Jeremiah, enough is known to-day to enable us to say this.

There is one conception especially, taken from the wide circle of such a God-fearing life, which admits of a primary reference to the prophets; viz. that of a "disciple" or pupil,[1] as employed by the same later prophet. As the good disciple must constantly turn the eye and the ear most intently to his master, eager to catch even the smallest hint or the faintest word, and when once convinced what his will is, must be ready to carry it out with the purest devotion and solicitude; so the prophet is to act in the presence of his invisible and eternal Lord. And if men commonly learn only of men, yet however it is to be desired that they act as confidently, as discreetly, as joyfully as if God Himself had taught them; so the prophets are to be taught constantly and immediately of God, as the hope is all men will be some day in the consummation of things, according to the same later prophet.[2] But if this habit of mind is to endure and to be ever the same in the life of the true, ideal prophet, he must, on the other hand, even if it were in a moment of rare emotion of mind, have previously known the true God, vividly and profoundly, in His whole truth and glory, as never before; he must have trembled before the divine holiness, and been touched impressively by the Divine Spirit, and received new and wondrous strengthening; he must have heard a clear call from God as from his immortal Lord; or he may deceive himself from the first as to his entering upon the career and doing the work of a prophet. Such a solitary moment of divine consecration has with genuine prophets a powerful influence upon the whole subsequent life, and some of the greatest of them, upon a retrospect of their protracted and changeful labours, seek to depict the rare sublimity and power of such a first memorable beginning

---

[1] Isa. l. 4. [The word in this passage is translated "*apostel*" in Ewald's *Proph.*, etc.—TR.]

[2] Isa. liv. 13, cf. Jer. xxxiv. 34 ff.

of all their divine work with a corresponding elevation of thought.[1]

But in everything that is properly designated revelation, the human spirit has a wholly peculiar mood and energy, and in such moments may feel itself absorbed into the divine, so that the Divine Spirit alone is active within it. Moreover, it may be surmised that where revelation struggles to communicate itself, another spirit stirs in man than that which commonly animates him. It is thus explained how the prophet may be called "the man of the spirit,"[2] or, as we should say, "the inspired man." Nor is it surprising that afterwards, when the prophetic spirit had for many centuries produced the most extraordinary results and authenticated itself in imperishable deeds, it should at last be conceived and described as itself a distinct mysterious power. That the Spirit of Jahveh laid hold upon a man with overmastering force is an old way of speaking; towards the eighth and seventh centuries before Christ some writers venture in higher discourse and narrative to speak of "the Spirit" without any additional phrase, when they mean properly the mighty power the prophetic spirit had in those centuries long since gained. And the fact that this term by itself may indicate even the seductive charm of the misguided prophetic spirit, shows how prevalent this way of speaking became.[3] Commonly, however, it is only the wonderful, mysterious influence of the prophetic rapture itself which is thus designated, especially in the peculiarly new phraseology of Ezekiel.[4]

Although the prophet could thus be called "the man of the

---

[1] Isa. vi.; Jer. i.; Ezek. i.-iii.

[2] Hos. ix. 7, but only interchangeably with the name for prophet in the other member of the verse; and this shows that it had not yet passed over into common speech. But even in Paul this name is by no means frequent.

[3] In the singular narrative, 1 Kings xxii. 21-23; in its mode of expression it stands almost alone in the Bible, and suggests an author whose style is not otherwise known.

[4] Nevertheless Ezekiel speaks in narration only indefinitely of a spirit which has penetrated him, strengthened him, carried him to this place or that, ii. 2, iii. 12, 24, viii. 3, xliii. 5, cf. with the contrary xi. 5, and the similar case 1 Chron. xii. 18.

Spirit," yet this name was not so frequently employed in those older times as might be supposed from later conceptions of what is "inspired." For in those days the healthy conception of the Divine Spirit, revealing itself manifoldly elsewhere than in the prophets, was still fresh and powerful. And another right feeling of high antiquity declared that in addition to inspiration as the commencement and the general basis of the prophetic activity, still other properties and powers must be found, before a prophet steps forth who really deserves the name. For

§ 30. 2. there is a very striking representation that every genuine prophet in his public appearance and work was to be a "messenger" of the true God sent to men. As a great lord cannot himself do everything the wellbeing of his house or kingdom demands, but instead of himself sends everywhere, where it seems good to him, one of his confidential servants[1] armed with his commands and his authority; so the prophet is nowhere to prosecute his own affairs, but only the business which God appoints in His kingdom. The figure of messenger with the word itself is taken from the administration of the great kingdoms of ancient time, and it is finally appropriate so far as it represents the world of humanity as the great distant realm to which God is always devoting His special care. According to primitive conception the prophet might also be held as pre-eminently "the servant of God," serving Him out of love and loyalty, and as a loyal servant sustained and aided by His protection; that is to say, not as a bond-slave, but as a free house-servant or client of his Lord, whose confidence he possesses, and whose will he executes. With the great Unnamed especially these are favourite images, by which he presents the ideal not merely of the prophet, but of every member of the community of the true God, and so ultimately

---

[1] Cf. concerning the signification of this "imperial messenger" in the old empires, *Hist.* iii. p. 641 f. Their name, מַלְאָךְ, received ultimately in Æthiopic (like our "statthalter" or rather "proconsul") the sense of a foreign ruler (Dillmann's *Christ. Æth.* p. 124, st. 73).

of all Israel as one man.[1] In the case of the prophet, however, the ideal is to have its primary and distinctest realization.

But the prophet receives his special divine call for a wholly special situation and period of human affairs; and serious complications and dangers threatening the whole nation and kingdom leave to the spirit of a truly great prophet no rest until of destinies so dark he obtains the divine solution. If, however, the condition of one out of many human kingdoms, and particularly of one suffering from grave defects, cannot be thoroughly estimated without an exact and comprehensive survey of all the rest, the prophet must be lifted up to such a high point of observation as will enable him at one glance clearly to grasp the entire position of all human affairs as before God. It is this calm and elevated, yet keen and watchful survey of things in their temporal variation and eternal similarity which from the first distinguishes every genuine prophet, and which he must constantly maintain; as, indeed, the ancient prophet Amos begins his prophecy concerning the kingdom of Israel with such a glance at surrounding kingdoms.[2] And as from this pure divine height all the different classes and families of his own people are alike comprehended in his view, so in the wider survey over all nations his own nation does not appear as a favourite whose profound defects he must not see and condemn. But if the prophet, in intelligent retrospect of the past, has obtained this wide sweep of vision over all human affairs of his time, it is not for him, with precipitate judgment and confused onward look into the future, to speak of anything that has perhaps moved and agitated him most profoundly. As a "watchman" of the night, continually alert but cautious,

---

[1] Isa. xlii. 1-4, xliv. 26 ff., with the passage previously explained, 1. 4-9. It is as if Haggai, i. 13, formed the name "messenger of Jahveh" for prophet, according to the then new expression, Isa. xliv. 26; it was imitated only in higher discourse, as Mal. iii. 1, but never became prevalent in common speech.

[2] Amos i. 2-ii. 16. No great prophetic writing, however, lacked such a survey, as I have long since shown.

marks every sound, even the faintest, and listens to every cry for help,[1] or as the "outlooker" at hot high noon peers forth from the lofty watch-tower far and wide to descry the distant approach of thunder-storms or foes,[2] so is he to remain in calm persistent watching, till at the favourable moment he discerns in the Divine Spirit what he must announce and hears the divine word he must repeat.[3] But, standing as he does upon his high watch-tower above the din of the world, especially is he to look stedfastly to heaven itself to mark betimes and distinctly the signs and the soft or louder voices that come from thence.[4] Such conceptions of the higher duty of every prophet were formed with increasing facility and growing completeness, so that, at least in the higher speech, the prophet is already characterized briefly as the "outlooker" or "scout." Yet such a name could not as yet be his common name, because everything hitherto described relates rather to the preliminary conditions under which a genuine prophet could arise and enter upon his work.

§ 31. 3. The function of the prophet peculiar to him, expected of him, and without which his further activity is impossible, is that in the complication and darkness of human affairs he should behold distinctly their necessary divine issue, and things which no mortal eye has seen as yet, he should see already close at hand and in all certainty. Now it must be noted here that there is a possibility of foresight in human affairs, because these affairs, however endlessly diversified and varied, however complicated and confused by the intermingling of human guilt, yet ultimately, both in the great whole and in

---

[1] In the old prophet, Isa. xxi. 11 f.

[2] The image of the sultry noon, Isa. xviii. 4-6, but there not immediately of the prophet; the image of the outlook is a very favourite one from Mic. vii. 4, 7, and Isa. lvi. 10; see Jer. vi. 17; Ezek. iii. 17, xxxiii. 2-7; cf. also Hab. ii. 1 ff.

[3] Thy "outlooker," *i.e.* thy prophet, Isa. lii. 8, indicating briefly and specially the watchful *foresight* of the genuine prophet. The figure of the shepherd is rarely used, because the idea of rule is connected with it (see *Proph.* i. p. 24); in Zech. xi. 4 ff. the reference is to the kingdom of the ten tribes, where the prophet might be actually held as co-ruler with the king.

[4] Hab. ii. 1; Isa. xxi. 6-10.

the minutest detail, have their possibility, their limits, their course, and their issue only in God Himself and His powers. Is there then in all human affairs connection and progress, and limit also, and an issue that differs according to the disturbance of human guilt, there is also for the human mind that moves in the midst of this flow of events the possibility, not merely of some foresight of their development and calculation of their issue, but also of an accurate foresight, if only that mind does not remain at a distance from the divine mind, and does not assume in such foresight more than is admissible, considering its conditions in this sensuous body. A capability of accurate foresight may therefore be spoken of as, amongst a thousand others, possible to the human mind; but at once it is evident how different it may be in degree as the individual (1) more or less is versed and watchful in human affairs in whose current he has placed himself, surveys with clearness the experiences and teaching of the past, knows with exactness the relations of the present, and is fully accustomed to draw from the one and the other conclusions with respect to the future; (2) more or less allows himself to be possessed purely by the Divine Spirit, and permanently led by it, so that he is not himself beclouded and enfeebled by obscuration through human guilt; and (3) more or less is from the first of energetic temper,—for this last weight is also to be laid in the scale. And then it follows that the foresight of the human mind, especially capable in the proportion that these qualifications exist, is in so far limited that it can only foresee (1) what, from the divine teaching of all history already experienced, and from certain insight into the actual affairs of the present, presents itself to the human spirit as it is quickened by the divine; and at the same time, which is just as important, (2) what is directly perceptible by certain inference from the smaller to the greater with which it is essentially related. Everything that goes beyond these safe limits may indeed be a more or less striking conjecture or guess, or may result from the noblest and purest effort of the mind to penetrate the darkness of the future, and to measure the temporal progress of the development of human affairs; but of more precise significance and of decisive truth it cannot be.

For many reasons it is well to bear in mind these limits of all prophecy so far as the foresight of things future is concerned. But what indispensable value, what wealth of knowledge, of admonition, of consolation belongs to prophecy when it is perfected in its own sphere, full of energy in itself, and rich in blessing from without! A good capacity of foresight in the small things of daily life is always useful; and the more extensive and complicated human affairs become, the more necessary is such a gift; but where can this necessity be greater than in the important affairs of whole nations and kingdoms of the earth? And it is just these which absorb the attention of the true prophet.[1] But prophetic foresight has in it something more than mere foresight: it starts from the divine certainty of the development of human affairs in conformity with their origin and continuous impulse, and it shows how the divine will, standing in its inviolability high above them, guides them ever and only in consistency with itself and to its own ultimate aim. It is this calm penetrating glance toward lofty heights and most difficult complications of human affairs, this clear retrospect into the distant past, and sure forward look into the future which are united in the genuine prophet, and which, in the consciousness that he beholds only, even against his human will, that which the Spirit of the true God allows him to behold, make him what he is as a seer. Since he always starts from some special and definite complications of human affairs, and seeks divine light upon their darkness, his glance into the future does not lose itself in indeterminate generalities; and there ever float, as in the most vivid forms before his seer's eye, the firm outlines and radiant splendour of pictures of the future, always new and always changing, as the rays of certain knowledge of the

---

[1] As the last prophets themselves confess most plainly, Jer. i. 4-19; Ezek. xxxiii. 2 ff.

divine harmony of things vivify and illumine them. And since the power of foresight was not to be preserved by artificial means, but to be sustained simply by the overshadowing presence of God, it was able in the free emulation of the efforts of great prophets to rise on this basis to an elevation otherwise unknown, and everything connected with prophecy could here perfect itself as, historically speaking, nowhere else in antiquity.

But just on this account can we here so clearly see the ultimate bounds that are set from the first to prophetic prescience. All the incomparable prophets, even the greatest, in the centuries intervening between David and Solomon and the first destruction of Jerusalem, prophesy within two high and insurmountable limits—that of the age in which they lived, and that of their own thought and foresight. Lying far back in the past, they beheld not only the brilliant origin and unchanging fundamental laws of the community of the true religion which alone are to fill the eye and all other senses, but also the noble indications never to be forgotten of a national prosperity and happiness, culminating in this community in the time of David, which already had more or less seriously deteriorated, and was at present profoundly imperilled. That the people themselves bear the guilt of this decline and threatening ruin of the nation of the community of the true God is just as much the firm conviction of these prophets as it is their sure and certain hope that the genuine fear of God here established would nevertheless not for ever remain without the eternal blessing of heaven, and that the deep underlying principles of this community of the true God, once firmly established, would never more be utterly destroyed. And so in the deepest darkness of the present they look into the future with no comfortless despondency, and foretell, even amid all the misery and subversions of the times, with the purest confidence and the most inflexible strength of divine certainty, the surely coming perfection of all the germs of the higher and better life once implanted in humanity in accordance with the will of God. With such firmness and assurance did their presaging spirit move within the utmost bounds of all human time, and thus are they the founders of a hope never to be quenched, and of a prophecy that in its simplest elements endures for ever. It is part of the assured serenity and divine truth of their prophecy that they nowhere discover in their immediate present this ultimate consummation of all human things, but at most see around them only the germs of it and the indisputable signs of its coming, and to these they point the despairing in the conspicuous darkness of their time. Certain stages and transitions they also on this account always depict as necessary between their present and that ultimate consummation. But he who should demand to-day that with historical exactitude and fulness they should indicate all the particular incidents, great or small, that lie between the then present and the last consummation of all human affairs, would not only make a great mistake himself, but would also attribute to them what is without justification and wholly inadmissible. All prophecy, even of the greatest and most accomplished prophets, can only express the divine truth and necessity of the relation of the present to that eternal development and consummation of human affairs that answers to the will of God: and the more correctly a prophet perceives and adjusts in this sense the most minute detail of confusion in the present, the more accomplished is he as a prophet.

Now it is certain that in the Bible no piece of prophetic writing, small or great, is found which does not open its glance into the mysteries of the future. Not as if the prophet in his thoughts and discourse ever broke out altogether abruptly into prediction concerning anything lying in the remote and wide future, or as if he would merely predict a thing for the sake of predicting it; rather does he always, whether he directs the mind at once to the future or points to it in the progress of his discourse, proceed from the firm ground of his present, and from important phenomena which then agitate the world, and mark in the future only what has its connecting link in the present, and may be either the divinely necessary and direct development of it, or its just as divinely necessary and certain reversal. But if he has firm standing-ground in the present, whence he looks into the future, and if his mind perceives exactly how the things of the present and the past project into the darkness of the future, or how their reversal must be accomplished in it, yet the true prophet nevertheless neither can nor will predict what does not already lie hid in the eternally predetermined development of all earthly things in accordance with the divine laws and truths; so that in the true prophet's prevision it is the infinitely manifold sides of this development that shift and change, and the measure of the clearness and certainty of the objects foreseen is thereby the less or the greater. But since, as already observed, his glance into the future never stops short with generalities, but always sees what it sees with the highest vividness and distinctness, and in strictly definite forms, whilst at the same time the human mind is unable newly to perceive in definite form what is not analogous or similar to that already seen or heard before, it is evident that the particular shapes the future takes to his view can only be pictures of these surely coming things themselves, —pictures borrowed from experience, yet in their last meaning and scope pointing beyond it, and causing phenomena to be anticipated which have first actually to occur in the earnest pressure and flow of events, before it is seen how in detail the fulfilment answers to the prophetic forecast. If any one shall say that so far the prophet with his pictures of the future only casts riddles into the world, whose right solution the fulfilment alone can bring,[1] it is to be added that because of the restraint of the present, and the suspicion or even the open hostility of men, the prophet, should he desire to place the solemnity of the future directly before the eyes of his oppo-

---

[1] This is the peculiarity of the ordinary prophet, which is conspicuous as so full of significance, in the lofty picturing of Num. xii. 6-8, to be further considered below; a passage which manifestly floated also before the mind of the Apostle Paul in his words 1 Cor. xiii. 12.

nents, might prefer to do this in brief significant pictures, stimulating curiosity rather than fully satisfying it; which again comes back to the idea of the enigmatical.[1] If, now, certain of the prophets were fonder than the rest of discoursing in skilfully pointed enigmas, and both Isaiah and Jeremiah rather avoided them, it yet admits of no doubt that prophetic discourse of the future does not seek, as a whole, to predetermine and portray a series of historical events already witnessed, and which, therefore, one need not really wait to see, but the truer the discourse is the more does it give only divine certainties, and in these certainties what is seen in vivid figurative form. And that all true biblical prophets sought to present such certainties only, is just one of the best marks of their simple unsurpassed veracity. Every one of their writings is in this respect a divine verdict.

Here, however, may be most plainly observed how the prophet in the midst of his discourse might lose himself, as it were, altogether in wide realms of thoughts, visions, and anticipations purely divine, and float away out and beyond the whole present, his eye being intoxicated with the wonders of another world. For that he is full of divine thoughts as he discourses, and is sustained and led by God Himself, is with him indeed self-evident; but when his spirit is once in train to behold only the consummation, as it must one day surely come, in opposition to the confusions of the present, and to touch those higher things after which he has so long and so often profoundly yearned, then his discourse expands with ease into an infinitude of ineffable delight and divine certainty, his eye hastens from one sublime picture to another, each enrapturing in its outlook, and the stream of his words swells, not indeed as if it would break through all bounds, but as if restrained within its full banks it would now flow along

[1] Without using the name, Amos (vii. 1-9) gives examples of it; but the name occurs in Hab. ii. 6 ; Ezek. xvii. 2 ; the so-called "Song of Judgment," Isa. xiv. 4-23, after the manner of Ezekiel (xvii. 2, xxi. 3, xxiv. 3), belongs also here.

with the more calmness and repose. Here, in fact, we plainly see the two boundaries of all movement of prophetic thought and discourse. The first overpowering seizure by the divine thought and luminous vision transports the prophet in the highest excitement beyond himself; he is lost in rapture, or, in Greek phrase, in ecstasy;[1] but then follow passages in which, nevertheless, in the midst of this at first so stormy enravishment of self, he sinks as into a long, peaceful, divine dream;[2] comes to far-extending rest and composure, after his most troubled unrest, merely by the happiness of beholding, and in the very beholding itself, of such divine glory; collects himself again with difficulty from the dream which oppresses him, and returns as by a sudden and violent effort to his customary thought and into the full veritable present.[3] All this with the older prophets is involuntary, and varies in each of them with the special occasion, and as the special spirit each happens to possess determines; the later prophets, however, accumulate artificially a multitude of anticipations of the future first awakened by the older prophets. But the less those men of God had actually seen of the further development of the kingdom of God in the following thousand years, and the more profoundly they yearned to see in the unfolding of it what in their past had been scarcely experienced at all save in its beginnings, the more readily is explained the free scope they give to their power, and their inclination to contemplate what no one of them actually witnessed in such perfection.

But here we must also remember, that in proportion as antiquity had no background of numerous and great all-comprehending experiences and teachings, such as we have to-day, the darker and the more dismal appeared the whole

---

[1] Cf. Isa. viii. 11; Ezek. iii. 14.

[2] As a poet once similarly expresses it, Ps. cxxxix. 17, 23.

[3] Such passages as Joel ii. 19–iv. 21; Isa. x. 24–xi. 14; Zech. ix. 9–xi. 12; Micah iv. f., are here meant: from which is seen that only in certain prophets did the power dwell of a vision so vivid and sure, and reaching so widely in all calmness hither and thither.

THE STAGES OF REVELATION. 65

future, and the more powerful must be the longing for new light to disperse this darkness; just as it is to-day in like manner when all the great light the past may have brought is again extinguished. As in the primitive time revelation was only sought the more vigorously because of the lack of it, so in this higher stage of revelation were visions sought; and we know that in the nation of Israel the oldest and most popular name for the prophet was "seer."[1] At the time of the prophets of the higher type, with whom we are here concerned, the new and exacter name, "beholder," "spectator," is preferred, and what was uttered was called a "vision" or "spectacle;" but these new names continue a long time in the narrower circles.[2]

§ 32. 4. But after Moses another name still came into use and obtained general currency, expressing in point of fact the idea of the prophet of the true religion much more completely, and describing exactly his proper distinctive work. For the right understanding of this, we must remember here more particularly how little the mere "seeing," necessary though it was, sufficed for the best aim of prophetic activity. The prophet is not to discourse for himself, or, as a poet, chiefly for his own pleasure and satisfaction. Of what advantage is it to him to have merely seen what no other mind has seen in the same way? To behold things most vividly and creatively only places him on a level with the best of poets. What he has seen and heard, in the spirit, of divine things of the future, must he rather with the same vividness and truth publish to men as revealed to him by his own and their God. But here

---

[1] According to 1 Sam. ix. 9; but that this name רֹאֶה maintained itself in the nation still longer, either poetically or provincially, is clear from Isa. xxx. 10.

[2] Historically it is of course important that the name חֹזֶה, "beholder," and חָזָה, "to behold," in the sense of "to prophesy" (as רָאָה, Isa. xxx. 10), with all further derivatives, properly distinguish the prophets after Samuel and David only, as is evident from Joel iii. 1, Amos vii. 12, and all other indications; thereby is seen the more clearly that prophecy in Israel ran through many different stages, and built itself up with increasing elevation and freedom through long periods of time.

EWALD I.   E

difficulties accumulate before him to the last degree. If the condition of mind in which a man seeks to penetrate an overshadowing present darkness, and to obtain a new, bright conception how the future must shape itself out of existing confusions, is one of unusual excitement, the excitement increases if, as a prophet, he desires to elevate his spirit above all his perhaps most cherished human purposes and wishes to the pure sacredness and awe of the divine will, and to obtain a clear image, in strict conformity with it, of what the future must bring. Yet the higher enlightenment does not come at his arbitrary beck and call, but as a surprise, and indeed the higher it is the more profoundly does it seize and agitate him.[1] If, now, in such moments, the most dazzling, and yet, in accordance with the divine righteousness prevailing over all human sin, the truest picture of what must come confronts him, how shall he not himself as a man tremble with fear in its presence? But his agitation may in the same moment mount still higher should his spirit be overpowered also by a vivid conception of the frightful perils to which he will be exposed in publishing before men, with all divine confidence, freely and clearly, everything the Spirit impels him to publish, and should he be the more deeply sensible of his own feebleness as compared with the task he is conscious the Divine Omnipotence demands of him. There are times when the prophet has to contend, temporarily it may be, or even a whole life long, against the most stiff-necked obstinacy and hostility of men towards divine truth and the best prophetic counsel.[2] A human tremulousness then readily overpowers him; and, even in the case of many an otherwise approved prophet, the divine confidence perhaps suddenly transforms itself into gloomy human fear, whose overmastering force leads him to persist more and more in the most perverse con-

[1] As later writers in the "prophetless" time experience the more definitely, and make the more prominently conspicuous, Dan. x. 8 ff.; Rev. i. 17; Acts ix. 4-8.

[2] As was the case with Jeremiah; with Isaiah, probably, also during almost the whole of his life; even Elijah desponds temporarily, 1 Kings xix. 2-15.

THE STAGES OF REVELATION. 67

duct.¹ But should he nevertheless remain faithful, as the true religion directly and emphatically demands of him, and as the early and fundamental idea of a prophet in this community presupposes,—for when once he was seized by the all-powerful hand of God and impelled to speak the word of God before the world, resistance on his part was inadmissible,²—then his zeal for that which is holy may be the more profoundly enkindled in proportion as the opposition and hatred of men, as he may be well aware, are directed with the more bitterness and blindness, not so much against himself as against the word of God he publishes, and his whole prophetic work; and still further, that zeal may culminate in the highest conceivable passion if he sees those who should be the foremost guardians of divine truth, even the prophets, advising and working corruption and ruin, seduced by the errors and blandishments of the time, and if he finds himself alone against the whole world in which he lives.³ Deeply hurt and bewildered by this ceaseless antagonism, his word, turned vehemently against all the world, may diverge into rashness; in such excitement even the best prophet may by his gesture and discourse seem bereft of his senses, if he does not actually become so for life;⁴ and since the prophet is called to action, his whole appearance as he enters upon his work may be that of a madman.⁵

Perhaps we understand now how the individual man, seized by inspiration, may sink down to this low level both in action and speech, as before stated (§ 27). But of the prophet who is to speak, not for himself but for others, something quite different is fairly expected; and therefore he alone was held to be a genuine prophet who was capable of proclaiming clearly and

---

[1] As the Book of Jonah teaches so picturesquely.

[2] As likewise the Book of Jonah teaches; but cf. also the express assertions in Amos iii. 3-8; Isa. viii. 11; Jer. i. 4-19, xv. 15-21; Ezek. iii. 14.

[3] As Jeremiah so often says, and expresses it in the clearest way, xxiii. 9-24.

[4] As Hosea says, ix. 7, with a clear reference to the peculiar peril to which he himself had been so near.

[5] That such instances are not wanting even in Israel in certain times of utter declension is evident, not only from the express words, 2 Kings ix. 11, Jer. xxix. 26, but also from such descriptions as Isa. xxviii. 7 ff., xxix. 9 ff.

in full possession of his faculties whatever he had seen in the hour of inspiration and had heard from his God. The prophet is to be the "spokesman" to men of the God who in Himself is silent; and the more suitably, with eloquent tongue, yet in harmony with the holiness of God, he publishes His will, the more perfect must he be held to be as a prophet. Hence it is that he receives what in Hebrew is by far his best and at the same time his ultimately prevailing name, Nabî;[1] but even the Greek name "Prophet" also signifies one who speaks forth clearly the word of his God,[2] and thus is essentially distinguished from that of the "Mantis," who, as individual revealer merely of his own private inspiration, according to the common heathen view, can discourse the more freely as one carried away by fanaticism and frenzy. Such a prophet, in the genuine sense of the term, was Moses;[3] but his word of Jahveh was of the most antique type, short, sharp, decisive, full of definiteness and authority, like the word of a field-marshal; and it took this form with him the more readily, in accordance with this oldest mode of its delivery, in proportion as he, being a prophet, was at the same time the leader of his whole nation. But in this respect also he was as good as unique in Israel; and in the times after him, as, on the one hand, new and grave dangers of all kinds became more

[1] Cf. *Proph. of the Old Test.* i. p. 7 f., 14 (Eng. ed. i. p. 8, 16). The true signification of נָבִיא, as a speaker discoursing distinctly and clearly, is not opposed to the fact that the genuine oracle of Jahveh is introduced or even closed with the archaic expression " נְאֻם, and this rather indicates the sound mysteriously coming forth out of the depth of the chest (cf. Arabic for "swan song" of the Phœnix, Harîrî, p. 172, 3 f. sac., and also for "to charm," p. 379, 1); for this word, heard by the prophet at first as in dark secrecy, is he to speak out clearly, and so as to be intelligible to every man. The newly-formed שְׁמוּעָה, Isa. xxviii. 19, Obad. ver. 1, signifies more clearly an "oracle," as "something to be heard," "a piece heard," as the prophet has heard it of God, that others may also hear it. Yet the usual name for it is " דָּבָר, "word of Jahveh."

[2] The *pro* signifies in this compound word, as in *pronunciare, proclamare*, the distinct loud sounding forth. The sense of "foreteller" the word does not give originally; but how much in reality the Greek προφήτης was nevertheless distinguished from the Hebrew Nabî will be evident below.

[3] See further, below.

and more oppressive to the community of the true God he founded, and on the other, the published word with poetry, prose, and all other forms of intellectual activity in Israel were cultivated with growing freedom and success, prophetic discourse also here fashioned itself from one stage to another, until the highest point was reached which in the whole of antiquity was possible. And by far the greater part of the literary productions of a prophetic character which we now possess come to us from this same period of highest development of prophetic work in Israel—the period in the midst of which we here stand.[1]

It is not to be overlooked, it is true, that although the prophet took the name which became so prevalent from his clear utterance of the word of God, he is by no means to be estimated by his mere capacity to express such a word; rather, indeed, when the fine mode of prophetic expression was once highly perfected, might the untruest word be dignified with the smoothest, most ravishing, or even most thrilling prophetic style, as was actually the case at times in Israel. Ultimately the great matter is what the prophet has seen (§ 31) in moments of inspiration previously to all discourse to other men, whether it contain truth or untruth, good or ill counsel. Moreover, since the prophet in his excitement and ecstasy may be too vehemently moved, and be scarcely capable of giving adequate expression to what he has seen or heard, or from other reasons, may not be very apt in clear, eloquent public discourse, persons were early found who were held to be capable of better understanding the obscure, fragmentary, hesitating word of the inspired man, and explaining it to the waiting audience, and their services were in request; these are interpreters, or if the inspired man is called a prophet, these are, so to speak, under-prophets, in Greek, hypophetes.[2]

---

[1] From the older time comes principally the fragment, Ex. xxiii. 20-33, as explained in the *Jahrb. der Bibl. wiss.* xii. p. 193 ff.

[2] ὑποφήτης, or as below, p. 75, he is also called the mouthpiece. Theocr. *Eid.* 22, 116.

Such a rather artificial development of the oracle was, from special causes, very prevalent in heathenism, and even in the Israelitish nation was not unknown, at least in the earliest times.[1] The creative prophet who could thus hold himself in the background was then regarded by strict analogy as the God, his interpreter as his prophet and mediator to men.[1] But it is one of the many marks of a healthy growth and unfolding of prophecy as a whole, that in Israel this artificiality in the progress of years found less and less approval; and at the time of the great prophets among whom we now stand every trace of it in actual life had been obliterated. What the seer had seen, it was understood to be fitting that as a prophet he should know how to express clearly before all the world.

It is wonderful to note how in general and in detail the word of God, or rather of Jahveh, took shape in the mouth of these prophets. They had no longer, as Moses had, the leading of the nation so completely that the mere word of Jahveh was implicitly obeyed as it flowed in inspiration from their lips. It is still, no doubt, the highest Ego alone from whose lofty elevation they ever discourse of the world, of the mightiest kings of their own nation and all other nations, to whose mind superintending and governing the world they have sole regard, and whose invincible word about the world they boldly publish with the same irresistible energy with which it flashed in upon themselves. Moreover, still bears sway within them as steadily as ever the old faith that this word of His, as the word of truth, is not made known in vain; that its consolation and its promise build up, its condemnation and judgment overturn and destroy;[2] that it will penetrate as fire, and as a hammer smite the rock.[3] But the powers of the world had undergone vast changes since the time of Moses. Kingly power in the State had assumed amongst

---

[1] As we see both cases in the narratives to be explained below, Ex. iv. 10, 17, vii. 1 f. But in like manner arises the same ἑρμηνευτής, also in that time as it were overflowing with never visible inspiration, 1 Cor. xiv. 27 f.

[2] See both in conjunction, Jer. i. 4–19.

[3] Jer. xxiii. 29; and already earlier, Micah ii. 11, iii. 8.

themselves an increasing rigour, and become more and more jealous of its own authority; even in the kingdom of the ten tribes it was so ultimately, and with the more one-sidedness, as it proved, after the long struggle with the purely spiritual force of prophecy. Intellectual culture among the people had become, step by step, after so many centuries, broader and richer, especially in oratory and literature; but their old spiritual freedom, fostered and favoured as it was by the fundamental laws of the community of the true religion itself, now turned itself in its high vigour against even the prophets themselves, and treated with suspicion, and indeed open mockery and scorn, their venerable authority; moreover, the office of the prophet, through the number of low-minded, mercenary men who had filled it, had itself sunk very low in general esteem, and now suffered severely enough under the prevalent impression that it was no longer, as in Moses' day, the safest refuge and the noblest redeeming force of the nation. Indeed, the better prophets had long been conscious that if in these times the word of Jahveh were to be published with the success worthy of it, it could keep no longer its severe simplicity, or stand on its old lofty height; it therefore deigned to take note of all the objections of opponents, to discuss at large and in full detail everything affecting its message, to change with rapidity, as the need of the moment suggested, the colour of its language and the mode of delivery, to adopt every varied resource of art—the sententiousness of the sage, the grace of the poet, and to carry its activity everywhere openly in every place before the people and before judges and princes when the higher aim demanded it. The prophet became a kind of popular orator, his word the most flexible and fluent, emulous in its form of the charm of all art, and ever ready as well and without trace of fatigue. It was no longer possible to make conspicuous at once the highest Ego in every passage of the discourse; the human feelings of the prophet also, his joy, his deep pain, even the blazing up of his fiery zeal and the sorrowful dejection he could scarcely hide, found manifold expression. Thus the strongest human element pervaded the prophet's word, and to men this was most ravishing, and where possible, instructive; while everywhere the higher dignity was still maintained, and in every suitable place there resounded freely the voice of that highest Ego by whom alone the prophet was consciously supported and upheld; indeed this Ego, with its unique elevation, is in the last issue supreme over all, so that the most human and the most humanly deferent discourse remains nevertheless the most divine. This is the true characteristic of this discourse, its wonderful charm, its undecaying power; there is absolutely nothing like it in all antiquity. Nor can we fail here specially to note that it is not in vain that man bathes his spirit thus completely in the Divine Spirit, suffers it, as it were, entirely to disappear before it, and to be invigorated and led by it alone in thought and discourse, even as in action also, provided only he does not thereby at any moment lose the distinct consciousness of his own limitation and weakness and the necessity for an ever uniform godliness of life.

Furthermore, mere speech of itself, even the aptest, most ravishing, and truest, does not suffice with the prophet. Just as certainly as clear, eloquent utterance of God's word is his chief duty and chief accomplishment, is it also certain that his whole higher duty did not end there. As in speaking he is to be the most active and unwearied promoter of the divine cause in humanity, so his whole life must be devoted only to this one true aim. Accordingly, in the case of all the great prophets, the more particularly and fully we contemplate them in the traces and evidences of their history preserved to us, the more certainly do we see that their whole life and conduct was ever in keeping with their public discourse. Besides prophets like Amos, who felt suddenly impelled by the Divine Spirit, and perhaps only for a short time, there were always some who from their early years devoted themselves wholly to this one vocation. In such cases the prophet found in every important experience of his life indications of the working and purpose of the same true God whose mind and word he felt himself called to publish; and everything he had to do in all freedom, he did spontaneously in the same mind and spirit; even his whole house was for him the seat sometimes of the living recognition, sometimes of the announcement and preservation of the same divine truths he represented openly before the world.[1] But if any truth, notwithstanding luminous image and parable in artistic discourse, would scarcely be plain to the people, or if the fulfilment of any important promise he had publicly uttered was unexpectedly long delayed, and it seemed necessary to keep a memorial and pledge of it distinctly and palpably manifest before the eyes of all, then, of set purpose indeed, through some action of his, he gave signs or symbols of it that should arrest the attention and not be easily overlooked, and instituted public witnesses that might speak in future in like manner; and in all this he acted spontaneously, as it were, sustained by the same spirit that prompted him to open discourse.[2] But even authorship, especially the collection and digest of public addresses, and the record of public acts, was to these noblest of prophets simply the appropriate continuance and confirmation of the chief part of their work, since it would serve just as well for the better preservation, diffusion, and perpetuity of their thoughts as for the calm and abiding vindication of their whole public activity; and the last consideration was by no means the least important.

§ 33. 5. But there is something still beyond all this about which the prophet is in the end to make no mistake. His prophetic work is to be regarded as closed, his divine commission, he may suppose he has received, discharged, with this fearless but prudent utterance of the word of God, and this action in a single given case otherwise supporting it. In

---

[1] Cf. *Proph. of Old Test.* i. 182 ff. [Eng. ed. i. 223 ff.], 280 ff. [Eng. ed. ii. 12 ff.], ii. p. 460 f. [Eng. ed. iv. 130 f.].
[2] *Ibid.* i. p. 27 f. [Eng. ed. i. 45 f.].

every suitable way it is competent to him to publish and advance the divine truth, and that he becomes its herald and defender at the right time and place, undismayed by opposition and unappalled by danger,—this is his virtue, his glory, his highest merit. But he is not arbitrarily and with violent hand to seek either to aid or anticipate the divine will, nor to invade with disturbing hand the sphere of other powers of human government. He has legitimately one single authority and force, that of divine truth; and this in a well-ordered commonwealth has its divine right and a use nothing else can serve, but it bears its divine fruit only as its activity is confined to its own authorized province and bounds. When, therefore, in a fixed case he has done all that his good offices can accomplish, and has done it often in the hot turmoil and conflict of the world, he is quietly to withdraw himself, and, as one who on his part has acted in all good conscience in harmony with the will of God, is to wait in patience the result and issue of his public work. All this is for him the more necessary, the more readily he may be carried away to all kinds of excess and violence, because of the storm-like outburst of his soul, and his glowing zeal for that which is holy (§ 32), and the more certainly every prophetic work is essentially an irresistible summons and command from above. If, now, the great prophets of the older time had not themselves gradually recognised more and more clearly and observed with an ever greater loyalty this last necessity and these divine limits, yet the later prophets act more and more inviolably within them,[1] and at length give distinct expression to them as fundamental laws.[2] So that it is here noticeable how the fruit produced by the steady action, the one upon the other, of genuine godliness and prophecy, was the riper and more abundant the longer such action continued.

---

[1] As the whole life and suffering of Jeremiah pre-eminently show.

[2] As is instanced by Ezekiel's words, which in their style have a wholly new and sharp definiteness. Cf. *Proph. of Old Test.* ii. p. 325 f. [Eng. ed. iv. p. 5 f.].

The genuine prophet may on this account, finally, be conceived and described with special appropriateness as the "interpreter" of the true God.[1] For the interpreter or dragoman is the indispensable mediator between two parties who without him could not understand each other, nor unite in a common beneficial work, and he has also nothing more to do than convey in words faithfully and intelligibly what the one commissions him to convey to the other; just so is it with the genuine prophet, he stands in this highest relation between God, who Himself continues altogether silent and hidden, and man. Or, as on the one side there is the high Lord and Ruler of all men, and the matter in question affects His kingdom and authority on earth, the prophet likewise is appropriately enough likened to a chief minister—not as if he had the material power of his sovereign, but only in so far as he has been taken into his secret counsel, and is his confidential adviser, and expresses and communicates publicly as the mouthpiece of the mighty and scarcely accessible or visible Lord what the royal counsel has determined.[2] It is evident that when such a first confidential counsellor does not answer to his trust, he must experience the more severely the anger of the king to whom he has access as no other has; so the prophet also, should he become unworthy of his name, forfeits implicit confidence and incurs heavy responsibility.[3] Or since love is the mightiest attribute of the true God, the most beautiful image offers itself, viz. that of God as the higher friend and older relative who honours the prophet as a younger friend with the charge of His house and goods, but only that He may have in him in the conflict with men the best advocate of His cause and defender of His right.[4] And

[1] This figure is not found till a relatively late period, at the time, namely, when the nation of Israel had learned most fully to appreciate the services of a good interpreter. Isa. xliii. 27, cf. with Elihu, Job xxxiii. 23.

[2] This image, borrowed from the Egyptian kingdom, is found in Ex. iv. 16, cf. vii. 1; Gen. xli. 40, 44; with this must be taken what Jer. xxiii. 18, 22, and Amos iii. 7, say of the secret counsel of the king.

[3] As Jeremiah makes this so properly conspicuous in chap. xxiii. 18-22.

[4] According to Isa. v. 1-7; but the representations so profound in contents

this conception of the prophet as "mediator" between God and the nation, representing as it does most finely and strikingly his entire character, becomes ultimately the prevalent conception,[1] and passes over at the right moment into that of "intercessor," when the nation is so deeply bowed down under sufferings of all kinds that only the prophet himself does not despair of its salvation, and fights for it in God with the most timely and heroic courage.[2]

Such are the essential characteristics of these prophets. That many of the people sought from them also help and deliverance in all bodily distress is easily understood; and also that they rendered help in such cases where they could, and that not a few of them were held to be equipped of God with wonder-working power in delivering men from all kinds of ill. But that this is the first and most necessary service expected of a prophet, the Old Testament nowhere holds, nor is it related of the genuine prophets themselves that they treated this as their primary vocation and business. It is possible, indeed, that to prolong his temporal life a while, or even out of pure sympathy with the sufferings of the people, many a prophet cumbered himself much with such needs of the people, and that the power of his mind, so wonderfully stirred and so wonderfully active, worked in this direction also with marvellous energy and helpfulness; and, indeed, we can very well picture to ourselves that greatest prophet Isaiah, who devoted his whole life to the prophetic calling, as early occupied to a large extent in the kingdom of Judah in such subordinate service.[3] But that an Amos, a Jeremiah, an Ezekiel, of whom nothing of the kind is reported, were on this account not such great prophets, the Bible does not even

---

and so perfect in art, Isa. i., Micah vi. f., Hab. i.–iii., Isa. lxiii. 7–lxvi., are, however, thus further explained.

[1] According to Jer. xiv. 11 ff.; Ezek. xiii. 5 ff.; in accordance with the image of the combatant stepping into the breach of the wall against the last rush of the advancing foe; but to this belongs Hab. i.–iii., cf. with Gal. iii. 19 f., and the like elsewhere.

[2] See last note.   [3] As may be inferred from Isa. xxxviii. 21.

remotely suggest; and we must be on our guard against coupling together as necessarily united characteristics which only occur together casually; although, to be sure, in this case accident is in the higher sense not accident, at least so far as we here plainly see how easily the quickening of one faculty of the mind tends to quicken another.

3. *The Revelation of Moses.*

§ 34. Moses was, as we have seen, a prophet, and his whole work was essentially a prophetic work, as will yet more clearly appear. Nevertheless he was at the same time very different from all the prophets hitherto particularly contemplated, and his work had a wholly other significance than that won by any one of them in his highest conflict. It is of moment, therefore, rightly to ascertain in what respect he as a prophet was yet a wholly different instrument of revelation, and how far his work was raised to a higher stage, and in so far altogether peculiar.

1. It must above all be borne in mind that a prophet, when he began to work, found the distinct God, whose spokesman he was to be, long since known in His definite character and special honour; for a special honour may here very well be spoken of as accompanying the knowledge and public announcement[1] of a God in antiquity which His prophet sought to maintain. But a prophet who was the spokesman of a God already known in His distinctive character would find also a circle of men who sought from such God counsel and salvation, for whom he proclaimed the divine oracle, and who, whether more or less exclusive, or of larger or smaller extent, might with fitness be called a divine fellowship of men, or briefly a community of such God; and the labour of

---

[1] What is announced in all opening words concerning the God of Moses, Ex. iii. 15, may here serve as an example: "This is my name for ever, and this my glory from generation to generation;" and only thus is explained the high significance of the name of Jahveh in the Bible; it is just this distinct God, so named and so famous, of whom one is to think.

prophets would serve not a little to increase or maintain the number of such worshippers.

If, again, it is asked, whence comes ultimately the conception and the first celebrity of such a wholly definite God, about whom a stricter or freer society of men gather, we cannot possibly mistake that at the first beginning of such a phenomenon there must always stand a man in whom were united in an exceptional way the first and second of the possible stages of revelation already mentioned. Upon that first stage lies the ultimate creative faculty which may here in general be active; the individual in whom this faculty of revelation is present in most original form and with truly creative power, may know God as no one before had known Him, in a wholly new and distinct aspect, and with new truth and certainty; he may possess also the special capability of influencing others by his own inspirations from this definitely known God, and of associating men together in larger or small numbers on the basis of His word and counsel, and in the hope of His salvation. If both these qualities met in a God-fearing and thus doubly-gifted man, and if, around a God known in a new aspect, and reverenced as dispenser of the highest word and salvation, he could thus gather for the first time a community, and establish a sanctuary for man, he would become in this way the founder of this new intercommunion between a distinct Deity and a large and unlimited number of worshippers, and would be the first of an incalculable series of prophets of the same God and the same sanctuary who might succeed him within these firmly-marked bounds.

Thus is explained at once how Moses could be a prophet, and yet at the same time something more than a prophet.[1] If as the announcer of a God known under a new and distinct aspect, as the founder of a new community, and as first of a multitude of similar prophets succeeding him, he resembled

---

[1] What is briefly suggested on this point in Deut. xxxiv. 11 f., cf. xviii. 15, corresponds with all the earliest and oldest authentic reminiscences and testimonies of the Bible.

many others who in ages before him had worked in like manner, yet he at once surpassed them all in each of these three characteristics, and became a prophet with whom no other, whether in Israel or elsewhere, in the whole history of the world can be compared, and raised the whole development of all revelation to the essentially new higher stage upon which we here stand.

But what above everything else is here of utmost moment is this, that Moses for the first time in all human history makes the perfect idea and vivid sense of the true God the starting-point of his activity. That the God whom in His sharp distinctiveness he placed over against all other gods, and distinguished by the name Jahveh, is really the true God, to be recognised as such by us for ever, can only be proved further on; but this indubitable matter of fact we here assume in order to explain what is relevant to our present subject. Not as if Moses was the first to conceive the thought of the only true God, and to raise his own heart to His pure and infinite height; rather was it the case that he and all the better members of the nation gathered about him were made glad and brave by the conviction that it was the same true God whom in remote and ancient days their noble forefathers had known and worshipped,[1] of whom Moses was now the new messenger and herald. For as a right conception, and especially that of the true God Himself, is capable of an infinitely expanding and more exact apprehension and definition, so Moses, by the experiences of intervening centuries, through the deeper wisdom of Egyptian sages and his conflict with them, and with the whole high Egyptian culture of his time, and from the pure, noble fire of revelation enkindled in him whose sacred hearth he knows how without intermission to guard, was much more definitely acquainted with the old true God of the patriarchs, at least in many aspects of His character. Above all, it was essentially the pure spiritu-

[1] The noble preamble to the higher history of Moses, as we have it in Ex. iii. 17 ff., vii. 3 ff., expresses only what the whole Bible attests.

ality of this God that Moses apprehended as no one before him, from which he sought the corresponding purification and strengthening of his own spirit, and to which he held it to be the highest task of his earthly life permanently to lift up the whole nation; and with this, as already remarked, there stood in closest connection that the highest attribute in this purely spiritual God was love to those who loved Him. In the certain and definite knowledge of this true God, Moses found the breath of life as no one before him, by His strength overcame the consuming evil passion of youth, and from His holy inspiration drew the pure nourishment of that gracious inextinguishable fire that glowed through a long life in all his words and deeds. To our modern view it has long been apparent enough what a mighty power of the knowledge of the true God animated him and his clear-visioned inflexible labour in harmony with it; and how in all this he is, prior to Christ, unique.[1]

The decisive significance with respect to Moses of this complete accord between the knowledge of the Highest and the conduct that professes to follow it, cannot be made too conspicuous; in divine things, as they touch our human life, everything turns upon it, as will be more and more apparent as we proceed. If the greatest temptation that can come upon man in this connection is that which the desire for earthly power and glory involves, and afterwards the possession of it itself, and if Moses was the potent ruler we know him to have been from reliable historical reminiscences, we know also besides how completely he resisted all such temptation; and there is especially one narrative in the rich store of these reminiscences which allows us to see in clear light the most striking example of such resistance. When Moses had attained permanently to supreme power over Israel, and had

---

[1] Cf. *History*, ii p. 60-323 [Eng. ed. ii. 47-228]. If in our days reliable contributions to the history of Moses should be found, they cannot lessen his true greatness. Already in the last centuries before Christ many heathen scholars took pains to darken his fame, but all in vain.

attained it after many and severe conflicts with the Egyptian monarchy, and with the errors and imperfections of his own people, and purely by means of his prophetic word and the sure and incomparable skill in leadership it gave him: and when already, as if from long and open gazing into the radiance of divine truth and glory, a reflected splendour played about his countenance before the eyes of the people, we ask, how now will he conduct himself afterwards before the nation and before its chief and prominent men? A ruler of the common type cherishes and fosters the halo of glory that surrounds him and his public appearance, especially in the presence of his own nation; he is quick and eager to do this if he has suddenly bounded to a position to which his bare birthright gives him no claim. The glory of a kingly crown was then directly enough suggested to the wonderful leader of his nation; and Moses had only by his own will and desire to make more brilliant and blinding still the glory which illumined his countenance before all eyes, and to turn towards every one with increased boldness and hauteur, and especially against the best men of the nation who might resist his new ambition, and against the rest who would timidly shrink back, and the king already stood before them, but a king no better than the Egyptian, or rather since he had originally proposed something the direct opposite of this, a king still more undivine than the Egyptian. But what was it he actually did? He would certainly have preferred that the people should have borne calmly and bravely the glory which with no cunning hand, of his own mere pleasure and greed, but by striving and wrestling with God, had come to play around his countenance; that they should have sunned themselves in it, and accustomed themselves to it in love; for then in thousandfold reflection would it have irradiated also all who thus held intercourse with him, without vanishing from his own countenance. But they were not yet prepared for this, and withdrew timidly when he showed himself openly before them. Nevertheless this did not prevent him, notwithstanding the glory of a light kindled at the fount of Eternal Light, from going amongst them in a friendly manner as equal with equals, and seeking to take away their human timidity, and accomplish what he must; but, in doing it, he henceforth put a mask upon his countenance, veiling all its effulgence, that the people might have no blind dread before a glory which was not the imperishable Eternal Light itself, but only a mortal reflection of it. So little did he seek his own aggrandizement, and honour from men,—the glitter and glare or the terror and force of common human kingship; so carefully would he wean the whole nation from anything like abject or blind reverence for human power or government, that they might more and more learn to fear and love Him who alone is ever to be feared and loved. Thus, too, he prevented all slavish prostration before himself, as if he were their king and lord,—a habit too common in antiquity,—and led the people in the hours of holy festival to render homage perpetually to Him whom all humanity should worship. In such complete and perfect accord even in highest things were his conduct and requirements as ruler with his teaching and aim as prophet.[1]

§ 35. If Moses is so great and noble in himself, he is nevertheless still greater and nobler in his prophetic activity. In this we see how he succeeded in emancipating his whole nation from temporal as well as spiritual servitude, in gathering them not so much about himself as about the true God and His inexhaustible and saving word, and in forming not a merely transitorily independent, noble, and prosperous nation, —one among the nations of the earth,—but rather a community of the true God. Here everything is equally wonderful. For the first time in all human history a whole nation

---

[1] This difficult and important incident (Ex. xxxiv. 29-35, xxxiii. 7-11) is here explained somewhat more fully and explicitly than in the *History of Israel*, ii. 315 [Eng. ed. ii. 223-4], and in the "Epistles of Paul," 2 Cor. iii. 7, 13. It is thus understood what a vivid group of manifold and lofty intuitions and truths of the Old Testament is found in this brief yet, if rightly apprehended, rich and clear narrative. Out of this wealth Paul only took what material he in that passage needed.

passes through such a purely spiritual new-birth that it puts itself under obligation to live henceforth only in accordance with true religion and her requirements, and to look for salvation in all time to come only from loyalty in its religious life and the love of the true God which this loyalty presupposes. Further, the groundwork and first principles of all true religion were at that time provided for a whole nation,— already great comparatively when its antiquity is considered, and they possess an imperishable life and may render the same service far beyond the circle and the changing destiny of this single nation to the whole of humanity. Still further, all this was attained purely by spiritual means, by prophecy, by the inherent truth and rectitude of this revelation and the wondrous charm of its word. And this last is so important in our contemplation of the power of all genuine revelation, that we cannot be too strongly convinced that it really was the case. But all careful investigation tends to dispel every doubt about it. For although obstinacy, disquiet, and revolt of various kinds that could not be suppressed without violence occurred subsequently under Moses himself, yet it must be remembered that the new constitution of the nation was based upon its own free compact and co-operation, and every constitution of this sort, both in its own interest and in the interest of those who remain loyal to it, must be protected against the outbreak of revolution. But what is truly grand and unparalleled in this matter is, that purely by his prophetic activity and power Moses succeeded in permanently gathering the nation together in Egypt around the centre of the word of the true God, and in eliciting the free desire and resolve to follow in a new organization of its whole life only this true God and His word. Prophecy thus in antiquity attempted the highest task and attained the largest success that was possible to it.

It can now be seen most plainly and in detail how far Moses differed as a prophet from all who were before or after him. An ordinary prophet is but the spokesman of a God already known in a stricter or freer community united about Him as a centre; he has not to lay the first firm foundation on this basis, not first to form a circle of such as are desirous of listening to the voice of this particular God; he makes his appearance therefore only when something new occurs in this circle, and a matter of special business urges him. Wholly otherwise is it with Moses. He announces, it is true, no entirely new God, and least of all puts himself into a more exclusive connection with Him, as did that crude untimely after-fruit of all ancient prophets, Mohammed; he but renews the remembrance of the true God of the patriarchs, defines afresh the idea of Him, and with so much greater exactitude that not till he works in direct relation with the mind of God, and announces Him, is the true God perfectly known. But a community has to be formed finding its bond of union in Him;[1] and this community, both in the nature of the true God now so fully revealing Himself, and in the mind and spirit in which Moses worked under His guidance, must be a community, the like of which till then the world had never seen. Thus an essentially new institution was required; and in addition to this, it was in a time of complete dissolution of all national affairs that Moses appeared, and he must make everything new in the midst of it. With the vocation of the prophet he must combine that of national leader and lawgiver, and become one of those mighty founders of new kingdoms, of victorious energy and toil, whom pagan antiquity honoured as the best of its heroes. Moreover, after the first powerful establishment of the new constitution and legislation, as befitted the new community, he must, in a long life, secure them against every new danger, supply their first deficiencies, and as the sole, acknowledged, chief leader of the nation, give new decisions continually as the daily course of events required, and for this purpose maintain the word of God in

---

[1] And how it was formed is so graphically and strikingly represented by the later narrator, Ex. iii. 11–xv. 27, that, as far as the profound meaning and higher truth of these narratives is concerned, there is nothing truer.

constant and perpetual flow. How far did all this distinguish him from the ordinary prophet! Everything is easier when the community of God is once for all firmly established; only some particular matter of business occupies the prophet's attention; his work is either more quickly done or is comparatively fragmentary and isolated; and only when a most difficult case surprises and takes possession of him has he to secure a new, sound, divine idea of it or insight into it (§ 31), or obtain, in short prophetic phrase, "a vision" from God concerning it. But Moses, up to his last life-breath, ordered everything in a way that, in his case, was divinely necessary, and indeed peculiar to him alone; in such character he survived in the stedfast remembrance of later times; and since it was pre-eminently the same tranquil knowledge of the true God which he proclaimed and from which he worked, the third narrator of the early history expresses the distinction between him and the well-known crowd of later prophets by an extremely appropriate representation in four long lines of higher discourse, and as a true word from the mouth of God Himself:—

> "Is there a prophet among you
> or a seer out of your midst,
> By vision I reveal myself to him
> and in dream discourse I with him;
> Not thus my servant Moses;
> in my whole house is he accredited;
> Mouth to mouth do I speak with him without vision,
> and not in riddles beholds he Jahveh's face."[1]

---

[1] Num. xii. 6–8; cf. Ex. xxxv. 11. In harmony with what I have said in the *History of Israel*, ii. 251 [Eng. ed. ii. 178, n.], I remark still further, that since the structure of these four long lines, composed in the higher prophetic style, is clear, the words of the first line, unintelligible as they are now, may best be restored by reading as above:—

אִם יִהְיֶה נָבִיא מִכֶּם ׀ וְאִם חֹזֶה מִתּוֹכְכֶם

"Prophet" and "Seer" are thus parallel with each other in the two divisions of the first line, and essentially the same as in Amos vii. 12–14; and the וְאִם חֹזֶה stands for the unmeaning יְהֹוָה. Besides, the narrator is not thinking of prophets like Isaiah and Jeremiah, but rather prophets of the northern kingdom, to which he assuredly belonged. Concerning the "dream," cf. further, below.

The image by which Moses is described is very ancient.[1] It is that of a chief servant or steward of a great lord, who, because he is implicitly trusted, is set over the whole house to order and manage everything as seems best to him, while his lord favours him continually with direct personal audience, speaks with him in familiar converse, and imparts to him counsel of which the world knows nothing. The ordinary prophet beholds divine things, as later writers would say, only in a mirror; sees distant events, in a sleeping or waking condition, as if suddenly present to his view, and made thus vivid to him by his God (§ 31); and hears veritable words of God, but yet not in all respects perfectly clear and immediately applicable words, but as riddles that need first the proper solution and explanation. Furthermore, his God is not so perfectly and constantly near to him that he converses with Him in full confidence as friend with friend, beholds immediately in highest clearness and with the same tranquil aspect the loved image of His countenance, and talks with Him and consults Him without any mediator. For then there is no longer need of mere vision and riddle; in the continually unvarying and pure divine clearness and certainty of knowledge and discourse all human sense and thought are lost. But just this describes as plainly as possible the higher stage on which Moses stands as revealer; and as to the conception of revelation itself, no passage marks the transition from the Old Testament to the New so luminously and surely as this.

Another narrator, presenting with equally rare elevation of form a reminiscence of the characteristics of Moses, starts from another side, but comes back to essentially the same conception of the higher stage upon which this prophet stood. If the gift of facility and skill in public discourse is with the

[1] How ancient this image is, is evident from what is said in the *History*, i. 421 [Eng. ed. i. 414]; yet such an οἰκονόμος is spoken of again in Luke xii. 42-44 in such a way that Matt. xxiv. 45-47 interchanges this name rather with the simpler old Hebrew-like δοῦλος. The image in Isa. xlii. 1-4 is different. Cf. *Antiq.* p. 287 f. [Eng. ed. 250].

ordinary prophet so necessary (§ 32) that without it he does not answer to the idea of God's spokesman and mediator with men, it is readily seen that such gift is no less necessary in the case of a recognised national leader who is primarily much occupied with most varied and urgent matters of everyday business. Now, an old reminiscence concerning Moses was that when he entered upon his divine vocation of emancipating his people he was not a ready and fluent speaker,[1] and yet the issue showed how nobly, in spite of this original defect, he fulfilled, as great leader of the nation, the duty which God had assigned him. The narrative, in representing his greatness, tells of his hesitation and doubt when, fully equipped and prepared for undertaking the whole charge of Israel's mighty deliverance, he suddenly remembers in his converse with God that he cannot use the Hebrew tongue as a fluent popular orator; it is then added that God strengthened and encouraged his spirit by showing that above such particular natural defects there stands an incomparably higher spiritual power that can make him equal to his task, and further, that there are always other men who might supply the want in a national leader of such a special facility and gift, as indeed in this case his elder brother might, and become thereby his prophet. And so it was. Before the king and all the wise men of the Egyptians, Moses stood as the mighty spokesman of the true God and deliverer of his people, but before the people themselves Aaron acted as spokesman and mediator—that is, prophet of Moses.[2]

With such thoughts, reminiscences, and narratives did the late time seek to preserve distinctly in the nation of Israel the truth that a prophet of a wholly new type might arise, who should stand far above all ordinary prophets, and that Moses alone had borne such character in antiquity. For it is

---

[1] This old reminiscence is certainly well founded, for Moses was trained from his youth rather in Egyptian than Hebrew culture, and not until late in life did he become a prophet, and then suddenly.

[2] Ex. iv. 10-20; cf. the words of the "Book of Origins," Ex. vii. 1.

not prophecy, or the capacity clearly to expound divine truths in all the charm of style and the force of words as a spokesman and deputy of God before the people that satisfies the deepest needs of revelation and perfects its highest aim in humanity; the constant tranquil intercourse with the true God, the continually repeated complete entering of the human spirit into the divine, and the clear radiant light which is thereby enkindled in man, glowing in his heart and shedding forth its effulgence in his life, so that the man becomes more and more a reflection of the eternal light, or in other words, the trusted friend of Him who is ultimately his only true friend; this, as was the case with Moses,[1] is, according to the Old Testament, a lofty height of life upon which the true God reveals Himself to the world far more than through mere prophetic speech and toil.

§ 36. Moreover, if Moses in his knowledge of the true God, and in his own prophetic work and effort, perceived what spirit is, and spiritless matter, practically realized spirituality and the perishableness of all visible things, and how the Divine Spirit should be specially active in man and in all affairs of the human kingdom, at length also is explained thereby the third point which just in this connection is still more important and decisive. The Divine Spirit, in whatever way it may move in men, and however manifestly it may work forth from the spirit of men, is not to be repressed, nor to be dreaded, nor in any instance to be checked with violence, if only it be in reality the Spirit of the true God; and as he himself, the greatest of all the prophets of antiquity, had led the nation, nay, had founded the community of the same true God, purely by the power of prophetic discourse and action, one may say with right that he could not but conceive that the prophetic activity must exist in this community with the

---

[1] According to the narrative, Ex. xxxiv. 30-35; cf. *History of Israel*, ii. 315 f. [Eng. ed. ii. 223 f.]. It is the narrative which may be best indicated as that concerning Moses' conduct with respect to the reflection of the visible glory.

same perfect freedom continually. It is not recorded that as a Samuel or an Elias in later times he founded schools of the prophets; he did not regard this as at all necessary, for through him the work of the prophet had become powerful in a way till then unknown on earth, and had acquired such glory that hundreds of their own accord might readily follow with pleasure the example he had given. Moreover, among all the reminiscences of his life the finest is that which shows how, when his subordinates looked with suspicion and envy upon the free moving of the prophetic energy and joyousness in a number of new men, and sought to restrain it, he rebuked their mistaken and officious zeal, and expressed the wish that rather all men without exception might speedily become prophets.[1] Thus through Moses the freedom of prophetic activity became a law in this community, a law which, if unwritten, yet by constant usage and as a matter of principle, was the more indelible, and was the very breath of its best continuous life and progress, as indeed throughout the long and changeful period of his leadership of the nation it had been the highest power that had fashioned and sustained the community; and what was held elsewhere in antiquity as either very difficult, or very dangerous, or as attached only to particular places and persons, was here, in these earliest times, and at the very beginnings of the everlasting community of the true God, a free art, having its limits only in itself, if it preserved its original purity as it was the unique privilege of this community to preserve it.

§ 37. 2. But further, with this great distinguishing work of Moses there was given in this community from the beginning, and by its own fundamental law, the most powerful means antiquity knew of perfecting further the revelation of the true God, of perfecting it, indeed, in an entire national

[1] Num. xi. 24-29; cf. what is observed in the *Antiq.* p. 333 f. [Eng. ed. p. 252]. That the addition וְלֹא יָסָפוּ here actually signifies our *dass sie nicht mehr konnten*, that is, "unsurpassably," "excellently," may also be concluded from the opposite, 2 Chron. ix. 6; it was manifestly a short standing phrase having this meaning.

community, both in a purity and an unrestrained extension and continuance that could not be surpassed. Prophecy was the oldest and most successful means of establishing more definitely and diffusing in wider circles the fear of God and all its good fruits; and if it was a matter of importance to preserve and increase constantly the fear of the perfectly true God, here in very deed was established a great national community in which this high free activity of mind could be exercised without let or hindrance if possible for evermore. Strictly speaking, there are only two of the higher accomplishments of life in which the mind moves with all freedom; the one is poetry with its kindred arts, and the other is prophecy; the former an individual gift called into activity by every strong experience of the mind, the latter having a wholly special province in which from the individual it works out upon a whole nation and even beyond, directing the great affairs of all human effort, and leading ever to the universal. All that we characterize to-day as freedom of mind most desirable for public life had full scope in this community at an early period, and with an absence of outward restraint unparalleled in antiquity. And so there sprang forth from this soil that marvellous fulness and glory of prophets known to us in the long series of centuries after Moses, working most zealously and in greatest numbers just when the higher needs of this community required it, differing very much in speech and skill, as in power and influence, according to the great spiritual freedom then prevalent, but in essential principle all in perfect agreement; moulding themselves manifoldly according to time and place in personal intuitions, pursuits, and habits, but amid all these transformations always progressing in the depth and purity of the prophetic faculty and achievement; bound every one of them to the ordinances of Moses, and not one of them to be compared with Moses as a popular leader or founder of new organizations,—not even the mightiest in external power, as Elijah, or the most distinguished in inward force, as Isaiah; and yet all of them, in their close, successive, most unwearied onward working, preparing unconsciously something new which should surpass incomparably the whole institutions of Moses. The most successful labours and conflicts of all human aspiration, with the most happy ultimate issues, are possible where spiritual activity and freedom — hazardous apparently, in point of fact easily deteriorating, though necessary nevertheless [1] — are united so inseparably with the fundamental constitution of a nation, that without them it could not be believed to be capable of life at all; only such freedom in public affairs is it we here contemplate; but as it is in a purely spiritual respect the purest and highest freedom, so it bore at last the richest and most incorruptible fruits. But even when this prophecy, after almost a thousand years of ever progressive development, gradually deteriorated, and on this account suffered a limitation by law of the freedom which had been so long unrestrained, yet were they then very far from wishing to abolish it in this community, whether for a time or altogether.[2] It continued to exist, therefore, that it might not cease until it had attained the very highest and best, the possibility of which lay in its nature.

It is in point of fact very instructive, and, moreover, in this place necessary, to mark somewhat more particularly the effects of prophecy upon the whole spiritual condition of the ancient people of Israel—not, indeed, such effects as were more remote in operation and period of time, but such as were apparent during the centuries when prophecy flourished. The most immediate and important were, that amid all change of time and destiny, and notwithstanding every new error that prevailed, the nation nevertheless, as it advanced from stage to stage, more and more surely perceived the highest truths

[1] As among the Romans the *tribunicia potestas*; in our days the freedom of election in Church and State, of transactions in all matters of law and government, and the freedom of the press.

[2] The Deuteronomic laws concerning prophets, Deut. xiii. 1-5, xviii. 9-22, are wholly new; earlier the prophets came into collision with other powers in the kingdom, and had often on that account to suffer severely, but laws for limiting the power of prophets were occasioned only by subsequent degeneracy as it acquired increasing prevalency.

which in this progressive development of all true revelation were given, and that it followed the known will of God in everything with increasing loyalty. Thus was gradually fashioned to growing perfection a nation that understood very well that, as with the individual man so with a whole people, there must be a higher end appointed than to be the victim of the caprice of an earthly king, or of the passion of a casually powerful faction, or of any kind of perverted ambition; that the unchangeable holiness and righteousness of the true God ruled equally over all nations, but that the one nation that did not idly deem itself specially admitted to His love and sanctity must find in its privilege an emphatic summons to pre-eminent fidelity to Him under all temptations. As now in this nation everything of the nature of prophecy, of which antiquity was capable, mounted up to its highest power and perfection, so its spirit penetrated both the fulness of its single intuitions and the usage of its speech and art, and indeed more and more all literature flourishing as it did in this nation with increasing variety and splendour; even poets of all kinds and historians also became profoundly touched by this spirit, and perceived with growing vividness what true revelation in humanity is, and transfigured their works by the spontaneous influences of ideas that had become fixed and luminous by revelations of the true God. The remembrance, too, of the sublime forms of antiquity, of the patriarchs, and ultimately of Moses himself, revived anew in such prophetic intuitions and impulses; and every scene and subject of the remote past suited for the flights of prophetic thought and speech was suffused with its spirit and hues. The profound fundamental conception of a Book of Job and its transcendent art now became possible. Even the ordinary language of Hebrew authors gradually received that point and brevity as well as vivid clearness of style which are peculiar to it as the mirror of oracular utterances.[1] And it was not through a

---

[1] Cf. the dissertation "on the brevity of Bible sentences" in the *Jahrb. der Bibl. Wiss.* i. p. 154 ff. All that is stated above has been hitherto but briefly

crude narrowness or any constraint whatever that all this so fashioned itself, but it occurred while the nation maintained fully with original energy and quick living capability its ancient independence, and like every nation of the kind unfolded its spirit on all the varied sides of life; for not till later times, to be spoken of below, did all this which, during the most glorious period of its life, side by side with all other pursuits and necessities, had been thus active in all original freedom, become gradually cultivated with much one-sidedness and rigidity.

Meanwhile there are still special indications by which it may very clearly be perceived how prophecy was cultivated in this community to the highest perfection. On the one hand, it is certainly a sign that an art and aptitude exerts itself most freely and powerfully, if it can afford to jest in an easy and natural way at its own defects and imperfections, or to listen to such jesting from others. If it was a mark of the prodigiously growing power of philosophy when Aristophanes was allowed publicly to ridicule it with impunity, we possess also in the Bible, in the narrative of Balaam, an extremely satirical and derisive account, presenting to us in a graphic picture all the mistakes of a debased prophecy, and how it always works in the long run to no purpose.[1] Somewhat about the same time we see also a great Isaiah inveighing in the chief city itself with annihilating scoff and scorn against all perverse prophets;[2] and the more simple prophet of the country, Micah, attacking them with the sharp sting of his earnestness and candour.[3] On the other hand, every art

---

noticed, and in general has been treated with too little of accuracy, although it is of great importance both for the complete history of the ancient nation and the right estimate of the Bible and its entire varied contents. Only a book like the 2 Macc. admits of an over-artificial, diffuse style of language.

[1] Num. xxii.-xxiv. with the explanations in the *Jahrb. der Bibl. Wiss.* viii. 1-41.

[2] Isa. xxviii.-xxxii., especially xxix. 1-12 ; also the *lying prophets* as the *tail* of the nation as it publicly makes its appearance, ix. 14 ; and the first words of the first discourse, ii. 6, are not to be forgotten.

[3] Micah ii.-iii., especially ii. 11, iii. 8.

and science perfects itself from the first in so complete an unconsciousness and serenity of earnest labour that it realizes its inner laws and proper limits in its very working and exercise, and for a long time does not think of them or regard it as at all necessary to make them the subject of special reflection or exact discussion; but if it has already a brilliant existence in its great works of immortal instructiveness, and has called forth also a multitude of bad imitators and blunderers, it is just as much a mark of its significance and power if it elicits at length a striking decision as to its own true nature and use. So an Isaiah and a Micah prophesy without pronouncing any doctrine of prophecy and its real characteristics; but at the verge of the whole activity of prophecy which had been cultivated to the highest point for so many centuries, we see at last, over against all who misuse and mistake it, a clear view given of what it is in itself, and a kind of doctrine pronounced, showing the marks by which genuine prophecy may be distinguished from false, and this by one of the greatest prophets of that very declining age itself.[1] Nor can anything more striking be said of it than Jeremiah has said in his homely words, and Ezekiel in his more ornate manner. Certainly, if after all the changes through which it had passed, and the ever-abiding effects it had produced, this prophecy, highly developed as it was, was destined to vanish at last from the public life of the nation and so find its proper close, it could not better go down, as an art and aptitude of life, than with this distinct exposition of all the innermost impulses of its beating heart, and this clear intelligent consciousness of its own nature.

§ 38. 3. For even the noblest kind of prophecy antiquity can show must one day work itself out and come to an end; this lies in the nature of all prophecy (§ 16, 2); and the

---

[1] No passage can here be more instructive than Jer. xxiii. 9–40, cf. with xxix. 8–32; but, to be sure, from such narratives as Jer. xxvi. is seen how far remote that age already was from the calm and even sportive prophetic serenity of an Isaiah, and what implacable hostility had arisen between the prophets of the same God. Ezek. iii. 16–21, xxxiii. 1–9, but also xii. 21–xiv. 11.

seventh and sixth centuries before Christ were the stormy and unrestful time in whose rapid changes this event occurred, approaching with gradual and sure steps; but no prophetic activity in the whole ancient time was so energetic and fruitful in its last healthier movements, and died at length at the seasonable hour of its ripeness with a bequest of such imperishable wealth, as this. On the one hand, after so many centuries the whole range of ideas and claims that formed the starting-point of the prophets who succeeded Moses had become less and less strange to the community itself, for whose benefit mainly they worked; the God whom at first they felt in their innermost souls as pressing hard upon them with His omnipotence and fixing their destiny in everything, from whom Elijah, as he stood before Him as a servant before his mighty Lord, became consciously armed with the most wonderful energy, and whom, in the highest excitement of his life, he found to be pre-eminently his God,[1] had been brought nearer and nearer to the whole nation, even penetrating the wall of partition between the prophet and his hearers; whilst the violence with which these men of the spirit had worked, impelled by the irresistible moment of inspiration, showed itself in Isaiah only in its very last traces.[2] On the other hand, fettered by the limits of the existing community and the whole age, they could not bring in the more perfect condition of things which, nevertheless, they so ardently long for and so correctly foretold; and as the best of them became more and more conscious that their work had no longer immediate and satisfactory efficiency, the respect in which they were formerly held was gradually and indeed rapidly lost, whilst great crowds of vain and frivolous prophets who flattered the power and passions of the hour, produced a fatal rupture in all prophetic work in this community, and suggested the wish and called forth the anticipation even in the circle

[1] 1 Kings xvii. 1 ff. ; Isa. vii. 13 ; more after a mere literary fashion, Deut. iv. 5 ; Isa. lvii. 21. Expressions such as 1 Kings xvii. 20 f. we exclude.
[2] Isa. vii. 13 f., xxii. 14.

of genuine prophets that the whole prophetic order would cease.[1] It is without doubt wonderful to mark how, after the first bloody persecution of the true prophets in the kingdom of Judah under Manasseh, a mere literary renovation and amendment of the old constitution by the fundamental thoughts of these prophets, as reproduced in the Book of Deuteronomy, could bring about a great transformation in the still existing kingdom. A manuscript breathing the prophetic spirit and accompanied by the ancient and sacred name of Moses seemed able to establish permanently a new order of things beyond the power of the living prophets themselves in their public work to establish! But, nevertheless, no mere book is really equal to this task; the quickly succeeding destruction of the kingdom involved in its own ruin the last efforts of the public activity of the true prophets, and only transiently did the immortal energy of this finely-cultured prophecy raise itself once again with irrepressible strength amid the early years of the New Jerusalem, in order that after this, its last and ultimately most glorious work, it might be extinguished for ever.[2]

Thus two causes of a wholly different kind—viz. its success in establishing divine truth, and its failure to bring the desired perfection—contributed to this appropriate end of all purely prophetic activity in the history of revelation. Publicity of labour in a free nation of the community of Jahveh had been from Moses downwards one of the two mightiest living impulses of this prophecy; such a genuinely free nation was not to be re-established in the New Jerusalem; but in it prophecy ceased the more readily, and was the less capable of restoration in its original type and form at any time subsequently, the more it had then no true place in the nation any longer so far as its essential impetus is concerned, whilst all

---

[1] The last in Zech. xiii. 2-6; but it lies at the basis of Jeremiah's words, xxxi. 33 f.

[2] Cf. *History of Israel*, iii. 713 ff. [Eng. ed. iv. 127 ff.]; and *Proph. of Old Test.* ii. and iii.

the sublime truths it had published in the community, throughout a period of more than a thousand years, and had at last made perpetual in the most magnificent literature, exerted their influence in it for ever after. But if its spirit, possessing as it were an ineradicable energy, was afterwards repeatedly active at least in literary efforts,—partly because it could not absolutely perish, and partly because the completion of the great work of Moses in the world was still an unaccomplished task,—yet these were merely aftershoots of prophetic power, and originated in the desire to imitate the older writings that were charged with the prophetic spirit, and on that account highly venerated. But, nevertheless, even in these imitations, the unsurpassed glory and living energy of the originals may be correctly estimated, since many a gem of vital truth is hidden in them, and some of them almost equal in artistic power and effect the earlier models.[1]

§ 39. 4. Something more, however, was found in this community in the course of the succeeding centuries, as the result and issue of the profoundly effective activity of this long compact line of genuine prophets, than the mere remembrance of their former high significance, or even the splendid collection of their imperishable writings. There stepped forth, indeed, no distinguished man dressed in the simple garment of hair, by which the prophets had once been known;[2] no one discoursed publicly to the nation in their marked and peculiar style, or was publicly honoured with questions a prophet only could answer;[3] still less did any one speak

[1] It deserves to be noted, as a remarkable sign of the tenacity with which in its decease the prophetic spirit sought to preserve itself where it could, even in its ashes, that these later writings were not written and were not read as if coming from the older prophets, but were anonymous, and were publicly used, for example, in festivals. Here may be classed the Book of Lamentations, Ps. lxxxv., the fragment of the Book of Baruch iii. 9–v. 9 [cf. *Proph. of Old Test.* iii. 267–282, Eng. ed. v. 123–137], all showing the genuine prophetic spirit, and in poetic art like the writings of Habakkuk, but designed only for public festivals in the temple and elsewhere. Concerning the similar "Psalter of Solomon," see *Gött. Gel. Anz.* 1871, p. 22.

[2] That prophets in their public appearances wore a special costume up to the first destruction of Jerusalem, is certainly evident from Zech. xiii. 4.

[3] Why nothing similar occurred after the last example that we find of this

publicly in the name of Jahveh, and with the demand to be heard as His immediate messenger. The prophetless time now spread the veil of its desolation and stillness over the land once resounding with the mighty voices of so many prophets, and since prophetic agency lay at the basis of the old constitution of this community, and was even one of the conditions of its life, the want of it now, everywhere so apparent, could not but be publicly recognised,[1] though no one had a clear conception how it was actually to be removed. Indeed, the special peculiarity of this time was that people felt vividly its real need, for the continuance of which there was no higher necessity and no divine predetermination even if there was no idea at all how that need was to be supplied. Moreover, as there was a vivid consciousness that in these centuries, as compared with the elevation and glory of the earlier, there prevailed a painful diminution of such energies as were essential to make a nation independent and free, contented and happy in its God, and highly esteemed by other nations, so there was a strong conviction also that revelation in Israel was not yet perfected, and that many things could not be so definitely done, and so securely adjusted, as would be possible if that consummation had come. Such was the prevailing view in these centuries, as it is expressed most frankly and most effectively in the finest and noblest moments of that interval between the golden evening and the dark impending night of the ancient nation, in the time of the Maccabees.[2] But in reality this obscure feeling contains a most important element, the very pivot, indeed, upon which in the meantime everything in this history of all revelation must turn.

questioning in Zech. vii. f., is clear from the explanation in the *Hist. of Israel*, v. p. 152 ff. [Eng. ed. v. 175 ff.].

[1] Strictly taken, the Deuteronomist, xviii. 15-22, already marks a time when there is no longer a generally recognised prophet, although it was desired that one like Moses should come again; so much the more readily were the later times, according to Macc. iv. 46, ix. 23, xiv. 41, regarded as prophetless.

[2] It is observable that the question is then concerning a new, supreme, free sovereign authority in the nation, and other highly important matters of the kind.

For if we ask more definitely whence then this feeling came,—a feeling which, it is true, found inevitably in the most decisive and elevated moments of those centuries conspicuous expression among the best of the people with the most important results, but which in fact, in the slow course of those centuries, penetrated, albeit obscurely and secretly, the whole life of the community of the true religion, and even when unexpressed determined its most important conduct and bearing,—we can answer only somewhat in this way: It cannot have had its strongest originating cause in the mere analogous feeling of the diminution of the old national freedom and power, for, as we see, it prevailed most distinctly just in those few intervals when the nation experienced once again greater freedom and glory, as in the Maccabean period; and, besides, the feeling of the need of a new and perfect revelation has in it elements entirely peculiar to itself. That the great prophets who worked in the last centuries before the destruction of Jerusalem, and at the commencement of the new city, had pointed more and more emphatically to the coming of the Messiah, exercised undoubtedly a powerful influence, because, amid all the diversity with which they presented His image to the thought, they had all with one voice declared: "the kingdom of the community of the true God has not yet found its consummation, but shall yet surely find it;" nevertheless, since the mighty sway of a king can be sketched in detail only very indefinitely, but little light was thrown upon the actual consummation of revelation itself by this prophecy. The most profoundly influential originating cause must therefore be sought elsewhere.

Now these great prophets, closing the long series of men who worked publicly in Israel, did not simply point onward to the future sublime King who should bring the consummation of Israel's hope, they also pointed back into the past, to the incomparable glory of the revelation under Moses, and to the happy time the community enjoyed under its protection so long as it remained faithful. And as a matter of fact, even so early as the calamitous times of the Judges, the remembrance of the glory of the revelation under Moses had become bright and vivid, and amid the heavier calamities of the last centuries of the old kingdom it became still brighter and more vivid. The whole period when the community of the true God was favoured with the leadership of Moses and Joshua, was very early felt to have been the period of His most lofty as well as most blessed and triumphant revelation, and was celebrated as such in the immortal words of poets.[1] If, now, incomparably the highest moments of that period were those in which the sacred covenant between Israel and its people was concluded at Sinai on the basis of the Ten Commandments, and if the best men in the nation in the early times of the Judges felt deeply enough that the thunder-voices of this highest law, that had once under Moses made the heart of the nation tremble, and transformed it to a new nation worthy of that new covenant, ought to shake and move it henceforth for ever, it is not surprising that this narrative of the most thrilling revelation of God a nation has ever received, took early a fixed and finished form.[2] Conceptions of this kind, and narratives which most vividly mirror them, were in fact only the plainest expression of the certainty that beyond the revelation of the ordinary prophets and its easily observable influence, there is a revelation standing far higher, corresponding to that whose transcendent influence this community had once experienced, a revelation never again to pass away. In this sense the whole remembrance of that revelation of Moses, its immortal result and indestructible monument, the written law, having come into existence, became, long before the end of the last great prophets, *i.e.* before the sixth and seventh centuries before Christ, more and more a highly transfigured remembrance. Why, therefore, with the gradual vanishing away of the guiding power of prophetic

---

[1] Judg. v. 4 f. ; cf. *History of Israel*, ii. 306 f. [Eng. ed. ii. 354 f.].

[2] Ex. xix.–xxv., with the special dissertation concerning this fully unique narrative in the *Jahrb. der B. Wiss.* xii. p. 198–211. In another connection it is already mentioned above, § 12.

activity, should not the need, now manifestly arising, be supplied by a return, the more decisive and faithful, to this old revelation, ratified as it was by the history of a thousand years, and distinctly recorded for each and all in the old written law? In this way already the Deuteronomist had aimed to afford in creatively prophetic style the true supply of the prevailing painful want threatening a thousand serious ills: his effort was not without result; and at length, after Malachi had in briefest and most decisive words pointed all the best minds of his time once again in the same direction, the broad path was fully levelled, and a new and great turn in the history of revelation in Israel had already been fairly started.[1]

This reverting to the past was for a series of centuries the best possible step, so far as it was of moment, to keep the community of the true God in the course of history. The mightiest incitement of all higher spiritual effort which had served hitherto to protect and advance the genuine fear of God in this community, and to avert its deterioration, was now dead; and indeed the living memory and clear conception of what prophecy and revelation really are, were more and more lost in these centuries. For a long time people lived in this community in the immediate after-effects of the sublimest and most fruitful activity of all revelation that had occurred anywhere in the whole of antiquity, or that occurred then amongst other nations of the earth; they read in writings grown sacred, multiplied a thousandfold, of its numberless words and deeds, and they moved everywhere as amid echoes of the voice of the true God, to Abraham, Moses, David, and to many others, like them, of prophetic gift; and they felt themselves once more withdrawn afar from the familiar nearness in which, according to Scripture, these favoured men stood to the true God; they yearned for His

---

[1] Mal. iii. 22 (iv. 4), by which may very well be observed that this last prophet by no means merely points back to Moses, but just as strongly, nay, rather far more strongly, points onward, iii. 1, 23 f. (iii. 1, iv. 5 f.) to the new period which must come; cf. *History of Israel*, iv. vol. throughout (Eng. ed. v.).

new living voice and heard it not, for prophets and found them not. Many new phenomena occurred and new pursuits were followed in this twilight; yet none of them actually sufficed to supply the want. The living activity of all revelation of the ancient type having exhausted itself, and these later men thinking that they moved as in cold dark rooms where no new ray of revelation any longer penetrated, the mind, saturated as it was with the rich blessing of the old revelations, and yet feeling itself in the present so dry, longed with more profound and eager desire to hear at least some short brief word from heaven, if only as a broken mysterious sound, and the hot eager longing did indeed hear the divine true word brought surprisingly near to the enraptured ear, which, moreover, already pressed overpoweringly upon the mind so prepared.[1] Of the possibility of such voices sounding mysteriously from the heavenly regions, which not merely the prophet, but every man, or indeed the whole nation, might hear, the heathen also frequently speak; but it is remarkable enough (p. 7) that they are foreign to the Old Testament, and are repeatedly mentioned only in those later centuries after the living stream of revelation, that flows through the times the Old Testament chiefly depicts, had been dried up. But how much the hearing of such abrupt heavenly voices depends upon the tension and mood of different minds, is clear; what the heathen supposed they heard[2] in this way was sufficiently unlike that which found similar expression in the circle of the community of the true religion,[3] or indeed in the schools of

[1] The Rabbinical expression, בּת קוֹל, is not so much Hebrew as Aramaic, and signifies (L. B. § 287 f.) nothing but a single voice, φωνή, as this Greek word expresses just the same idea in Hellenistic speech and in the N. T.

[2] It may be said with truth that the first voice of this kind in which the nation extensively believed, and with which was given an example of far-reaching influence, was that of the Hasmonæan Hyrcanus I., according to Josephus, J. K. i.; 2, 8; arch. 13; 10, 3; in him the oracle of the high priest appeared in this way in these late times to be revived; but the powerful precedent once given in his case produced effects in the nation to an incalculable extent afterwards.

[3] It cannot be denied that the powerful inclination of that time towards such kinds of revelation had its effect also upon young Christianity, although, to be

the Rabbis. In fact nothing is to be seen here but how the stream of genuinely prophetic revelation in Israel, wholly interrupted, sought at last in this way to restore itself in single drops falling here and there; and another means, similar in kind, with which the deficiency sought to supply itself, will be further noticed below. But how little, in all such ways, the void could be filled up is readily evident.

§ 40. 5. When now the old revelation, as the Pentateuch presented it, and in the application of it which logically followed, had become as law the firm basis of the whole spiritual life of the community, and the teachers of the law had accordingly made their appearance as the highest judges of this life, and more and more the sole successors of Moses, in the place of the prophets, then the thread of further development of revelation appeared to be entirely broken, and broken for a future no longer capable of measurement. The learned schools, established for the exposition and application of the holy law, in reality presupposed this, and based upon the presupposition their tedious toils and the whole confidence of their work. In this new state of things in the community centuries elapsed, and the position became more strongly and immovably fixed. Anticipations and promises of the old prophets that ran contrary to it were easily disregarded or were wrongly explained; and those of the Pentateuch, fewer in number and more difficult to understand, were still more readily set aside. In fact, this age of the Hagiocracy, resting upon the holy law, intervened in order to remind the later days, and to remind them at length when the need arose with the greatest emphasis, that all prophecy, even the most potent and the most freely obeyed, fails to bring the highest revelation.

sure, in this case the method was wholly new and the purport altogether different. Instances of such a φωνή as John xii. 28-30, Acts ii. 2-6, ix. 4 ff., x. 13 ff., afford us a sufficiently historical glimpse of the possibility of the occurrence of such experiences and reminiscences; but very early such higher representations as Mark i. 11, ix. 7 followed. That what is to be called, whether in the best and purest or in a less pure sense, the piety of such thoughts and conceptions, was of a deeply-tinctured and saturated type, the Rabbinical narratives almost superabundantly show.

For prophecy, pursuant to its nature (p. 23), expresses divine truths as demanding unconditional obedience. If, therefore, a larger series of divine truths once made known in this way form a law-book in conformity with which all the spiritual life of a community is to be directed, the entire spiritual life, even if the truths so prescribed actually coincide with all true religion, as is the case here, yet is bound to this law as to a restraint; what should be the freest purpose and act of the human mind, becomes, notwithstanding the fact that here it is divine truth with its light and power that alone has to rule, a matter of outward constraint, to which submission is to be rendered out of mere slavish fear if it is not comprehended or approved in the heart, so that the choice offered is servile submission or revolt. This inconvenient state of things, tolerable at first when divine truths are only seeking their entrance into the world of humanity, becomes more and more injurious when such truths, surrounded by a glimmer of ancient sanctity and in the midst of a world altogether differently fashioned, are dealt with by learned schools, and become subject to the contingencies of such treatment. If a man has an inclination to submit himself slavishly to every sentence and thought from which he expects salvation, so much the more does every divine word expose him to this danger, especially should it be radiant with an ancient sanctity. But how much greater must the danger be, if a great collected work of old divine words is regarded as the basis of all spiritual life, and yet has to be explained by learned schools and applied as they think proper; if men suppose they have all the divine wisdom of life summed up in such work, and might well have it indeed, but they know not how rightly to estimate and use it! What at first was a living stream of divine truths and salutary precepts, becomes then a stiff and benumbing lifeless form; what was thought to be held in the hands as the word of God, is turned into arbitrary command of man.

Another disclosure was also made in the time of the Hagiocracy. The immediate power of the prophets of the last centuries having been gradually broken (§ 38), as their activity divested itself of the violence that originally characterized it, these prophetless days must show conclusively and with growing distinctness that even this violence, with which the oldest revelations, now regarded as law, had first entered into the world, and had in reality formed the sole dominant power of those centuries, did not in the long run suffice. In this is found the true primary cause that led the entire development of all revelation not to rest at this stage, and that unveiled more and more the deep want inherent in the prophetless time, and made it more heavily felt. The old presentiments and prophecies that a higher consummation, as of all the immortal blessings of Israel so also of its revelation, was to be expected, united their living power the more readily to this most urgent feeling, with which indeed they were akin. In fact, the last of the great prophets had not departed without indicating briefly, but with most luminous glance, what here was felt to be lacking, and must in the future come; so rightly sensible were they themselves of the imperfection of all that till then had found place, even of their own prophetic activity. Isaiah complained that the religion of most men was only human command learned by rote, as was most distinctly shown when the dangers and distresses of public life became suddenly most grievous.[1] The Deuteronomist concluded his renewal and spiritualization of the old sacred law with the most emphatic suggestion, that every divine law of the true religion is at the same time most human, not something seeking to remain over against man as simply outside him, or too obscure or too difficult for him;[2] and still more simply and distinctly Jeremiah declared the necessity of a new covenant between God and man, in which man should no longer contemplate what is divinely needful for him as a written command, constraining him, standing over against him, but should already carry it in his heart, and

[1] Isa. xxix. 13, cf. with i. 10-20, but also xxix. 18, xxx. 19-22.
[2] Deut. xxx. 11-20, cf. xi. 26-28.

fulfil it freely from the heart.[1] So in this community there remained at last only the question how the swanlike word of all the old dying prophecy could find fulfilment, and how in this fulfilment the thread of all revelation, long broken off, could be picked up again and woven in afresh? And when the hour was ripe the right answer was given by the revelation of Christ.

4. *Christ's Revelation.*

§ 41. At the expiration of the prophetless time, it had become clear to the best part of the nation how little the rigid reverence for the old written law, and the national illusion based upon keeping the law sacred in this way, were really well-pleasing to God, and how certainly both must rather lead to the inevitable destruction as well of this nation as of the true religion thus ineffective and quiescent in its midst. As soon as this was fully realized, we see, in a wholly new form it is true, the most vigorous efforts made which could possibly be made in this community to reach that consummation of the divinely-human life which the old prophets had foreshadowed, and which alone could be the consistent issue of this whole great development. But since the days of Moses the prophetic spirit alone, notwithstanding all the imperfections inherent in it, and all the aberrations into which it had often fallen, had nevertheless been the profoundest, and in its deepest purpose the most indestructible, power that had preserved and further unfolded, as well as creatively called forth, the main thoughts upon which this whole development was based. Accordingly, now at the close we see this spirit quite unexpectedly yet nevertheless irresistibly raising itself anew, and attempting the ultimate task that was possible to it. First of all, in keeping with the nature of the times, new writings of the most diverse

---

[1] Jer. xxxi. 33, with which stands appropriately in close connection, according to the sense the word of the great Unnamed, Isa. liv. 13.

kind,[1] whose inspiration was entirely kindled at the inextinguishable fire of the ancient writings, now become sacred, poured themselves over the new world after the Maccabæan age as a stream rising continually higher and higher; and these contributed not a little[2] to soften the frozen and benumbed ground of those centuries of winter, for the sowing of a new spring, and to quicken to intensity the expectation of a great harvest long since fervently desired. Afterwards occurred the advent of the Baptist and of Him for whom the Baptist broke the way, Christ Himself, both of whom, it is undeniable, were regarded during their public work as prophets who at last, after long ages, had once again arisen in Israel;[3] and this view of their character found currency in the nation, although neither of them directly aimed at being accepted as a prophet of the earlier type.

The event showed, however, how little these new prophets in Israel resembled the old prophets. The Baptist, it is true, started in his public ministry, as they did, from the fundamental thought of God's kingdom, considered properly what was its present condition upon the earth, and especially in this nation, and renewed the demand for a return to the better state of things as urgently as the time desired it,—the very demand with which the last great prophets had closed their labours. But nevertheless he could not work, as they did, from the very central point of the community, still less did

[1] [Cf. *History of Israel*, v. 461-491 [Eng. ed.]. Ewald means the four Books of Maccabees, the Books of Judith and Enoch, the Wisdom of Solomon, and the Greek Book of Daniel, etc.—TR.]

[2] According to most recent discoveries and investigations, this may with justice be maintained; and it is equally certain that for these two or three centuries these writings had a great influence upon the whole widely-scattered nation, and even reached to the heathen. I have proved this abundantly in earlier writings.

[3] Of the Baptist this is self-evident. Cf. Matt. xi. 9, xiv. 5, xxi. 26; John i. 21-25. Of Christ, however, it is certain from such reminiscences as Mark vi. 15, viii. 28; John iv. 19, vi. 14, vii. 40, ix. 17; but John shows himself most acquainted with the opinions of the learned and unlearned of that time, so far as he gives it to be most clearly understood that with the more learned the question was whether in Christ the prophet promised in Deut. xviii. 15 were come or not.

there revive in him that Ego, bending everything before it, which had found utterance in them.[1] Christ, however, from the very beginning of His public life, professed to be something wholly different from them, and He was so. He brought the consummation of all revelation, so far as an individual spirit encompassed within the limits of the earthly body can bring it. Let us now explain this more particularly, and according to the twofold aspect the sentence just expressed presents.

In the outset it is above everything certain that, from the first moment of His public work to the last act He could perform in the flesh, and the last word that broke from His mortal lips, Christ always, with absolute uniformity, felt Himself to be the Messiah whom all true prophets long since expected, and whose coming was desired with purest longing by all the pious in Israel. It is of no consequence when He regarded it as the suitable time to be recognised as such by the Twelve as the basis of His community, by the whole ancient nation, and at last by the heathen magistracy;[2] certain it is that from the first moment onwards He acted in the conviction and inner certainty of it, and that nowhere, even before His express announcement of His full claim, unfolded step by step, did He deny Himself to be the Messiah where such denial would have been an offence against the truth.[3] If, however, the idea of the "kingly" among men has in general more than a casual signification, it can only imply that which proves itself in human affairs to be purely elevated above what is defective and erroneous, or, indeed, what is perverse and corrupt. For that the king knows how to take up and maintain such a position in his nation, is the presupposition

[1] Since we possess only the few fragments of his discourses which the Gospels contain, we are not able to come to any other conclusion than that he did not renew the Ego of the old prophets; but this is very probable also for other reasons.

[2] These are the three stages which, with such perfect accuracy, the Gospels well distinguished, Mark viii. 27-30, xi. 1-10, xv. 2; and essentially in just the same way John vi. 66-70, xii. 12-36, xviii. 33-37.

[3] Just this is most essential in the matter.

about him, and the necessary reason that he is desired and honoured; but if an individual king may make himself unworthy of this presupposition and honour, as he may, it does not then follow that the idea itself, and the special dignity of the kingly among men, become beclouded or illusive, and are to be cast aside to the mass of other confused thoughts as superfluous or misleading.[1] What there is in the idea that is really true and ever elevating, what is unique in it, and not to be otherwise supplied in the circle of human relations, it was not Christ's business to render conspicuous in detail, though He peacefully acknowledged in national affairs the legitimate kingly authority.[2] In discoursing, however, of the "kings of the earth," He made prominent also the feebleness and imperfections which clung to them as they were in His time.[3] But there is still another idea which is not borrowed simply from human relations, bears a universal signification, and comes back essentially to the same conception. It is the idea of the "perfect," which is to be put, in the main, on a level with the divine itself, yet is set up also before men as their divine goal; and so by Christ Himself, where the context of the discourse makes it suitable, is conspicuously presented as an aim that is at once highest and most necessary.[4]

But what a thought is this idea of kinghood, if it is raised to the height to which, in this case, it was to be raised; if it should have its real import in that sphere of all human relations into which Christ, as Christ, entered! For the true King was to come for the community whose every member was already bound to lead a divinely-elevated, *i.e.* a kingly life, so that no earthly king was needed, and in which should then be peremptorily issued to all earthly kings—since they were nevertheless necessary—the demands of all true religion. He was to establish, as the long-expected One coming from

---

[1] Cf. further upon this, vol. iii. [2] Matt. xx. 25-28; Luke xiii. 32.
[3] Matt. xxii. 21.
[4] Matt. v. 48. The idea of perfection in its relation to God and to men is here more exactly described than in Gen. xvii. 1, although this relation is at least correctly indicated there.

God, armed with His full authority for the work, a kingdom which should start, it is true, from the immovable basis of the old community of the true God, but a kingdom that was the fulfilment of all the sublime hopes inspired in this shattered community, and the consummation of a divine salvation such as never within nor without this community had ever before been experienced by man. He was to establish it, indeed, with the inherited treasure of all the wonderful powers of spiritual knowledge, of faithful activity, and blessed hope vouchsafed to this community since the primitive times; but as a King who must know best of all how to apply anew, and to increase the inherited treasure of the ancient kingdom, in order to found a new kingdom, manifestly necessary, but never yet actually begun by man. He was to establish it as a kingdom of pure divine knowledge and love, grace and freedom, as opposed to all kingdoms of human unwisdom and caprice, and of dark, stern human force, that in heathen kingdoms had alone been dominant at all times, and now also had long since broken in upon the old community again, overwhelming everything; as a kingdom standing above all humanly-limited kingdoms, immovable to all eternity, of continually progressive salvation for all humanity, and yet, notwithstanding all imperfections and difficulties, forthwith as such in the midst of them to begin. He was to establish a kingdom of God as His Son, who had been predetermined for it in accordance with old sacred hopes, and was to be its human judge and king. But, above all, He was to become its first subject and citizen, in order to show to all men, by His own obedience and service, how they also must first be genuine subjects and citizens of it if they would rise up to be its freemen and lords.[1]

Such was the position which Jesus, as Christ, must occupy in this community; such the height of the work to which He must uplift Himself, if He would fully answer to the

[1] Matt. xx. 28. Cf. how a similar thing already occurred with Moses, Num. xii. 3 with Ex. xi. 3.

divine summons which here went out to Him. Only in this community, and at this stage of the long, changeful development of all true religion in its midst, was His public advent and work possible. It is wonderful how, upon a firm basis once laid, and by the struggling of all beneficent forces once properly started towards a high, divinely-prescribed goal, everything may combine at last to make possible the actual attainment of this goal. Thus there pressed upon Him, who was the right man to carry off this prize, all that the past had wrought; whilst in the present all that was old lay in a state of dissolution and ferment, tending with potent energy towards a new formation. The times of Moses had come back again, so far, but it was only that what it was possible then but to initiate amid severest conflicts might now be perfected. That Christ came only "when the times were fulfilled," is the right acknowledgment of the New Testament;[1] and the mightiest lever to this fulfilment was the perfectly accurate and prompt realization of the nature and duties of the Messiah demanded.

But if the thought of the expected and demanded kingly and perfect One was itself, in this whole, great, and stedfast coherence of all relations and of all times, an influence in the highest degree impelling and elevating to all that was here necessary, three things must yet be added, that this Jesus may, as Christ, become the right instrument of the highest revelation. In the first place, the possibility, as a matter of fact, that feeble, mortal, individual man may also actually suffice as such an instrument; that is, of course, at the appropriate time, and in the right conjuncture of all humanly-divine affairs. But this possibility is given from two opposite points, which include everything in question. On the one side, it is firmly established that the individual man can indeed form and attune his spirit by the knowledge and admonition of another, or even of all the rest of men, and in his own knowledge and action receive aid from them; but in

[1] As this is said in the briefest and plainest way in the latest writings of the New Testament, Eph. i. 10; Titus i. 3.

everything which the will of God demands of him he stands face to face with Him alone, because his spirit is something firmly shut and hidden to all save itself, but can immediately participate in the divine spirit, and must participate in it if he will actually fulfil that will. No man can either violate or fulfil the will of God for another, as the Old Testament most emphatically teaches.[1] If, therefore, the will of God can be perfectly fulfilled by man at all, one man must first so fulfil it, or it will never be perfectly fulfilled in the human race, and the whole aim of man's creation will thereby be missed.[2] On the other side, all human fulfilling of the divine will in the individual man consists in an unbroken series of temptations to the contrary overcome, whether with less or more difficulty; but if even one temptation may be overcome by the individual man, which no one denies, then an individual has power to overcome all temptations, and to breathe that perfect divinely-human life in which the whole good pleasure of God, and the whole happiness of man, meet and coincide. Thus then the possibility here in question must be conceded; and how little the Bible contradicts it, whether the Old or the New Testament, will be further shown in the following chapters of this work.

Secondly, it is evident, it is true, that the practical possibility just mentioned may take shape and form in very different ways, in accordance with the incalculable variety and force of natural gifts in individuals, and that not all human spirits as they step into history are from the first equally competent to lead the way in attaining the highest aim here proposed, still less to maintain such competency for a length of time. But what may rightly be called the divine spirit is in itself ever a whole, and endowed, moreover, with the special faculty of striving intelligently and effectively for

---

[1] As Ps. xlix. 8 ff., li. 6.

[2] These general propositions, as well as that immediately following, can only be more definitely discussed and demonstrated below, vol. ii. and iii., but in this connection they must at least be briefly stated.

the whole,[1] although it is confined in the limited and frail body of an individual man, and works from this limitation. Here, however, the question is not general, does not concern the infinite detail of everything man in his mental activity may inquire into and know, or may attempt and accomplish in the world; the problem is simply that of never at any moment violating the principles of true religion, that of obeying thus the divine will only, even where it is most difficult to obey it, in thinking and speaking as in doing and suffering; and for such a task the spirit which an individual has received may suffice, even where the utmost measure of attainment is demanded of it. It is said also, where from the context it has its proper import, " not by measure "—as if He were Himself a heathen god, and so possibly envious, who likes to give what he gives only piecemeal and in scant measurement—" does God give the Spirit," [2] but if He gives it at all, and to any one in special mode,[3] He gives it wholly, so that it can accomplish, through that man from whom it works, even the most perfect and abiding results. Christ proclaims it as a universal truth, not one merely applicable to this man or that; He does not say it immediately of Himself. But the truer the general proposition is, the more vividly and obviously it is realized by the individual by whom it is actually realized; and how it was realized by Christ in a peculiar degree, is evident enough from the whole phenomenon of His life.

But if this practical and this so to say personal possibility were both realized by Jesus as Christ, there must still be added at last, in the third place, the one possibility, which to have made a reality is His peculiar and immortal merit alone,

---

[1] [*I.e.* contains in itself all possibilities open to it, and the capacity to realize them.—Tr.]

[2] John iii. 34. [Ewald ascribes this saying to Christ.—Tr.]

[3] To what is special there is already reference in that the discourse here is of a special giving of the Spirit by God, and of Him whom God sent. But the idea of " not by measure " leads back also essentially to what is said in John i. 32, cf. 52 (Eng. version 51), of the special manner of the descent of the Spirit upon Jesus in baptism.

viz. the perfect, unobscured, conscious submission to the divine will, and harmonious co-operation with it in every moment of His public activity which we can observe; and this, too, in a life-work incomparably important for the salvation of the ancient community, and through it of all humanity, and just as incomparably burdened with temptation, difficulty, and sorrow, and whose only joy was the pure realization of divine assurance and hope. But through this, and through this alone, did that wondrously elevating thought of the kingly and perfect, demanded in this community by old prophecies and expectations, and sustaining Him all along from the beginning, receive at length its fulfilment and satisfaction; and when a king had come, who, standing infinitely abased amid all other so-called kings, yet eternally overtopped them all, and transfigured at once and for ever the idea of the kingly, and when a kingdom was founded, differing from all others, yet alone able to give to all others salvation and perpetuity, and unite all together in a common divine security, then already the whole development of millenniums of antiquity in this community and all the rest of the nations attained its perfect consummation, but only to make room for a wholly new fellowship, whose light and whose revelation now at once begin.

For Christ's revelation is His public appearing and work in themselves, as they must take shape and form by the full living concurrent action of all these four potencies.[1] It is the consciously-certain word of a King who founds His own kingdom of the perfect true religion, expected in the disintegrated ancient community of the true religion, and who calls all who will listen to Him to participate in it. But as certainly as the kingdom He founds as its human King is none other than the kingdom of divine truth itself,[2] so certainly He

---

[1] [These four forces (*mächte*) are—1. The idea of the kingly and perfect demanded by ancient prophecy and expectation; 2. The practical or objective possibility of its realization within the limits of our humanity; 3. The personal, or subjective, possibility of its realization by the God-given Spirit; 4. The actual realization itself in Christ's own experience and work.—Tr.]

[2] John xviii. 37 f., with all similar sayings in John.

has but to lay down in all calmness and all clearness the fundamental conditions of it, and by His own work corresponding to these conditions, and by the formation of a community resting upon them, actually to begin it. And as certainly as the expected King coming at length into His kingdom has to apply afresh for the purposes of His kingdom all the old inherited treasures and forces increased by His own, so certainly nothing is lost to Him in itself and in His new community,—no truth spoken, no blessing secured at any earlier period of this community's history. Still further, just as certainly as He knew that the God whose kingdom of truth He had to found by all such means in the new community, is ever the same both in Himself and towards His own people in the world, so certainly He never at any moment despaired of the victory of the kingdom set up by Him on earth, but discoursed and worked even in the conspicuous destruction of His own mortal body as the King of this kingdom, and by the divine Spirit eternally triumphant.

Therefore from the very beginning of His public work He does not, in an individual case or generally, first seek divine truth, as the prophets do, who often become certain of it and publish it only after most violent unrest and agitation; He has it already, working always as a King in the divine kingdom in blessed repose, and He obeys it without hesitation even where, from the vicissitude of the times, it is of importance to be ever freshly certain of the divine will in particular affairs; so that even the most fearful experiences from without shake and thrill Him indeed humanly, but yet leave Him divinely undisturbed. He does not, as the prophets, struggling often with the darkness of other thoughts, first transpose Himself into the divine mind, and then from the sternly authoritative and sharply reproving Ego of God Himself, discourse over against the world (p. 48); He speaks and works directly from His own Ego, but as if that Ego were never accustomed to be without the divine light, and in no case were without the divine will. The divinely-human life exists in Him already as a sure boon and most blessed possession, and revealing itself more widely to the world, it acts in all repose, whether others, as they observe it, make it their own or not. He can therefore calmly say, Every one may know, even from his own earnest will, to obey implicitly the divine will, whether His doctrine be an arbitrary invention of His own, or that of God Himself.[1] The prophetic element in Him, apart from the clear glance into all the future, is therefore also the inner certainty of mind as it reveals itself in its truth over against the world. But on this account also, words and works, doctrine and conduct and suffering, are with Him in such perfect agreement and harmony, that the former only illustrate the latter, the latter the former; in everything He presents equally a revelation of what the divine life in man should be. And not till this is reached do we find the supreme revelation (p. 72). It is because the separate works a man performs may without doubt be most easily known in their true character, whilst mere thoughts and doctrines, notwithstanding their inner certainty and absolute clearness, may involve truth so high and so new that many to whom they are made known may not be equal to the task of raising themselves at once to the most entire acquiescence in them, that He says, He who will not believe in His divine mission on account of His words, ought at least to believe Him on account of His deeds, since to deny the light of facts is pure sin.[2]

It is thus, in fine, one of the best witnesses for the truth of His revelation that His whole public work is devoted so purely and so singly to His vocation as the glorious King of the kingdom of the perfect true religion, that, in fact, He fulfils this vocation in the most complete way imaginable, and that neither in word nor deed does He intermingle with it

---

[1] John vii. 17.
[2] All the earlier Gospels allow this to be inferred. John, however, at last expresses it throughout his entire Gospel most clearly. Cf. *The Johannean Writings*, i. p. 27 ff. The principal section, John xiv. 11 ff.

anything in the smallest degree that is irrelevant and would only disturb or obscure it, and inweave error afresh into the most unsullied and transparent truth. Where power that is unalloyed and so far immeasurable holds itself in act, in knowledge, in judgment, in speech on all sides every moment, voluntarily, discreetly, firmly, within its proper and therefore inviolable human limits, and where the highest display of energy shows the greatest self-restraint, the most laborious work the serenest joyfulness, the most vehement unrest and agitation and the keenest smart the happiest repose, there all the divinest that is possible in man may reveal itself, not only most perfectly as to its nature and contents, but also most clearly and most conspicuously over against all the world, and most convincingly over against all convictions. But the most searching and repeated investigation attests how absolutely and firmly Christ observed due limits; and most readily is it seen how He observed them in public action with unsurpassable accuracy as well in the least as in the greatest affairs. Just as prudently and firmly did He keep within them, also, in all family concerns; by His mere authority He would not forestall the decision of any lawful tribunal, nor strain a right to any one's advantage or disadvantage.[1] And if with one who is held to be a sage, a teacher, or a prophet, the temptation is always great to make a display of superior wisdom by giving judgment upon some abstruse subject, or to show transcendent prophetic power by foretelling whatever men desire to know; yet in His case we never find even in the least that He speaks and judges so that, from His assumption, error and injury must sooner or later necessarily accrue. On a question of critical knowledge, He gives a decision only where and so far as it was necessary, —in the right place, and then with striking completeness;[2] foretelling what only God could know, He expressly dis-

---

[1] The reminiscence in Luke xii. 13-15 shows this pre-eminently.
[2] As cases like Matt. xix. 8, John v. 45-47, vii. 22, show most plainly; also Matt. xxii. 41-45, if it is taken accurately.

claims.¹ And as He could thank God,² when prepared for death, that from the ranks of those who were truly His own not a single one had been lost through Him, so there never came from His lips a word of corruption or even of error; and indeed this was the less likely, from His own strong assurance of the wondrous power of the good word and the deeply pernicious power of every evil word in human affairs.³

Thus, then, in the only true and therefore most beautiful manner, was fulfilled on this side in Christ everything that the old anticipations finding expression in this community had fervently desired (p. 98). As the truth and love, and thereby the definite will of God to men, may become in a man most perfectly living and effective, so this truth and this love of God and His eternal will to men were now manifest in the most perfect clearness and certainty,⁴—no longer as from an invisible distant Deity, or according to the demand and prescription of a law; and the Word of God which, comprehending in itself the whole mind of God, penetrates and orders and sustains the whole universe from the beginning, but before all the universe is addressed to and seeks to guide mankind,—this Word, as we may now briefly say upon a calm retrospect of the appearing of Christ, was embodied and made human in the life of this one man, and in His perishable mortal body itself, that it might be manifest to all humanity as it was first manifest in Him.⁵

5. *The Consummation of all Revelation.*

§ 42. It would be a great mistake, however, to suppose that the revelation which is the subject of our discussion was already perfected during the earthly appearing of Him who brought its consummation, or that there is any one

---

¹ Matt. xxiv. 36.   ² John xvii. 12.   ³ According to Matt. xii. 36 f.
⁴ Cf. how this is expressed just as briefly as appropriately in John i. 17.
⁵ For the introduction to John's Gospel, i. 1–18, was after all the only introduction with which a Gospel could be most suitably prefaced.

moment of His human life, or any single word or deed of His, in which it is already perfected. For the first certainty of this whole development takes us back to the conclusion of § 19 f., that not single words, were they the eternally truest, and not single deeds, answering exactly to the import of such true words, but only a finished history, embracing everything that is relevant to the subject, can give the complete revelation which, for the needs of our present-day knowledge, we here seek as in reality entire antiquity had sought it. Even the last divinely-joyful surrender of Christ to death, and His last words on the cross, perfect this revelation only so far as He as this unique special man could contribute to it; it was perfected only as this whole human appearing and activity of Christ Himself was for ever perfected, and now by reason of its entirety and its finished and settled significance it stood in connection with this long development as a divine whole before the world. For if an individual life can be rightly estimated, as well in itself as in its connection with the rest of mankind, only when, being fully concluded, it becomes conspicuous as a finished whole, but then, however, this right estimation, disconnected from the will of him whom it adjudges, becomes irresistible, by reason of the pure working back of divine impulses and powers whose activity the individual history itself has occasioned; how much more must all this have been the case here, where the lifework of this unparalleled personage had been the most difficult in itself and of the highest nature, and, moreover, had formed the conclusion of a most protracted and changeful development, upon which depended the deepest spiritual life of all mankind! When, therefore, the apostles, and soon incalculably many others, gazing upon this wholly perfected divinely-human life, became certain of its infinite significance and purely divine glory, and, notwithstanding all mistaking and hostility of the world, maintained this significance with unshaken faith; and when, as they were suffused with the radiance of the glorified Christ, they found their own enlightenment and that of the whole world only in His light and in His truth, their own immortal life only in His immortal life: then was the revelation perfected, which since the time of Moses, nay, since the beginning of all human history, as will be yet further evident, struggled all along towards its consummation. But this perfected humanly-divine life having entered into the world, produced already, even in its first body of disciples, fruits of imperishable life, of which we shall soon speak more particularly.[1]

But there is yet another point of view from which a perfecting of revelation may and indeed must now be affirmed. For if the utmost that the perfect true religion demands of men (§ 41) had first to come in One who is in full reality so perfect, that His whole conspicuous historical manifestation was in everything—in all He spoke, taught, or strove after, in all He did, attained, endured, or suffered—nothing but one free outflow of that perfect true religion itself, and one unparalleled effulgent transfiguration of it for all the world; now had this unique personage come who must thus first come, and He had come not in the simpler conditions of the higher antiquity, but in circumstances already the most developed and the most gravely complicated into which human society could grow, and not among the heathen, but in that society which from its peculiar world-old culture possessed in all these things the longest experience, the most intent expectancy, and the ripest preparation, but also the sharpest glance and suspicion, and when once inclined to the right the most accurate judgment as well; a society, indeed, in which before such a claim as Christ raised His work must be regarded as everything or nothing, and could find only either the most terrible end, well-deserved in the judgment of all the most sagacious, upright, and incorrupt of His fellow-countrymen, or at least with some, and these an ever-

---

[1] Cf. § 46 ff. One cannot refrain in this connection from involuntarily referring to the word with which John concludes his preface, i. 14–18, and whose further elucidation his great Epistle gives.

increasing number, the highest reverence and the most faithful following. If, however, He had now come in this way, and by the whole of the now concluded phenomenon of His life had so completely stood the test, that at least with the few whom He had first of all gathered about His own person in close attachment, and had taken into His full confidence and love, He found the purest faith; then the acknowledgment must also have been made, that no other man could come in whom should be manifest a yet higher king of the kingdom of all true religion, and who should fulfil the will of God more perfectly both in his humanity generally and in the special capacity of spiritual kingship. Therefore, as they banded themselves together around Him,— notwithstanding His invisibility to the sense,—the immediate duty [1] could only be to participate in the kingdom He had founded, and in its requirements and hopes; the immediate task, too, was to obey Him in all things as the faithful subject the King, or rather, as He Himself most loved to indicate the relation, as a friend the friend, or a younger brother the elder; and the consecrating bond that made all one was that everything material and sensuous was with this King excluded, and only the purely God-like and the divinely-transfigured had authority in the whole kingdom. And in point of fact there is no change in the position of things to-day, for we still hold that revelation is completed with Christ's historical appearing, since a higher and more conspicuous revelation has neither actually come in the ages succeeding Christ, nor upon closer consideration is it even possible.

With all this coincides ultimately the idea of the Truth as its highest generalization. The Apostle John, indeed, in all his three Epistles loves no idea more than this, with that akin to it, Light. He characterizes it in his Gospel also as the

[1] The idea of divine duty incumbent upon men now the oldest apostolic preaching made in reality very prominent (Acts ii. 38-40, iii. 12-26, iv. 8-12, etc.).

conception in which the whole now finished manifestation of Christ culminates,[1] and he makes it recur in Christ's sayings themselves[2] with the same high significance in which he otherwise renders it prominent. Why truth in this whole sphere should not from the first arise to men save from its own necessity, is indicated above (§ 16), and will be yet more evident subsequently (vol. ii.); but if it has become known in a matter affecting, as truth in this department must affect, all men alike, then it lies in its nature, which is above human caprice, that it should secure its own preservation among men; and we saw above how it had constantly been preserved in the great several portions of it which had come to be known in the old community, and had formed its very ground and basis. But just as much does it lie in the nature of truth also, that in a definite department of knowledge and activity it should become the more conspicuous and incapable of being lost again, the more completely in the whole range of it it has found manifestation. And this was just the case now. As in the highest question of the relation between God and man, so also in all other principal questions, truth had arisen in such absolute lucidity and trustworthiness, that Christianity itself, as it had now once for all come to be known in the world, might be regarded, as John regarded it, as virtually synonymous with it.[3]

Nevertheless this is not equivalent to saying that truth in this whole sphere has not still to struggle for its further unfolding in special particular aspects of it, still less to asserting that among Christians it is everywhere always conspicuously heeded, and, as the divine will enjoins, practically used, even indeed in those portions of it long since become a sure possession. Revelation is now, it is true, completed in

---

[1] John i. 14, 17.

[2] From John iii. 21, iv. 23 f. onwards often; and with no word is it more distinctly felt than with this. How spontaneously to the grey-headed apostle this word so exceptionally dear to him flowed into Christ's sayings, as they became freshly vivified again in his own mind!

[3] 2 John 1-4; 3 John 1-4, cf. with 1 John i. 6, 8, ii. 21, iii. 19, iv. 6.

itself, perfectly and historically, in the sense that no higher revelation is yet to be expected; but concluded and become unnecessary as an activity it is not; rather may its activity be still further highly desirable, nay, indispensable in the right place. But if the spirit in its purest, and, so to say, most spiritual sense (§ 36) was in the earlier day held in Israel to be the true spur of revelation, so now, after the highest revelation had been manifest in Christ, must Christ's spirit in a wholly analogous way be contemplated as itself alone capable of carrying forward the work which He Himself had once so powerfully begun. This is the all-prevailing feeling which dominates all apostles and other writers of the New Testament, as in reality it completely penetrated the whole of youthful Christianity.[1] And thus the principle still stands good, notwithstanding, and most palpably so with every Christian, that revelation is essentially perfected and finished with Christ.

§ 43. By this perfecting of revelation is understood—

1. As far as the past is concerned, that of all the truths of this sphere nothing which has been already won upon any previous stage is allowed to be lost on this highest and last. For if there are actually divine truths, which should guide the life of all men equally, and which the more surely and completely they are known, and the more deeply and many-sidedly they have become part of living experience, are the more fit to guide this life, it becomes possible, with a continuously progressive development especially, that no truth should be lost upon a higher stage which has already been won upon a lower, since this higher stage itself can only be reached by means of the gains of the lower; and further, that least of all can an essential truth be lost when the highest stage is reached, and when it is thenceforward without interruption maintained. But this continuously progressive development

---

[1] Thence in purely prophetic writings the Old Testament, "Thus saith Jahveh," passes over into the new expression, "The Spirit saith," Rev. ii. 7, ii. 17, etc.; then with special emphasis twice, xiv. 13, xxii. 17.

here presupposed is possible where, upon the basis of at least some entirely irrefragable truths of this sphere, a community is once upbuilt of such as find in them the only true salvation of their whole life and effort; for then the efficacy and preservation both of an individual truth that belongs to this sphere, and of the coherence of all truth, no longer depends upon the frailty of one man, or of a few men, but finds security in the abiding aims and regulations of the community itself, and in the continual succession of generations of men born, or newly naturalized, in it. Since, now, such a community had been already firmly established from the time of Moses, and had become, at least in its deepest foundations, more and more immovable through all the long and stormy centuries that had succeeded; and, moreover, since Christ had upbuilt the new community of His perfect truth upon just the foundations of the old community that were firmest, and the treasures that had received the longest attestation, it is evident how in the new community no single fragment of true knowledge, and no single means of reviving it ever afresh, could be lost. This, indeed, Christ Himself in His whole public action had shown,[1] and the immediate and best continuers of His earthly work at once further attested it.

In fact, however, this supplementing of what Christ had said and done was the more necessary, since Christ neither had the intention nor found the time to teach every individual thing Himself that belongs even to the fundamental truths of this wide circle. It is true, indeed, that, according to all our most exact investigations, it is incorrect to say that His public activity lasted only for a year; it extended rather over three or four years. But even in the wider course of

---

[1] That by Matt. v. 21 ff. Christ would not even remotely put Himself in real opposition to Moses and the prophets, I have long since proved; the men of old time He opposes are wholly different men, and perhaps the same as those meant in John x. 8, as the latter passage is explained in the *Jahrb. der Bibl. Wiss.* ii. p. 40-47. Just as certain is it that such words as Gal. iii. 19 f., 2 Cor. iii. 7-15, John viii. 5 ff., are not even remotely intended to detract from the high authority of Moses himself, which in its measure is rightly conceded.

these years He had other pressing business than to teach once again everything that already stood secure in this community, completely verified by the labours of the old great revealers and the experience of all earlier centuries. What is of moment here is that He could presuppose so calmly and self-certainly, as He continually did, the anciently-attested rich treasures of revelation as a divine and acknowledged possession. Upon this wonderful structure, for the founding, defence, and further progress of which the whole antiquity had laboured, He placed only the still wanting last coping-stones and sheltering roofs, without which it must certainly have become disintegrated by exposure, and have fallen into decay.

As those old verified rudiments and mighty fragments of revelation, by their very contents, and by the imperfection which still characterized them, side by side with all their indwelling truth that could not easily be destroyed, spontaneously tended and led to an actual consummation of revelation, so long as a breath of fresh pure life still animated this community, and as the best prophetic minds had just on this account with increasing confidence ultimately anticipated, and as it were challenged this consummation, so when it had now come it threw back its luminous splendour upon all the separate truths which had been won in earlier days in this community, or even elsewhere, sporadically in all antiquity. The profoundest vision of the great unnamed prophet of the Old Testament,[1] and the most difficult task he had in his time demanded as Israel's higher duty, unattainable then, listened to fondly long afterwards as a beautiful tale of antiquity, but lying as if spell-bound and dead upon the ground, woke up anew, one wonderful word after another, till all became wholly living again in the new higher light that now flashed forth;[2] the radiant splendour of Moses also, obscured by the later

---

[1] Cf. *Proph. of Old Test.* iii. 21 ff. [Eng. ed. iv. 245 ff.].

[2] From Matt. iii. 3 to 1 Pet. ii. 21-25 what progress there is! And yet it is only one direct and necessary progress.

scribes, now emerged from eclipse;[1] and the stories of the patriarchs of the yet freer, clearer, remote time, irradiated by this new and intense effulgence, became luminous with meaning never known before.[2] And so the same new light would arise at that time upon all the scenes and fragmentary records of the earlier stages of revelation,[3] the light which from other causes and yet similarly to-day amongst ourselves is shining, and might still further and more freely be diffused.

But just as the consummation of revelation looked back upon this its peaceful height with brighter vision upon all things historically developed during its own earlier stages, and projected into the present, so it was also keen-sighted enough rightly to perceive the deficiencies that were there prevalent, and, moreover, felt itself energetic enough at the same time to liberate itself from them. Yet, indeed, there is nothing more difficult and critical than emancipation from conceptions and usages of life long since deeply rooted, irradiated widely as by a divine splendour, and upheld by the dominant schools; and should the individual recognise also with sufficient certainty what is pernicious and perishable in them, the most careful reflection is continually needed to determine how far he might venture to go as a member or leader of the community, in order, in some definite matter, not to produce at the time greater mischief. But it had been seen already how, with respect to old sacred customs, Christ Himself had moved in that spirit of perfect piety which was destined to prevail in the community;[4] the new community, therefore, that gathered about its heavenly Head immediately after His

---

[1] Heb. xi. 24–28, cf. 2 Cor. iii. 13–16; above, p. 82.

[2] John viii. 39–58.

[3] The example of Heb. xi. 3–40 is only the most manifold and in so far most masterly and greatest which the New Testament affords us; the copious treatment of a thought in harmony with the Old Testament by Stephen, Acts vii., is to be coupled with it.

[4] Not merely with respect to the law of the schools concerning the Sabbath, but also otherwise frequently; the lasting impression the certain and variously attested reminiscence of this must make in the earliest time of the apostolic activity is too much overlooked to-day.

glorification, attempted to shape its actual life in accordance with His;[1] and the further step which Paul somewhat later boldly ventured upon with the certainty peculiar to him and victoriously accomplished, is so instructive for us in this case chiefly as we have so clearly in view the unusual difficulties which then presented themselves, and were yet so happily and harmlessly overcome. Thus the apostolic age shows with what power and success the new original force of the perfected revelation can work retrospectively in order rightly to apprehend all that is incomplete in past historical developments, and establish something better in its place; as Christ did this Himself everywhere, and once incidentally gave expression to it clearly enough as a principle.[2]

§ 44. 2. For the present, however, it must be matter of importance to discourse in spirit about all serious questions as Christ Himself had been heard to discourse about them. It was not in the garb of the old prophetic speech that Christ discoursed, but with an inner certainty, clearness, and by consequence simplicity, that reproduced the old prophetic speech in its finest characteristic, and caused all His words to be soon customarily designated prophetic sayings.[3] Now, therefore, that which once seemed to have belonged to prophets only was to be among Christians common custom, so that every one, even if speaking of other subjects and occasions than Christ, should yet discourse with the same inner certainty and simple truthfulness as He had done; and the incomparably high significance which Christ attributed fundamentally to sincerity of word as the corresponding outcome of sincerity of spirit,[4]

---

[1] Also often overlooked, although as a model for the time immediately following it must have been of the greatest importance; but we overlook it because we no longer possess such copious witnesses of it as of the changes introduced by Paul. But the vast importance of these earliest changes is shown in the *History*, vi. p. 138-193 [Eng. ed. vii.].

[2] Matt. xiii. 52.

[3] In Greek or Latin, according to p. 24, much more simply and briefly, λογια, *oracula;* the German *Sprüche* is less adequate. As to the subject itself, see *Die drei ersten Evangelien*, 2nd ed. p. 63 ff.

[4] Matt. xii. 36 f. may be taken with Matt. v. 33-37, xxiii. 16-22.

anticipated this requirement. As a matter of fact, the language of the two writers of the New Testament who had once stood very near to Christ, and who at the same time, as writers in the Greek tongue, are more independent, answers most faithfully to this demand; pre-eminently the language of John in his great Epistle and in his Gospel, then that of James also. Peter, however, although his Epistle inclines more to the type and colour of Greek discourse that became customary through Paul, expresses most plainly the original Christian requirement in the sentence, " Let every one, when he speaks, speak as God's oracle."[1] Paul himself discourses indeed with less simplicity, with less absolute directness and absence of all consciousness of his own Ego and adornment of Greek colour; but where he enters into the discussion of special difficult questions (and just in this he is altogether peculiar among New Testament epistolary writers), it is felt at once how the nervous brevity and simple directness which Christianity brought into the world again in such thoroughly new form, seeks to take possession also of questions which are properly speaking scientific. The Epistle to the Hebrews follows Paul in this only at a wide interval in its principal discussions and dissertations. The three pastoral Epistles are colourless; the transition to more artificial discourse we do not mark until the Epistle to the Ephesians and the Second Epistle of Peter, the last being parallel especially with the Epistle of Jude.

What better conclusion could there be of this whole matter, than that without continually introducing God as the ultimate originator or pledge and witness of truth, as the greatest prophets of Israel had once done, always in the highest and purest sense, nevertheless human discourse should be commonly spoken as if it were His discourse and His word! For even

---

[1] 1 Pet. iv. 11. All this is to be taken into account, that we may understand what new healthiness and quickening of mind in this direction Christianity brought. In the Old Testament only Jeremiah touches upon this demand for simple transparency and plain directness in human discourse, xxiii. 25-40.

in word, nay, first of all and most necessarily in word, the true God was not now to come among men and make Himself audible and perceptible to them as it were ever anew and from His lofty and remote height; He was to be present with men always in all repose and equalness, so that nothing should be thought and nothing should be spoken which had not the mark of veracity He required, and was not, though in humble and limited measure, a kind of revelation of His mind and thought, or at least could not be answered for at last before Him as a conscientious word.

§ 45. 3. With all this, however, the eager looking for divine enlightenment with respect to the darkness of the present and the future, and the special department of ancient prophecy to which this belonged, were so little to be repressed, that they rather freshly awoke with new ardour and new boldness, and seemed capable of entirely recovering once more the old power. Whilst for many centuries the prophecy of the palmy days of the nation had been as good as dead, and dragged on but a poor existence in anonymous writings (§ 38), now it renewed its strength, as did all the deeper life of the spirit, which in the nobler times of the old community flourished spontaneously, and it reappeared openly with its task and its whole entire effort in the different new Christian communities.[1] Yet certainly its slumbering fire was first vividly enkindled with special force amid the new and severe persecutions which so soon broke out, threatening afresh the whole existence of this community; and accordingly, in the first larger book of prophecy, replete with art, that issued from the midst of its life, the short all-explaining sentence is given : " The witness of Christ "—uplifting itself boldly even amid the direst temptations and pains of the world—" is the spirit of prophecy ; "[2] the former called forth the latter, and is virtually one with it, so that he who is most ready for that " witness " is also easily most irresistibly possessed of this " spirit." This is as much as to say, it is

---

[1] Cf. *History of Israel*, vi. p. 185 f., 694 ff., vii. p. 361 ff.
[2] Rev. xix. 10.

only the genuine spirit, which shows itself active in Christianity in so perfect a form, that can now possess the prophets and speak forth from them. And if in a book so highly esteemed at that time as the Book of Daniel, it might be read how the prophet, falling down and doing homage, humbled himself profoundly before the radiant form of a mighty angel that appeared to him,[1] the new Christian spirit rather felt aversion to such slavish fear and adoration of an angel,[2] since it seemed as if every other spiritual existence must now vanish before the solitary grandeur of Christ. Accordingly, Paul also, regarding it as opportune to seek to confine within its appropriate bounds the stream of prophetic ardour, soon overflowing again in the new Christianity, briefly counselled that all Christian prophecy should shape itself "according to the proportion of faith," or in that measure and in those contents that agree with the faith that is established independently of the prophet, and with his own conscience, and should be approved only in so far as the prophet would be answerable for it to these authorities; and it is self-evident that this "faith" is in Paul's mouth the Christian faith.[3] In another passage, where he sees himself obliged to deal very definitely and copiously with all the diversified manifestations of higher inspiration as they occur in youthful Christianity,—partly in an altogether new and even strange form,—he concludes the long discussion with the brief general proposition: "Even the spirits of the prophets are subject to the prophets," so that they are under control and orderly if only the prophet knows how to curb and guide them.[4] There is no need to suppose that the maxim, the motto of a golden seal, impressed at last in the New Testament upon all prophecy and to be legible for ever, contradicts the view of the best earlier antiquity (p. 63 ff.) concerning the relation of the prophet to the spirit impelling him; it only

[1] Dan. x. 4–10; which passage probably floated before the mind of John of the Apocalypse.

[2] Rev. xix. 10, xxii. 9; with which must be taken as the counterpart, i. 17. Thus also the end of the Apocalypse points back to the beginning.

[3] Rom. xii. 6.   [4] 1 Cor. xiv. 32, cf. with the discussion, xii., xiv

supplements it, while it admonishes the prophet in the very midst of his self-surrender in some obscure matter to the urgent and all-powerful impulse of the true spirit, not to suffer anything undivinely conceived to intermingle, and to hold the bridle of the horse the more firmly, the more swiftly it runs. For the whole individual man and prophet can ever stand superior to a particular thought that has seized him.

But it is worthy of note, and instructive to mark well and somewhat more closely, how Christian prophecy, suddenly springing up thus with unanticipated boldness and independence, actually shaped itself in detail. The highest art in which prophecy could ever clothe itself together with the sublimest and most lasting contents were already found in the treasury of the Old Testament prophets, and the reading of old writers in conjunction with immediate authorship were then two of the living impulses that flourished in the highest degree. It is quite in harmony with this that Christian prophecy, newly struggling forth, should throw itself with youthful zeal into the glow of that imperishable centre of divine fire; should nourish to still greater vigour by its warmth the Christian hopes now so wonderfully attained, whose mighty life was kindled chiefly at that central-hearth; and should not merely replenish itself afresh with the contents of those old sacred works, as far as they appeared applicable to the present, but above all should be newly vivified and sustained by their unsurpassable art. The Old Testament prophecy, with every charm of its high art and holy word, born again, however, in the Christian spirit, found once more a resurrection to life, and the old shadows, freshly animated by a new spirit, stepped forth anew into the full light of day. Of such works, of which, according to all indications, many appeared, the best, the Apocalypse of a John otherwise almost entirely unknown to us, has alone been preserved in the New Testament. Who would wish to hinder this kind of resuscitation of the old sublime prophecy of the true religion? Or if, in quite a different sphere, the unsurpassable art of Homer were to-day imitated for a new purpose, who shall prevent it ? But the resuscitation of the art of Old Testament prophecy was at that time only one of the many means by which the consummation of all revelation in this its right sphere sought the more surely its own preservation and defence. But because this renewal of existence was possible only by means of literary art, and by no means proceeded from the midst of a great public life, as did that immortally perfected Old Testament prophecy, it could well serve its special aim as a wholly appropriate instrument, and illustrate one and another of the finest Christian truths; but the real old prophecy in its living art, it could neither completely renew nor surpass, as indeed from that day to this has never happened, notwithstanding varied and successive attempts.

Christ Himself, however, even in the midst of His public activity as it became more extensive and difficult, and its day was felt to incline to its end, had spoken more frequently and at large words which after His departure were rightly felt to contain the presages of His prophetic spirit, and on that account were the more carefully weighed and the more eagerly collected.[1] They were spoken, as their occasion and varying special contents demanded, in very manifold form,—in significant parables, in abrupt sentences, and in longer discourses, and also as additions to a special word of prophecy from the Holy Scriptures;[2] but they were all without exception just as purely creative, and therefore as simple and transparently clear, as all other words of His revelation; and even the least fragment of them showed that artistic beauty and perfection which marks everything that is truly creative. They were spoken, moreover, as publicly as all that Christ spoke,[3] and,

[1] That the prophetic words of Christ taken from the "collected sayings," and as a whole well preserved in Matt. x., xiii., xxiv., xxv., are in all that is essential really His, no competent critic can deny. John, who regards it subsequently as superfluous to give a similar collection, shows rather how Christ expressed such anticipations in living connection with His other thoughts and discourses, experience and acts.

[2] As in the addition to the words from the Book of Daniel, Matt. xxiv. 15.

[3] That Christ said nothing to the Twelve alone that had it been advisable at the moment He could not have said before all the people, and that was actually

as the occasion offered, in a wider or narrower circle;[1] but they concerned, as did everything that proceeded from His spirit, only the great affairs of His kingdom. And since in these prophecies, as collected and compared one with another, was presented in all simple brevity an adequate image of the whole infinitude of the future development of His kingdom, so far as its founder in the midst of the limitations of His particular time could present it, revelation in this aspect of it was perfected as far as was necessary for its absolute and supreme aim; as, indeed, this might be perceived with the greater certainty as soon as the most vital part of those prophecies began to be fulfilled.[2]

It is true, however, that not every Christian at once and in all situations of life has that higher rest and unshaken composure in which Christ Himself, amid temptations and sufferings which He only could experience, ever looked forward to all the future, and in which He lived, as if wherever He might sojourn a longer or shorter time, He carried about with Himself everywhere, in the frail perishable human body, a continually uniform perfect revelation of God and His will. Nor is it less certain that, face to face with the darkness of the present and the inscrutable enigmas of the future, not all even of the most intimate chief witnesses of His glory and heralds of His gospel could constantly maintain this same unclouded serene repose—all sharp dissimilarity notwithstanding—as the Apostle John had won it according to the testimony of his

said before them as soon as possible, is partly self-evident and partly follows from the right sense of the words, Matt. xiii. 13-17, cf. with v. 13-16, x. 27. The same thing is true of what He said to His specially trusted three disciples, or to one of them; but what was elsewhere said to an individual, as in John iii. 1 ff., iv. 7 ff., is only in its ultimate import what, the occasion being different, He said also everywhere.

[1] See preceding note.

[2] It is well worthy of note that the Apocalypse of the New Testament was written in the midst of the exceeding unrest and insecurity which might well take possession even of the best Christian hearts, before the destruction of Jerusalem had brought the first great confirmation of Christ's prophetic words. It can therefore be rightly appreciated only as it is firmly held to be the last mighty outcry of Christian longing ere the first great realization of it.

three Epistles and of his Gospel narrative. Every Christian may always find himself still in a position of things in which, with respect to great Christian affairs or the experiences of his own life, he yearns for new revelation, that he may clearly and confidently know how he has to act so as to conform to God's will; but as to the glance of the soul that longs deeply and painfully for new revelation in great universal humanly-divine issues, this, during the whole continuance of youthful Christianity, might really be excited most vividly, nay, to over-measure and intoxication, not only by the greatest wonder which so far human history could experience, and which, as seen in Christ's history, still stirred men's minds with all freshness, nor merely by the severest straining of all expectation and hope thus occasioned, but also by the rare abundance of what may briefly be called (p. 97) apocalyptic writings, which, in the glowing heat of those years, excited the imagination most vehemently, and could easily throw susceptible spirits into a similar fervour of intuitions of heaven, of hell, of the judgment of the world, and the ultimate eternal consummation. A man of such glowing thoughts, longings, and imaginations was Paul, and especially so as being yet a wholly new disciple of the Lord; but he not merely possessed at that time the most burning longings for revelations concerning the infinitely great last Christian things, he had also subsequently to fight resolutely enough with all the world, nay, even with his own sick body, that he might not ever be struggling anew in most urgent prayer for immediate divine revelation. But from the way in which in his later riper days, under special but unavoidable circumstances, he once expresses himself [1] concerning two things, different in themselves, but with him very closely connected, his word may be taken as the soundest doctrine upon the subject. For he was perfectly conscious, indeed, that a Christian in his highest excitation and most blessed rapture could feel himself transported to heaven and hell, nay, to the

---

[1] 2 Cor. xii. 1–10, with what is said in the *Sendschreiben des Apostels Paulus*, p. 301-308.

near vision of the glorified Christ and the judgment of the world, and he did not reject such extreme inspiration with the revelations received in it concerning the last things; but he knew also that a man must not lose by means of it his composure and presence of mind.[1] And once in the wrestling of his prayer he thought he heard an immediate voice from God Himself and the glorified Christ, and he was not deceived in this; but that he was not deceived lay merely in the clear truth, firmly established, independently of his excited feeling and perfectly normal character, of the brief twofold word he had heard in the way not infrequent in his age (described above, p. 102), and whose normal character consisted just in this, that it finds its response so perfectly in every genuine Christian mind, and, moreover, contains in itself for him as for every one similarly suffering the most wonderful uplifting and consolation. If, now, Paul presents, in general, a typical example of the individual Christian in all situations of life, he also may show us here that, in the two great directions which can occur in practice, the universal and the special, the potency and truth of revelation, of course in the midst of the consummation of all revelation brought by Christ, may be active continually, if it but keeps itself within those firm limits which this apostle has himself traced out from his own living experience. For the perfecting of a spiritual and so an eternal beneficent activity is not to bring for the future its cessation, or indeed its ignorement and disregard, but only the proper laws and limits within which henceforward it has to move. And as the perfecting of the creation of human speech does not demand the cessation of this activity, or seek to hinder its infinite application and extension, although never again may its proper unalterable foundations be destroyed, so similarly this activity of all divinely-human speech is never again to be restrained where it keeps itself in its right limits as they have now been won.[2]

---

[1] In ver. 2 he speaks as one may discourse of every Christian, so little does he seriously wish to boast of himself only.

[2] That revelation might go on in the community, indeed, even without Paul,

Special Marks of the Consummation of Revelation.

§ 46. In all that has just been said, there lies the general proof that upon its fifth stage revelation is in reality so perfected that to expect or attempt a higher would be folly indeed. But there are yet distinct marks by which this perfection may ever be recognised with the same certainty in another aspect, and by all.

1. As touching its expression, revelation has come in Christ to a stage which, because it is the highest, is also the simplest; this must be said if what is essential is considered. The particular outward husk and variegated diversity in which it made its appearance all through the previous stages, so long as the pure divine Ego still suppressed as it were every human Ego, it has now stripped off; this Ego still speaks down from its lofty height only as a lingering echo, and more perceptibly in the imitations of learned writers. The proud, high growth and luxurious bloom vanish ultimately in the firm, solid fruit, and the most motley and manifold as it perfects itself changes to the most simple. When divine thought feels itself now no longer strange and foreign in the world, and sure divine certainty needed no more the distinct affirmation of God Himself to accompany it in order to find acceptance among men as divine word and be regarded as divine certainty, then it is that according to the will of Christ all human thoughts and words are to be full of divine assurance and joyfulness. Now sounds indeed from the lips of Christ Himself the certifying " Verily," or rather, according to John, still more strongly the " Verily, verily, I say unto

---

and in a particular matter run counter to his way of thinking, he says himself, Phil. iii. 13, cf. with 1 Cor. vii. 40; upon the same belief rests the whole Apocalypse of the New Testament; and this does not assert that with it any future revelation is to be excluded. But the most general witness for the faith in a continuance of revelation in great communities, and strictly taken in the individual also, lies indeed in the faith in the Holy Ghost, as this is indicated above, p. 122 f.

you," mingling in all earnestness with His words in the proper place as opposed to common thought and discourse; for that not every Christian as he speaks is moved by God's Spirit, and that this Spirit, even where it is dominant, may readily be misunderstood, Paul tells us definitely enough;[1] also nothing whatever is to be lost of all the mighty words and commands of the pure divine Ego which, thrilling the world of mankind, became the support and stay of its higher fellowship; but just in order that the highest Ego should have neither been revealed in vain, nor where it shows itself less discernibly should be actually mistaken, is every one to hear the divine word speaking even in the simplest word if it accords with the Holy Spirit called forth and become luminous by the fulness and clearness of the supreme revelation now vouchsafed. For—

2. As a second mark of perfected revelation, there is now apparent the full agreement of this essentially mediate (§ 12) with the threefold immediate revelation which is collateral with it, and just as infallible, only it is mute in itself, and has not reached the distinct light of word and clear thought (§ 11). If revelation, briefly so called, just so far as it is genuine, and especially when it is perfected, but expresses in clear words and thoughts what without it lies already in the relationship of the human and divine spirit in the whole creation as the spirit-informed work of God and in divinely-ordered human history, then it may be cultivated somewhat exclusively by itself alone never so long, albeit affected consciously or unconsciously more and more by influences from the three kinds of immediate revelation, yet at last a time must come when it perfectly coincides with them all, announces nothing as God's will and word that contradicts them, but expresses all that lies unspoken in them, and so attains in that very circumstance its supreme consummation. Precisely this had now happened. For during this somewhat exclusive development, the mysteries of the human spirit

[1] Cf. 1 Cor. xiv. 32 with vii. 40.

had become more and more profoundly understood, the things of creation had been investigated with an ever-extending research, the grand teachings of history had grown irresistibly clearer and clearer; and the longer revelation had continued to work, the more completely had it quickened the spiritual eye and ear to note all this. The great Old Testament prophets already found support for their oracular utterances in the reason of men,[1] in the indications of God in creation,[2] in the divine teachings which history may offer.[3] But when Christ in His revelation had pointed so simply and with such deep creativeness to all that the inner light and salt of the human spirit when well-guarded might effect,[4] when He had placed in bold relief with unsurpassed and thousand-fold variety what the infinite analogies of the whole human and not-human creation could witness for the kingdom of God,[5] and when He had set up for the light of it at every fitting point the inexhaustible teachings of all history,[6] then at length the two sides of all revelation exactly met in a new and still higher revelation, such as never before the world had seen. Not that it was necessary that all details of the knowledge of things of the human spirit, of creation, of the history of all ages and of all nations, should thereby be exhausted; they are not yet exhausted to-day, notwithstanding all the new eager attention bestowed upon them; and for the matter in hand nothing depends upon this exhaustion. But that revelation had now placed itself with such absolute clearness and confidence in the midst of this whole circle of thinkable things,

---

[1] In cases like Isa. i. 3, xxviii. 23–29; Jer. ii. 31 ("see ye yourselves," as Luke xii. 57, ἀφ' ἑαυτῶν, "of yourselves ye judge"), and elsewhere in so many passages, especially by the style of discourse more and more strongly appealing to the hearer's own conviction.

[2] As Jer. x. 12–16; Isa. xl. 12 ff.; it is in this case chiefly the later prophets who more and more strongly take this way of proof.

[3] From Amos vi. 2, ix. 7, down to Jer. ix. 24 f. and beyond.

[4] Matt. vi. 22 f., xii. 34–36; Mark ix. 49 f.

[5] To which belong so many parables, as Matt. vi. 26–28, xiii. 3 ff.; Luke xii. 28–28.

[6] Mark ii. 25 f.; Matt. vi. 29; Luke xiii. 1–5, and the passages mentioned above.

and was conscious that its high conceptions were in the most perfect harmony with all that could be thought and known beyond its primary sphere, so that it brought all the sources of immediate revelation of God flowing into one channel, and mingling completely with its own word of God, and knew that it derived from them nothing whatever that is dark and obscure,—this is the mark of its consummation also on this side. And accordingly—

3. Having founded for itself through the collective labour of its millenniums a new bright world, the world of divine thoughts and truths and words now manifest, it was able at length to address itself without distinction to every human mind, that it might replenish it with their light, and awaken it to new life. For the perfected revelation no longer, as in its youth, is ever putting itself here and there spontaneously to the test, and aiming in this or that more limited circle towards a firmer self-development; it knows that for every man without exception it possesses the same all-embracing truth, and for every foe that opposes it it has the same overmastering strength. And that already upon its fourth stage, and still more absolutely upon its fifth, this full consciousness of its destiny for all the world and for all eternity has been won, here is the last and most palpable mark of its perfect consummation.

III.—THE RESULTS OF REVELATION.

§ 47. It has now been seen that revelation, just as its activity shaped itself upon the highest and therefore simplest of its stages, having reached in antiquity its high perfection, can continue also without let or hindrance for all the future; that, from the special aspect it assumed in prophecy, enough that is imperishable and eternal ever remains, and can continue to work in other ways when the modes of action in which it appeared for a time are laid aside and destroyed; and that this whole energetic development returns in its last stage to its first, but with the infinite gains superadded the intermediate stages alone could secure. It is therefore open to us finally to contemplate in particular, and now with the more absolute and complete accuracy, just this gain itself, or rather the results of all revelation, and the fruits this whole potent spiritual movement of antiquity produced. Not that are thereby meant the more remote consequences of revelation, different in different places and times, and compared with the chief matter somewhat more contingent, as, for example, that a special and moreover very rich and eternally fruitful literature could arise from its activity; this is to be discussed in detail by and by. Rather are meant the consequences which are first of all to be found upon its path, which attest to us that its mighty toil was not without its immediate effect upon the wellbeing of humanity and the advancement of its divine destiny, and from which only a complete and just estimate can be formed of its whole effort. They are such results as are in all that is essential alike at every stage, but are necessarily greater and more noble upon the higher stages.

1. *The higher Community among Men.*

§ 48. The first great and splendid boon revelation can bring is the possibility, which it alone possesses, of establishing among men any higher fellowship. It is true there are impulses enough which bring individual men, and even many of them, into fellowship with others, but there is only one impulse which can make such fellowship firm, enduring, and salutary. Where outward pleasure, or the pursuit of temporal gains, or force, or artifice and persuasion, found among men a society, whether of the most exclusive or broadest character, the germ of death lies in it; and this is the case even where the companionship is the most exclusive and isolated of all, viz. marriage; for all these impulses unite men, indeed, for the moment, but still sunder them again even more sharply and destructively. The power to establish a better fellowship between men must proceed from what can alone subject their spiritual efforts, readily going asunder to infinity by the impulses just mentioned, to a unity which stands over their spirits according to their own obscurer or clearer feeling of its spiritual nature. For in the last analysis, man, in opposition to all other creatures, is a spiritual being who alone can be led by his spirit, so that two men come into permanent agreement only if that which impels them in common, and which therefore, itself of a spiritual nature, stands over each of them singly and both of them together, has become obvious to the spirits of both. But what stands over the spirit of the individual, and of all men simultaneously, itself of a spiritual nature, so that men can come to a common understanding in it, and find, through repeated new understandings, a permanent union, this may in general be rightly designated the divine. The earliest nations already felt this, and so there arose, even thus early, among men of all nations an eager desire to hear the voice of God, or the oracle, and to suffer themselves to be guided by it. The longer the seat of an oracle could maintain its authority, and the more widely that authority extended, the more numerous was the spiritual fellowship of men that gathered around it, as we shall have yet further to consider below, § 52 ff. The fellowship so formed may, however, be called a higher fellowship, because it is essentially spiritual, and so necessarily rests upon such foundations as are far more enduring than those upon which unspiritual communities are based. From all this it is evident that the higher the perfection revelation attains throughout all its stages, the more indestructible must be the foundations of the fellowship which such revelation yields.

Meanwhile the particular elementary materials, essential to the construction of such a fellowship from the first, stand out upon the higher stages of revelation accurately distinguishable, and more and more clearly conspicuous. This is the place to examine these original elements more closely.

1. The idea and influence of the "light" are pre-eminent, and receive through revelation a higher significance. What the will of God to men is comes by revelation into the light, first of all in detail and specialities, afterwards with growing completeness in all its parts and as a whole. At length man can enjoy the light of revelation irradiating his spirit more and more as the light and warmth of his own best life, can permit himself to be enlightened, yea, to bask in the light of the old, already granted revelation, and can also seek in every new darkness of his life new light in that light which has been kindled for perpetual guidance. Last of all, he can recognise that this light is inseparable from God Himself, and for him, from this point of view, God is light. This progress in the apprehension of the light, in the course of time, may be traced clearly enough, so far as it is relevant to our subject. Isaiah, on the point of discoursing to the men of Israel, calls upon them "to walk with him in the light of Jahveh,"—to suffer themselves to be enlightened and guided by the old revelation, as it is just about to arise again in increasing effulgence;[1] and it becomes a brief, firmly-established principle that His word is this light, or rather, in further application of this image, "a lamp," the right use of which is necessary in order to have for the earthly course the higher light of all life.[2] But when it is said further on, in elevated prayer, "in Thy light let us see light,"[3] there is expressed quite generally the truth that men must ever raise themselves anew to this light, and the graciously-conceded possibility of this is joyfully greeted; nay, we instinctively feel here what ineffable blessedness, in the devout remembrance of this possibility, now streams through man's heart. Last of all, He comes manifestly into the world, in whom the Christian heart exulted, as He could say concerning Himself, "I am the light of the world," for the Word (the Logos) of God, who by His life and action in the world was its light from the beginning, had now become in Him the divine light for all

---

[1] Isa. ii. 5.   [2] Ps. cxix. 105.   [3] Ps. xxxvi. 10 (A. V. 9).

men, so far as that Word could be manifest as a mortal man whose whole life was for all humanity the most conspicuously luminous exposition of the divine will.[1]

This light may also be designated the plain evident "truth" which in this whole province has its validity for men. Whilst light is something self-active, and according to its peculiar property efficiently working, truth is the unalterable and positive ground of things, to the weak and enfeebled eye wholly dark and quiescent, to the spiritual eye becoming apparent at length just as it is and as in its nature it must be; the ground of things which neither is nor can be other than it is, of which therefore account can be given and for which proofs can be brought, although it does not depend upon them. For this reason, as revelation tended more and more to its consummation, one might say, according to this way of looking at the somewhat different conception of truth, that revelation is, in briefer, more incisive language, truth absolutely;[2] or, somewhat more definitely, that the aggregate or sum of the word of God is truth,[3] so far as every various detail which was in later times reckoned as the existing revelation is comprised under one head or sum, and this very sum-total comprehending all that detail in itself comes to be estimated with revelation. And such short expressions were the more proper at a time and place where God Himself was already characterized as "truth."[4] In the New Testament, however, the idea of the truth is connected immediately with that of light.[5]

2. But this light is not kindled and this truth is not firmly

---

[1] John viii. 12, cf. with i. 4 ff., and 1 John i. 5–7, ii. 8–10.
[2] Ps. cxix. 142, 151.
[3] Ps. cxix. 160, as the words in themselves run,—
   The sum of Thy word is truth;
   Thy judgment is ever wholly righteousness.
As the two parts fully correspond if מִשְׁפַּט is read for מִשְׁפָּט
[4] Jer. x. 10; said similarly as, God is Spirit, is Love, John iv. 24; 1 John iv. 8, 16.
[5] As follows in particular from John viii. 32, cf. with 12; but it is also apparent here that the idea of light is easier of comprehension and earlier.

held that the one or the other should exist for itself alone and remain inoperative. Nay, in revelation, from the very first the more purely and creatively it breaks forth, these twin-forces of light and truth never appear without teaching how man should act so as to conform to them, as already has been shown in § 13 ff. To know and to maintain firmly the right way of life, both in its whole conduct and in every special embarrassment and difficulty, is for every man so much a matter of primary importance, that the light and the truth do but serve ultimately to this end.[1] Properly speaking, therefore, every revelation, if it be persistently active and vital on all sides, proposes to make or ensure a special course or way of the spiritual life;[2] or, in other words, every religion has its own type or character and mode of life.[3] But revelation, the more perfect it is, affords the more surely and adequately the possibility of their attainment; and it does this not simply by the clear shining light of its pure truths, but also by the equally luminous models of life presented by the revealers of those truths and their immediate and most loyal followers.

But the ultimate goal of this course can only be the true God Himself; and this whole conduct and life of individual men is to bring them nearer and nearer to His truth, to His will, and His whole life.[4] If, then, to our thought the truth that is known and walking in the truth are indeed separable, to him who reveals it they are essentially one; thus we understand how upon the highest stage of revelation He who could call Himself the Truth, can also call Himself the

[1] In such older utterances as Ps. xxxii. 8, Isa. xxx. 21, the mere showing of the way stands, it is true, more alone; but in Ps. cxix. both are equally prominent; cf. vers. 27–32 with 142–160.

[2] This is so necessary, that Christianity, in the very first years of its existence, and before Paul became a Christian, had already its own peculiar "way," and it was characterized in the language of its confidential friends with appropriate brevity as "the way" (that known to all its confessors), Acts ix. 2, xix. 9–23; cf. *History of Israel*, vi. 386.

[3] As already Micah iv. 5 intimates, otherwise than Isa. ii. 5, yet similarly, and more plainly because later.

[4] Cf. in the prayer "Thy way," Ps. v. 8, xxv. 4, xxvii. 11, lxxxvi.

Way; but we comprehend also how it is He can put the Way before the Truth, since the movement of the light, it is true, takes place first,—to repeat here that great image,—in order that the Truth, in conformity with which this movement proceeds, should come to the day;[1] but for men since His glorification, the first and most necessary thing is that they enter upon the way with which for them He has now become identical. Furthermore, what at first we seem unable to say, viz. that a man should be the way which every one who strives towards God must take and traverse, we can now say, if He is in reality the historically unique personage who by all He said and did can become to all who look to Him and make Him spiritually their own, Himself the way that leads to God.

3. Yet this mere way is not, furthermore, the object and aim itself to which revelation points as its end, and which alone it seeks ultimately to serve. Its purpose is, in the last issue, life, the promotion and so far as possible the diffusion of life,—that life which, more closely considered, is for the creature the sole highest conceivable good, the participation in the divine life, restricted it may be, but, as far as understanding and actual entrance upon it go, complete; a life which, conceded to men by the will of the Creator, is only too easily forfeited and lost, but is brought near to them in such a way in its whole purpose and claims, even as in its clear contents and worth, by no new impulse as it is by revelation. For what do that light and that irrefragable truth ultimately afford, but the sure glimpse into this life of infinite duration and blessedness? And whither can that way lead but to life as the highest good, destined for man indeed from the beginning, but to be won by struggle and conflict? Now the brief term life, taken in its whole possible infinitude of contents, is employed here, it is true, in its proper connection with perfect fitness; but it is not to be overlooked that it has become capable of this its highest possible comprehensiveness

[1] John xiv. 6 f., cf. with ver. 4 f.; but already the light and the truth were spoken of, viii. 12, 32.

first of all in Hebrew, and is the favourite and customary term, because Hebrew prefers to avoid compound words. In Greek and in all languages akin to it, the idea of "the immortal" expresses the same thing, and is readily interchangeable with it, not merely in the Greek parts of the Bible, but also in the Hebrew.[1] But what is this idea of the immortal, when referred to man as mortal, other than that of "the resurrection"? This also in the proper place is interchangeable with it.[2] In another aspect, however, the idea of "salvation" is equivalent to it, and is ultimately inseparably connected also with all that revelation has in view, and in the high signification of the "divine" salvation, as alone worthy of the name, it is made distinctly prominent by the revelation of Moses.[3] But still more clearly and fully it may be characterized "the eternal salvation."[4]

Accordingly, on the highest stage of revelation, no utterance is found more briefly and appropriately comprehending everything here relevant than that of Christ at the close of His earthly course, "I am the way, the truth, and the life."[5] Yet here again is the main ultimate principle indicated, that not one of these blessings, desired by revelation and supplied to

[1] Sentences such as Ps. xxxvi. 9 (where in the other member "light" corresponds to it) may be taken together with Prov. xii. 28 ; and ἡ ζωή still more plainly passes over into ἡ ζωὴ αἰώνιος in John, and then even more so in the pastoral Epistles.

[2] When Christ says, John xi. 25, "I am the resurrection and the life," He makes the first emphatic only because of the special occasion of His words ; the chief thing, however, is that not till now is this third and highest idea added to the others, "light" and "truth," and that where everything is to pass over into the life and conduct of the community, they are placed in the enumeration after the "way," John xiv. 6.

[3] In the first flush of the salvation of indestructible continuance then obtained, how could this be expressed more exactly and for us also more significantly and memorably, than in the name Joshua. Cf. Num. xiii. 16, with *History of Israel*, ii. 332 [Eng. trans. ii. 236].

[4] As the thought and eternal hope of it in the song of the community in the primitive age (Ex. xv.) are already expressed, but in its conclusion most briefly, ver. 18.

[5] John xiv. 6 ; it is here seen how, according to the plan of this Gospel, everything which it seeks to make conspicuous as duty for man, just as the course of this earthly appearing of Christ up to the very end had taught it, culminates in this saying.

the measure of its power, is given to any one individual man simply for his own use, as if intended merely for him and to remain his own exclusive possession. Every one of these three blessings is, as revelation desires, for every man; and any one of them also, if only put into activity and made effective in the right way, is of such a quality by its very nature that it is able to form a fellowship among men. Therefore where all coincide in the right way and find their proper activity there, the essential elements of a permanent fellowship of spirits are given; and it is this we call the community of God, or, more briefly, the community, which again under another name is itself the Church.

The community, therefore, in this higher sense, or the Church, is the first result and abiding fruit of revelation upon its higher stages. With it is established among men a fellowship which, as it is created by these three first elements and fundamental powers alone, so only by them can it be further sustained and preserved; consequently it must ever expel all foreign material that may possibly penetrate into it, if it will not become a prey to dissolution. These first elements and fundamental powers are, however, of such a purely spiritual nature, that the fellowship which is continually upbuilding itself anew, and is preserved by them, cannot deny its own essential character, and so a fellowship arises among men whose sole and simple function it is to exhibit and promote none other than that humanly-divine life as it should be upon earth. However difficult its task may be, however much there may yet be wanting to it on all sides, here now at length it has stepped forth on earth a veritable reality, and it will for ever continue to exist. If, however, those first elements and fundamental powers are the only forces which can found and preserve such a fellowship, and if they are given here in purity and perfection, then the fellowship they produce must be capable with humanity itself of perpetual duration; and notwithstanding every vicissitude to which as historically arisen it has been subjected in the further course of history, it must bear in itself an indestructible life, so that it can see, it may be, all other communities dissolve at its side, but neither with them nor by them be itself dissolved. Already present in the germ, and indicating its profoundest struggle and ultimate aim in the Old Testament, it sustained the extremest and most painful shock which could befall it in its earthly existence,—the breaking up of its own national home under whose shelter and protection alone it could first arise and grow strong; and even thus it but emerged, papilio-like from its sheath, that it might find in the New Testament a fuller and freer life. Such is the fellowship which made its appearance with the consummation of revelation as its first and abiding fruit.

2. *The Priesthood.*

§ 49. A further result of the consummation of revelation is, that in the fellowship thus established the right instruments are found to undertake the special charge of its preservation, and to bear at the same time the responsibility of upholding all its principles and activities. Prophecy, it is true, is throughout the creative power, standing in the midst of the whole movement, described above and advancing the power of revelation in all its stages; and much of its inmost essence still works even in the fourth and fifth stages, as we have seen. But just because prophecy is the creative power in this case, it is also in its time the freest and most spontaneous, deriving its origin from special urgency in most pressing circumstances, and displaying subsequently on suitable occasions a wonderful activity, but having from its very nature no uniform continuance, and at best being never intended as a standing office. Only in heathen religions was it readily made into a standing office;[1] the purer and the higher its

---

[1] As among the Egyptians, where in the latest times the prophets still remained externally at the head of the whole hierarchy. Cf. *History of Israel*, ii. p. 201 [Eng. tr. ii. 140].

development, the less could it assume this character. Having accomplished its mission in founding a community, it is relieved as a matter of course by another activity and power, whose task and business it is to preserve and advance the fellowship thus founded; and this may properly be termed the priesthood. Priests are elders, in the sense in which elders are the primary leaders of every community. It is almost accidental,[1] however, that this term means pre-eminently the leaders of the higher fellowship of men of which we are now speaking. Elders arise after the community is established, not before; but they become then indispensable. Undertaking the leadership of the society already founded, their office, unlike that of the prophet, at once becomes perpetual, continuing with an uninterrupted and uniform necessity. Upon them principally does the continuation of the aims and efforts of the community now rest, and its increasingly beneficent influence in the world; but they can actually preserve these blessings only as they revert constantly to the first principles and fundamental truths which, as dominant in the minds of the prophets themselves, were the true founders of this community. So side by side with Moses arose in Aaron the whole priesthood of the Old Covenant, stretching as it were in one long unbroken chain over a period of a millennium and a half; and the twelve apostles were in their turn the true first priests of the New;[2] for we ought to accustom ourselves to restore to the good word priest its proper rights, since in German we have now no other name with which intelligibly to replace it.

Of all this a subsequent volume must speak more at large. Here only it is maintained that the priesthood is a result of revelation and the community founded upon it, but a result necessary in its nature, and therefore perpetual in its continu-

---

[1] Accidental, so far as the Greek word πρισβύτεροι passed over into the Christian community among ourselves, and our own "priester" arose out of it.

[2] That the Twelve actually were the first priests of the Christian community is unquestionable. Cf. *History of Israel*, vi. 186.

ance, as already Jeremiah has very definitely said,[1] at a time when it was threatened most palpably with destruction. Of what kind of men the priesthood should be formed is a question by itself; but whoever makes some important contribution, from the free impulse of his spirit, to the maintenance or new enforcement of the principal truths of revelation, may here be called, in a certain sense, a priest.

3. *The Spiritualization of Humanity and its Pursuits.*

§ 50. But neither with the rise of the priesthood nor the founding of the higher community are the results and noble fruits of the consummation of revelation exhausted. Each of them is but an organic instrument through which the spirit of true religion, that has its source in revelation, actively works. The result of utmost importance and the fruit of noblest growth is the larger final issue which by means of its organic instruments, distinguishable indeed, yet intimately allied and never fully separable, the spirit of true religion produces. This is nothing less than the formation of a new humanity; a humanity in which the imperfections and mistakes of immature youth no longer prevail, but there rules more and more absolutely and perfectly that spirit alone which, upon its higher stages, revelation demands with increasing precision and indicates with increasing clearness, and whose vital and salutary influence it gradually extends through its whole realm. This genuine divine spirit is to be absolutely and solely more and more, from the midst of its own organization, the informing and guiding spirit of all other organizations, and ultimately of every individual man, as indeed the perfect true religion now expects and demands that it should be. The clear and convincing proof of the possibility of this is afforded by the entire history of the nation of the Old Covenant; for who will deny that within the period that elapsed between the founding of the Old and the New

[1] Jer. xxxii. 19-22. Cf. with the narrative, xxxii.

Covenant, more than a millennium and a half, this nation underwent a complete inward transformation, and, notwithstanding all the grave errors by which it allowed itself to be gradually ensnared to its deep and final destruction, was nevertheless in intellectual culture highly accomplished and wonderfully capable of every new spiritual development. And what greater praise can be given to it than that at last it was the only nation qualified to be the source whence Christianity could go forth into the world? Moreover, how Christianity, immediately upon its establishment, could produce a wholly new humanity, spiritually superior to all earlier generations of men, we know sufficiently from the New Testament and other books, as well as from the great history of all mankind. Yet all this in detail can be discussed only in a subsequent volume.

But humanity does not consist merely of an infinite number of individuals, but also of an incalculable number of common interests. As a whole, of many parts and organs, and all in their last issue related to mind, humanity has necessarily very different activities and aptitudes, that make its great life possible, and fit it to reach by progressive steps its ultimate goal. Every one of these activities and aptitudes has its part in the collective intellectual existence, and has also its peculiar inner necessity. But however different in themselves these activities and aptitudes may be, and however divergent they ever anew tend to become, yet, classified according to their fundamental differences, in addition to revelation and priesthood sufficiently described above, they may be reduced to three, which may briefly be designated Law, Science, Industry. All things, for example, have by creation and the unvarying uniform eternal will of God, and by inherent nature, their original right relations with and towards one another, relations which may change through the mistakes of men and because of their own progressive development, but which must ever revert to their normal determination if humanity is to continue its existence happily and make good progress. These are the bases of law, and fully to respect this law everywhere in its whole range and establishment, and to maintain it among men wisely and successfully, demands an activity and aptitude which has its proper place and high value in all humanity. There is also a not less necessary activity which investigates the grounds of all visible or merely conceivable things without exception, and ascertains the interdependence to the thought of all the most diversified parts of creation, as well as their relation to God; science also has its proper place in humanity, and is in large measure indispensable. And from all this may be distinguished countless arts and activities, in which not any one of the previously-named activities is conspicuous, which as such are purely of the mind, but in connection with which physical labour predominates, however little they may be able to dispense with the elements of science and the protection of law. But all these activities, — revelation, priesthood, law, science, industry,— in which we may truly say all human pursuits and efforts consist, different as they are in themselves, do not stand side by side with each other in such a way as that one of them can dispense with the aid of the others, or that the individual man engaged in any one of them as his special pursuit can be truly successful should he ignore all the rest. If, however, they are all to work together to a happy final issue, it is revelation that has rightly recognised this final issue, and showed to the others without exception what it is and how it is one and the same for them all; and it is to the priesthood that the destiny and duty primarily belongs to lead them all forward ever anew towards this final issue, and unite them in seeking it. That all this is possible, is a result of revelation; and how it is possible that a single higher spirit should guide all the different activities of a broad, wide fellowship to one far-off divine event, the long and changeful history of the continuance of the Old Covenant is fully competent to teach.

True, unfeigned piety, such as genuine revelation produces in humanity, gives, it is true, in itself nothing but the right attitude and tendency of mind; a boon simple and inconspicuous, yet affording the sound basis for every human activity and experience, and involving as a consequence infinite joyfulness. But if this right attitude and tendency of mind gradually exercises increasing influence upon all men individually, upon all human fellowships, and upon all their different activities and pursuits, this influence shows itself also in magnificent results upon such apparently remote lying provinces as it would not at first sight be expected to reach. The Bible itself offers sufficiently instructive examples of this. Thus in the narratives of the creation, with which the Bible opens, there is, without any need to overestimate or misapply the details, a higher dignity and truth than similar ancient representations and narratives possess, as in modern times it is at length beginning to be felt; but it should not be overlooked that it was the whole life and movement of the spirit of true revelation that contributed to make these narratives so finished in their form, and so incomparable in their grandeur. Again, though monogamy is not, it is true, required by any precise command, yet it wins its way in the Bible nevertheless chiefly through the growing power of the whole spirit of the more perfect revelation. In fine, a short maxim touching everything that is relevant to our subject is found in one of the latest books of the New Testament, " Genuine piety is profitable for all things,"[1] — penetrating humanity with its spirit more and more deeply, in full harmony with the ultimate purpose of true revelation, and transforming it to a higher divine life.

[1] 1 Tim. iv. 8 ; cf. Tit. iii. 8 and 2 Tim. iii. 16.

PART II.

REVELATION IN HEATHENISM AND IN ISRAEL.

§ 51. SCARCELY, however, have we ascertained what revelation is, through what stages it has reached its consummation, and what benefits, indispensable for the salvation of all humanity, result from it, than there obtrudes upon us the more irrepressibly a question, the answer to which we have hitherto taken for granted, viz. why is revelation perfected in antiquity, and why has it attained this perfection in Israel only, and in no other nation of antiquity whatever? Simply to evade this double question by asserting that both these events actually occurred, and that to investigate such matters of fact minutely now is useless or presumptuous, as it might prove embarrassing,—this is impracticable. Amid the prejudices so widely diffused to-day, and everywhere penetrating so deeply, such evasion would be of little avail. The objection would always be confronting us, it is inconceivable that antiquity should have had an advantage of so large a kind over our presumably so much more cultivated age, and still more, that amid so many great and renowned ancient nations, and at the time of Greek and subsequently of Roman culture, this one nation, seemingly so insignificant, and partly by its own fault so contemptible, should have carried off this prize over the heads of them all. The careful consideration of these questions is not therefore to be avoided. Moreover, the right answer to whatever comes within the scope of them will serve, not merely to scatter all prejudices now entertained, but will carry us still further into the apprehension of those great truths upon which in this matter everything depends, and finally

THE FOUNDING OF A TRUE COMMUNITY OF GOD. 155

lead to our holding the more firmly and consistently from another point of view the result obtained in the previous discussion.

It is not to be denied, however, that the task that lies before us is not an easy one, involving as it does the contemplation and full knowledge of history, of the history of antiquity especially, but still more widely of all experiences of a similar kind which modern history may afford. Unless the precise points this whole question raises are definitely handled, the task cannot be discharged, and for this an accurate knowledge not less of all other nations than of this special nation is requisite. At the same time, if a comparison is instituted in conformity with such knowledge between the history of this particular nation and that of all others, and if the few but marked differences which grow into prominence during the course of two, or it may be said three, thousand years are fully grasped, it will be perceived that everything essentially belonging to our inquiry proceeds from three impulses, which in the slow but at last so much the greater progress of events arose one after the other, and ultimately all of them co-operated to produce the result at first sight so wonderful.

I.—THE FOUNDING OF A TRUE COMMUNITY OF GOD.

§ 52. The significance of this first impulse will best be seen if we recall, from the close of the previous discussion (§ 48), the fact that the establishment of an enduring higher fellowship among men is one of the greatest and noblest immediate consequences of revelation. But it is not this bare special consequence alone that we have now more particularly to consider: where it was found, the expectation of the best effects that antiquity looked for from revelation was realized. For, besides the light and divine guidance which the individual man desired for himself, it was principally the higher unison and guidance of a whole nation, the impression a divine oracle would produce far beyond its primary sphere, that might, it was thought, be justly anticipated from revelation. That the divine voice alone was capable of reconciling antagonism in the conflicts of public opinion, of investing the laws with sacred authority and respect, of showing in the most helpless position of affairs the true way of national deliverance, was the prevailing view of all the nations of antiquity. Enfeebled at times, and in certain localities, this faith ever grew strong again, and at least, in the hour when dire calamity befell the land, was irresistible. It was regarded as the greatest possible misfortune for the whole nation, nay, as proof of the implacable anger of the Deity, if in great straits no divine voice were to be heard.[1] In comparatively peaceful and happier times, the principle held good which a didactic poet of the Old Testament, in the midst of the finest development of Israel's national glory, once expressed briefly and incisively : " Where there is no revelation the people are dissolved," *i.e.* are without discipline and order, without morality and cohesion.[2] Wholly in the sense of this principle does the corresponding second half of this wise poetic maxim echo back : " But he who instruction," that higher instruction and teaching of which alone the poet speaks, " heeds," so that he does not violate it and go contrary to the will of God clearly expressed in a definite situation of life, " salvation to him." And if the voice of God were rarely heard in distress and embarrassment, because no great and acknowledged prophet was found, it was held to be a misfortune for the national life.[3]

[1] If such complaints were expressed at a late period in the community of the true religion, Lam. ii. 9, Ps. lxxiv. 9, it can readily be conjectured how much more frequently and heavily they broke out among the heathen. In addition to this, the distinction may be noted between Lam. ii. 9, when the prophets can find no oracle (Jeremiah could often find none for days, Jer. xlii. 1-7), and subsequent times, Ps. lxxiv. 9, when there was not even a prophet in Israel at all.

[2] Prov. xxix. 18. The תּוֹרָה here and Isa. ii. 3, as elsewhere, devolves upon the prophet; in Jer. xviii. 18, Ezek. vii. 26, upon the priest only.

[3] This is the meaning of the narrative, 1 Sam. iii. 1.

THE FOUNDING OF A TRUE COMMUNITY OF GOD. 157

These were the sentiments and experiences that prevailed in antiquity, and unless we note them carefully we cannot understand the histories of ancient nations at all.

1. *The Origin and varying Feeling of the Need of it.*

§ 53. Although it is unquestionable that such convictions pervaded the whole of antiquity, and could not be repressed, it would be a great mistake to suppose that they were felt with equal clearness and certainty, and the like vividness and strength, in all nations. More or less distinctly the necessity was realized of founding a genuine community, in which the divine will should always have the supreme place of power, and all men might readily know and obey it. But what is the mere consciousness of a need, especially in things purely spiritual? In climate and in fertility of the soil there is an extraordinary variety in different lands, and obscure causes, not yet adequately explained, make the seasons here very unfruitful, there very fruitful, elsewhere moderately good, and so on in hundredfold gradation; but the deficiencies such variations produce are soon removed by a general readjustment of things, and it is only lack of foresight or of industry that occasions intolerable hardship; for this whole physical order of the universe is so beyond man's control that he cannot alter it if he would. But in everything spiritual the individual man has incomparably freer and wider scope for expectation and choice, and on this account there is far more difficulty in basing a powerful common interest upon the bare feeling of spiritual need; and what a distance there is here also between this mere feeling of need and its satisfaction, or even the true beginning of satisfaction! It cannot, therefore, surprise us that nothing in antiquity varied so much among different nations as the consciousness of this need and the supposed methods of satisfying it.

But just for this reason there might be found, in the long course of all these varied changes, special historical situations, when the essential conditions favourable to such a satisfaction would be present, at first only in some particular place, but resting on so firm a basis that, a true beginning having been made, the desired blessing could more and more perfectly be secured. What is, above all, to be noted here, however, is that in the period we now designate by the name antiquity, a period of great length and of highly diversified character, there were important changes which cannot be overlooked. As the eye strains to penetrate the more remote expanses of all past human history, very hard for us to measure, it may be seen surely enough that the need we speak of could begin to be strongly felt only at a very definite point in the life and development of collective humanity; and if it is difficult for us to speak with certainty of these wide and now most obscure realms of remotest antiquity, yet because of the great interdependence of all these things, we cannot here omit what, according to traces still discernible, may to-day be said about them.

Now, with respect to the remotest periods of human history as a whole and generally, we can without doubt distinctly see—(1) that they were very different from one another in their immediate needs and dominant tendencies; and (2) that they followed one another, as the needs and tendencies determined, in necessary succession. As much as this may be discovered, because the imperishably great results of every period lie clearly before us, nay, at every moment we live upon them, as upon fruits every one of which has matured amidst the mighty labours of some past age; for fruits won by the mind, unlike material fruits, do not perish with the using. These great gains, indestructible as long as humanity endures, it is our special aim now rightly to estimate, and the significance of each of them, and the order in which they must have been won, well to understand. It is not admissible, it is true, to suppose that at any of the great successive periods of all these highest human efforts some principle or factor made its appearance not already given in the divine determination, not given, that is, in its germ or rudiments, from the beginning of all human creation; not in this sense is the succession we here speak of to be understood. But the needs of all historical humanity, and the corresponding great efforts and tasks, are too numerous and too varied, and, considered separately, too mighty and too difficult, to take their rise simultaneously, and to reach their consummation side by side. The consequence was, speaking generally, a succession; the one or the other was called forth powerfully at an earlier period, and became operative in an ever ascending scale of activity through the pressure of indispensable need. And if we put together exactly all that we are able, from universal historical testimonies, as well as from the things in themselves, to infer to-day concerning this great course of the development of humanity, we can maintain that—

1. The high task of revelation described in the previous discussion by no means fell in that period we must here distinguish as the first. Not that humanity could have at that time no conceptions of God and divine things, and no names for them; these undoubtedly are of very early origin (§ 16); nor that the power of revelation could not then have commenced its activity, for this activity goes back likewise to the remotest primitive ages (p. 17). But the earliest task and first immortal fruit of the efforts of the human mind must have been of another kind, viz. the fashioning of human language as the firm basis for all subsequent endeavours in the supply of the needs of the human spirit, the smallest and commonest needs as well as the highest, and those at first virtually unanticipated. It would be irrelevant to discuss here the origin of human speech and the ever invariable principle underlying its formation;[1] in a special instance and

---

[1] No existing work meets the demands of our present knowledge and aims, least of all Renan's; cf. *Gött. Gel. Anz.* 1859, st. 1, 2. How the solution of the problem must be approached step by step I have sought to show in the *Sprachwissenschaftliche Abhandlungen* (i.-iii., Göttingen, 1861-1871).

pictorial sketch the biblical history of creation gives the briefest and most striking outline of the true representation.[1] But nothing is more certain than that the whole of the first period of human history is filled up with this preliminary task, and that the fulness of language and its ever unvarying solidity could not easily be attained. For that language arose altogether historically admits really of no doubt, least of all to-day; it is the ultimate successful issue of the full co-operation of two different capacities of the human mind, viz. the capacity to represent by means of sounds the numberless different sensuous or mental impressions received, and the capacity to put together in the same sounds all such impressions as rational thoughts. But that the perfecting of each of these capacities is easy, and still more that their subsequent thoroughly-harmonious working is easy, are suppositions possible only if there be no close investigation of all that is germane to this subject. On the contrary, searching inquiry convinces us that as all other great possessions of human society have been won not without mutual co-operation, so it was only after repeated commencements and protracted attempts that language grew to the perfection in which, without essential change and as a means for different purposes, it has since been preserved. And as in the perfecting of all other human capacities that are only historically developed, some prominent individuals led the way, so was it also, we doubt not, with the primitive language of mankind; its last firm shape was given to it by the commanding influence of the few who incited the many to imitation; whilst there is no ground to question that at that time humanity was confined to a very limited area, and made up a comparatively small but compact and homogeneous whole.[2]

2. When mankind had already tasted the good and bad fruits of this its first imperishable gain, a wholly different age

[1] Gen. ii. 18-23, above touched upon (p. 15).
[2] The original unity of the human race will be further discussed in a subsequent volume.

must have supervened. Language, when made capable of the perfect and easy use just described, is the first and most necessary means whereby the many may act as with one mind and one hand, and human efforts and toils be directed to one common goal. But it serves just as well also to disclose the more quickly and surely, and make palpably manifest or even deceptively to veil and hide, the incompatibility of the thoughts of different men; and the higher the development, by means of language, of reciprocal interest in human pursuits for the attainment of a special good, the deeper the disunion and division become as soon as, by means of language, from honest or dishonest motives, the emptiness of this fancied good is pointed out, or perhaps the passion for evil possessions is inflamed. It was at such a time mankind began to be scattered over the face of all the earth, manifestly rather from inner estrangement than mere love of roaming; and the incident the Bible somewhat casually connects with the remembrance of ancient Babel has so far its good significance. Mankind fell apart into different nations and languages; the sharper and the wider the separation, the more quickly would languages vary. But when once such a universal spirit of unrest and wandering had taken hold of mankind, thousands of years might pass away before, in this ceaseless whirling and surging to and fro, the current would steadily set towards the formation of distinct nations and the culture of definite tongues. Even then the first and second attempts would not secure permanent results; and nothing can give us to-day a clearer idea of the long continuance and the many successive stages of this conflict and commingling of the people of the earth, when once separated, than the careful comparison of the oldest known tongues, and the endeavour to find out their closer and more remote affinities.

3. The breaking up and disorganization of a Whole so infinitely divisible as humanity, when once it begins has no limits; but after it has gained ground and the evil of it is sensibly felt, the desire to check it must more and more

strongly be aroused. No longer, however, could language merely be the instrument by which a closer bond of higher community of interest could unite men's minds again; for the subtle process of dissolution might ever begin afresh in a nationality held together chiefly by language. It is true, nevertheless, that the means to a new understanding and union must be found in language; but this language could only be the higher language of revelation, the voice coming down from above, as explained in § 11-48. Only the power of revelation, and of practical religion arising from it, could now offer the strong attractive force by which men should be brought together again, and form the firm bond by which they could be permanently reunited,—a bond consecrating every other, and making it perpetual, whether in marriage, government, guilds or fellowships of any kind. It might be only upon some particular spot, and in a wider or narrower circle, that revelation should prove itself the power that could raise mankind out of its condition of dissolution and ruin;[1] but it was this power alone which in some such way actually created at first enduring fellowships, kingdoms, laws, morals, and gave birth out of its own life to the earliest civilised nations.[2] As it works towards this goal, the history of all nations becomes for the remembrance of later generations illumined with clearer light; and as far as we can look back into the known history of distinct nations and kingdoms, we see them clustering around the seats of oracles, listening to the voice of prophets of all kinds, or it may be spiritually led by priests, and living according to customs and laws the more difficult to keep in proportion as they depend upon a divine sanction, and suggest the divine earnestness of life. Revelation and religion, with all their large demands, were thus a necessity for nations and kingdoms; and mainly according to the depth of this feeling

---

[1] That every nation has its own special god or gods the prophets themselves say, Micah iv. 5; Jer. ii. 11; Deut. iv. 7; but the history of all antiquity shows it as well.

[2] According to the bold but true image, Isa. i. 2, lxvi. 9.

of need, and the reality and fulness of its satisfaction, the spiritual life and effort of the nations varied, especially in the remotest antiquity.

But just when the need of revelation and religion was thus sensibly felt in all its urgency on the part of whole nations and kingdoms, a relapse to barbarism, which had made its appearance amidst the great division of mankind into different nations and their violent streaming and surging to and fro for the possession of the fairest portions of the earth, had spread so widely, that it threatened to hinder with insuperable obstacles all progress to a better national condition. Every degeneracy and relapse to barbarism, with individuals and mankind in general, but increases the darkness which, by its very creation, lies about the human spirit, and makes more and more dense the sensuous rind in which this spark of divine life is enclosed awaiting the coming and awakening of the higher light. The temporal development of humanity, or in other words "history," by changes dependent upon the bent of the human will, determines whether this sensuous rind, growing perchance harder and harder, can be effectually reached and penetrated by the higher light; and as there is an historical illumination and transfiguring of all human effort and toil, so there is an historical darkening and induration.[1] But during the previous wild conflicts for the acquisition of the primary earthly possessions, and for the primary security of the earthly life, and during the first great misuse of human language that attended these conflicts, the darkness had become deeper, the sensuous rind harder. Nevertheless, the first sure beginning of a better life for a whole nation could never be made until first of all in its guidance and moral bearing, and chiefly in the culture of its deepest convictions, of its faith and its whole spirit, and then in its permanent constitution, a reversion to the original rectitude

---

[1] Apart from its pre-eminent final Christian teaching, the Bible nowhere represents this so boldly and clearly as in the important section, very applicable here, of the history of Pharaoh and Moses, Ex. i. 8-xv. 21.

and purity of the human spirit had not only been attempted but also firmly established, against all growing perversity and prevailing miseducation. If, therefore, the need above described were now to be in reality as fully and permanently satisfied as obscure desire and longing suggested, a double task must be undertaken, involving the indefatigable straining of all the better spiritual energies on the part of those who would lend their aid to it. The advent of heroes as, in the original acceptation of the word, mighty founders of mighty kingdoms, ancient legend places very appropriately not before the beginning of the third age of the world, but even earlier traces of them are to be found in the Bible.[1]

Such being its origin and the problem it had to solve, the great diversity in the realization and satisfaction of this need among the oldest nations of the earth is now understood. For in those far-off times, the duration of which is no longer precisely determinable, as the seats of oracles arose here and there among the nations, humanity itself in its great essential constituents was unusually broken and dissolved, and the condition and predominant aims of the greater or smaller, and the more or less powerful of the nations of the earth were very dissimilar, notwithstanding all higher resemblance in general circumstances. Especially had the struggle for the fairest and most fruitful regions, and the mutual enmity and estrangement it occasioned, become very violent; and nothing now appeared less practicable than the formation even of a national earthly community with the necessary provision for its long continuance, whilst here the task was to found a community of the true religion that should continue for ever. Nay more, it was simply an emphatic expression of this dismembered state of mankind, and of national diversity in condition and aim, that every nation had its separate deities, or at least its separate chief deity, whose worship and whose oracles formed the centre of its life. Moreover, since revelation and religion are not the only means by which a

---

[1] Cf. *History of Israel*, i. p. 367 ff., 412 ff. [Eng. trans. i. 288 ff., 381 ff.].

confederation may be established among men, and whilst it is possible that mere human compulsion, for example, may uphold it by arms and punishments, an explanation presents itself why this need was by no means everywhere equally realized and still less equally satisfied. Hence most nations had recourse to revelation only occasionally, and chiefly when driven to it by severe straits, or they relied too exclusively upon various additional perverse means of establishing and preserving the common bond. All this, however, makes it intelligible that at first

2. *Imperfect Satisfactions of the Need*

§ 54. Were manifoldly conspicuous, and seemed, in spite of their imperfection and variety, to find nevertheless an abiding foothold in human nature. So difficult was it to attain to even the beginning of right action in this matter, as will be sufficiently evident in the subsequent course of our inquiry. The unusual importance of this phenomenon, however, makes it the more necessary to explain particularly every detail of it relevant to our subject, at least in its main features, and to note the significant points of difference which became prominent in imperfect satisfactions of the great universal need. Everything that is yet imperfect, as it enters into free open history and develops itself vigorously according to all its impulse, makes sooner or later repeated experiments testing its adequacy to supply in this or that new way the deeply-felt but still unsatisfied needs, and its insufficiency may be shown not less clearly in every fresh trial. In matters of a grave and far-reaching significance, we can observe this the more distinctly. At the same time, however great, upon close and detailed examination, the diversity of all these imperfect attempts appears,—attempts which even to-day in a large section of the nations of the earth still have force and acceptance, nevertheless if we look at what essentially distinguishes them, both in relation to their inner nature and their historical rise and issues, we find that they diverge mainly in three directions, and in the third branch off forthwith into three different subdivisions. There are thus five distinct species of communities, all of which may be called " sacred communities," because they seek to unite and rule men by their need of higher truths. On this account, too, they are the antithesis of worldly kingdoms or States, which hold men together by the mere external authority of laws or mandates, and they are able to maintain themselves purely by their own inner or spiritual energy, notwithstanding the mutations of these earthly kingdoms. We may call them sacred communities, in so far as their inviolable and perpetual bond of union is that which is most sacred to man; and they might be called communities of God, if the last of the five did not reject the living idea of God and seek to be content with a mere equivalent, which, however, in that case has always a kind of sanctity. Into these five kinds of imperfect sacred communities, then, everything is divisible that does not yet rise up to the perfection of a true community of God, or that this community alone with all its power strives against; and we may briefly designate them as the communities (1) of prophets; (2) of prophets and priests; (3) of the pure; (4) of the saintly; (5) of the learned.

§ 55. (I.) 1. The original and essential power of that species of divine oracle that must be indicated as prophecy, may have such large influence as to assemble about it not merely a small and in many ways limited fellowship of men, but also a very wide and varied one, or a whole nation and kingdom; and it may do this not merely once in a way, but so that its reputation seems to stand, as far as this fellowship is concerned, firm and stedfast for ever; and a nation or kingdom, in all times when the higher counsel is needed, may, either of its own free will or at length as an old custom or law, invariably apply to it. That everything in the case in hand springs from this definite sort of oracle, is shown in § 28 ff.; and that this is the simplest and most ancient way in which the more durable fellowships reaching beyond the circle of mere house and tribe were formed among men, is evident from all that is adduced in § 48; indeed, we possess proofs enough how great in this respect was the power and activity of the oracle. Moreover, how sacred and highly-esteemed the prophetic power ever remained from the earliest times in the consecrated centre of the Egyptian kingdom, has already been mentioned (p. 148); by this conspicuous example we may perceive most clearly with what persistency and, so to speak, conformity to the laws of the realm, the prophetic power could, in this highly-cultured nation and kingdom, be regarded as an ultimate means of union and safety. But nothing prevented nations and kingdoms that had not a unity and power so ancient and so firmly based as Egypt, from deriving such counsel from a foreign source, and allowing themselves as mighty nations to be influenced and led by the fascination of a renowned prophet; and if Israel even, during the prophet labours of Moses, suffered themselves to be led a long time by a Balaam, as an old and in its essential contents certainly authentic reminiscence affirms,[1] we see how in later times, when the high reputation of Israel's prophets as men of God, of rare elevation of character, had been long established, foreign kingdoms much more depended upon their utterances, were eagerly bent on receiving their active counsel, and hoped to constitute themselves anew in improved and more compact fashion by means of their word of God.[2] But how significant in antiquity the power of such oracle-seats was in the guidance of whole nations and mighty kings, how their efficiency was acknowledged over the entire old world, and how until even

[1] The purely historical element in this narrative is pointed out in the *History of Israel*, ii. 301 ff. [Eng. trans. ii. 213–216].

[2] Not merely such longer and more definite narratives as those preserved from the reminiscence of the life of an Elijah, Elisha, and Jonah (*History of Israel*, iii. 575, 609 [Eng. trans. iv. 128, 196]) prove this, but also such (rightly understood) wholly clear utterances and intuitions of the prophets themselves as Isa. xxi. 11 f.; Zech. xi. 4 ff.; and utterances like Jer. i. 10 are only late echoes from times which so far for those prophets had to be sure already greatly changed.

later times the primitive reputation of many of them was preserved, may be seen most obviously in the writings of such Greeks as Herodotus and Strabo,[1] who best knew the old world and most copiously described it; and even Roman writers also say enough of such things.

But if such a seat of divine oracles remained isolated, and unconnected at all with a great national sanctuary of sacrifice, presently to be described, a permanent community could not easily be formed around it; and even if eagerly resorted to at first, and in favourable times subsequently, it was with difficulty that it preserved its original reputation for any length of time. For it is true every such seat must have first arisen from the exercise of a new power of prophecy, and in this found its special incentments and stay (though these were very manifold, as will be evident below); but since there always intermingled much that made the stream of prophecy flow rather artificially than purely (as this will presently have to be explained in detail more precisely), it was not possible that any one of these kinds of revelation of divine oracles should long preserve its reputation on a wide circle undiminished. Everything lacking in transparency, and on this account artificial rather than self-active and purely spiritual, may indeed for the moment, so long as it is new, seem to be satisfactory, and draw the eyes of the world upon itself, but it does not satisfy for any length of time; the artificial element appears soon to be the chief thing, and is cultivated with increasing one-sidedness; and as thus the small streak of purely spiritual vein operative at first was more and more enfeebled, the power of beneficial revelation, originally hid in such oracle-seats, was gradually and inevitably lost; whilst in such case, because there has been no pure beginning, no possibility of progress in that which is better presents itself.

---

[1] All through Strabo's Geography it may be observed that he (otherwise than Herodotus) had purposely directed special attention to such things, appearing as they did in many ways so strange in his time; and he even seeks to entertain his readers facetiously with them.

Neither the very ancient oracle of Dodona nor that of Delphi, whose reputation continued longer, nor the foreign Egyptian oracle of Ammon, whither at last their eyes were turned, remained permanently in extensive influence among the Greeks, or could assemble about it a more settled community of adherents; and what is so plainly observable in the case of the Greeks, repeated itself in like manner more or less through the whole of antiquity.

But this is not all. Such an artificial means of obtaining oracles, if it had once won for itself a wide reputation by a notable instance of success and through a highly-esteemed prophet, might be carried, by mere imitation on the part of men of inferior spirit and more doubtful calling, into ever narrower circles, and thus it would become less and less capable of forming around itself a great community of sufficiently broad aims and common pursuits. A conspicuous example of this has been preserved from the most ancient times of the community of the true God. Scarcely has the new species of revelation, one that seemed compatible with the higher religion, gained its high credit with some measure of permanency in the nation of Israel through Aaron, the elder brother of Moses, than it sinks into caricature at the hands of a grandson of Moses himself, and is degraded to a miserable paltry means of livelihood. The story is frankly told in the Old Testament,[1] it is true, but every attentive reader can mark, for it is self-evident, how gravely censurable the transaction is, and to what serious errors and misfortunes and multiplied ill effects it led in later times; and he must surely be a man of very little discernment who professes not to perceive this from the whole tone and purport of the simple narrative. Now this trivial-minded grandson of Moses, seeking his worldly hire, had at least inherited so much of better sense that, furnished as he was with a new and at that time highly-reputed piece of workmanship for obtaining oracles, he desired

---

[1] Judg. xvii. f. ; cf. *History of Israel*, ii. p. 491 f. [Eng. trans. ii. 347 f.], and *Antiquities*, p. 295 [Eng. trans. 264 f.].

to preside as leading priest over as large a portion of the entire community of Israel as possible; but when once, through him and other young people like him, the broad way had been opened to the dissolution of the great community Moses founded, and to more and more paltry and narrow prophetico-priestly guidance, this mischief grew and spread, so that soon every single house in the nation, if perchance it could defray the cost of it, sought to have for itself a similar oracle-giving piece of workmanship, and readily forgot in selfish interest the common good.[1] For a long time the tendency in the nation to this miserable state of things and this secretly progressive dissolution of the great community could not be prevented; for it always seemed to be a voice of Jahveh that was thus drawn forth. Not till the great prophets of the time of the kings arose, and the lurking corruption had caused such great and palpable mischief, was this degeneracy resolutely grappled with and resisted; and many centuries passed away before the wounds Israel had inflicted on herself were thoroughly healed.

§ 56. (II.) 2. Something altogether different must arise, if an organization for revealing divine oracles, and a permanent place, were not left for this purpose in solitary isolation, but became elevated, in inseparable connection with a great sanctuary of sacrifice and a priesthood belonging to it, to the position of a centre, or even the sole sacred centre, of a whole kingdom. This wholly different possibility must be fully and accurately considered, that we may understand wherein its peculiarity essentially lay, and why, notwithstanding its superiority to the previous means of founding a community, it nevertheless could not form a community much better in character and of permanent continuance.

In the outset, it is to be distinctly noted that the revelation of divine oracles does not of itself suffice for the needs of religion, if religion is to have an enduring and even uninterrupted significance and authority for man. The oracle shows

---

[1] Cf. *Antiquities*, p. 296 ff. [Eng. trans. 264 ff.].

THE FOUNDING OF A TRUE COMMUNITY OF GOD. 171

simply how man should act; but he who desires to fear God continually, and to be loyal to Him amid all the most manifold temptations of the world, or if he has done amiss, to return to Him with new energy and enlightenment, will not be satisfied with hearing new divine words addressed to him, as the growing darkness of the time may demand; he needs also, and above everything, the continually new participation in truths long since given, and the powerful influences of godliness,—an ever fresh baptism, so to speak, in the unexhaustible tides of the ocean of divine purity, grace, and glory. And if this is true of the individual man, how much more of a whole nation! Now the priesthood, in its distinction from prophetism (§ 40), is exactly fitted to maintain continually in life and practice the firmly-standing truths of revelation; and prophetism associates itself spontaneously with the administration of the corresponding offices of religion, or, what is essentially the same, in the sense of the earliest antiquity, the performance of the sacrificial service. Such service must have in its perpetuity a very definite order, which may constantly be observed, especially and most conspicuously amid the changes of human life and destiny; and precisely in the exact maintenance of this sacred ordering of things lies a great part of the power and influence of this service. If, now, an accredited seat of oracles were connected with such a sacrificial sanctuary and priesthood, if this double sanctuary were elevated to the position of a true centre, and formed, as it were, the living heart of a whole kingdom, and if it were made perpetual, with its constant repetition of the order of its services and its whole splendid ceremonial, it might very well be thought that the whole of a great nation might be captivated by the charm and authority of such a sublime sanctuary, and that even far beyond the primary circle of its influence it might attract to itself the sympathy and conciliate the goodwill of men.

The way in which such a thought could occur to the mind, and could be carried out more particularly in detail, is explained if the following considerations are taken into account. There was certainly, long before this close, intimate union of prophetic and priestly activity on a large scale, such an alliance often attempted and much accredited on a small scale. As soon as it had been recognised anywhere in the wide circle of humanity how indispensable the prophetic office is, and how not less necessary also is the priesthood, an attempt might be made in the very earliest times, and in the smallest circle, to unite both as closely as possible with each other, and become accustomed to such a union. The smallest original circle of a human community is that of the family or house, the next that of the tribe or clan, which is but the extension of the family according to ancient usage. The head of the household or tribe could then regard himself as likewise the natural priest of this often very numerous community; and how long this relation continued, especially among the old shepherd nations, the ancient reminiscences of the patriarchs of the Israelitish nation still sufficiently indicate. For the official service of sacrifice, partly very laborious, the first-born sons were, however, regarded from the oldest times as having special obligation and right,—a primitive custom of which, until the times of Moses and farther down, many traces were preserved.[1] The image of a household god, which served as a source of oracles, completed this simple equipment according to primitive usage; and we know with sufficient certainty how difficult it proved in the ancient nation of Israel, long after Moses, to abolish a custom that had become sacred by its antiquity.[2]

If now, in the chief city of a kingdom, a great sanctuary was established with a united order of high prophets and of numerous priests of all kinds, the clearest example of which

---

[1] Cf. *Antiquities*, p. 349, 377 [Eng. trans. 263, 302].

[2] Cf. *Antiquities*, p. 296 ff. [Eng. trans. 223 ff.]. The old sacred tradition held, and rightly so, that the three patriarchs were too elevated in their ideas to seek oracles in such ways; but that a Rebecca or Rachel was not considered to be above this ignoble custom, follows from the style of discourse in Gen. xxv. 22, and from the narratives, Gen. xxxi. 19 ff., xxxv. 2-4.

is seen in the old Egyptian kingdom (p. 148), this in its constitution would still be only that old house sanctuary raised to its highest stage of splendour and magnificence. The whole kingdom was now regarded as the wide household, in which this sanctuary formed the centre of all that was sacred, and where the prophetic and sacerdotal office was ever ready to serve the king as well as the whole nation. If the separate provinces which belonged to the kingdom chose to serve different gods, as in Egypt every Nomos had its own specially sacred god and cultus, the great sanctuary at the seat of the government and in proximity to the king was regarded as the consecrating bond which should enclose and guard the whole kingdom. Here, therefore, one might suppose, could have been formed a great compact national community; in point of fact, however, this was impossible from the very constitution of the sanctuary. For the prophetic as well as the sacerdotal office stood altogether apart from the nation as a sacred order by itself, which required, indeed, that the king should take an immediate part in its sanctity and its sacred aims, and become himself a kind of priest, that he might not be the enemy and opponent of the priests, but contemplated the nation itself as standing far below. The three constituent parts of a human kingdom with which we are here concerned, the kingship, the priesthood, and the people, still therefore remain as three ever widening circles surrounding an invisible sanctity, the exclusive knowledge and the sole guardianship of which the middle circle arrogantly assumes to itself; and which is not equally near to all three circles, and cannot accomplish the same ultimate salvation for all. Thus, then, is wanting even the beginning of all true unity and equality, the first characteristics of a community, and the great nation takes part either not at all or only superstitiously in that sanctity which is nevertheless the best refuge and defence of its whole earthly life.

Precisely the same thing occurs where there is not, as in the old, highly-cultured, and more compact kingdoms, a great visible sanctuary, as that of Egypt at Memphis or Thebes, and that of Assyria at Babel or Nineveh, but where, through a peculiar development, a special race succeeds to the priestly dignity, as the race of the Brahmins in India, or that of the Chaldæans in later Babel. Indeed, in this case a true community is even still less likely to arise, because distinctions of race and mere external advantages become much more strongly and oppressively conspicuous. Such a priestly caste has ever originated from a race or stem dominating the whole nation in the beginning; it has lost, indeed, the supreme power, but still retains enough of ancient culture or knowledge to desire at least to take the lead as a sacerdotal caste. But just on this account the petty inner jealousies and quarrels of the nation become at length only more and more incurably incited, as the early and middle history of India throughout such long centuries may attest. Of the formation of a genuine community here, then, can we still less speak.

§ 57. (III.) The inadequacy of an isolated prophetic activity, and of an artificial blending of prophetism and sacerdotalism, for the leadership of a nation, at last more and more strongly felt, called forth in many regions other endeavours, proportionately more energetic and victorious, but not the less perverse, to found an enduring sacred community of men. But to this end a radical improvement in the prevailing type of religion itself was needed. And it deserves the highest attention that even in those early times the powerful amendment of the prevalent kinds of religion was essential for the formation of a better community. For the conscious feeling of the need of an organized community, compact but just and beneficial, is something in itself desirable; even though only a single nation should thereby be fashioned after such an ideal, a higher good is won, worth all the pains and effort it costs. Moreover, in kingdoms raised to such a high measure of power and wisdom as the ancient Egyptian, it might be seen early enough how little the mere force of weapons of war enable a government to secure a permanent good understanding and union in a nation. Only a higher religion, subduing self-seeking and all other evil desires, and a moral life in harmony with it, can permanently establish a better community among men, and especially among members of the same nation; but just in this was ever, and is still given, the necessity to rise above the lower views and perverse tendencies of a religion once prevalent to such as are better, and to bring these to sovereignty; and thus the earnest desire and powerful effort to create a morally improved, and so more united and happier nation, may be a means of amending the traditional usages of religion itself. Nay, it is to be said that never is a great and enduring reformation of the underlying elements of all human piety attained without the spirits of men being seized deeply and powerfully with an eager desire either to heal or to avert the mischiefs and miseries that have oppressed the life of the nation. And it is just as noteworthy that such a genuine reformation, wholly independent of biblical religion, was accomplished at an early period in two ways, sharply divergent in themselves, but of far-reaching influence, and for the entire history of humanity of the most decisive character.

These two entirely opposite ways may be said to move along the two paths which, speaking generally, are available, if the aim just indicated is to be reached. Either the path long since, nay, from all primitive time, opened, as is evident from § 21-24,—that of religion itself,—may be kept, as the direct path which in reality, however earnest the desire is to avoid it, is not to be permanently avoided, as further experience and even the case itself alike show; but in keeping this path, clearing it also from the perilous and evil obstructions upon which so many have stumbled and which indeed must ultimately make it, for whole nations and the mightiest kingdoms of the earth, a mere path to destruction; or, purposely diverging from this, a cross-path rather than a side one may be taken, which at first promises to lead the traveller aright in safety and ease, but soon proves itself nevertheless only too certainly as by no means tending to the wished-for goal.

Now it is instructive to note how that first path was taken by the people who, apart from Israel, must be regarded as by far the most cultured, sensitive, and tender in religious feeling of all that higher antiquity, whilst they distinguished themselves above so many others, and particularly above Israel, in obtaining, for that early time, a widely-extended power and influence; we mean the Indian people, who also adopted two very different modes of effectually clearing the path, in the sense indicated above.

3. One of these modes, originating in the higher antiquity, and spreading powerfully from the primitive seats of the people towards the west, took such a deep and lasting hold upon many west Asian nations, that only by violence was it ultimately broken. It is connected with Zoroaster's name of old-world celebrity, but became powerful and successful principally through the ancient Persians. This mode of action, in direct contrast with that presently to be mentioned, though springing from the same source, starts, in the ancient way, with the reformation of an entire existent nation, and carries it out on the two sides which in point of fact perfectly correspond, and taken together but make up the whole higher life of man. On the side of religion, in energetic counter-action against errors already formidable, it rejects a too sensuous divine service, stands rigorously by an ultimate order and unity in all that is divine, and seeks to reduce everything that must be reverenced as holy to the elements and forces which are simplest but purest and most wonderful, and apparently primordial. On the side of human affairs and correspondent duty, it seeks, by a strict separation of the pure and impure for man, and by a series of high moral requirements, to train up an energetic, self-conscious, proud but strictly exclusive race; and its principal achievement was the preparation of the Persian nation for the victorious part it played in the history of the world, the after-effects of which

were destined to be so powerful and long-enduring.[1] But since the ideas and assumptions concerning the divine powers, and the distinction between the pure and the impure, were very erroneous, and since a one-sided development of a nation to a proud, dominant, martial people, accustomed to victory, can nowhere produce a healthy national life that shall endure, it is easily understood that here also no such community could arise as should become the nourishing mother of a religion in any sufficient measure both salutary and true.

4. Altogether different was the new mode, springing out of the high and rare culture of the life of the Indian people in a comparatively speaking later age, whose chief movement was mainly eastward. This purity and holiness of life, which all prophetic and priestly activity did indeed demand ultimately of every man, and which nevertheless was always so little visible in general among the people, nay, was often in times of prosperity and abundance so painfully wanting even among priests themselves, was not this to be possibly won by the individual man, independently of all traditional prophetic and priestly aid? And may not the individual man who wins it completely, become for every nation the most living and persuasive exemplar of this life, and even a new sacred centre around which shall gather a new world of better and purer men? Such a living centre must be incomparably mightier and nobler than any mere seat of an oracle or any altar-furnished sanctuary, even the most resplendent and alluring. Such was the latent drift of thought which in antiquity, in regions most dissimilar, early enough forced its way with overmastering power, and wrought at last the most far-reaching and wonderful results. Even where an actual community of genuine religion already exists, as is subsequently to be explained, this new thought may at times be very powerful,

[1] Only fragments of the old Zoroastrian writings remain to-day; it is far more difficult, therefore, to pronounce a final judgment upon these matters than in the case of Buddhism, but our short summary contains what may be said with certainty. When and where Zoroaster lived, and what was the fortune of his faith in the pre-Persian time, are, moreover, questions still not satisfactorily settled.

and produce a multitude of new creations: in the Old Testament there was no other ground for the origin of Nazarites, Rechabites, and Essenes;[1] and in the mediæval Christian times it was from the like impulse that Franciscans took their rise. But altogether differently must this impulse have worked where as yet no actual community of the true religion had been established; and in this the old Indian peoples are distinguished above all others. From an early period many individuals among them threw off the Brahminical rule, and sought by an escape from society and a life of lonely seclusion to attain the more readily the highest purity of character; and at length out of this vast mixed and motley multitude Buddha issued, to become the founder of a purer life that should serve as a luminous example to the rest of men, to break the restraints of caste imposed by the Brahmins, and all merely national limitations, and to make himself for now nearly two millenniums and a half the divinely-honoured saint of an innumerable host of disciples. Whether from such a movement a genuine community could possibly arise, no other precedent helps us to determine so correctly and with such certainty and clearness as that of Buddha. What then has been the result? To the competent judge it is evident that in the whole nearly two millenniums and a half during which it has existed, and amid all the varied and changing forms in which it has established itself firmly in different lands of the earth, and still maintains its powerful sway, Buddhism has never anywhere taken the shape of a true community. Rather does it break up everywhere, to speak briefly, into two communities: the body of saints who teach and who have to live as Buddha lived, and the men of the world who support them with temporal resources and catch the reflected glory of their sanctity as they submit to their spiritual guidance. Only the inner community has perfect holiness, and, moreover, in this there is no equality, since one only of its members is

---

[1] Cf. *Antiquities*, p. 118 [Eng. trans. 84–89], with the subsequent observations, p. 150 f. [Eng. trans. 152]; *History of Israel*, iv. 483 ff. [Eng. trans. v. 370 ff.].

the representative ever self-regenerating Buddha. It is not to be denied, it is true, that the conception taken of the pure life is, in this whole wide institution of renovated religion, on the one hand much more rigid, and on the other much more tender than in Brahminism or elsewhere in ordinary heathenism, and that the thorough discipline of the whole popular life resting upon this basis worked very salutarily in many directions. But there is something one-sided, overstrained, and contrary to nature underlying this whole system, and showing itself prominently at almost every point; the severance and dislocation of all that is highest in the efforts of the human spirit—in that as a matter of principle the saintly stand upon the one side and the less saintly and perfect upon the other—leads also as a direct result to a new chilling and repression of all human aspirations, when once this institution of life is firmly established in a nation; and there is, further, no proper beginning even possible of the varied, flexible life, progressing in the freest rivalry of all its members, that marks the true community.[1]

5. If, then, the old prophetism and priestism, even in their artificial combination, could not create an enduring community, could not give to a people that firm, compact unity which a large or small empire requires, was it not the best conceivable course to abandon both ways, and the piety that arose from them, and to hold fast simply and suitably, and develop

---

[1] A correct knowledge of Buddhism ought to obtain amongst us. The importance of Buddhism in human history is unusually great. It is the only kind of religion which independently coincides in so many points with that taught in the Bible, is indeed most similar to it, and though of an earlier date than Christianity, yet resembles it in so many directions. The knowledge of it therefore contributes largely to the better judgment of Christianity itself in its further development. That Christianity is liable to fall into the Buddhist error of separating the community into the saintly and the secular, its history teaches; yet it possessed in its youth energy enough to reject the Sabæan heresy as well as the Manichæan, which was still more inclined to this error (*History of Israel*, vii. p. 172-184). Only in the Middle Ages was it too feeble and too perturbed to save itself from injury by such a division into the saintly and the secular which pressed in upon it powerfully through the Papacy: there needed the mighty labours and efforts of the Reformation of the sixteenth century to deliver it from this relapse.

further what had proved itself a surer possession as the result of the noblest endeavours and spiritual toils of the past, viz. the wisdom of life and the best morals? This is the fundamental thought which in the extreme East, in the Chinese lands, where civilisation was almost as early and as highly developed as in Egypt, became ultimately dominant, and obtained at length through Confucius so decisive a victory that it is to-day the true soul of the vast Chinese Empire. Confucius did not immediately assail the old religions of those wide and populous lands; he let them subsist so far as they were able to subsist by their own inherent force. But his own thought turned away from them; he imagined that the empire, and the government over it, if it were small, and still more if it were large, could flourish purely by the best morals and the healthy principles of a righteous administrative wisdom; and he based upon this supposition a system of doctrine which, propagated by schools, is to-day the foundation of that vast empire, embracing the finest and most populous parts of the earth. Confucianism demands our attention here, partly because it belongs to the pre-Christian era, and coincides in point of time very nearly with the attempt of a directly contrary nature which Buddhism made towards founding a better community; partly because its fundamental thought is one very likely to be entertained by a highly civilised nation, and recurs to-day amongst ourselves with great force; partly also because the truth we here seek to set forth may become the more evident by its direct antithesis. For the course which Confucianism takes involves conduct and aims the very reverse of those which result from the direct way of religion, is indeed as a cross-way which of set purpose intersects the way of religion, and would, if it were at all possible, lead men further and further away from it.

But, as a matter of fact, this whole view of things and mode of action rests upon an entire misconception of what religion is in itself, and what it ought to be for man; and, moreover, only becomes possible when in the long course of human development religion has given to nations as to individuals so many noble fruits that living men can forget the more readily upon what stem alone they could have grown and ripened. By the long persistent practice of the commands of a definite kind of religion, certain moral usages are firmly established in a nation; by long experience of the changes of human destiny, certain intuitions relating to the best possible conditions for the continuance of human kingdoms become fixed and permanent; and subsequent reflection develops in addition a new insight which shows how the best of these moral usages and intuitions may be applied in governing men. The clear, fine racking off of such better morals and principles appears, moreover, to be the most effective expedient in ruling simultaneously many different races with their different kinds of religion and religious cultus; and it must be confessed that in this respect it has proved an admirable means of holding together, even amid the constant change of the most dissimilar ruling houses, the different peoples of a most powerful and widely extended empire. Politics here take the place of religion, the rigid penal law that of public freedom; and the wisdom of one man, Confucius,—preserved by means of a well-graduated series of schools, and by an official system in which promotion from stage to stage depends upon passing the severest tests,—this is to suffice in all the highest and most intricate questions of life. But the result is, that the human having to enter, after it has reached a certain divine culture, into the position of the Divine itself, the Divine avenges itself against it unceasingly in thousandfold reactions. Religions are not suppressed and extirpated as this State policy intends; deprived of their higher guidance, they only degenerate more and more deeply and perniciously; while statesmen superstitiously burn incense and offer sacrifice before the statues of Confucius and virtually worship him as their true God. Still further, if the wisdom of this man-god, as it is treasured up in sacred books and reverenced above everything, but barely suffices through long ages to keep a tight rein upon a confused crowd of people, it becomes also to the rulers themselves a bondage and barrier, a hindrance to all higher understanding of things,—the more disastrous the later and more changed the times become,—since it is only the manifoldly narrow and limited spirit of this one man, and not the infinite Spirit of God, under the power of which they permit themselves to unite, and then again to spread out and extend. In addition to all this, whilst apparently this broad empire forms the greatest single community, in reality it is divided into a community, on the one hand, of those who know, rule, and punish,—for the empire is held together by stern law and the sword;—and, on the other, of those who are ignorant, ruled, and punished; and beyond the needs of the outward life the whole range of education and discipline does not necessarily reach.[1]

3. *Its Perfect Satisfaction.*

§ 58. It is certain, then, that by none of these forms and regulations of religion among men the need of a true community has either been met in the earliest or latest times of antiquity, or can be met to-day, although in the historical phenomena presented there is a wide difference, and the beginnings of such a community are more observable in some cases than in others. So much the more wonderful is it that this need was perfectly satisfied in Israel in those ancient days under

---

[1] From all that is said here about the Chinese Empire, it is evident how entirely our modern European kingdoms, especially as they have sought to shape themselves since 1830, 1848, and 1866, are in a fair way to sink down to a thoroughly Chinese condition of things. It is not a question of mere names, that of Confucius or any other, nor of accidentally similar phenomena; alas! under a smooth and ever splendid exterior it is just the spirit of Atheism and the contempt of all true religion that brings on such a condition, only those who are responsible for it are far less excusable than Confucius or the philosophers among the Greeks, who in many things were equal to Confucius, but inferior to him in the practical issues of their wisdom. There is no danger to-day of our sinking into Brahminism or Buddhism, but there is great danger of our falling back into a Chinese condition of things.

Moses, and yet nothing is more certain than this, if we follow accurately all historical traces. But we must also consider—

1. That if this need was to be satisfied in those early times and in this nation through Moses, then all the pre-conditions which alone made it possible that a true community of God could arise there must already be fulfilled. Now what were these fundamental conditions, and how were they certainly and really found in those primitive times, and just with this so far unique nation of antiquity?

The first, that which is primary in this whole question, relates to the nature of the conception of God Himself and of the hallowing of His will. Certainly in few places of the whole earth at that time, when by a conjuncture of most favourable circumstances the community of the true religion was to arise in this nation of Israel, had a simpler and truer kind of piety been preserved than among this people. It is evident that out of the mist that had already arisen in the earliest ages of humanity (p. 163), a simpler, less firmly developed indeed, but truer godliness might emerge, here and there at least, in regions where the heavy vapours of all error had less thickly and densely gathered. Now, shepherd nations with their simple life, their free upward glance to the stars glowing in the clear heavens,[1] and their plain moveable sanctuaries, might readily remain a long time accessible to a simpler and yet true religion. That the forefathers of the nation of Israel belonged to shepherd-tribes; that they preserved strictly their simpler, freer manners when in conflict with long-since settled but degenerate southern peoples; and that the nation itself, even in the changed circumstances of its life long after Moses, held fast tenaciously its peculiar and simple manners: all this we know certainly enough. Such circumstances must already in that age, three thousand years before Christ, have favoured an unusually lofty movement under national leaders like

[1] It is remarkable that the grand images of the stars of heaven are nowhere so largely conspicuous as in the reminiscence of the patriarchs, Gen. xv. 5, xxii. 17; picturings such as Isa. xl. 60 but follow these old reminiscences.

Abraham and men of kindred spirit, the victorious result of which was, for the first time, a deeper knowledge of all genuine religion, and a stricter faith in the one true spiritual God; so that a foundation was laid for such belief, which at least in this populous circle it was afterwards difficult to shake, and which was never again to be completely destroyed. To be sure, during the centuries after Moses, the reminiscences of this once powerful spiritual elevation of its first great leaders and heroes gradually became more and more feeble, but the hold upon some of the more tenacious elements of it was sufficiently strong and unrelaxing, and the whole subsequent history of the development, as well of the manners and customs as of the religion of the nation, is unintelligible without this first energetic beginning of a very definite religious culture.[1] However far, therefore, scholarship in more recent days may have thrown doubt both upon the historical character of that early time everywhere presupposed in the Bible, when the formation of a community of the true religion took its rise, and upon the significance of the formula, "the God of Abraham, of Isaac, and of Jacob," we have nevertheless an unquestionable right to see here the first mighty step taken towards such possible formation, and the first fundamental condition of it.[2]

The second was, that this nation, Israel, in a wholly new position, into which it fell through the national entanglements of the time, and in which it experienced and painfully endured what was the direct contrary of a genuine community of God, nevertheless did not abandon again the true religion deeply rooted in it from the beginning. In Egypt at that time, human government, with a national community which, as its counterpart, may be designated a merely human community, already flourished in a high degree. All human

---

[1] As all this is so fully shown in detail in the first three volumes of the *History* and in the *Antiquities*, it may here be taken for granted.

[2] Cf. *Hist.* i. p. 454 ff. [Eng. trans. i. 317 ff., ii. 34 ff.] with the Dissertation in the *Jahrbücher der Bibl. Wiss.* x. p. 1-25. The hackneyed doubts of some recent writers rest only upon ignoring or mistaking what is already scientifically proved.

pomp and glory might be seen there; kingly authority embracing and upholding firmly a great composite, well-administered realm, and a people progressive, inventive, familiar with science and art. Every nation that came, like Israel, into close contact with it, allured by its charms and influenced powerfully by the discipline and rigour of its singularly elaborate government and highly-cultured national community, was dissolved and lost in its midst. But perversity in its religion and in its rule of prophet and priest was also, as we have seen, p. 168 ff., very fully developed; and the kingly power, touched by the degeneracy that had found place in the high spiritual impulses of the whole life of man, had long since grown into an arbitrary and violent despotism. Judged by the motives and forces of the true religion, here then was an example of the very antithesis of what a national community should be; and not in such mean and obscure circumstances as might elsewhere easily be found, but on a grand scale, and to those who did not wish to be in subjection to it, of the most oppressive and burdensome character.[1] If Israel would not yield to pressure that first commended and then enforced the perverse religion and rigid mandates of this fully-developed and despotic government, and of the similarly organized national community which it controlled, and so far felt itself strengthened by the healthy vigour of its own religion, yet it could and must see here how civil and religious government and the national community should *not* be. But is it of any service to be obliged simply to see and endure all this? The nation *did* endure it for a long time, and without entirely despairing of the better religion inherited from the patriarchs, or becoming at once completely broken and destroyed. But even the most tenacious national energy may at length be impaired and exhausted, if it is not reinvigorated anew from the only source from which such reinvigoration can come.

Thus, then, has the third fundamental condition, viz. the

[1] On this whole subject, cf. *History*, i. p. 552 ff., ii. p. 5 ff. [Eng. trans. i. 386 ff., ii. 3 ff.].

advent and whole mission of an unparalleled God-sent man, like Moses, its all-decisive significance. Without his coming, the long deep sighing and yearning for redemption from Egyptian bondage which, according to the brief and striking reminiscence of the Book of Origins,[1] went up to heaven and to the God of heaven, would not have been answered; but how far he could appear upon the scene as in the hand of God the only efficient instrument for this task, and could bring the only possible true deliverance, has already (§ 34-36) been discussed.

§ 59. 2. For, indeed, everything that Moses established that is immortal and unchanging culminates in the founding of a community of the true religion. This is the eternal sum and crown of his work.[2] In directest contrast to an Egyptian national community, and a government corresponding with it, which, in all its seductive sensuousness, and all its terrible reality as irreconcilable with the true religion, floated vividly before the vision of the great prophets and leaders of the people, and before the vision of the people themselves;—this community, speaking from a purely historical point of view, could arise only in the midst of constant observation of that great mistaken system, and after sensible experience of its frightful effects. But, once arisen, it is of eternal significance and validity, reaching far beyond the circle of its first historical origin and establishment, forming the sure basis of all real persistence and all real progress of insight and activity in true religion, and being, in fact, the indestructible beginning of a development corresponding to such persistence and progress by its incalculable duration and inexhaustible fruitfulness. The full handling of this subject comes properly in a subsequent volume, but we must here offer something of an explanation of it.

---

[1] Ex. ii. 23-25 ; cf. xiii. 19-22, xiv. 30 f.
[2] What is here so briefly sketched is shown more in detail in the *History*, ii. p. 193 ff. [Eng. trans. ii. 135 ff.], but it is so important and decisive in itself that nowhere can it be made sufficiently conspicuous.

Pre-eminently and emphatically, all possibility of the rise, much more of the development, of a community of genuine religion rests upon the perfect knowledge of the true God and its all-embracing significance for men. He who recognises, as Moses did—(1) that there is only one true God, and all men without distinction are equal before Him; (2) that only the government of this God, and His will in all human things, are indestructibly eternal, and amid all changes of human condition immutably the same; and (3) that this one true God is He who embraces all men in the equal measure of His power, punishing their deviations from His will, and still more in that of His infinite love approaching them with condescension and grace; he who recognises this—if, at the same time, he is animated by as pure and ever equal and even glowing a love to his people, and to all men, as Moses was, and is adapted also, as he was, to be the leader and builder of his nation—will be able to sketch also the proper outlines of that community of the true God which is the only genuine community; and he will not simply trace these outlines as a teacher and introduce the details as a legislator, he will introduce them into the world as Moses did, luminous in their own splendour, and by the living example of his own character and work. Thus, then, it is already of incomparably great significance if, for the first time in the history of the world, a community is founded in which all men, without exception, are contemplated as equal before God, and as having in Him only their inseparable cohesion, because finding in Him their inextinguishable light, their better mind, their common wellbeing, so that the distinctions of prophet and priest, or not-prophet and not-priest, of human king and ruler and human subject, of learned and unlearned, of rich and poor, of free citizen and slave, completely vanish, and are recognised as necessarily vanishing before the true God of this community, but only in order to emerge again in a second series, illumined by the sun of righteousness and love of the same true God who is common to all, and of His will, and henceforth to pass for as much as they are really worth under the light and will of God. But of far greater significance is it that, having been born from the noblest energies and efforts of all true religion, in the most wearisome and painful conflicts with the perverse government and national community that were its direct antithesis, it has known from the beginning, by deep and most memorable experience, something of all human suffering, and also the true salvation, divine love, and redemption. The sublime primary ideas and forces of the true religion are thus, all of them, efficacious in its midst from the beginning; and it is these that are able, after they have once established the solid structure of this community, to maintain it unshaken for all time to come. For this reason also this firm basis and healthy germ of a community of the true God does not thereby admit at all that its circle is at once closed with the one nation, Israel. If this had been the case, it could never, in accordance with the historical conditionedness of all development of human things generally in those early times, enter into the process of growth; but sustained, first of all at least, by the firm concentration and inner energy of one nation, taking deeper root in its sacred enclosure during a long series of centuries, and bearing the finest bloom and fruit, it becomes capable at length of embracing all nations.

The founding of this community of the Old Testament goes back into an age so remote that we no longer possess reminiscences of it so direct and lucid as those of the founding of that of the New, which, indeed, is the consummation not the destruction of the Old community, and in which the Old community preserves for ever its simple irrefragable foundations. But we can still recognise with certainty that, in point of fact, this achievement, as it was the most arduous, was also the greatest and noblest of that ancient time—an achievement incomparably more important and richer in results than a hundred victories on the field of battle. By means of it the nationality of Israel became seized by a pure

divine thought, and more and more completely transformed,
—a thought uplifting this single nation, of scanty numbers
and scanty earthly power, to a nation of a wholly new kind,
and with wholly new influence, the like of which all antiquity
cannot show, and which just in this its community lived on
ineradicably after all that was imperfect and perishable in it
had found its end. What the whole of antiquity, in its very
different nations and national institutions, strove after in vain
(§ 54-57), or at best attained only in imperfect organizations, was here attained even before there was any particular
recognition of it in the wide realms of antiquity, and before
its whole significance was properly appreciated.[1] For in this
case no one-sided predominance was possible, either of the
authority of the priesthood or of that of the learned; and the
power of the prophetic office, most essential and fundamental,
as we have seen, in a nation not wishing to live without
divine sanctity, found here both its freest scope and its wise
limit and divine law. All members of the community, guided
by the inviolable principles of the true religion, and upheld
by the same firm unchanging foundations of fellowship, could
strive toward the same goal of pure divine salvation, and
enjoy the same fruits of such effort, without any one having
the occasion or right to feel himself unsatisfied, or in all
seriousness to withdraw for a time from fellowship. Here
was that which is truly pure and holy; and here was set up
at length a government which was to be the very reverse of
a government of human caprice and unrighteousness, and
which, in spite of all earthly imperfections and changes
possible to it, could nevertheless offer the firm beginning of

---

[1] The unusual and joyous images with which the restoration even of the later community after the exile of Israel is delineated in such passages as Isa. lxvi. 7-9, Ps. lxxxvii., cxxii., cxxiv.-cxxvi., xlvii., lxvii., lxviii., suggest with what effect the creation of the original community would have been described to us if we had sufficient literary memorials from that ancient time. We are able, however, from the narratives, Ex. xix.-xxi., and from other reminiscences given and elucidated in the *History*, ii. p. 305 ff. [Eng. trans. ii. 216 ff.], to gather what was the nature and influence of the original creation of the community.

an unchangeable power, marked by continual progress in all divine blessings humanity can enjoy, and by eternal salvation.

§ 60. 3. For the purest and highest advantage which a community of the true religion can afford is this :—when once well established and making good progress, it becomes an abiding safeguard against all perverse efforts as they newly intrude, and the best security of all further progress. If with every better fellowship among men and every well-organized civil community this is the case, how much more is it possible with a community of the true religion, and, indeed, has it actually occurred with this community in the course of the long series of centuries! And just this is the best proof of the unsurpassed perfection and glory of this new creation, going back into that high antiquity, and standing alone in the history of nations and in the history of religion.

Every well-organized community indeed especially tolerates and protects, it is true, the most diversified efforts and labours of its individual members, so long as they have in themselves a good aim and do not run counter to the highest and chief aim of the community; nay, by the closer unions of a spiritual kind among men, of its own creation, it calls forth whatever is possible in this direction, but assigns to everything its proper bounds and demands that no single movement overstepping its true limits shall be dangerous to others; and in this not only is the healthy rivalry of individuals incited, but the highest and best service one man can render as against others is the more fully elicited and its advantage secured. Thus, too, must the power which in this whole sphere is most creative and commanding, the prophetic, exert most profoundly its noblest energies and learn to work altogether with its own peculiar means ; and we see therefore in this nation prophecy more highly developed and more vigorously and happily working than in any other nation of the whole of antiquity. But, still further, how government over men must shape itself at its purest and best, does not appear so plain and is not so suggestively taught for all time to come in any other ancient nation as in this, in which in almost all the most different eras of its history there arose a numerous and brilliant series of men most serviceable to the State, the larger and more luminous stars of which afford us joy and guidance to-day.[1]

Moreover, should new errors and perversities arise, as is possible within this as every other organization that is not purely but only humanly divine, should they press in often with stormy violence or maintain themselves in its midst for long periods of time, it was proved again and again that here they could not produce such devastation or work such destruction to the deepest foundations of society as in other national fellowships. For at the right time one of the good and necessary powers of this community always acted with a beneficent regulating and restorative influence upon that which overstepped its due limits. Should priests degenerate through pride and luxury, the common people, who had their just rights as well, rose up against them; should prophets or learned men or authors lapse into love of idle thinking and insincere speaking, the whole nation exercised a check upon them, for the freest access to all arts was open to it, and the remedy of direct divine thought and discourse was not denied it; and should the rulers abandon themselves to caprice and despotism, the other existing powers of the community could at once take vigorous action, and the courage to rush in antagonism against this solid bulwark of defence would soon fail them. All this lay in the fundamental laws of this community of the true religion, and in the moral usages that from ancient days established themselves more and more broadly and firmly in it; and in spite of the many raging storms that disturbed its repose, the higher equilibrium ever recovered itself again and peace returned.[2]

[1] To this Zech. ix. 16, x. 4 very significantly alludes; a witness all the more important because referring to times from which we have not so many witnesses as from others.

[2] I give here but a brief reflected image of historical details that meet us on closer contemplation.

But that ultimately all good progress becomes possible from imperfect to perfect development of the least that is obtainable through the unshaken continuance of such a community as well as of the greatest and most decisive, is not less certain. In point of fact, this last possibility already lies in the two previous ones; for where they are not present in vain, but grow more and more irresistibly into realities, there in the onward stream of all higher efforts once powerfully called forth this possibility presses from goal to goal to the gradually more complete attainment of the ultimate goal, or if there is one, and from the beginning there was in this case, to the very highest of all. He, therefore, who is perfectly acquainted with the entire history of this nation in all its aspects will not doubt that within the two thousand years, or nearly so, of which we now speak, it passed through the most violent changes and most extraordinary transformations that any nation can experience, and that these occurred with respect to all the very manifold, nay, even conflicting tendencies and efforts for which the life of a nation can complicate or divide its organization. But he will just as surely find that in spite of all the errors and declensions into which at times it fell, nevertheless a series of progressive movements was made in it, most memorable in themselves and important in their consequences, varying no doubt as the needs of the time varied, but in their entire tendency all of them, so far as they met more than transient needs, verging coincidently at last towards the only highest goal, to which the first steps of the series, conditioned by the original beginnings and fundamental aim of the community were directed, and which is none other than the perfect true religion at length to be won. But this last and highest goal could not be reached without the steps to it being taken within the irrefragably firm deep foundations and high mural defences of this community.

II.—THE CONFLICT AGAINST ALL DEGENERATION OF REVELATION.

The Opposition of Heathenism and True Religion.

1. *In General.*

§ 61. The correctness of our last observation must now be fully shown by a distinct but great and all-prevailing phenomenon, the right understanding of which, and the knowledge of all aspects of it in their indubitable certainty, are here specially relevant. We must come now to the more particular consideration of the danger of degeneracy to which all revelation may be exposed; and we take the word revelation, as often in common discourse, in the double sense it may bear, viz. as indicating its inner impulse and original activity (§ 13–20), and also its enduring noble fruits, or the divine truths which are ripened by it and already work anywhere in humanity.

Now it is certain that every activity of the mind, even the noblest and most necessary, when once vitalized and more or less developed, may in various ways deteriorate, and in like manner its fruit may in various ways be perversely sought and perversely applied. Why should this not also be the case to the same extent with revelation, which, considered on its primary, that is, its human side, is likewise an activity of the mind, historically arising and historically developed, and whose fruits, that is, the divine truths it seeks to reveal and make familiar to humanity, must first find a true domestication in this human world, and therefore must encounter and contend with all impulses and powers hostile to them! Precisely when such a special facility and activity of the mind has already won high credit among men, and become much in quest, may it be most readily and persistently misused by those who practise it and those who resort to it; and precisely when its fruits have been longest admired and most highly honoured may they become most easily disesteemed by the concupiscence of men, and also wrongly applied by their unwisdom. The higher revelation stands among all the spiritual efforts and activities of antiquity, the more possible was its perversion; and the more strongly the divine truths and commands it brought to light as the fruits of its arduous toil impose obligations upon the human will in its deepest impulses and determinations, the more vehement may be the resistance and hostility of that will against them, and the more obstinate its entanglement in delusions and a whole wide network of new and grave errors.

Revelation in the nation of Israel under Moses had developed an activity for the true religion, and as its best fruit had created a community the like of which till then the whole world had not seen. For the first time in the world's history, a whole nation had been born again through the spirit of the true religion; and true religion, in order to facilitate its longer continuance and its progress on the earth, had found, in a broad, well-organized national community, a firm hold and a sacred seat for further development. Those sublime days and years of more remote antiquity under Moses tower on high in the midst of all the millenniums of entire antiquity as for the history of the true religion the lofty boundary beyond which true religion has as yet as good as no sure seat at all among the nations of the earth, and on this side of which only it could begin its consecutive and extended efficiency for all mankind, although it was provisionally limited to this one nation. And if the times of Moses had not the large far-reaching significance of the early days of Christianity, a millennium and a half afterwards, yet from the first creation of mankind onwards there had been no such decisive revolution as this, which alone was capable of preparing the way for Christianity that should at length complete everything, that is, all perfect religion.

But wonderfully elevated and glorious as the revelation of Moses was (§ 34–37), it nevertheless suffered from the first from two somewhat serious deficiencies, less noticeable perhaps in its new powerful and splendid commencement in the world, yet making themselves gradually more and more perceptible in the long course of the following centuries. This revelation remained in its inner impulse and spirit essentially of a purely prophetic character; but the more imperfect element in prophecy is the violence (p. 23 f.) with which the divine truth it proclaims breaks its way as if from without irresistibly into humanity; and this peculiarity showed itself in its fresh and undiminished strength as the revelation first became conspicuous in those still early times, and took for such long centuries its limited but immovable seat upon the earth. The other deficiency is in itself, it is true, of a wholly different kind: this revelation, as it ran its course in its whole most wonderful power, could find nowhere else upon earth than in this one nation a favourable place for intelligent acceptance and firm ground for efficient working; and it must confine itself to this one nation at least provisionally, if it would make for itself and for true religion in general a home upon earth, and find as it were a refuge and sacred seat of operation in some spot, limited it may be, but secure on all sides because of the firm bounds of a nationality. That it could not for ever seclude its community in this narrow space was indeed certain; it had in it from the beginning too much pure truth for all humanity pressing to overflow its bounds, to be able to stay for ever within a limit into which it was directed for that early time only by the comprehensive and guiding law of all historical development.[1] But that which is once so deeply settled in the life of a nationality, and becomes so much, in accordance with national sentiment, its defence, its pride, nay, ultimately its sole highest good,—as to this nation was the case with the true religion more and more after the time of Moses,— finds also its primary limit in such national life increasingly strong; and the merely provisional element in the life of a

[1] Cf. *History*, ii. p. 169 ff. [Eng. trans. ii. p. 117 ff.].

nation at first, an element that could not from the very nature of that life restrain it for ever, extending itself in this narrow bound over many centuries, becomes thereby at length all the more a hindrance to the freer movement desirable for such life. This second deficiency, however, ultimately coincided quite closely and in new form with the first. For the earlier and more necessarily it was adjudged that this revelation, in its first and most energetic action, should find its place only in this one nation, the higher mounted that violence essentially cleaving to it, since its community became now also a national community, and the spiritual power provisionally blended with the national which can nowhere be maintained without external constraint.

All this, indeed, was but the operation in this special case of the general law of all new historical development in human affairs,—a law which works with the greater stringency the more creative the new element is that seeks to become historical. Nothing new that is in itself purely spiritual, and tends to take immediate effect in humanity, enters into the world of human relations which are restricted in a thousand ways as to time and space, without confining itself first of all within the limits in which it becomes historical,—limits which subsequently are obstructive to its essentially boundless energy and to its innermost movement struggling after wider and wider extension, but which surround it at first only as its protecting walls, that, however, must remain as long as it is necessary. But these limits within which all revelation of the true religion was to produce new fruits from fruits already matured, were not so impenetrable as to prevent many impulses more or less incompatible with the spirit of this revelation forcing their way through and attempting to mingle with the better impulses or to stifle them again. Many old sacred customs irreconcilable with the innermost impulses of the genuine revelation and its continuous progress were preserved from the long days before Moses, or returned with fresh vigour after the time of Moses, especially in periods of new confusion and despair; and a series of centuries passed away before the last traces of these old sacred usages were lost, since in a nation not disloyal to its youth nothing maintains its existence more tenaciously than such old inclinations and customs. But from the foreign nations also, with which Israel in all the turning-points of its long and complicated history ever remained in the most manifold and unavoidable contact, there penetrated many ways of obtaining oracles irreconcilable with the instincts and truths of the genuine revelation, which were sought after in times of prosperity in Israel from wanton desire of innovation, in times of disaster from dull despair.[1] In such continual seeking with curious and itching ears after new kinds of oracles, all antiquity, especially in the livelier and more cultured nations, occupied itself the more unweariedly and insatiably, the more the oracle itself in general was unperfected, and in so many places in the full bloom of its youth; and Israel also had times when it yielded to this disposition and temptation only too wantonly, as the excitement grew to find new and higher oracular responses, and to become acquainted with the religions connected with them.[2]

Furthermore, in the use of the genuine means of obtaining divine responses, and in the application of truths long since acknowledged among them, Israel did not always show the wisdom, loyalty, and perseverance without which progress is so little possible that the want of them must sooner or later lead to the most dangerous retrogression, and to new obscurations of the light of all true religion. No nation in the midst of the complicated and difficult course of its history, and after it has once made the surest headway in disclosing grandly all

---

[1] That Israel is a nation of most peculiar kind, calmly dwelling alone, becomes conspicuous first in Balaam's mouth, Num. xxiii. 9, then in somewhat later prophetic passages, Deut. xxxiii. 28; Micah vii. 14; rather, however, according to a pious wish which became increasingly strong after experiences of ill, but was only partially fulfilled in history from the eighth century before Christ.

[2] See all this picturesquely described, Isa. lvii. 9 f.; Jer. ii. 18, 36.

the tasks and activities of higher spiritual effort, is safe in the presence of relaxations of strength and mistakes which may throw it back again; and if, indeed, a much larger and mightier nation like the German, to whom as to no other the guardianship and furtherance of Christianity have fallen, nevertheless ever since it should have known its better divine determination has been so much mistaken about it, and is still to-day so seriously wanting towards it, how then should not such human infirmities manifoldly visit a nation much smaller and far more exposed from its situation to conflicts for its very life, and where amidst all of them and so with the greatest difficulty true religion first sought an enduring community upon earth! For in a nation once energetically aroused and vivified, all such purely spiritual aims and aspirations, and most of all this first and yet most elevated and arduous one, float before it in purest essence and intent, remain always unattainably beyond it, and absolutely independent of it, and as it were wait to see whether in favourable times it will by such influences be developed from stage to stage more widely and nobly; but they never cleave to it like earthly material, and they easily pass over to other nations. Nevertheless revelation, in its purest effort, its most active beginnings, and its inexhaustible pains, was, according to § 36, subsequently to Moses the profoundest occupation of every mind, and the beating heart of the community he founded. And as revelation was placed in indispensable and unceasing reciprocal action with the unshaken basis and innermost impulse of all true religion, so the latter depended in its purer continuance and its progress upon the former as its motive-fire ever impelling onward, and at the same time as its necessary and radiant light. Nay, it may be truly said, if revelation or the oracle is in question, the faith of man is also above all in question, whether, for example, he will believe or not in this or that word, this or that thought, as giving him counsel and strength in the needs and doubts or temptations of his life; or whether, if he cannot directly find such higher word or such thought, he will believe in this or that means of finding them. For such thought, whether consisting in a longer or shorter series of clear or obscure words, will always be that higher power he seeks, and from which he expects at the moment his salvation. If the question were therefore essentially of the movement and direction of faith, it was also at the same time concerning the movement and tendency of the deepest needs of the seeking and struggling human spirit, and of its corresponding energy which stands in the centre between the impulse to seek new light and help, and the light already given and the means of seeking further light. But if, now, since the time of Moses faith was in this community to be placed wholly and uninterruptedly upon God alone, and the spirit in the new needs and despondencies of life, struggling for new light, was to find again by further care and toil only in Him all light not yet revealed by Him, in this was given the possibility of always rejecting both the perverse seeking of oracles and the fruits of it. And the basis of the true religion, as it lived in this community through the institution of Moses, was so sure and firm, and the treasure of radiant eternal truth so highly valued, that all perverse means and supports of faith were at the right time always rejected; and accordingly revelation itself in its inner impulse and essence, and in its fruits, became gradually from stage to stage riper and more perfect, till the highest development was reached possible in antiquity, and the profound yearning after an ultimately completed revelation in some measure met.

In such a manner, indeed, may this development as a whole be conceived, incomparably wonderful as it was in the whole of antiquity. But what an immense multiplicity and diversity of hindrances of perverse enterprise and endeavour presented themselves in the course of more than a millennium and a half which must elapse in this community before they were all fully known in their perversity, and strenuously avoided! In what did not man fondly believe in order to find for himself, if he could, the confidence and salvation of faith! And to leave nothing of the kind untried seemed to be the lot of this community, because by dint of its own irrefragable foundations it had to do apparently the most difficult thing which man ever learns, and so often would fain not learn, viz. always and only from the true God alone to seek and expect the true light and salvation of all human life.

§ 62. This whole incomparably great and eternally significant transaction which was here accomplished, we can most briefly explain by the antithesis a name offers whose proper meaning it is now necessary to fix. That name is "Heathenism," or as it runs still more vividly and originally in the Bible, "the nations," that is, the nations in general, in opposition to this one nation which, as the nation of the true religion, separated itself from them in the course of centuries more and more sharply and definitely. Only by the nature of its religion and its oracles, different from all that had hitherto arisen among men, was this one nation strongly and perceptibly distinguished from all others from the beginning; but the distinction was in its essence so necessary and grave, that it gradually became a solid partition-wall which never seemed capable of being broken through again. In the earliest ages, when this nation had first to win for itself a firm position among all other nations of the earth, this opposition, showing itself rather in sharp warlike expedients and old national badges,[1] becomes more and more a purely spiritual one, and thus has the deeper hold, and is for all time, as it were, unconquerable. Accordingly the distinction appeared in the language, at first gradually, but at length with greater firmness and graver significance. That this nation early felt itself sharply and incisively separated from "all the nations," or more briefly, from "the nations," is intelligible enough, and living as it did in Palestine in a restless tumult of nations, it learned to look upon its neighbours, and soon upon all the

---

[1] Cf. *History*, ii. p. 219 f. [Eng. trans. ii. p. 154 f.], and *Antiquities*, p. 102 ff., 118 ff. [Eng. trans. p. 76 ff., 89 ff.]; cf. with what subsequently was to enter as an open badge as if in the place of circumcision, p. 307 [Eng. trans. p. 231].

rest of mankind, as "the nations;" and to designate them chose a word somewhat rare and foreign,[1] using it ultimately in this sense as a short and standing expression.[2] A similar distinction obtained in Hellenistic Greek[3] when Israel, widely diffused amongst the nations, felt its distinction from them the more deeply. So arose the conception now expressed in the words "heathen" and "heathenism."

It was not, however, the bare national distinction that raised this barrier between Israel and the rest of the world; there was a spiritual significance connected with it from the beginning, and this grew in process of time into fuller meaning. At the same time the spiritual significance, in so far as Israel formed itself into a community of the true God, overleaped all national limits so constantly that even from the first foreigners could enter;[4] and as foreigners were never altogether wanting in it during the long succeeding revolutions of its history,[5] this community passed over into all nations ultimately, under Christ and His disciples, without being in any way hampered by national restrictions. Nationality played its part, but never alone, rather only as conditioned by the nature of the development in the higher antiquity of all true revelation and religion (p. 193), and it vanished, as at last in actual fact, so already very early in the desire and longing of the best prophets of this community.[6] If, then, the distinc-

---

[1] גוֹי, גוֹיִם in the ancient Hebrew are rarer and more poetic than עַם, עַמִּים; somewhat like our "nation," in opposition to "volk."

[2] In the old portion, Lev. xviii. 24, הַגּוֹיִם are not yet briefly and simply the foreign nations; but already in the Book of Origins the short expression occurs, Gen. x. 5, 32; in Balaam's speech, however, the opposition is sharpest, Num. xxiii. 9. As the word in common speech became more and more a proper name for the foreign nations, it could lose in the higher discourse the article; yet גוֹיִם without the article is rare in Isaiah's time, and not frequent until afterwards.

[3] ἔθνος, not δῆμος; τὰ ἔθνη. Such short words as ἐθνικῶς, Gal. ii. 14, and ἐθνικός, Matt. vi. 7, xviii. 17 (from the hand of the last editor), do not occur in the Old Testament.

[4] Cf. History, ii. p. 118 [Eng. trans. ii. p. 82].

[5] Cf. History, iii. p. 195 [Eng. trans. iii. p. 144], iv. p. 457 ff., 517 f. [Eng. trans. v. p. 350 f., 396 f.], vi. p. 531 ff.; and Antiquities, p. 316 f. [Eng. trans. p. 237 f.].

[6] This was a great and indeed the finest part of the Messianic hopes, from the

tion between heathenism and the true religion has the all-penetrating significance it unquestionably has, this significance must lie elsewhere than in the sphere of nationality; and at this point of our discussion we perceive the distinction most palpably. True heathenism exists everywhere where revelation and religion, once won, and whether in a high or low condition of cultivation, fall back and deteriorate, and cannot find again the path by which they may be led out and beyond the increasing power of error and decay. The characteristic mark of true religion and revelation, as of their impelling fire and clear light, is that at the right moment and by the original truth already surely won, they always find again the way that leads out beyond every new darkness and confusion obstructing and hindering their progress. Heathenism, on the contrary, is enervation and torpidity upon this way; and as there is always movement in the world, a declension upon it further and further, even to death itself, may follow. But since revelation is the innermost and most essentially potent impulse to remove every obstacle checking its progress and to increase the clear light already won, it is evident that heathenism arises most immediately and multiplies its power most perniciously just where the living energy of revelation is becoming paralysed and its light is on the point of going out.

The more important the great opposition between heathenism, in its innumerable forms, and the true religion is,—the latter becoming ultimately the perfect true religion,—the more indispensable is it to have exact ideas of both, and of their relations the one to the other. Nothing would be so perverse as to place the distinction in something merely accidental. To suppose, as is often done, that it lies only in this, that heathenism accepts the principle of polytheism, the true

old portions of Joel in Isa. ii. 2-4, Micah iv. 1-4, to the latest times; also peculiarly in Zech. xiv. 16-19, but most copiously and beautifully in Isaiah himself, chap. xix. Nowhere can we see how the fulfilment corresponds to the prophecy so definitely and clearly as here.

religion that of monotheism, is not sufficiently determinate, since every heathen nation has ever sought to think of and hold fast in its faith one God as its supreme deity; and, on the other hand, in the circle of true religion, a plurality with respect to the divine subsistence at least is admitted, and only Islamism has suffered the doctrine of the divine unity to become petrified through exaggeration. But this distinction is also wholly insufficient in itself, since it extends to one only—an important one, certainly—of the many pure truths upon which in religion everything depends. Heathenism has, however, a general significance, affecting all the great truths religion involves, as well as its moral principles and its human home, the community; in short, heathenism is religion that has made a substantial beginning but is arrested in its free development and progress to perfection, and so has become retrograde; and it is less in its commencement, or in its course up to a certain stage, than in its lacking direct and proper onward advancement to the real ultimate goal, that it is seen to be the contrary of all true religion, much more of true religion in its perfect consummation.

It is not denied, therefore, that heathenism may have its better elements. Historically it arises from the same common source as true religion; and side by side with its superadded error there is in it what it is difficult wholly to suppress, the originally direct aspiration of every human spirit. The first beginnings of all revelation and religion as they appear in all human history (§ 13 ff.), and as without them history is not to be thought of, are also the beginnings and original impulses of all heathenism, and so the very mainspring of its existence and of its otherwise inexplicable continuance before our eyes to-day. All heathenism has also its gods and its revelations, and whether they are more or less living and true, whether they are reminiscences from the primitive age and obscurely inherited traditions or not, is at this point matter of no concern. But it has also its flowers of Vedic songs, sprung from the bright childhood of the world; its Homeric poesy, charming and simple in its art, yet with all its exuberant life unhealthy in its sensuousness; its Egyptian priest-religion, sternly severe, and menacing with the dark shadows of death and the rigours of eternal judgment; its community-founding Zoroastrianism and Buddhism, struggling painfully and self-sacrificingly with the problem of extirpating the infirmities and ills of human life; its lofty Chinese State-wisdom; and, finally, its manifold attempts, through the doctrines and morals of schools of deeper reflection and inquiry, to supply what the old and worn-out ways of revelation and religion would no longer afford. Moreover, in those nations where it flourished in connection with a happily-thriving high culture, heathenism had attained by such means so conspicuous a development of the powers of conscience and reason, powers original to the human spirit (§ 14, 2), therefore God-given, but capable only historically of manifold growth and discipline, that the apostle, who had these nations constantly under his eyes, could appeal to this active twofold power of their mind as a witness in themselves against their own deeply-seated moral corruption.[1] Thus heathenism and true religion flow at first from the same source, and resemble, so far, two streams which, taking their rise from one spring, flow together undivided a longer or shorter distance, but subsequently parting at this or that rock, one diverges into side streams which, following different courses, run on a longer or shorter time, some of them with much grandeur and magnificence, but all at last alike losing themselves in the sand, while the other goes pouring on in its straight direct course, is never again completely broken or divided, and grows mightier and mightier as it flows.

§ 63. For it is certain, furthermore, that everywhere where in antiquity in the special development of each nation, heathenism, in order to strike out upon its side-ways, broke loose sooner or later from the more innocent and oldest kind

---

[1] A union of the two powers of conscience and reason is implied in Rom. i. 19 f., although their names are not given.

of simple revelation and religion, it formed itself in the highest degree differently, since just caprice gaining ground with power determined its nature; nay, it must shape itself more and more differently, the less it was able thoroughly to overcome the thousand hindrances opposing the direct perfecting of all revelation and religion. It may still be recognised with sufficient certainty that all the Semitic nations in that primitive time, when they had not yet separated from each other as they did afterwards, possessed in common a simpler religion, the visible remains of which may still be met with in them all; but after their separation how utterly diverse was the development of the religion of the Aramæans, the Phœnicians, and the Arabians![1] Similarly with respect to all the nations of the midland family of languages, at length spreading much more widely and freely than those of the Semitic, it can still upon closer investigation be clearly seen how in their earliest age they were held together in their original seats by a common simpler religion, whose traces, after their separation further and further from each other, could never be fully effaced. But among the western portion how differently did the religion of the Greeks shape itself from that of the old Italians and Romans, and from both of these that of the Germans and the Celts! whilst in the eastern portion, among Persians and Hindoos, though religion for a longer time was fashioned in common after a peculiar type, it finally fell asunder into very different forms quite distinct in type, and more and more irreconcilable with each other. But what is so observable, according to authentic and manifold testimonies of antiquity, in these powerful and for all the higher culture representative families of nations, occurred unquestionably everywhere else, and has continued till to-day in an increasing degree in Africa, Australia, and

---

[1] I have shown this in many ways, in the *Antiquities*, in the *Dissertations concerning Sanchoniathon and other Phœnicians*, in the *Gött. Gel. Anz.*, and elsewhere. A summary of Renan's errors is given in the *Jahrb. der B. Wiss.* x. p. 283 f.

America, so far as heathenism in such lands is at present an actual potency of life.[1]

Still further, the various forms of heathenism, developed to the utmost by means of art or science or any honest effort, even should they seek ever so assiduously, and for a long time perhaps ever so brilliantly, powerfully to strengthen themselves by such aids, are never able to reach the goal of genuine perfection and unbroken continuance. Looking at the infinite diversities which appear in the historic course of heathenism, it is observed that in many nations attaining early a high culture or aim of life, the pure original energies of all revelation are just as early overtopped and overgrown by other energies and activities of the human mind, not less noble perhaps, but still heterogeneous. For example, among the Egyptians and many Semitic nations, and then more especially among their later scholars the Greeks, they were completely surpassed and thrown into the shade by the wonderful efforts and splendid works of art and science, among the Romans by the single and powerfully-cherished ambition to conquer and rule all nations far and near. Since, however, the needs of religion and of revelation lying behind it were irrepressible, even in the midst of the eagerness to follow wholly other impulses, the endeavour was made to satisfy such needs by closely connecting these impulses with them. The nations that specially cultivated art and science, by art sought to glorify their gods, by science to investigate their nature more profoundly, and so give to them a more vivid existence, while the Romans thought they should renew revelation and religion sufficiently if they introduced from foreign sources the oracles and faiths that were most famous. But how little could the consummation of the energies and truths of revelation and religion, thus blindly sought, be reached by such intermingling of the most different objects

---

[1] The Fetisch is the last outcome of this, *i.e.* any visible thing you please which any man accepts as his god, to-day in this way, to-morrow in that; cf A. Bastian's *Besuch in San Salvador*. Bremen 1859.

of human aspiration! Wholly different phenomena present themselves among heathen nations within which, after a higher culture had been acquired, the original energies of all revelation and religion nevertheless remained active, put forth new, peculiar, and powerful efforts, and so created new forms, some of which had the most wonderful consequences and a long existence. This was early the case with the Egyptians, so far as we now can judge;[1] but it is seen most clearly and is of longest duration among the ancient Hindoos and Persians; and Buddhism, by a genuinely creative transformation of the old Brahminism, in accomplishing which it was inspired by some of the purest impulses of all revelation and religion, has won that high significance and capacity of life which, in the remotest lands of Eastern Asia, still characterize it to-day. Only here, indeed, do we see the noblest development, the most commanding power and persistent duration of which heathenism is capable. Moreover, thus is explained how it is that precisely these most flourishing forms of heathenism show the greatest similarity to true religion, and are most easily, though superficially, mixed up and confounded with it;[2] and still further how it is that just with them the true revelation and religion has had the severest and most obstinate encounters. The conflict of Moses and Aaron with the Egyptian priests and magicians (p. 87 f.) is the eternal type of all such struggles. But, however far isolated sections of heathenism may carry their development, they are never able to reach the true goal of all revelation. The history of nearly two thousand years, with all its costly and painful experiences since the establishment of Christianity, enables us to maintain this with more simple definiteness and universality than is found in the brief assertion or prophetic anticipation of Scripture.

Thus, then, heathenism is the potency of all error and misguidance that stand in the way of the direct progress and

[1] Cf. *History*, ii. p. 56 f. [Eng. trans. ii. p. 39 f.].
[2] As in earlier times Manichæism with Christianity, in the Middle Ages and later Buddhism with Popery.

perfect consummation of true revelation and religion. In point of time it is the first, in point of extent and force the most pernicious and powerful of all errors; revelation and religion may indeed have an incomparably wider and more permanent influence, but not till first of all these hidden and secret toils have been escaped. All error is infinitely diversified in contents and changing in form, and this most potent and pernicious of errors, in all its possible ramifications and combinations, is not to be evaded or anticipated; whilst here, as everywhere, truth is one and unchanging, and its progress resembles a straight line and course. The direct and complete antithesis of true revelation and religion, and their onward progress, heathenism thus interposes with manifold and mischievous effects before the goal is reached, and may afterwards penetrate again and again by new efforts of greater or less significance into the wider circle, as did, for example, mistaken Islamism, or into the narrower circle, as Popery has done. But it is the divine destiny of all human error to serve only as a palpable contrast and antithesis to truth, and of truth to recover itself from the toils of error and disclose its real nature; and thus the true revelation in its first conscious and clear beginnings extricated itself from the hidden snare, in its further and greater advances struggled forth from amidst entanglements of increasing difficulty, till at last it reached its ultimate and highest goal, and now stands there the bright, clear mirror that shows in their true feature and image all forms of error, whether descended from antiquity or newly arisen.

As, therefore, the community of Israel, sprung forth under Moses in sharpest conflict with heathenism, and appointed by its very origin to the continuance of this inevitable and direct conflict, was the community within whose firm walls this conflict actually reached at last its ultimate goal; so the Bible shows us as a whole and in detail the history of this conflict in all its different aspects and stages up to the highest victory which could be won in this community, and then the gradual breaking down of these walls, now become too narrow, that the whole wide world of men might share the struggle. This conflict with heathenism—for the first time and so in the severest form in human history, begun on all sides with deep earnestness and the assembling of the human forces of a smaller circle, continued with yet deeper earnestness and more powerful concentration of all forces as every new inroad of frailties and discomfitures furnished the occasion, and finally perfectly victorious after the direst distresses and perils—is the chief phenomenon and indeed the summary of the whole history of this community; and that it was fought out within the firm stability of its walls, and could only be fought out within them, is its highest glory. Moreover, as the nation of this community in its difficult and long course gradually came into closer and closer connection with the most different nations of the antiquity that lies nearer and is better known to us, so also the passages of the Bible which incidentally or at large discourse immediately of heathenism, are very different in character. In the oldest portions of the Bible, the peculiarity of heathenism as it affects individual nations, Egyptians, Canaanites (Phœnicians), and others lying around and in part akin to Israel, is rather referred to, and as the occasion offers somewhat particularly indicated; and the more vivid the reference in the writing, the older that reference is.[1] But after Israel, from the eighth century before Christ, was flung out in great numbers into the wide world of nations, and its conflict with heathenism must be carried on in a far more complicated and severe and wholly new form, then the first attempts are made to deal consecutively and exhaustively with the nature of every kind of heathenism on earth without exception, and to portray it in living colours and sustained descriptive pictures.[2] What a change! In the earliest

[1] The oldest laws in the form in which we find them in Lev. xviii., xix. show this; and the very peculiar passage, Ex. xxiii. 20-33.
[2] In Deut., Nah. i.-iii., Jer. x., and then still more in many longer passages,

times this nation in deep and perilous tumult of life, and in quest of a fixed abode on earth, had fought with heathenism; but afterwards for long centuries had found its joy in calm, secure, peaceful dwelling in the beautiful fatherland, and had accustomed itself to this as the sweetest happiness of life; and now pitilessly thrust forth amongst far-removed and mostly ruder nations, it was to maintain even among them its peculiar revelation; nay, as it no longer possessed weapons of war, to seek peacefully to draw them over to itself! And this, too, was only the prelude to the dispersion in the Greek period when Israel must learn to know heathenism more intimately from a wholly different side, and when the picturings of its seductive art accumulate in the Bible in wholly new form.[1] In the New Testament, on the other hand, the inner strife in the community is renewed once more, and now as never before; and yet the New Testament, too, closes nevertheless in the Apocalypse with just this opposition to heathenism and, as not before depicted, the unfulfilled profoundest opposition in its extremest power and most frightful violence. So true it is, that according to the entire Bible, the all-pervading, all-penetrating conflict is simply that between the true revelation with its community and heathenism.

We must, however, now all this,

2. *In Special Detail,*

§ 64. More particularly consider, since only such more exact consideration of all the details can give us an adequate image of the whole; and it is the more necessary since the direct progressive impetus of all revelation, becoming more and more powerful and at length wholly perfect, has con-

---

Isa. xiii. f., xl.–lxvi., Jer. l. f., and in the piece Bar. iii. 9 ff.; also Ps. cxv. and the Psalter of Solomon.

[1] Daniel, the Greek Jeremiah (*Proph. des A. B.'s*, iii. p. 382 ff.), Book of Wisdom (cf. *History,* iv. p. 626 ff. [Eng. trans. v. p. 479 ff.]), the Books of the Maccabees, and the like.

tinued its development only by its opposite, and therefore cannot be understood in its progress without it. For from the beginning of the creation God placed man upon the earth, it is true, with this purpose and destiny;—to acquiesce in His will more and more perfectly and obey it, that is, to learn from the midst of the universe the will and so more plainly the voice and words of Him who does not discourse to the senses, and to behold the whole being of Him who is not perceived by the senses; but He left to man to put forth the necessary effort, and find and employ the right means to this end, as might be requisite in the gradual progress of his inquiry and task. Such means, therefore, if they answer their end, are upon each of the many stages pure and innocent, until some stage is reached upon which their insufficiency to advance the necessary further progress of revelation is clearly proved, and a better and more adequate way has been found. Now every means to an end is in the hands of men by mere repetition and imitation readily impaired and becomes duller and less effective than it was originally; but if merely from custom and indolence it is firmly retained when already a better exists, the insinuating error that claims to be right in its methods becomes more serious and obstinate continually; and all kinds of low cunning and artifice are then the more readily connected with the growing perversion. This is the nature of the perversion which shows itself in the course of this highest spiritual effort of all antiquity; whilst in the midst of this course only in the nation of Israel was a community established which from the time of its sound and better beginning of things was destined to withstand all deterioration in revelation already influential, and subsequently to become influential in the community. Not till then does there occur, therefore, a more concise, definite, and continuous development of this great incident; and as we depict its stages in detail according to history, we shall at the same time be able to survey with more luminous glance the infinite particulars the consideration of which now opens upon us.

It is not necessary, however, to describe all heathenism as it unfolded itself in its endless diversity in antiquity, and as it may be seen to-day in the best and highest form possible to its peculiar spirit in the lands of Eastern Asia with their ancient culture. Sufficient for our aim will it be to consider particularly the various types of heathen thought and feeling in the search after revelation as the Bible presents them; and indeed the subject itself requires no more. For not only did this whole singularly earnest and consistent conflict of genuine revelation with all its opposites start from an earthly surrounding in which heathenism had attained among the Egyptians and Canaanites the highest, finest, and most varied development possible to it at that time, but it was also continued in the bosom of the community itself still more earnestly and extensively, until the consummation was reached. And so there is no species of heathen feeling and thought which at least in its drift and tendency is not mentioned in the Bible either incidentally and by insinuation or more definitely and at large. The impulse itself which in heathenism and in the sanctuary of the community of the true revelation is alike the spring and source of all activity, we may briefly designate "faith" (p. 198 f.); but how the heathen form of it, which may be designated "superstition," lays hold of ever new and subtler and seemingly more divine expedients in the whole course of this long development, may be best seen under the three great decisive periods which divide the whole history of the community wherein everything is perfected. These three great periods of change we must take, however, rather in accordance with the underlying characteristic of each of them than with respect to external limitation.

In the first period, the primary means of drawing forth revelation or communicating its contents to others to which faith turned were just those chiefly which since primitive times had become increasingly powerful almost equally among all nations, and with the more cultured were in a high degree of artificial development. They take their rise amid the simplest conditions of all human civilisation, and lead us back to the guileless innocence and childlike trust of the earliest ages of all nations. They were resorted to, therefore, in the days of the patriarchs up to the time of Moses in all the natural ingenuousness but broad manifoldness and diversity peculiar to that primitive era; and indeed Moses' revelation had to fight earnestly against them from the beginning, just because they were so steadily practised in those remote early times, so deeply rooted in the life and conviction of the nations, and so prevalent almost everywhere with the like fascinating power, although in very varied development. Even after Moses some apparently less pernicious, and one may say more innocent, usages were retained, on account of their ancient sanctity, a longer or shorter time in the customs of the community; and the entire atmosphere these world-old practices and conceptions breathed, pervaded the regions where the true revelation gradually grew to perfection, and to such an extent that without the recognition of it many passages of the Bible cannot be understood.[1] Moreover, in themselves and apart from the seductive art with which their votaries have loved to clothe them, they are all so congruous to common human thinking, that not merely did they seek to penetrate more and more into this old community of the true revelation, and in times favourable to them often became extremely dangerous, but so far as their inmost essence is concerned, they are in our days still in existence everywhere, spontaneously or of set purpose, even where it might scarcely be expected.

In number, these and the more artificial kinds of superstitious usage following later, are, if the whole length and breadth of their development is traversed, incalculable. Since, however, the conflict in this community after the days of Moses was in principle at least directed against them all without

[1] Where, for example, as in Job, Gen. xv., or with respect to Balaam, Num. xxii.–xxiv., the higher antiquity is artistically depicted.

exception,[1] whilst they sought ever again in continually new and manifoldly seductive art to force their way in, it is not to the older laws of the community,[2] but to Deuteronomy that we look for a brief, round enumeration of the worst kinds of them in its time.[3] For the satisfactory understanding of all the different kinds mentioned in Deuteronomy and elsewhere in the Old Testament is involved in difficulty, partly because most of them are only briefly and abruptly mentioned, partly because the designations of them come from the oldest Semitic nations, and many such usages first found their way into Israel from the Phœnicians, Syrians, and other alien Semites. Great caution therefore is needed in speaking about them particularly.[4] If we look, however, at their significance as expedients to obtain revelation, and at the same time at the great historical development of all human impulses that in this matter are active, we may very well distinguish them according to the three following tendencies:—

[1] It is undeniable that the better men in the time of the patriarchs and their kinsfolk opposed them; this, indeed, is presupposed in the narratives of Genesis and by the poet of Job, who was well versed in history (esp. xxxi. 26 f.). But the more general and earnest conflict against them did not begin conspicuously until the days of Moses.

[2] These describe superstitious usages generally as in the Ten Commandments, Ex. xx. 4 f., and in the oldest explanations of Lev. xxvi. 1 f., or forbid specially dangerous species of them, as Lev. xix. 31, Ex. xx. 7; thus also may the oldest documents be recognised.

[3] Deut. xviii. 10 f. Enumerations in the round number 7 are preferred by the Deuteronomist; cf. *Hist.* i. p. 342 [i. p. 238]; here 9 are given together. The early estimation of this passage is seen from its imitation, 2 Chron. xxxiii. 6; for that it is an imitation is apparent by comparison with 2 Kings xvi. 3 f.

[4] To understand the obscurer names in this chief passage, it is well to observe that the series is not accidental, for (1) the Moloch oracle is placed first because at the time (2 Kings xvi. 3) it occupied special attention, as follows from Deut. xii. 31 also; (2) from קֶסֶם to וּמְנַחֵשׁ three kinds of oracle by omens are given; (3) two connected with sorcery succeed (here the existing division of the verses is at fault); (4) three resulting from artificial questioning conclude, so that necromancy is the last. The two that were regarded as most mischievous close the long series (2 Kings xvi. 3; Isa. viii. 19), whilst those in the middle fall into groups according to their likeness to each other. The actual life of such prophets of superstition is depicted nowhere so copiously and with such graphic irony as with respect to Balaam, Num. xxii.-xxiv. Elsewhere, apart from various Eastern writings, see especially Æschylus, *Prom.* 483-499; Porphyry's chief works; Just. *Apol.* i. ch. 18; Tatian *to the Greeks*, ch. 33; Origen *against Celsus*, 7, 1.

§ 65. FROM THE FIRST PERIOD.—1. One of the first and deepest impressions upon the spirit of man would be made by *the place itself* where once, as if unawares, a divine voice, or a heavenly vision, or some unexpected divine help had touched and strengthened it. This is the simplest and most innocent way in which a special place could become sacred. Ever again the desire would be to return to such place in the hope that some new voice and help from God might be received, because once known and experienced there. So the whole record of the life of the patriarchs in the Holy Land is full of such reminiscences.[1] Yet, innocent as this belief is in its beginnings, other anticipations and thoughts that are more from the very midst of the life of the higher revelation indicate early enough how little a man's being touched by divine words and influences depended upon mere place, whether the beloved and hallowed native land or any special locality in the patriarch's world.[2]

But the belief that signs and voices from the Deity may be received better in one place than another was once deeply rooted, and all kinds of efforts were made in harmony with it. The high places of the earth, especially some peaks of mountains sought out with special skill, seemed to bring man nearer to the God of heaven, and to facilitate the survey of human destinies on the plains below; but, according to the Old Testament, it is only a diviner like Balaam who purposely selects such places.[3] On the other hand, no places seemed to be able to send forth as if from the mysterious depths of the dark earth such earnest, solemnly-warning, divine sounds as certain caves and chasms; but whilst such places were more and more misused by superstition chiefly amongst necromancers, the oldest law of the Old Testament warns against all oracles of the dead.[4] If also deeply rushing subterranean water

---

[1] *History*, i. p. 434 f. [Eng. trans. i. p. 302 f.].
[2] For that is the real meaning of such narratives as Gen. xxviii. 11-22, xxxi. 3, xvi. 7-14, and similar ones.
[3] Num. xxii. 41, xxiii. 14, 28.   [4] Lev. xix. 31.

could be heard in such positions, there would readily be associated with the dreadfulness of the place the primitive feeling of a certain life of the water and awe of its sanctity, which among the ancient Persians and Indians expressed itself so strongly in reverence for springs and rivers ; and the awe thus occasioned led to the Sibyl-oracle, which, according to all traces, was artificially practised at an early period in anterior Asia and Syria, though accidentally it is not anywhere mentioned in the Bible. Throughout we see here a feeling of awe, originally harmless enough, obscured early in its childlike innocence, and misused as an artificial oracle, whilst nothing bears less all artificial change and formal repetition than the impulse of genuine revelation, and the Sibyl-words so extremely celebrated at length through the gross superstition of the Romans acquired a more enduring fame by their complete transformation in the spirit of Hellenistic and Christian poets.[1] Or if hot springs and vapours issuing from deep caverns seemed in an unusual way to transport into inspiration by restlessness and heat men who sat above, and to carry them out of themselves into a divine ecstasy, it would appear that there was the best place for divination. To this also by accident there is no reference in the Bible.

It is true that after Moses, in the course of the earliest centuries of the founding of the community of Israel, the sacred ark of the covenant became gradually regarded as a sacred instrument near which it seemed possible that the voice of God to this community should be again and again expressed distinctly and without interruption ; indeed, the traces of this belief are strongly impressed upon some passages of the Old Testament. But the early destruction of Shiloh,[2] and the admission still early enough into the innermost sanctuary of

---

[1] Cf. the Dissert. concerning the origin, contents, and value of the Sibylline Books, Gött. 1858. The name Σιβυλλα, which the Greeks could only interpret as Διὸς βουλή, appears to me to be derived from שִׁבֹּלֶת, "stream." For if the Æolians say Σιός, yet the abbreviation to Σι has still to be established. The שִׁבֹּלֶת is, however, more Aramaic than Hebraistic.

[2] Cf. *History*, ii. p. 582 ff. [Eng. trans. ii. p. 413 ff.].

Solomon's temple of this holy relic, inherited from the grand days of the founding of the community, and since too much reverenced, checked for the present any possible germ of superstition beginning to show itself; so that the transfigured remembrance of it, taken up into the circle of Messianic hopes, held at length an honourable place. The temple itself, however, with its restoration by Zerubbabel and Herod, especially since the thousandfold glory of heart-stirring song and inspired prophetic hope made it illustrious, seemed, in the last century before its first destruction, and again in the last before the second destruction, to win anew a sanctity which might have become a hindrance to the free perfecting of all true religion and of genuine revelation as well;[1] but before the overthrow of the first and second temple the best oracles always sent forth earnest warning against the indulgence of such superstitious reverence.[2]

§ 66. 2. But the charm of flowing and rushing waters, in those lands especially great, forms an easy transition to another series of such primitive fascinations for the human mind. Vegetation has an inner strange life, and much about it surprises and captivates the attention of simply reflective but keenly discerning men, especially in the case of particular kinds of it, and pre-eminently trees, tall, or apparently ever-living, or rare trees, such as terebinths, oaks, cypresses, balsams, and the like.[3] Their tardy or rapid, their ordinary or extraordinary putting forth of bud, leaf, and blossom, seems to indicate something wonderful; and some usages of a varied kind arising from this belief long maintained their existence in Israel.[4] But it was principally the agitation and whispering of the tender leaves on the top of the trees in which, as

---

[1] *History*, iii. p. 795 [Eng. trans. iv. p. 265 f.], vi. p. 678 ff.

[2] As in the Old Testament strongly, Jer. vii. f.; in the New, Christ Himself, Matt. xxiii. 37 f., xxiv. f.; John iv. 21.

[3] δρῦς μαντευομένη in Tatian *to the Greeks*, xxi. xxxiii.; concerning the balsam plant, see 2 Sam. v. 23 f.

[4] As is clear from Num. xvii. 16-24 [Eng. ver. 1-10]; cf. *Antiq.* p. 344 [Eng. trans. p. 259 f.].

in other sudden, strange rustlings and seeming voices, signs of the Deity approaching and making Himself audible were found,—a divine speech whose meaning the soothsayers professed to be able to decipher.[1] This is a kind of soothsaying that was apparently much in favour among the oldest ancestors of the people of Israel,[2] and was retained as it were involuntarily long after Moses, sometimes, indeed, being put upon a level with the existing oracle of Jahveh.[2] And if ancient Israel could with difficulty wean itself from the belief in the sanctity of certain trees, because the entire old world was full of it,[3] the employment of such trees in prognostication and soothsaying in the primitive age certainly formed the main cause of the difficulty.

Whilst now all this practicable effort to obtain divine oracles from visible things by careful listening, and to publish them to others, was continued with the highest diligence when once begun, different kinds of *audible oracle* were further cultivated—a special oracle to which in the metaphors of genuine prophets very graphic allusion is made.[4] To these various kinds of audible oracle there were soon added as counterparts several very diverse *oracles of vision*. Strange occurrences suddenly and unaccountably taking place were

---

[1] The עוֹנֵן, according to all indications, means divining by means of mysterious sounds; the old expression אֵלוֹן מְעוֹנְנִים, Jud. ix. 37, is thus explained, "Terebinth of whisperers," *i.e.* of those who hear and interpret the whispering as the name of the place; cf. 2 Sam. v. 23, 24, and the order in Deut. xviii. 10. This art of the עוֹנֵן is one of the oldest and simplest in this nation; and the word is frequently employed. It is derived from the Arabic and Syriac, not from עֲנָנָה, "cloud;" in the circle of the old omens is no inspection of the clouds. The Greek exactly corresponds, κληδονίζεσθαι, from κληδών, *i.e.* φήμη; the LXX. actually render עוֹנֵן in Deut. xviii. 10, 14 by κληδονίζεσθαι, and so elsewhere. The *omen* in Latin arose perhaps from *audmen* = "signs heard in the air," as *augurium* is the "hearing," and *auspicium* the "beholding" of birds.

[2] In that passage, 2 Sam. v. 23 f. The LXX. little understood the words, although the translation συσσεισμοῦ (to be read instead of συγκλεισμοῦ) for צְעָדָה contains an anticipation of the right meaning.

[3] *History*, iii. p. 199 f. [Eng. trans. iii. p. 146 f.], vii. p. 534; *Antiquities*, p. 160, 439 f. [Eng. trans. p. 120, 331 f.].

[4] Such vivid picturing as Hab. ii. 1, Isa. xx. 7, is specially to be regarded.

supposed to give, in the first sight of them, divine tokens affording counsel and suggesting decisions for difficult situations of life. Nothing of this sort so obviously presents itself as watching the flight of birds; the bird comes out of the heights of heaven as if to betray heavenly secrets, and from the nature or direction of their flight, as well as from the diversity of the birds themselves, signs and indications of the divine mind were sought. That this observance of birds was one of the oldest expedients for obtaining oracles, and was widely diffused among all nations, is shown by the usage of words found alike in the most different families of language.[1] And just as readily intelligible is it to us now that the notes or cries of certain birds at unusual times and on special occasions were regarded as giving divine prognostications and warnings.[2] It cannot be doubted, too, that in Israel from ancient times such customs prevailed,[3] many relics of which were preserved long after the time of Moses, although only in reminiscence and speech. When, however, the oracles of vision were in this way in high favour, there was no reason why diviners should be always content with watching the flight of birds or similar rare phenomena, an expedient tedious in itself and often tardy in its results. Balaam is fetched

---

[1] Among the Arabians "bird" signifies "destiny," "fate," although it is not the oldest Semitic word for this idea, Sur. xvi. 14; and long before Mahomet, Porphyry, *Concerning Abstinence*, iii. 3 f., 5, iv. 9 f. (326–328), spoke of the divining birds; so also Cicero, *de divin.* i, 2, 92, of the *aves* of Asia Minor and Arabia. The same usage is found in Æthiopic. The almost lost old Semitic עוֹף in this signification reappears in Arabic compounds, Hamasa, p. 121, 127.

[2] Thus *augurium*, spoken of notes, is manifestly distinguished from *auspicium*.

[3] Since עוֹף, "bird," nowhere bears the superstitious sense, it appears doubtful whether among the ancient Hebrews reverence for birds was known. But the doubt is removed by Gen. xv. 11 (*History*, i. 473 [Eng. trans. i. p. 330]). נָחַשׁ was apparently the primitive word for augury. The Syriac corresponds, and the root is found in Arabic in the signification of "to inquire," and with a bad sense, "misfortune." To this agree Num. xxiii. 3, xxiv. 1; the verb נִחֵשׁ, *augurari, ominari*, "to forebode;" the LXX. translation of מְנַחֵשׁ by οἰωνιζόμενος, Deut. xviii. 10, and of נְחָשִׁים by οἰωνοί, Num. xxiv. 1, cf. xxiii. 23. But it cannot be proved that נַחַשׁ itself ever means "bird;" the root suggests only "to inquire after." See below.

from afar by a prince, and seeks in the open air the right place for obtaining an oracle, and looking out with special care for omens lights upon them at last, as the Bible recalling ancient times relates with fine irony and in agreeable fulness;[1] ought all princes or even prophets always to take such pains in seeking divine counsel and decision? Thus there came into use early a substitute for this looking out for divine hints and tokens that could more readily be employed. Reliance was placed upon an image of the god most loved, the eye was fixed upon it during petitions and prayers, and it was thought perchance a favourable answer might be read as the eyes of the image moistened. This is the deeply-cherished reverence for the Penates amongst the ancestors of the nation of Israel from which many families and branches of the people could in many later centuries only with difficulty be weaned, and which ought after the time of Moses to have been rejected by the whole community. The best prophets ultimately complain bitterly of the questioning of staff and stock.[2] Or a sacred luminous ornament of precious stones or an actual mirror was taken, fastened to some part of the body upon which the eye could rest intently, and moreover the consecrated medallion was watched in the solemn hour, in ceremonial robes, that during prayer an oracle might be found in it; which in particular cases through the powerful efficacy of art could be made to assume very different aspects.[3] Or with greater facility a costly cup of hallowed

---

[1] Num. xxii. 41, xxiii. 4, xxiii. 14–16, xxiii. 28, xxiv. 1; cf. *Jahrb. der Bibl. Wiss.* x. p. 46 ff., 178.

[2] Hosea iv. 12, cf. iii. 4, with *Antiquities*, p. 296 ff. [Eng. trans. p. 223 ff.].

[3] According to the list in Deut. xviii. 10, and the description Ezek. xiii. 17–23, it is probable that the קֶסֶם was a decision, *i.e.* an oracle which was won in such method, deviating from that of the Urim and Thummim, yet somewhat similar; it may perhaps have been first used by kings in judgment and been introduced from Syria, and manifestly was only gradually perverted by abuse. In the ancient proverb, Prov. xvi. 10, it is found still in a good sense. The LXX. commonly render it by μαντία, which only expresses its meaning in a general way; on the other hand, in Prov. xvi. 10 by μαντεῖον. In the bad sense קֹסְמִים, *præsagia*, is used; and the Arabic "to swear" is taken from the "higher" or "inspired" discourse.

associations was taken, and by the ringing sound of it, or the mixing and bubbling of the liquid poured into it, signs and intimations were sought as to the incidence or flow and mingling of things in the world of mankind.¹ But although by an arrangement of a species of glittering ornament in the old way the high-priestly oracle was obtained in Israel (the Urim and Thummim), yet this was originally regarded as a supreme judicial resource in doubtful matters in the community rather than in civil affairs;² it was substituted, moreover, for the purer oracle of Moses only when that was wanting; and though it was long employed by the successors of Aaron as a means of answering the questions proposed to the priests, still it never had even as a priestly oracle (§ 49) so high a respect as the free prophetic oracle, and it vanished from the life of the nation on the destruction of the first temple as an ancient mystery, of hallowed memory according to Scripture, but not to be restored. In the great history of the development of these things all this properly attests nothing but the singular vitality of the desire for oracles as in all the higher antiquity so in Israel, and in Israel still more from the best motives, so that the people were content with a confessedly lower means of obtaining them³ when and so far as the freest and best kind could not be had. The divining cup, it is true, is mentioned in connection with Joseph,⁴ but in connection with him only as an Egyptian prince, and as something naturally understood according to Egyptian usage.

§ 67. 3. All audible and visible oracles have, moreover, this in common, they depend always upon what is casual, that is,

---

[1] Cf. Isa. ii. 6; *Proph. of Old Test.* i. p. 301 [Eng. trans. ii. p. 37]. The Greeks called it κότταβος; concerning the Persian custom, see in the *Shâhname Bischen*, xi., xii., xiv.

[2] Cf. *Antiquities*, p. 385, 389 ff. [Eng. trans. 290, 294 ff.].

[3] The Book of Origins, to which alone we owe the exact description of this oracle, because in its time it stood in full respect, Ex. xxviii. 15-30, Lev. viii. 8, regards it, according to the whole sense of its description of the old laws, as something of less importance. Moses, according to this book, did not need it; rather is it assigned by him and limited only to the priest.

[4] Cf. *History*, ii. 96 [Eng. trans. i. 419, ii. 66].

upon a casual coincidence with, and in the case of those described more particularly at last a casual mood and determination of, the mind that seeks the oracle. On this account for the sake of simplification a step farther is at length taken, and the *lot* is regarded as the simplest of all means of securing a divine decision, *i.e.* a decision binding the human will. In point of fact, the lot as the simplest expedient certainly, but one presupposing much of deeper reflection, is the close of this whole development. What men do not venture to decide is, when decision is nevertheless felt to be necessary, decided by a man's freely taking and choosing from a given number of equal possibilities casually; and yet in so far as the will of the person drawing the lot decides, the decision is by him and for him rather than purely casual. This simplest expedient, as it may mark the close of this whole development, we therefore find chosen rather in highly-cultured times as a last resort in cases of indecision, and employed also in connection with urgent questions, among the common people, too, after mutual agreement. The more noteworthy is it, however, that according to an old sacred custom it was always associated with the oracle of the high priest, the better to avoid all human caprice in the oracle of mere vision.[1]

All the formal expedients hitherto explained for facilitating recourse to oracles are the simplest and most ancient. If we regard the motive which first calls them into existence, we see only what powerful longing and irresistible impulse to elicit in the dark present divine counsel and determination marked that long period of human history. In their origin therefore and in the first attempts to employ them they are innocent, and resemble the childlike urgent seeking for the invigorating voice and sure guidance of a God who is felt to be rarely present and never for any length of time. The

---

[1] *Antiquities*, p. 385, 391 f. [Eng. trans. 290, 294 f.]. Reference is made in Ezek. xxi. 21 to a lot very common amongst the Arabians, viz. by the shaking of arrows, as a then existing Chaldæan custom.

heart sighs amid the dark moments of life for some decision, some reliable determination of the will, and that such help comes from the Almighty Being whose mysterious reality is felt, fills it with new pure confidence in seeking thus what it so eagerly desires. But let it be granted that one particular place can inspire the spirit of man more than another and suggest to it what is divine, that the artificial straining of the whole attention to hear and see divine things can perhaps bring them nearer to man, and that the chance of the lot can deliver him from painful uncertainty and indecision of purpose, and give him a kind of divine confidence; yet belief in all this is not faith in the true God and His already revealed eternal word; rather does such belief, as it becomes a habit of life, lead men away from God and His word, if already known, and if not, instead of bringing them nearer, it but blocks up the way, especially if the mind is more and more exclusively and obstinately occupied with it. Since, now, the unsatisfactory nature of all this to nations that had already made progress in various pursuits and many kinds of culture must at length be sensibly felt, there arose,

§ 68 IN THE SECOND PERIOD, new and stronger attempts to draw forth out of its seeming hiddenness and aloofness divine aid for human salvation. As, however, there was no abandonment of the more or less perverse methods just described, but a further extension of them in various ways by means of newly-won appliances and newly-developed powers of mind, the ultimate issue was rather worse corruption than greater salvation. Moreover, as in everything of this sort there is a tendency to extremes, the number of such new methods increased very largely; and, since all that advanced culture brings shows itself, so far as living activities are concerned, in arts and sciences, and, so far as individuals are concerned, in extraordinary men who gain wider confidence for their special exercises of skill, we can see readily, in this way of looking at it, how belief in those simpler expedients for obtaining oracles and all possible divine certainty sought to renew and strengthen itself by the aid of these new branches of culture. Among nations of such early and high civilisation as the Egyptian and some Semitic nations, these artificial kinds of superstition were much resorted to long before Moses, so that even he had to combat them very sharply; but since they penetrated with a new and greater seductive power into the community of Israel, imperilling its interests, after it had already walked in the way of true religion, and had won a peculiar high cultivation and repose of life, we direct our attention to them now. For, as with everything original and creative, so with the true revelation and religion when they transformed Israel into a new community, both were in the highest degree simple as well in their principles as their appliances; and it was only when the nation, by virtue of the strength which this salutary transformation gave, had attained a new position in the earth, and a luxurious repose of life in which simplicity would no longer suffice, that there pressed in these new and more or less heathenish practices, in contrast with which the true revelation and religion had taken all pains to continue to advance in their direct path.

1. Among the arts by which it was sought to facilitate largely the quest of oracles, one of the earliest in certain nations was the *inspection of sacrifices*, an art that arose from combining with the sacrifice itself the observation of all the movements and rarer peculiarities noticed especially in the inner and secret parts of the warm victim. Sacrifice was regarded in itself as a supreme and awfully mysterious transaction; how easily, therefore, by careful and intent examination, might signs and foretokenings be found, not only in all the different movements in the sacred act, but also in all the varied peculiarities of the innermost organs, which were held to be the subtle and delicate seats of life— signs and foretokenings which Deity itself might give in so hallowed a moment through the medium of the skilled interpreter! Thus an art of inspecting victims, cultivated

with unusual care, arose amongst many nations; but the examination of the viscera of sacrificial victims was never conspicuously introduced in the nation of Israel, probably because in their view the blood only seemed to be sacred.[1] It was more in favour among northern nations, and is mentioned in the Bible only once, viz. in the account of the proceedings of a Nabu-Kodrossor.[2] The old Semitic custom was to pay heed only to the movements of the victim itself, and, indeed, mostly when the victims were children offered in sacrifice to Moloch.[3]

On the other hand, the manifold arts employed to get the absent, and especially the dead, to discourse, as if the truth sought everywhere in vain might be learned from dear absent ones, and still more from the highly-honoured or even much-feared dead, were certainly first called into existence in Egypt, which lived upon a religion of the dead, and was early gifted with unusual skill in all rare arts; and from Egypt the custom spread widely, not merely in Palestine and other neighbouring lands, but elsewhere.[4] With the prevalence of these practices the peculiar delusion of superstition began to play its part, and it was the more mischievous, when true revelation was already exerting its power, in proportion as the

---

[1] *Antiquities*, p. 48 ff. [Eng. trans. 38 ff.].

[2] Ezek. xxi. 21. How the Shamans still prophesy from the fractures of the shoulder-blade of the burnt sheep-offering is described in the *Ausland*, Febr., p. 194, and in Vambery's *Sketches from Middle Asia* (1868), p. 232; cf. Spence-Hardy's *Eastern Monachism*, p. 152.

[3] As is seen especially from the narrative 2 Kings iii. 27; but it is even yet to be perceived clearly enough in the story of Gen. xxii. 1-19, trembling, as it does, with the heart-beat of the noblest piety, and transfigured by the light of all the highest genuine struggling for true revelation.

[4] אוֹב, plural אֹבוֹת (*Lehrbuch*, § 177 d), "leather bottle," or "a hollow thing," "the belly," designated in Hebrew one who could imitate perfectly another's voice; the ventriloquist בַּעַל אוֹב, according to 1 Sam. xxviii. 7 ff., or shorter אוֹב; the LXX. render it, Deut. xviii. 11, by a newly-coined word, ἐγγαστρίμυθος. It may very well be used of the necromancer who practised his art by aid of ventriloquism, but in Deut. xviii. 11 it is distinguished from the necromancer, and it is therefore evident it could be used of those who knew how, at their pleasure, to make discourse, say a god whose words it was desired to hear, as the priests of Isis did.

skill used in these frauds was highly cultivated, and a dull feeling of despair led men to desire extraordinary excitements and violent agitations of mind. But precisely for this reason there are from the earliest times more stringent admonitions from the mouth of true religion against this superstition than against any other.[1] Closely related to this there was, however, according to all indications, the equally primitive application of the Egyptian art of serpent-taming for a similar end, although the sense in which the serpent had significance in revelation and religion was ultimately so manifold that the different cases must be well distinguished. In the end it was regarded as the biting and healing creature, the most artful, and in a good sense the most sagacious;[2] but originally it was considered as to men certainly only the beast of the abyss, dismal, ferocious, and frightful;[3] and as the imagination figured to itself the dreadful outermost abyss of the universe inhabited by a huge serpent, a dragon, so a similar monster was supposed suddenly to fill the lower heavens in the black thunderstorm. But after taming was practised a long series of new conceptions, and soon also of corresponding arts, became attached to the serpent. As the great monster appeared to be the epitome of all corruption and death, the serpent-tamer juggled before his credulous public as if he were just as able to call up and bring hither the dead as to tame or untame these serpents; and as the underworld was considered the inexhaustible seat of all the mysterious forces and treasures of the earth, the same conjuror could show the serpent under his hand as the wonderful creature entirely in his power, and acquainted with all the more hidden things of the universe. In the earliest time, nevertheless, the serpent-oracle must have

[1] As the old laws show, Lev. xix. 31, xx. 6, 27.

[2] The proverb, Matt. x. 16, is plainly suggested by the words of the well-known narrative, Gen. iii. 1; the Greek, indeed, has in both places the same word, φρόνιμος.

[3] Clearly to be seen in the old poetic image, Gen. xlix. 17; but in heathen mythology this is the oldest conception of serpents, as it has been preserved so conspicuously in Brahminism and Buddhism.

been a kind of oracle of the dead or of the underworld, and the reasons for this are obvious enough;[1] later it was employed in many other ways, and it declined more and more to a feat of jugglers. But against the old horror this superstition awoke, Moses guarded the faithful of the better sort by setting up overhead the image of the dead serpent, therefore no longer to be feared; similarly as, according to an old reminiscence, he once contended victoriously with Egyptian magicians whether he or they could the more readily change the serpent into a rod that would be of service for man.[2]

The art connected with man's dream-life was harmless. The belief that divine forms and divine words come near in dreams with special clearness and intensity when one is sleeping hard by a sanctuary was a world-old belief, and very prevalent among the ancestors of Israel.[3] But all dream-life is too mysterious and captivating not to tempt the addition of many kinds of art and stratagem, in order to excite more

[1] For example, the word יִדְּעֹנִי stands everywhere in the closest connection with אוֹב, and, according to its derivation, corresponds fully to Πύθων as signifying "much-knowing;" just as certainly this is originally the ὄφις πύθων. But if the Vedic *Ahis budhnjâs*, that is, "the serpent or the dragon of the abyss" (hell), preceded this Greek term, then the Greeks could the more readily find in it their πύθων, since the second word of the term in Sanscrit admitted of a play upon the word *buddha*. The LXX., to be sure, translate the word in Deut. xviii. 11 by τερατοσκόπος, and in Lev. xx. 27 understand it less accurately; in the last passage both words, אוֹב and יִדְּעֹנִי, placed close together, indicate merely the πνεῦμα πύθωνος, or, according to a better reading, πύθωνα, and appear also in a phrase corresponding to ἔχων πνεῦμα, Acts xvi. 16. They understand it better in Isa. xix. 3 as "that which speaks out of the earth," and translate it well by γνώστης, 1 Sam. xxviii. 3, 9; 2 Kings xxi. 6, xxxiii. 24. Ironically, Isa. viii. 19, cf. xix. 3, imitates the ventriloquists, as they make innocent children, called from the underworld, speak delicately like chirping birds, and old men growl hoarsely and heavily; but these really black arts, by which it was thought evil might be banned, were preserved the longer among the heathen; cf. concerning שַׁחַר, Isa. xlvii. 11, 15. How serpents are still worshipped in Africa, Livingstone describes in his *New Travels*, 1866, trans. i. p. 50.

[2] Cf. *History*, ii. p. 249 f., 90 f. [Eng. trans. ii. p. 176 f., 63]. The Greek figure of the serpent as tame to Esculapius offers a resemblance here.

[3] The typical instance, Gen. xxviii. 10-22; narratives such as Gen. xxxi. 10 f., xxxvii. 6 ff., xxvi. 24, and especially the graphic representation Gen. xv., show this; cf. also Judg. vii. 13.

strongly feelings of awe of deity and the desire to hear divine words of consolation and prophecy, and so the aid of sacrifice and various holy preparations was employed to make sleeping by the sanctuary more effective.[1] Since this custom was held sacred in Israel from of old, and manifestly by ancient traditions of the patriarchs, it sought to find points of new connection with Jahveh-worship for some time after Moses. Indeed, it cannot be denied that different kinds of dream-oracles were long considered compatible with Jahvehism;[2] but in high esteem they never were in Israel. The poet of the Book of Job represents the pious of the world's patriarchs as hearing divine words in dreams without any special artificial preparation,[3] and at length Jeremiah's simple rigour rejects briefly and decisively all such oracles,[4] whilst in highly cultured heathenism, for example among the Pythagoreans and in Athens, they remained always in high honour.[5]

With all such arts did man, now at least with peculiar freedom, seek for expedients to obtain divine oracles. Very numerous, too, were the arts of magic also, using that term in the stricter sense; the magician by a play of the hands or the eyes, or an artificial instrument, sought to draw man to himself, and as it were put him within a certain circle under a spell, that he might chain him as with divine power and compel him to listen to the words of the oracle; and yet there were men enough who soon learned to believe in the power of such arts, and readily placed themselves under their

---

[1] The ἐγκοίμησις; cf. *Antiquities*, p. 344 [Eng. tr. p. 259 f.].

[2] As follows from incidental references, Num. xii. 6; 1 Kings iii. 5 ff. They are distinguished as appertaining to priestly arrangement, 1 Sam. xxviii. 6, 15; Deut. xiii. 2–6; and opposed to waking face-to-face vision, and ascribed to the aged as coming slowly, Joel iii. 1 (ii. 28).

[3] Job iv. 12–21, in splendid picturing which the later poet imitates with respect to Elihu, xxxiii. 15–17. But nothing of the kind is said of Job, who stands far higher than Eliphaz, so finely does the poet discriminate.

[4] Jer. xxiii. 25–32, cf. xxvii. 9. But far earlier the Unnamed had already (Zech. x. 2) briefly referred to the vanity of all oracles by dreams.

[5] Cf. the writings of Hippocrates, c. I. iii. p. 167 n., 4331, and elsewhere; *Iamblichos Pythag.* ch. xv. (65); Porphyry, *On Abstinence*, ii. 41, 53; Tatian, *To the Greeks*, ch. i.; Justinus, *History*, 44. 5, 2.

influence that they might hear divine words, or be delivered from ill by divine salvation.¹ Moreover, binding and banning by such magic arts was well represented to the senses by the tying of magic-knots.²

Furthermore, all such arts were supported by the charm of verses, songs, or words otherwise regarded as sacred, designed and employed in various ways as appeared best to suit the special aim, but everywhere with the most assiduous skill, so that such as were aptest or were united with new arts were again specially distinguished.³ Speaking generally, it is hard to say how many kinds of expedients were used in order to secure the help of the oracle. When the interrogation of the ancient house-gods appeared no longer altogether suitable, the more ornamental and agreeable "Heights," as they were called, were introduced.⁴ A prophet of Israel too, it is true only an Elisha, had recourse to music to transport himself into the right elevation of spirit;⁵ and almost playfully is it related what means Isaac when feeble with years adopted in order to put himself in the right mood for prophesying.⁶ But how little all the various, more sensuous arts above described could permanently secure high respect in Israel is evident from the fact that they were early abandoned to women, as this also finds expression in Hebrew

¹ I regard מְכַשֵּׁף as the old name of the magician, especially of one working with the hands, with a magic staff or in a similar way, according to Micah v. 11. The word stands with חֹבֵר in Deut. xviii. 10 f., Isa. xlvii. 9, 12, which bears a similar signification; the existing plural form of each, כְּשָׁפִים and חֲבָרִים, is the same (cf. also Ps. lviii. 6), and corresponds to such Latin words as *præstigiæ* ("allurements," "magic arts," so called from "tickling," "alluring," cf. *instigare*). The idea of alluring, captivating, is also alone predominant in 2 Kings ix. 22, Nah. iii. 4, Mal. iii. 5, and the φαρμακός of the LXX. leads to it on another path. That the word is very old follows from Ex. xxii. 18.

² חֹבֵר might owe its origin to these witches-knots, only that elsewhere, Ps. lviii. 6, Isa. iii. 3, the charm of words is more appropriately connected with it.

³ The LXX. rightly express (Deut. xviii. 11; Isa. xlvii. 9, 12) by ἐπαοιδή these incantations.

⁴ *Antiquities*, Eng. trans. 120, 227.   *History*, Eng. trans. iii. 306, iv. 27.
⁵ 2 Kings iii. 15.   ⁶ Gen. xxvii. 3 ff.

speech.¹ Now, where a sacrificial priest must be employed, it was not held to be proper that a woman should officiate; the same remark applies to the introduction of the aid of

§ 69. 2. Science in this matter, which indeed is of such great significance that this stage of the whole question must be specially noted. The term science, however, must be understood in the strict, limited, and somewhat prejudicial sense in which the ancients spoke of mathematicians. The wonders of the heavens were profoundly recognised, the course of the stars accurately traced and determined, their great diversities observed, in ancient Babylon and among their rivals in Egypt. After these wonders, for which the common eye of men has little discernment, had been investigated with scientific precision, the new science, which embraced such a wide range of material, and involved so much that is mysterious, came down from its lonely height, as every riper science does, and gradually penetrated into the thought of humanity in general, and sought to serve common needs and aims. To apply the knowledge of those mysteries for the gratification of the desire, now become so intense and shown in so many ways, to know divine mysteries, and to have palpable guidance by visible revelations; and to meet in this way the want which, it was beginning to be felt on all sides, existing arts, old and new, had not yet adequately met,—all this followed as a matter of course. So arose a vast science of the relation of heavenly mysteries to human affairs, and in particular of the influence of individual stars on human destiny. The assistance hitherto afforded by rude arts, already for the most part deeply touched with moral deterioration, seemed now to be proffered in an incomparably better and more appropriate way by the fascination of the most exact calculations and predictions the new science gave. And,

¹ Cf. the old word מְכַשֵּׁפָה, Ex. xxii. 18, and עֹנְנָה, Isa. lvii. 3, formed after the same manner; and especially the narrative, 1 Sam. xxviii. 3 ff. It was the case among other ancient nations. The plural form, however, is, with all such names, masculine in Hebrew.

indeed, before the consummation of all revelation, why should not this grand and earnest attempt to promote it be made? How this new doctrine, with its professed unveiling of divine purposes and powers, spread in heathenism is otherwise known; what is here to be noted is that from the eighth century before Christ it had an influence in the circle of the community of the true religion which was the more dangerous just because at that time the earthly prosperity of Israel waned, and a longing arose among many of its prominent men for innovations from without. Among Biblical writers the shepherd Amos is the first who, still in the ninth century, discourses much of the particular wonders of the heavens; yet what he says is simple and steeped in the spirit of true religion. But we know that in the eighth century the arts, the scientific discoveries, and beliefs of Babylon and Nineveh were in growing favour at the court of Jerusalem;[1] and the poet of the Book of Job refers throughout the whole of his poem very frequently to the sublime wonders of the skies,[2] which are also much mentioned subsequently in other writings. But presently we see also the strong admonitions of the Deuteronomist against the worship of sun and moon and the whole heavenly host;[3] and then Jeremiah teaches how little the signs of the heavens should occasion alarm, since merely the heathen had any cause to fear them.[4] So thoroughly was his new superstition banished from the midst of the community of Israel, whilst for many centuries it spread most powerfully among the heathen.

§ 70. 3. All expedients for obtaining oracles hitherto described, whether the simplest or the more artificial, were necessarily dependent upon the action of men, and flourished as exercises more or less of special skill and habit. Thus arose not merely a belief in the efficacy of such means and aptitudes them-

---

[1] Cf. *History*, iii. 664 f. [Eng. trans. iv. 169], and later, iii. 798 [iv. 208].
[2] Cf. *Poets of Old Test.* iii. 62, 282; later, especially Isa. xlvii. 13 and Daniel; a later Biblical allusion is Matt. ii.
[3] Deut. iv. 19, xvii. 3. [4] Jer. x. 1–10.

selves, but, on the part of the multitudes who sought thereby their own advantage, a belief also in the few men who possessed and employed them. However innocent and even desirable and beneficial such a belief may be, and indeed in the Bible itself, but only in the proper place, it is commended and called for,[1] yet it may easily deteriorate and become a superstition if it does not rest upon the divine truth of the prophet's message rather than upon the prophet himself as a mortal man. Among the heathen, prophetism degenerated early in this way, and could never free itself again afterwards from this most dangerous of all corruptions that threaten it. Especially was the idea early prevalent among them that the prophet was the more deeply seized by the spirit of a deity the more that spirit, as it were, unmanned him, and by its overpowering violence deprived him of his senses;[2] a danger to which also the true prophet in the community of Israel might easily be exposed (pp. 44, 54, 64), but from which all the great prophets following one another in so long a series always knew how to keep themselves free. A heathen prophet therefore liked to have his interpreter as an under-prophet, whilst all the genuine prophets in Israel were too fully and absolutely qualified for their task, and therefore too self-possessed, to think they needed, any of them, expounders of their utterances. If, however, the prophetic gift were held to be something exclusive and connected in an obscure way with the prophet,

---

[1] Ex. xix. 9 declares how desirable it is that the nation of the true community *believe in* Moses; but this is from the fifth narrator of the primitive history (*Jahrb. der Bibl. Wiss.* xii. p. 211). With Christ also, in relation to whom "faith in Him" had from the first a wholly different basis than with the prophets, the high word, "whoso believeth in me," runs only through John's Gospel, and in such brevity only from vi. 47. The reading of Mark ix. 42 is inaccurate. It appears in Matt. xviii. 6 in place of the simpler reading of the "collected sayings" Mark retained; cf. also Matt. ix. 28 with the older form of the narrative, Mark v. 36, ix. 23 f.

[2] If the old μαίνω, "to rave," is derived originally from a Zendic *mainju*, i.e. "spirit," as the later δαιμονίζομαι and δαιμονιάω in the same sense from δαίμων, so μάντις again was not so called from μαίνω, but from the same *mainju* as one "driven by the spirit;" but it early received the same secondary signification as δαιμονιζόμενος, and is in comparison a much older name; but just this name was the customary name for their prophets with the Greeks.

it might be thought further that it clung to the individual man as one of the many physical and psychical peculiarities, and was transmissible to his posterity; thus, indeed, the Greeks had races of hereditary prophets.[1] But where public opinion was sufficiently favourable, prophetism readily became a mere high dignity in the State, which, as others, had its uninterrupted continuance and definite place in the departments of official life.[2] How free from all such impediments and limits did prophetism flourish in Israel; in times of distress and great need withdrawing into itself in self-confidence by means of schools, and becoming stronger from without;[3] yet never by such rare efforts long diverging from its higher freedom and direct onward development! It is not surprising then, as a further consequence, that in so many places heathenism entrusted prophetic power, obscure as it seemed, to women rather than men; whilst in Israel a woman, possessing the whole power of a genuine prophet, was tolerated certainly, according to the freedom which every purely spiritual impulse and enterprise claims for itself necessarily the higher it goes, but the prophetess was always exceptional.

The decline of prophetism is to be attributed in part to the people of the nation itself, who sought divine decisions on so many questions. It is in many respects really useful, and even inevitable, that in cases when uncertainty and suspense are too painful, some decision should be found which precludes all further uncertainty; individuals desire it when they have to act and they do not know how; magistrates, too, when they wish to follow a decision acknowledged by all on account of its divine origin. A word from God, however, was held to be the supreme and final decision—it had either this unique

---

[1] As the Melampodides, similar to the Homerides, but more limited locally.
[2] Cf. above, p. 148. With what dignity did a προφήτης τῆς Ἰσιδος enter! Aristophanes in the "Peace," v. 1085 ff., favours the high estimation of the prophet; so amongst the heathen in Africa to-day the prophet stands high, Livingstone's *Travels*, ii. p. 81; Bastian's *Journey to San Salvador*, p. 91 f.
[3] Cf. *History*, ii. 599 f., iii. 70, 544 ff. [Eng. trans. ii. 424, iii. 311, iv. 129].

significance or none at all; and the prophet had just on this account in the high questions of the guidance of the national government and in the crises of the national destiny an incomparably high importance. As, according to old custom and the old way of looking at things, no treaty of moment could be concluded without sacrifices, which were made specially impressive and solemn in order to remind men in a way they should never forget that divine punishment must fall upon the covenant-breaker;[1] so in those times, when the prophetic power in Israel aspired most disinterestedly after its inner perfection, no covenant with a foreign nation was regarded as properly entered upon without the counsel and approval of the prophet.[2] But since it is certain that the prophetic activity is from the first purely spiritual, and must find in its relation to the true God alone the eternal law of its right exercise and application, the decline of prophetism was owing in far larger measure to itself, if it yielded to these allurements which pressed in upon it from without, or sought to facilitate its task by any of the perverse means above indicated, or by others lying closer to hand. In point of fact, however, these two different kinds of corruption easily run into each other, since the prophet, if he does not withstand outward allurements, will readily make, what should be the most spiritual and therefore independent activity, an indolent art and a profitable and mercenary craft; and the more resolutely and persistently prophecy in Israel withstood such inner and outer seductions without doubting its divine vocation, the more strictly and happily did it widen the distinction between itself and that of the heathen. When in the kingdom of the Ten Tribes, in which, conformably with its origin, prophets as a class received the highest consideration, but also earliest degenerated, the elder Micah, as the only undeceived prophet, held firmly the real divine truth against 400 of his contem-

[1] Cf. concerning such treaty and covenant sacrifices, *Antiquities*, 91 f. [Eng. trans. 21, 68 f.].
[2] This is clear from Isa. xxx. 1 and xxviii. 7, 15; cf. *Lehrb.* § 156 e.

poraries,¹ and when an Elijah had also been possible, there was given the possibility that even this seceded kingdom, which succumbed to its fate so early only because a heathen element was more and more predominant in it, should not go down without seeing before its ultimate overthrow a great true prophet like Hosea working in its midst. When in the darkest distresses of the eighth century also, Isaiah, in a weary and heavy conflict against degenerate national leaders and their prophetic counsellors, maintained with the greater stedfastness the eternal truths by which alone nations and kingdoms can subsist, there was secured by him even more than the continuance of this kingdom of Judah for nearly a century and a half longer. Even the delicate and tender-hearted Jeremiah could become inexorably severe when defending these same eternal truths, as against all the world, so against stiff-necked and erring fellow-prophets especially;² moreover, in his old age, after the destruction of Jerusalem, when he was the only prophet in whom the nation generally had confidence, and in a most difficult case he was urgently entreated for an oracle from Jahveh, so little did he hasten to pronounce an inconsiderate judgment, that it was only after being absorbed in prayer for ten days that he found the divine response.³

The heathen oracle declined more and more, not only because of a perverted zeal to serve men without delay, but also because of the eagerness to give divine decisions, when they were called for, upon all possible affairs. The temptation to do this in Israel was felt in times of prosperity the higher the respect in which the oracle of Jahveh was held; in times of misfortune, too, there was a readiness to enter into all questions, and at least to anticipate the prevailing inclination to procure heathen oracles.⁴ These were the two hidden rocks upon which the better prophecy in Israel in the earlier as

[1] 1 Kings xxii. 5-28.
[2] Cf. especially Jer. xiv. 1-xvii. 18, xxvii., xxviii., and xliv.
[3] As in the case of Saul's inquiry of Samuel, 1 Sam. ix.
[4] As Elijah's history abundantly proves, 1 Kings xviii. f.; 2 Kings i.

well as in the later times might be wrecked; it was not able to avoid having to do with obscure and more complicated questions of human affairs of purely material significance,[1] but it ran the risk at first of mixing itself up with matters of too trivial and casual a character, and subsequently of engaging in perverse rivalry with heathen oracles. It must therefore be borne in mind that the range of subjects about which prophetic decision was sought in Israel, and also the knowledge and aptitudes which such decisions required, were alike extensive, as indeed the large number of contemporary prophets proves; and in this breadth of comprehension and the increasing multiplication of prophets there lay new danger of growing corruption. The more wonderful is it, therefore, that prophetism in Israel, amid all such allurements, always at the right time found its way back again to the higher tasks of its mission, and followed these alone with firmer decision; and thus when the better prophets considered it wise to enter into the more casual perplexities of common life, or into questions of temporal wellbeing, they did it with that freer superiority of mind which would prevent any detriment to their higher vocation.[2]

There was still another snare to which the heathen oracle was exposed, viz. the mode of expression supposed to be most suitable for divine decisions, and which in its verbal form and colour was at once recognisable. An oracular utterance must carry its truth in itself; it does not wait for the proof to make it a truth, just as indeed every true proposition does not first become true when its proof is brought forward, and proof is necessary simply for what in its announcement meets with no acceptance. If the oracular utterance is able to keep this absolute elevation, it may be as brief as it will, provided

---

[1] In cases such as 1 Kings xvii., 2 Kings i., and for the most part iv.–viii.

[2] As all such older and more extended narratives as 1 Sam. ix. f. show. The narratives from Elijah's and Elisha's life are of another kind, partly because they present to us the deeply-distracted and severely-strained condition of the kingdom of the Ten Tribes, partly because they have passed through many stages of tradition; cf. *History*, iii. 548–554, 573 ff. [Eng. trans. iv. 63–70, 80 ff.].

always it is definite and exact. But the men who delivered the heathen oracles exaggerated this peculiarity, and endeavoured to compensate for the uncertainty of their thoughts by ingenious brevity and equivocation in expression; it is well known how in this way all Greek oracles became at length ridiculous; and even the many long Sibylline sayings, often merely imitations from the heathen by those who were not heathen, have this characteristic of compression, and conceal half-obscurely the pure truth. How entirely different were the oracles of God in Israel! It is remarkable that in the Biblical collection of prophetic books we possess but two brief, concise divine oracles which give evident illustrations of this style;[1] they are certainly from a very old prophet of the kingdom of the Ten Tribes, and indicate the peculiarity of those prophets. Usually it was in the mind of the great prophets, much more perhaps in its delivery, that the oracle took the form of beautiful, simple clearness and superabounding vigour of expression, without losing thereby any of its pure elevation and sharp conciseness. Short sententious utterances are peculiar rather to the higher antiquity,[2] or to the artificial oracle of the dead;[3] artificially veiled oracles arose only with the later merely literary aftergrowths of the once so highly developed prophetic literature.[4]

§ 71. But the more the divine oracle kept its original absolute elevation, and the more it rejected such merely outward and sensuous preparations and helps, with which as we have seen heathenism could not dispense, the more difficult must it be for the grand prophets of Israel to find at once and always belief for their responses, while at the same time only belief in the truth of their utterances assured their efficacy. If, therefore, in the community of the true religion

---

[1] Isa. xxi. 11 f., 13 f.
[2] Such as Ex. xvii. 16, xix. 4-6; Lev. x. 3; Ex. xxxiv. 6 f., xxxiii. 19; Num. xiv. 18; the Decalogue, and Lev. xviii., xix.
[3] Cf. *Jahrb. der Bibl. Wiss.* xii. p. 189 ff.
[4] Cf. above, p. 102, and *Prophets of the Old Test.* iii. 251 [Eng. tr. v. 107] to the end; the *Dissertation on the Book of Enoch*, 1854, and other things specified in the *Prophets*, iii. 490 f. [Eng. tr. v. 324].

the question is more and more, whether in spite of all new darkness of the times and doubt of men they will or will not remain loyal to the eternal truths already revealed and struggling for further revelation ; then the purer and more elevated the truths are which faith should embrace and maintain with firmness in the direst temptation, the more difficult does faith become to those who have not yet reached such serene heights ; and yet there are gloomy complications of public life when faith in such truths as are announced by the prophets appears for the moment most necessary. In the midst of such heavy complications and conflicts, prophets otherwise of the noblest and most perfect character began to think they could not more emphatically render aid to the feeble faith of their contemporaries than by pointing to wonderful deeds and works performed outwardly before their eyes, or yet to be performed, as proofs of purely spiritual teaching, and of promises the senses could not grasp. Everything unusual that strikes the sense may serve as a sign and token to men that there is very much in God's universe which surpasses their present conceptions and expectations, may rouse them from their stupidity and indifference, and may liberate and strengthen the feelers of their faith so that they may realize the existence of invisible divine forces and truths. In particular, such rare yet palpable deeds and works as a prophet, by faith in God and the deepest efforts of his spirit, executes before the world, so that it is not himself as a man like other men, but rather God in him who appears to do them, and thus to reveal Himself in His actual existence to mankind, may very well tend to strengthen the conviction that the same God whose power is so visibly working through this man, may also work in him yet further by publishing to the world through him truths and promises the senses cannot apprehend. Thus it was men learned to ask for such signs or provisional proofs of the truth of the prophet's announcements, or the prophet himself offered to give them when men doubted. All this formed in Israel, as it were, a school of faith as well for the prophet as for the nation, a reciprocal exercise and training which, upon this high level, and with this end in view—referring always only to the highest truths and to God Himself as the verifier—was possible nowhere else but in this community. But if this school was beneficial for the community during many centuries,[1] and Isaiah was a master in it,[2] it does not follow that it always worked so well. For in reality the proof which is given by such signs is from the less to the greater, from the sensuous to the supersensuous; and if the sense and mind in other respects are not directed with a wholly youthful freshness of interest to the supersensuous, and prepared gladly to behold its wonders still further, but are already too surfeited, too unreceptive, and too old for this, then the proof if offered may not be obtruded;[3] and further, it is improperly demanded where it is not necessary, and where from love to the prevailing unbelief and from obduracy it may be employed merely to evade that renewing and invigoration of faith in the supersensuous which is in the highest degree desirable.[4] But thus from what was at first an aid to progress in revelation and religion there grows up what is rather a hindrance to progress, which indeed occurred in Israel during its earliest times, but especially as its greatest prophets endeavoured zealously to lead on the community to

---

[1] This benefit is presupposed in the conflict of Moses with the magicians of Egypt, Ex. iv. 2, 9, vii. 8–12; but also Isa. xxxviii. 7, by Isaiah himself.

[2] Isa. vii. 11, xxxviii. 7; only more remotely similar are the two cases, Isa. viii. 1–4.

[3] The conflict between Isaiah and King Ahaz, Isa. vii. 1, 17, was specially significant and fruitful in results, because the king (although only in order to find a pretext for his superstition) appealed to the principle manifestly taught even then in the best books and schools, viz. that one ought not by the demand for signs to tempt God. Incidentally this shows that before Isaiah's time the highest problems of faith and true religion were much investigated in Israel, and indeed in everybody's mouth.

[4] The history of this community from the time of Moses onward shows this —especially the narratives in the Pentateuch, cf. 1 Cor. i. 22; yet there is a great distinction between cases like Ex. xvii. 1–7, Num. xx. 1–13, when the people from actual want of the necessaries of life fall into despair and tempting God, and cases such as are meant in the New Testament. In the one we observe the youth, in the other the surfeited age of the nation.

its higher perfection. Moreover, since the attempt to give such sensuous proof of something supersensuous may easily be misused by prophets of all kinds, the Deuteronomist warns the community expressly and strictly against every prophet who seeks to work upon such a principle;[1] and the last great prophet Jeremiah, even as his successors, by no means desire to confirm the truth of their words by such proofs. Thus a formidable hindrance to the consummation of all revelation and religion was removed, a hindrance which in its whole perilousness was possible only in such consummation. But the more

§ 72. IN THE THIRD PERIOD do the last and most serious hindrances of this consummation show themselves; they come all along from two different and even opposite sides, and developing themselves first, to speak briefly, on the side of the *unbelief* just mentioned, at length, from the opposite side of *perverse faith*, they assume the extremest power possible in this whole long course of things.

Unbelief, as we just remarked, was not introduced into the community from without, but sprang up from its own soil; and not first in late times, but occasionally and very readily passing over from the most ancient times. But still it may intrude at a later period from a wholly different quarter, and then indeed with the greater danger, because emanating from the very substance of all religion and revelation itself. Genuine religion claims the whole man; it claims him not merely as a reflective and energetic, but also as a practical being; it demands not simply his thinking and reasoning faculties, but also his sentient and imaginative faculties; pre-eminently it requires also a distinct and certain perception not only of earthly and visible, but also of invisible and divine things. Now all invisible and still more all divine things can be known and apprehended by man only by the help of the faculty of imagination. But what is known by man by means of this faculty only, even when it has sunk

[1] Deut. xiii. 2–7.

most deeply into his spirit as though it were an eternally abiding possession, may nevertheless, as soon as the first glow in which it was warmed and illumined by the fire of imagination has passed away, again and again be doubted by the understanding. That is to say, the understanding may be at issue with the imagination or its images, and may reject, as incongruous with certain already accepted truths, the whole luxurious brood imagination has called into existence. Now it belongs, it is true, to the very nature of all genuine revelation and religion, that, when and where they are in full activity, the mere faculty of imagination can no longer exercise itself so exuberantly in relation to supersensuous and divine things; rather is such exuberance a characteristic of heathenism and the result of a perverted impulse which contributes not a little to its ever deeper degeneracy.[1] The extraordinary superiority of the community of the true religion over heathenism in this respect is attested indirectly in that its sacred tradition never degenerated to a heathen mythology; a matter lying somewhat remote perhaps, but of great importance, because sacred tradition is most closely connected with all revelation and religion, and, as remote reminiscence, is their ultimate support. But without the activity of the faculty of imagination true revelation and religion did not arise among men, nor can they continue to exist. Indeed, this faculty has preserved in all vividness the most imperishable and truest representations and pictures of the primitive age of our race when revelation and religion were all-powerful; it produces also in times of new, more general, and stronger religious interest, when it is itself also powerfully stirred, a fulness of new intellectual growths; and, moreover, by means of it every original poet and thinker creates fresh, striking, and appropriate images which enter into the existing circle of ideas and seek to adjust themselves with it.

The creations of the imagination, springing as they do from

[1] Cf. *History*, i. 20-69 [Eng. trans. i. 13-45].

the quickened life of the spirit, can nevertheless, even in the circle of the true revelation and religion, maintain themselves vividly and fruitfully only in the like warm glow of feeling. If, however, to the first creative years of the community and its happy development there succeed years of lassitude or despair, and the impulse of scientific investigation becomes likewise sufficiently dominant and commanding, this moral lassitude and despair readily unite with the boldness and indeed the cold arrogance of the new wisdom of the schools, in doubting the congruity of ideas accepted as valid in revelation and religion, in rejecting the necessity of these pure activities of the spirit, and ultimately denying both the accuracy of their perceptions and the soundness of their works. And thus doubt as a spiritual power, and consequently in the end Atheism, open their paths in this community, not indeed chiefly from the influence of heathen nations without, but from influences working in its own pale, as a careful study of its history shows. Such paths were ventured upon with increasing peril during the centuries of the old kingdom's decline,[1] but they were reopened the more readily in periods favourable to them, and repeatedly even in the regenerated community of the New Jerusalem, now in occasional and feeble attempts, now more widely and formidably.[2] The schools and morals of the Sadducees were, it is true, ultimately best known as of this tendency, but it would be a mistake to suppose that similar schools and morals did not seek for power in Israel in yet earlier times. If we see, therefore, that the true revelation and religion always in due time obtained the victory in this community (as is indeed historically established), whilst heathenism, even amongst the most cultured nations of antiquity, sank deeper and deeper, not a little also through the growing mischief of unbelieving wisdom; we anticipate what deep and inextirpable roots

---

[1] Prov. xxx. 1-14 is the chief witness of the Atheism that prevailed in Israel; cf. *Jahrb. der Bibl. Wiss.* i. 100 ff.

[2] Cf. *History*, iv. 249 f., 357 ff. [Eng. trans. v. 193 f., 274 ff.].

revelation and religion must have had in the community of Israel. And, strictly speaking, short sayings[1] from the more ancient time, all-decisive words[2] from the later time of Jeremiah, suffice as a defence against this danger, which might well be much more serious in the prophetless days than earlier.

§ 73. But just when the power of true revelation and religion in the community obtained this victory over what we should now call the philosophy of religion,—in that case, however, a philosophy made foolish,—and when everything so shaped itself in the great world that the sacred truth in Israel, after it had become more deeply and securely established in its own limited community amid all temptation and change during a millennium and a half, appeared to be competent as it broke through its temporary bounds to overcome the whole heathenism of the world, there intruded a perverse faith, which, precisely because it is in appearance the very antithesis of all heathenism, is fraught with the greater danger. That is the belief that in the Scripture which gives the essential contents of true revelation and has become sacred to the community, the holy and the divine itself is possessed and is to be reverenced as such. It is this faith in Holy Scripture that becomes ultimately comprehensive and determinative of everything in the ancient community; it is faith in a visible object, cherished as its only precious and sacred treasure, nay, as its very deity, and tenaciously and spasmodically grasped in the deepest trials;—a faith with which as the surest product of its whole changeful history it supposes itself to be perfectly in the right as against heathenism, and which, nevertheless, on the contrary, tends to make the community familiar with a most pernicious element of heathenism, and threatens to hinder all progress to real perfection. It well deserves, therefore, to be considered at this point with all attention and carefulness.

[1] Such as Prov. xxviii. 4, 5 ; ver. 4 has תּוֹרָה, as ver. 7 in the old prophetic signification, noticed above, p. 156.

[2] Jer. viii. 8 f., ix. 23 f. ; cf. what is said below, p. 249.

Now the origin of this faith itself is very readily explicable, and the error that creeps in with it and becomes at length so extremely dangerous is at first very harmless, nay, hardly an error at all; just as with the oldest kinds of faith that in their course became superstition, so it occurs here with this last kind, which precisely because it is the last involves the greater peril. Two observations will suffice to open this question so far as it is proper to do so here.

(*a*) Writings that contain what is elevating and permanently instructive for the mind of a nation, and of an almost indestructible force, become by their own beauty and splendour gradually so indispensable, so worthy of honour and even sacred (using the last word in a general sense), that they are raised to a position far above the current value and common destiny of all other writings; and the actual or accepted authors also come to share the radiance of this glory which gathers about the writings themselves. This is especially the case in the particular circles in which these writings have their immediate significance and importance; as indeed the best grammatical works of the old Indians have thrown a broad halo of glory around the name of Pânini, and the works to which the name of Hippocrates is affixed make that name illustrious to all physicians. But they readily attain even beyond such special circle a yet higher and typical or even unique significance, a significance almost on a par with the notion of sanctity, *i.e.* inviolability and supreme reverence, if from special causes they become the sole all-important writings for the instruction and elevation of nations generally. For example, Homeric poetry, chiefly, it is true, as poetry of imperishable inborn splendour, is the standard of all poetry, and for the purposes of criticism and imitation cannot but be so regarded, but it has at the same time for the later Greeks a more general significance as presenting to view the beautiful and immortal forms of their noble past. So in the case of the writings composed or approved by the Chinese Kung-tsö (Confucius), intended especially only for his pupils, yet because they were held to contain for the entire Chinese Empire the very highest wisdom, they obtained so high a significance that they might be called the sacred books of the Chinese, did not all such writings answer to the idea of superior or classical rather than that of sacred; for only if writings of this kind contained something that reminded members of a smaller or larger holy community of that which for them is holy or divine, could they be considered as sacred, or can we so consider them. Finally, it is easily understood that such writings possess their whole peculiar utility and charm chiefly for the people among whom they first came into existence, whose interests they were intended to serve, and who alone at the time they were written could understand with perfect certainty their language and import. But nevertheless by special fitness and destiny such writings, after once winning for themselves high respect, may also find currency in foreign nations, and amongst them, for reasons more or less sound, obtain perhaps a far higher respect, and be abundantly employed for wholly different ends.

(*b*) The other thing here to be noted relates to the special impression all writings as such may readily make upon men, and which in those ancient days they could make far more readily than to-day amongst ourselves, seeing that now they are far more generally estimated aright in all their inimitable excellences and in all their less favourable qualities, inasmuch as their diverse nature, their varying fitness and uses, have become incomparably better known. A writing serves, when well preserved, to immortalize thoughts and doctrines unchangeably for all time; and in its minute and manifold characters, seemingly dead and cold and for most men, too, it may be illegible, it conceals perhaps the highest truths that may suddenly vivify and can continually instruct mankind. If it comes down from distant, perhaps better and happier times, or is brought from remote lands reputed to be the abode of sages, there is a special charm about it. The charm is the greater if fame has already prepared its way, announcing it as coming from the hand of an unusually holy man, or an honoured founder of religion, or as containing wonderful divine suggestions and predictions. Hence spring up many applications of sacred writings which often seem to us so strange. When Mahommedans turned to their Koran as a book that, in anxious desire for divine help, they had only to open to find in the first word or sentence that caught the eager eye the best counsel and guidance for the decision of some urgent affair, they were not the first who thus acted; even Roman priests did a similar thing with their Sibyl-books that were brought to them from afar. A sacred writing appears at least incomparably better, more divinely suggestive and distinctly decisive, than the glance at the mere image of an idol; and the clear word that is found in it has its surer significance which may be further pondered with collected mind.

These two things thus presented are not to be overlooked. Both were contributive to the formation of a comprehensive Holy Scripture, and to the higher regard felt for it in the very community which was founded under Moses, and which flourished for the longer and more independent period of its pre-Christian existence without any such aid. In this Scripture the community had not only the richest collection of precepts concerning the whole round of duty, but also the sublimest declarations concerning God and concerning His kingdom and its history and future upon earth, and, moreover, the plainest admonitions for the religious life as presented in the whole grand and typical past experience of the community. All the divine voices and doctrines which had directly or indirectly quickened genuine piety and promoted true blessedness were now, in the form in which they were first known, compactly treasured up for further and perpetual service, and could never again be lost. This, too, was the more useful and necessary, the more the immediate activity and living power of all genuine revelation as developed by the prophets gradually came to a standstill, the probable duration of which no one seemed able to fix. And thus this Holy Scripture, although it corresponded only to the present Old Testament, yet included in itself so much that had wonderful interest and fascination for all men, that it became with each century more known and admired among the heathen, nay, was soon recognised as the most powerful means of diffusing among them true religion; so that it could throw upon the community, even from the heathen, the radiance of the splendour and truth of this religion, differing as it did essentially from all forms of heathenism.[1] Among the sacred books of the other nations, however, those of the Persians and Indians were scarcely known familiarly to the Greeks and Romans even by name; of the Egyptian books something more was known; but, as far as we can judge to-day,[2] they are so much inferior in intrinsic value and the charm of style to the books of the Old Testament, that they could hardly come into serious conflict with them at all.

But apart from the reverence which these sacred books of Scripture found amongst many of the heathen, and the increasing sanctity with which they were thus invested in the eyes of the old community, everything in the course of the latest centuries conspired to add to their sanctity and strengthen the faith with which they were regarded. As these books, not merely because they were indispensable to the continuance of the community, for that could not be said of all of them, but mainly because of their own intrinsic excellence, were raised to a high position and rendered incapable of being lost, the

---

[1] Cf. *History*, iv. 331 ff. [Eng. trans. v. 255 ff.], v. 109-112, 116 f. [Eng. trans. vi. 81-84, 87 f.], vii. 396 ff., 638, vii. 384 ff., and elsewhere. Not simply up to the Roman destruction of Jerusalem, but until the Hadrianic extirpation, with every closer contact with the heathen, the heathen reverence for the Old Testament grew, and this reacted upon the growing reverence for it in the community. Not till the issue of the Hadrianic war did the great change in this matter come.

[2] The so-called writings of *Hermes Trismegistos* are not to be regarded as containing the latest elements of the old Egyptian sacred writings; they were written in the third, or fourth, or fifth of the Christian centuries by some who wished to freshen up Egyptian heathenism by Christian phrases and thoughts, or rather to show that Christianity is not absolutely necessary to those who desire true religion; they were therefore written originally in Greek, and afterwards translated into the languages of Oriental Christians. The Book of the Dead, and what has been otherwise preserved of the genuine sacred writings of the Egyptians may here be put in evidence. Cf. Herm. Tris. *Poemander*, ed. Gust. Parthey, Berlin 1854; and the Arabic H. Tr. of Fleischer, Leipsic 1870.

admiration of them would become more and more general, and especially would this be the case the longer and the more carefully they were read by large numbers of the people who were eager for knowledge and salvation. The community also found in them the permanent standard and law of all its higher life, and had not merely an incomparable treasure of higher wisdom, art, and culture, but also, and conspicuously, the most brilliant testimony to its whole past with all its imperishable glory. And if in these later days it was almost always subject to heathen power, and had lost the living breath of revelation by the prophet, and the vivid feeling of the nearness, help, and grace of its only ruler and Lord, yet did He seem palpably recognisable and near enough still in this His written word, if only it were rightly understood.

But the more readily could an exaggerated reverence for Holy Scripture now also arise; and as in all times unjust contempt of what is sacred only in the long run increases its sanctity, so this feeling of the sacredness of Scripture reached its highest point when the perverse wisdom of the schools (§ 72) had for a long time energetically turned itself against its authority, and the Maccabæan struggles had embittered very much the conflict with the heathen and their wisdom. The scrupulousness of the Essenes and the busy officiousness of the Pharisees completed this exaggeration. Holy Scripture became the sole foundation, not only of all decision concerning what is lawful in the community, but also of all higher instruction [1] and of all permissible wisdom; heavy penal statutes soon avenged the contempt or violation of it, and even touching it with unclean hands was deprecated as if its very leaves were the inviolable God of the community; [2] and the more ingenious and severely orthodox a new school of scribes pretended to be, the more did they seek by new arts

---

[1] "Higher," because besides Holy Scripture various accredited school-books were used as Catechisms; cf. *Die drei ersten Evangelien*, p. 264 f., 2nd ed., and *Sendschreiben an die Hebräer* (Göttingen 1870), p. vii.

[2] *History*, iv. 251, 641 [Eng. trans. v. 194 f., 491], vi. 551.

of exposition and affected sublety to extract wisdom out of the mere letter.¹

§ 74. The Deuteronomist, it is true, at a time when grave offence had already been committed against the contents and spirit of genuine revelation and religion, long since vouchsafed, —offence as well on the side of frivolous school-wisdom as on the side of too punctilious reverence for the sacred letter, —earnestly admonished against either withdrawing from the word of God, by perverse denial, what necessary belongs to it, or adding, through anxious fear, what is unnecessary and pernicious;² as indeed it is generally speaking the characteristic of precise, and precisely to be followed, truth, that it may neither be augmented nor diminished; and more than this is not intended by the Deuteronomist when he points to the true revelation long extant, and the necessity of being loyal to it, while not denying that in the future a great advance may be possible through a second Moses.³ Still earlier also Isaiah had warned against those to whom the word of God, that ought to be taken and understood in the very depths of its divine meaning, is merely human command to be learned by rote;⁴ as also against those who in like manner make religion the formal repetition and multiplication of sacred exercises and rites such as prayer and sacrifice.⁵ Still more definitely had Jeremiah rejected all perverse wisdom and authorship,⁶ and sharply rebuked the folly of seeking a magical charm in old sacred words, as false prophets were fond of doing.⁷ He, therefore, who took all these things in their true sense, would be able to find in existing Holy Scripture the right course to pursue; and it is one of the finest proofs of the excellence of the Old Testament that it guards, equally and securely on the

---

¹ *History*, vi. 269 ff., vii. 53 ff., 379 ff.
² Deut. iv. 2, xiii. 1; cf. with the image of right and left, v. 29 f., xvii. 11, xxviii. 14; Josh. i. 7, xxiii. 6.
³ Deut. xviii. 18 f.; cf. xxxiv. 10–12, and above, p. 97.
⁴ Isa. xxix. 13.
⁵ Isa. i. 10–17; Micah vi. 6–8; cf. Ps. l. and xl. 7–11; Jer. vii. 22 f.; cf. xxxi. 31–34; and already Amos v. 25, and Hosea similarly.
⁶ Jer. viii. 8 f., ix. 22 f.   ⁷ Jer. xxiii. 30–40; cf. Ezek. xii. 21–xiv. 11.

two opposite sides, both the whole compass of the higher knowledge already won, and the whole practice of genuine religion. But that Holy Scripture, so complete, so well collected and preserved, as well as the exercises and usages it prescribes and allows, could be so seriously abused, and that this whole perverse tendency of mind could be so fatally fostered as it was in these last centuries by schools of learning under the old true religion,—this was something new, something of which there was no experience in the times of the old prophets. It was a new kind of heathenism [1] that, in those half-obscured days when at length everything pressed forward to the consummation of all true revelation and religion, ever yet refusing to come, poured its seductive influence over this community just as it thought of fighting most bravely and indefatigably against the ancient heathenism of the world, and even boasted most loudly of this conflict and its cost. As, however, all errors diverging from the same truth are related to each other, and one mightily prevalent error can overpower all truth more and more fully; so the danger was now imminent, that at last through the perversity penetrating into the deepest heart of all true revelation and religion already won, both the one and the other with the community in which they arose would be completely obliterated from the earth. For nothing could be worse than that, amid the luminous splendour of true religion as it struggled onwards so powerfully on all sides to its final victory, a new heathenism in veiled form should insinuate itself in its place and obtain the pre-eminence.

[1] So Christ Himself regards it, Matt. vi. 7, cf. xviii. 17 ; but Paul also speaks of this whole tendency quite similarly, Rom. ii. 17-24. In the face of modern error all this is very important. The Hegelian school, flattering heathenism too much, has done mischief ; while some modern Jews, with their misstatements of another kind about Sadducees and Pharisees, are already forgotten and scarcely deserve notice.

3. *The ultimate Victory in this Conflict.*

§ 75. But in point of fact it is shown from another side (§ 41) how certainly Christ alone brought this consummation. The revelation of the divine will man may not seek through any insufficient or wholly perverse, *i.e.* purely sensuous means, nor by such aid hope to fulfil what is already revealed. So long as something of the kind, whether subtler or coarser in form, is mixed up in the matter, genuine revelation cannot be fully attained nor genuine religion in all its power and blessedness be fully realized. Only as it purely and uprightly strives after the true God can the spirit of man be touched by the light of His revelation, and only as he works just as purely and uprightly in this light can man hope to live in harmony with his revealed will. In the long conflict with every type of heathenism before Christ this was the result surely won; to have recognised it as such and to have made it an inalienable possession, is the glory and, in the noblest sense of the word, the pride of this community; and the faith thus shown is the ground of the bright confidence and ineradicable eternal hope of the nation. But only when Christ —over against the means of revelation and religion held to be sacred and right, which as they had arisen in this community and had been highly developed in the practice of centuries were also generally esteemed the most genuine, and nevertheless were perverted—followed purely with the direct divine means the direct way of all true revelation and religion up to the very highest goal; only as He throughout His whole life taught the right use of Scripture, suffering nothing of its higher sanctity to be wrested from it by the mere sacredness of the letter,[1] and also in harmony with all this as He allowed neither Himself nor His disciples to darken in the least living divine holiness and righteousness by the whole round of old venerable usages:[2] only then was the victory complete over

---

[1] Cf. *History*, v. 308 f. [Eng. trans. vi. 233 f.].   [2] *Ibid.*

everything which must be held as heathenism, *i.e.* defection from the true religion and hindrance of its power. For it is readily understood that in this way was annulled, not only for that short term of all human history in which He sojourned till His death in the midst of the old community, everything that till then had attained a perverse sanctity in this community contrary to its original destination and tendency; but now also the condemnation is pronounced beforehand upon every perverse sanctity which may arise in His own community, and appeal for support to His own word and institution, as He Himself anticipated and explicitly enough declared.[1]

§ 76. This form of heathen superstition, concealed under the guise of the utmost sanctity, did not, it is true, thus gradually and imperceptibly take root and spread mischievously until the centuries when the vigour and bloom of the ancient nation declined. Although it wanted then some five hundred years to the public advent of Christ, the beginning of this tendency in the community led more and more to prepare the way for the subsequent great defection, which no one more quickly perceived and combated in all simplicity with more certainty of victory than Christ. It was this five hundred years immediately before Christ which He Himself well distinguished from the old splendid era of purer faith, and, when it was necessary, severely condemned.[2] But if any one asks how it was possible that this tendency, which is most appropriately designated in one word as that of the hagiocracy,[3] could be so overpowering that no less a personage than Christ Himself must come in order to open again the direct way of all true revelation and religion which had thus been barred, the answer takes us back to the very founding of the com-

---

[1] Matt. vii. 21-23, xxv. 44 f.; cf. xxiv. 11, 24.
[2] By "those of old time," Matt. v. 21 ff., and by "all" who came before Him, "thieves and robbers," John x. 8, are manifestly meant the same persons, since He condemns the former; the context made the different designations necessary; cf. *Jahrb. der Bibl. Wiss.* ix. 40-49.
[3] *History*, iv. 3 ff., 213 ff. [Eng. trans. v. 1 ff., 165 ff.].

munity by Moses. It was remarked above (p. 195) that two deficiencies adhered to this community in its establishment, the first of which was that it was not founded without the immediateness and violence of spirit which is peculiar to every prophetic work the more it comes into activity purely in the ancient time. The light of the stream of divine truth as it looks forth radiantly from the words, the irresistible violence of conduct in conformity with it as it displayed itself in the spirit of this purely prophetic and sublime national leader, overpowered the nation. Thus the truth and will of this highest Ego, revealing Himself by Moses, took at once the form of law, *i.e.* compulsory precept for the life, and did so necessarily in proportion as the community, which gathered itself in all severe earnestness solely about this word of God revealed and authenticated in it, and desired to recognise no other Lord and King but God, was one and the same with this single nation, Israel. A single nation, however, in order to maintain its own existence, and to continue independent of all other nations, cannot dispense with outwardly compulsory law, so that the divine law must become national, and its penalties be inflicted by bodily punishment. If, then, revelation and religion as they created this community under Moses bore in themselves the character of law, afterwards, it is true, by a movement of more than a millennium and a half in duration, they unceasingly aroused in this community its native force and freedom, and already the imprisoned butterfly long desired to break through the narrow bounds thrown round it in its first immature youth, as the history of the whole first thousand years of this national community shows. But the law had become since that early age the firm all-embracing sheath of this wonderful form, which no power could break through with safety, and, above all, without mortal injury to the life of the true revelation and religion hidden within it, if it were not a power which stood as to its spirit high above that old type of revelation. But just because this immortal treasure might be manifoldly injured and wasted by base and destructive hands, the sheath encompassing it had hardened and thickened anew in the last five centuries, so that now it was as difficult as possible to break through it. All revelation and religion had become law as never before,[1] a law, moreover, contained in the great book of law written in ancient days, and to be derived from it by the scribes as the true spiritual masters of the time. Thus the imperfectness which originally adhered to this type of revelation was now obstinately preserved, increased a thousandfold in force, just as old deficiencies everywhere when most urged to vanish altogether are fond of seeking to maintain themselves tenaciously; and whilst the whole freedom and glory of the second five hundred years of this community, with its great prophets, was forgotten, a mere deficiency of the initial period of the community became now the sole mighty means of its full upbuilding and whole perfection.[2] But then it was that, with sure glance and peacefully fearless mind, Christ showed clearly how even Moses, as a lawgiver, must be estimated if the divine contents of his law were not to be dissolved, but, on the contrary, what the law imports were to be perfectly fulfilled.

This is the wider significance of Christ's conflict; in waging it, however, He went at once far beyond the limit of the tendency that had prevailed for the last five hundred years, a tendency which in its opposition to the true religion can only be characterized as heathen, and He touched immediately the high boundary which a millennium and a half ago the founding of the community of this nation in the midst of all antiquity had set up as a barrier of rock. Indeed, the Apostle Paul quite justly perceived that in Christianity the question was essentially this—whether a system of things that had obtained since Sinai, and had become, to be sure not

---

[1] "The law and the prophets" paraphrases the whole condition and innermost life of the community, Matt. v. 17, xxii. 40; transposed Matt. xi. 13, because spoken of Messianic things; restored in this sense in customary order, Luke xvi. 16. But still more briefly "the law" now means both the whole of the Old Testament and the condition of the ancient community.

[2] *History*, iv.-vii. [Eng. trans. v.-viii.] passim.

till the last times, so elaborately complete, should or should not continue; that is to say, whether the true revelation and religion should or should not remain under the constraint of the law?[1] But this sacred law, as it had been understood for centuries by the scribes, and been made by their use of it into so irksome a yoke of faith, a yoke which the Pharisees, as the predominant national party, had in the most perverse way devoted themselves to make as comfortable as possible, had now created out of itself the existing spiritual, and, as far as it went, also secular, magistracy of the national community, a magistracy which had ruled for centuries, and which, as a member of this community, and having a just claim to work in it, Christ recognised as a magistracy existing according to outward right.[2] If, now, in the presence of this law so existing and so administered, Christ taught and acted as we have said, and the entire power of the law as it culminated in the government of the community at that time fell upon Him at last in deadly conflict, deeply conscious that the government and the law itself thus administered could not exist side by side with Him, then, in that very moment, as may be said perhaps boldly but still with truth, was death inflicted, not upon Him, but rather upon the government and its law, since with the irremediable fatal shock death itself begins. For if it is an eternal divine ordinance that what is truly holy, when the attempt is made to destroy it, turns round rather with irresistible energy upon its destroyer and destroys it instead, so upon this law, that with all its imperfection cleaving to it, and all its perversity developed to the highest degree, directed itself in hostility against Him, who rather sought to elevate

---

[1] According to Paul, everywhere this is to Christians self-evident. He proves it, however, more definitely in the Galatians, the 2nd Cor., and in new form in the Romans. If he does not start from historical investigation and the criticism of details, as we should do to-day, so much the more is his simple keenness of discernment to be admired.

[2] Matt. xxiii. 2-36 does not therefore contradict Matt. v. 21-40. In the higher sense, too, it is correct that the scribes were thieves and robbers, John x. 8, seeking more or less forcibly to lay hold of and appropriate the more pious souls of the community, and yet finding amongst them no true audience.

it to its perfect sanctity and splendour, was death self-inflicted ; that is to say, the law as it then was proved itself incapable of coming to Him and making Him its own, and it could now no longer hinder the direct progress to the perfect true revelation and religion He would give to the world, and whose way He broke by all He did, and especially by the death of sacrifice He freely offered for the world. On the other hand, also, all that was imperishable in the law and in the community till then, and that had more and more perfectly unfolded its power since the community was established, liberated now from the fatal deficiency which had ultimately led to the worst heathen aberration, could at length be recognised the more distinctly and work the more freely.[1]

With the death and resurrection of Christ, therefore, was also removed, as by a single quick and sudden stroke, the other deficiency which adhered to the community of the true religion and its law, as they had hitherto existed. The breaking of the hard sheath in which the law had imprisoned the better soul of the true revelation and religion, broke also the limits of its community, and opened to all nations free access to the community, of transfigured revelation and perfected true religion, a community born again by the new law of divine love and redemption one and the same for all men. Israel as a nation might now decay and vanish away, and, in point of fact, it did so soon enough, so far as it offered resistance to the better way; but it vanished only to live on immortally in the better community expanded into a divine home for all humanity, and enriched by all the possessions that had ever been won.

[1] That Paul was the first to perceive and express all this is a grave error of modern writers. The breach that could not be healed without full conversion to the better way was by Christ's death and resurrection so sensibly and powerfully effected, that the apostles from the beginning could never think and speak essentially otherwise than Paul (Acts ii. 22-40), and all later controversies between Paul and them, however important they were at the time, altogether vanish in comparison. Indeed, in accordance with Messianic hopes, reference was already made to the admission of the heathen in the words, Acts ii. 34 f., 39 ; cf. xxii. 21 ; Eph. ii. 13, 17.

In this way the same result is obtained which has been obtained before from a wholly different side (§ 42), viz. that not till the apostolic time could the conclusion of this two thousand years' development be reached. What has already been shown in the history of the inner forces and pure impulses of all revelation is here attested in the very complicated, manifold, and changeful aspects of its great conflict from without, i.e. against heathenism. The issue is the same there as here, and the same Christ is in both, at the end of convergent ways, the sole person who perfectly attains the goal. Yet it is not the mortal part of Him, but only the immortal and indestructibly eternal that attains this goal, as the apostles could not experience until after His bodily departure, and could not till then announce it to the world as they thus perceived it. When, therefore, the apostles summoned the entire old community, in which alone all this could be consummated and whose limits could not be broken through but by His death, to a repentance and conversion now incomparably more urgent, and for all who had the mind to see it obviously the more necessary than for those whom Christ at the beginning of His public work in the community had Himself admonished, and when they turned soon enough with still more urgency where it was possible to the heathen to invite them to enter the old yet fully new community of Israel,[1] then only was everything heathen in the ancient Israel overcome for all who did not cling to its last and hardest shreds, and thereby imperceptibly, yet surely, seek to fall back again gradually under its power; and then only was the right time come to call the heathen with all good confidence into a community so purged from the last im-

---

[1] The Epistle to the Ephesians, standing alone amongst New Testament writings as written purely for heathen Christians, presupposing as established their full equal right with the members of the old community to everything Christian, yet regards the commonwealth of Israel ($\dot{\eta}$ πολιτεία τοῦ Ἰσραήλ, ii. 12) as continuing to exist in Christianity, and lays emphasis upon the fact that heathen Christians have the same part in it as Jewish Christians.

pulse to heathenism that every relapse to it is henceforth inexcusable.[1]

§ 77. If, however, Christianity, contemplated in this aspect of it, is nothing but the consummation of all that with clear consciousness and true earnestness was already striven after in the community of Israel long before this its transfiguration, the consummation of that which, strictly speaking, already lies in the spirit expressing itself creatively in the founding of this community and its simple original law, the Ten Commandments, the consummation of that which, a thousand times injured or obscured, more and more powerfully and surely combated its contrary as it arose, and that could only in the midst of this community be perfected as Christ at last perfected it; then no view is so incorrect as the view which declares that Christianity originated in its time from the working together of the now so-called Judaism and heathenism, and is therefore a kind of mixture of both. Such a view could arise only from the monstrous confusion of historical comparisons now-a-days so freely, and for the most part so perversely instituted, and from the not less vast mistakes in judgment concerning the three great spiritual powers here compared; but besides this, it has sprung principally from the weak preference for heathenism with which more recent scholars among us are afflicted. The question as to the thousand better aims, wholesome, or at least useful fruits of their genius, the most cultured heathen nations have left behind for our perpetual enjoyment and unfeigned gratitude, is here a wholly foreign question; we need not ignore or deny the smallest of them. But that Christianity did not arise from a mixture of heathenism and Judaism is certain. That it did cannot be proved from the ultimate prevalency of the Greek language

---

[1] Not in vain does the Apocalypse in Old Testament words make conspicuous the necessity of the purity of the Christian community (xxii. 15, cf. xxi. 27), agreeing in this with Paul, 1 Cor. v. 1-8, and reject indeed the existing, *i.e.* non-Christian Jerusalem decisively, but picture heathenism as the direct antithesis to Christianity, and as the foe against which the glorified Christ must Himself fight in the last decision of the destiny of the existing world.

and of Greek authorship, *i.e.* from the spread of Hellenism: nay rather, it was Christianity itself, far more than the pre-Christian Hellenism of adherents of the true religion, that impressed its own spirit upon everything Greek. Nor can it be proved from the elementary intuitions and popular conceptions, or indeed tendencies and aims, which Christianity derived from the existing heathenism, or by which it was, so to speak, unintentionally overpowered: if by this anything more important is meant, there is no ground for it. That the idea of the Logos was not borrowed from Greek philosophy has been abundantly proved. Youthful Christianity in its prominent upholders was in all such things dominated far more by the deepest spirit of piety towards God, and was much more circumspect and chaste than, for example, the Alexandrine Philo, of whose influence upon new Christian thought there are no traces until the Epistle to the Hebrews. Christianity is, in point of fact, nothing but the consummation—surprising perhaps in the highest degree and in its definite creative form unexpected, but still, strictly considered, the most direct and consistent consummation of the true revelation and religion whose development went on unceasingly in the profounder striving of the community from its very beginning. The stream of revelation and religion was never wholly interrupted, the life-breath never stifled, till by a last mighty movement this new and transfigured life was won. Then, indeed, all that was noblest and most imperishable, that in two thousand years and more had become an inalienable possession and pure good, passed over into Christianity; and not less a benefit was it, that just in its most tender and susceptible youth Christianity entered into the enjoyment of all this large wealth, approved and inherited from old time, and especially that it received from the Holy Scripture of the mother community the most salutary and strengthening nourishment possible. Historically, however, it is notorious that Christianity, even leaving Christ out of view, issued purely from Israel, so far as its first heroic preachers and champions are concerned, and upon them the earliest heathen Christians, who like Luke clave to Israel with their whole heart and laboured earnestly in the gospel, were conscious that they were virtually altogether dependent.

Christ Himself, as the power of the purest divine love and salvation become human, was just as kindly-disposed towards all heathen men, as men, without exception, as towards the members of His own nation; but He held firmly (p. 201, n.) with sure insight and consistency to the irreconcilable opposition between heathenism and the community of the true religion, and He knew perfectly well how and where as Lord in His domain to maintain or relax the limits of this community.[1] And just as Lord, and Lord in His domain, must He everywhere be first contemplated, if all that is still higher in Him is to be properly estimated. The bitterest foe, ultimately the most faithful servant of the glorified One, transformed as no one else into an apostle to the heathen for many years, speaks everywhere about the heathen calmly and respectfully, nowhere mentioning their name with a curt and harsher word;[2] and yet he, too, firmly and constantly holds the complete irreconcilability of heathenism with Christianity, whilst he feels only a sorrowful regret for the stiffneckedness of his Jewish brethren who persist in their hostility.[3] The Apostle John, in his old age, throwing himself back into the times and conflicts of Christ, spontaneously becomes, in the speech of Christ Himself, a severe but not unjust judge of his former countrymen,[4] so that nowhere else in the New Testament is language so peculiar held concerning them; and yet, looking back in Christian light to the beginning of the Decalogue, and once again as with the final effort of his mind making conspicuous the sharp opposition between all true and false religion, he concludes his own last great word with the short

---

[1] Cf. *History*, v. 454 f. [Eng. trans. vi. 347 f.]; and concerning His relation to the Hellenists, p. 526 f. [*ib.* 402 f.].

[2] As 1 Pet. iv. 3; the long description of Rom. i. 24–32 was, on the contrary, unavoidable in that connection, and, moreover, is calmly historical.

[3] Rom. ix.-xi.; earlier somewhat otherwise, 1 Thess. ii. 14-16.

[4] Cf. *Die Johanneischen Schriften*, i. 10 f., 37 f.

saying, "Little children, keep yourselves from idols,"[1] as if this were the last will and testament of his whole life to all Christians. At the same time, however, it is seen here how after the conflict of true revelation with heathenism had come to its proper end, the idea of heathenism found a wholly other import than it had found formerly, if passages of the great prophets of the middle period, which anticipate the later view, are excepted.[2]

§ 78. But, speaking generally, it is altogether wrong to wrest Christianity perversely from its spiritual and historical connection, and to seek one-sidedly to estimate by its last great phenomenon the entire changeful conflict of true revelation with its thousand-headed foe, a conflict extending over more than two thousand years. If we survey this conflict on its purely national side as it took form and shape in the whole long history of nations, we do not see this one nation of moderate numbers, upon whose better life alone the decision turns, withdrawn in silent seclusion from the theatre of the great history of the world; this was only the case in a very limited sense (p. 195). On the contrary, no nation of such moderate compass ever lived in such a constant changeful turmoil of nations as this, or was involved so deeply with its whole best life and effort, nay, with its entire heart and soul, in conflict with such different nations, great and small, or maintained in such a conflict its better nucleus and noblest aim so indestructibly, and in the best sense of the word so purely, in spite of all its distresses, errors, and defeats, and all the great vicissitudes which marked its course. That in this sharp encounter with the most different nations it was always the soul of the nation that was sensibly touched, and that participated therein with the most lively emotion, is, in relation to a people so profoundly seized by a higher aspiration of spirit, as self-evident as that its spirit was manifoldly

[1] 1 John v. 21.
[2] So, from their connection, Isa. i. 24-31, xxx. 22-32; and similarly others, precursors or successors of Isaiah; also Ps. l. and lxxiii. speak thus of heathenism, *i.e.* of the idols in Israel itself. Jeremiah's words, ix. 24-x. 16, strike especially deep.

and often deeply and fruitfully stirred. All quickening and close contact of this kind must, however, more or less influence the religion of this nation and its idea of revelation, since it was just these forces of religion and revelation, powerful in themselves and lying near to the heart of the people, that could be variously excited and newly adjusted or even transformed by some judicious development in a particular direction; and even new materials brought nearer to the mind of the people would largely influence it. If it is remembered, too, how one-sided the spirit of every nation is before it comes into close and vigorous contact with other nations; how much this particular nation in its first youth and even higher cultivation had still to learn; how greatly seductive and manifold the dangers were (§ 64 ff.) which menaced the tendency of its spirit that since the time of Moses was a settled question; how high was the culture, in other respects so different, of most of the nations with whom its intercourse was familiar; and how incomparably difficult notwithstanding the problem appeared which this nation had to solve if it would not be disloyal to its proper divine origin as the community of the true religion,—then we shall readily concede that by all these close and intimate relations it could obtain many and extremely useful aids and encouragements to its spiritual life.

It is worth while to follow up this subject more in detail; and although the farther back we go into remote antiquity the more difficult it is to get exact knowledge, yet some elements of valid knowledge are obtainable. But even with these it is most difficult indeed to determine trustworthily how far the old Egyptian ideas of God and their other wisdom influenced the structure of religion in Israel and of its new community at the hands of Moses, trained as he was in Egyptian schools; it is just in the certain disclosure of the more spiritual side of remote Egyptian antiquity that our science to-day is very backward; and whatever else found its way into Israel from that powerful source is of little moment compared with these all-important matters. But when it is considered that the question concerns just the most peculiar and creative element in the knowledge of God and the application of it to the community, and that what Israel under Moses partly defended and partly acquired anew in vehement strife with the Egyptians is precisely the opposite of what the Egyptians desired, it will not be expected that this was derived from them. According to ancient tradition, the Egyptians allowed their ceremonial vessels and festive dresses to be stolen from them by Israel under the guidance of Moses;[1] but what Moses is thought to have stolen from them was in reality something which they ought to have defended a thousand times more than mere costly vessels and dresses, if they had possessed it and knew properly how to defend it. But from the primitive times long before Moses many a precious fragment of reminiscence of more than national and human things was preserved;[2] and after it had found its home in Canaan, how much did this nation appropriate from old traditions and other spiritual treasures of this land even of the oldest times![3] In the happy days of the kings when the blessings of a long peace and of wide commercial intercourse were enjoyed, and in arts and sciences even the most distinguished nations were rivalled, a multitude of higher conceptions and wonderful traditions of divine things streamed in from the neighbouring Phœnician and other nations, and from far distant eastern lands, and blended with the old treasure of like conceptions and traditions the nation long had possessed.[4] The dispersion of the nation,

---

[1] Cf. *History*, ii. 95 f. [Eng. trans. ii. 65 f.].
[2] As the story of creation, Gen. i. ; cf. *History*, vii. 529 f.
[3] As the tradition of Sodom ; *History*, i. 347, 449 f. [Eng. trans. i. 242, 312 f.].
[4] Cf. *History*, i. 60 [Eng. trans. i. 39], iii. 378 [Eng. trans. iii. 276]. The name of the mother of mankind, חַוָּה, *chavva* (ιὤα, LXX. Gen. iv. 1), *i.e.* Life (LXX. Gen. iii. 20), is apparently derived from the Phœnicians ; this is indicated by the sound of this non-Hebraic name, which nevertheless was not unintelligible to the Hebrews, Gen. iii. 20 (for just these sounds are in the root merely Phœnician for "life"), and by the way in which in Gen. iii. 20 the name is interpolated. Cf. *Jahrb. der Bibl. Wiss.* ii. 165.

when its earthly power had declined, taking place early, introduced from all sides, but chiefly from the Assyrians and Persians, new and highly attractive doctrines and images of things divine, and completed the remodelling of its religious phraseology, giving it greater freedom and flexibility, a remodelling initiated long before by the great prophets and poets, and rendered desirable by the over-simplicity the rigid doctrine of the divine unity had occasioned.[1] With the Greek and Roman dominion came the freest intercourse with nations from the remote east to the remote west, and the widest diffusion of Israel, increasing its susceptibility to foreign impressions still further, giving richer fulness to its circle of conceptions concerning things divine and to its practice of the divinely-human life,[2] and thus facilitating more and more the transition of its type of religion, and finally of its community also, into the great wide world.

But amid all this contact with foreign nations, foreign opinions and customs, and even amid all changes in universal history, the divine fundamental thought, which was the life of this nation, remained untouched. It had sunk too deeply into its spirit, since the regeneration of the nation under Moses and the founding of its community; it had grown with its growth too firmly amid all the sorrows and joys of its changeful career; it had become too much its sure consolation and pride, and, above all, it was in itself too perfectly and absolutely true, not to maintain itself in such a way that it should never more be lost. At times, however, it was in great peril, and seemed about to suffer eclipse. But as the earthly fortune of the nation rose higher and higher in the first half of its long history, reminiscences of its sublime origin restored this thought to its full vigour and integrity; and during the deeper and deeper decline of the power of the nation

---

[1] *History*, iv. 237–239 [Eng. trans. v. 180–185], and *Dichter des A. Bs.* iii. 62 f.

[2] Whether the sacred customs of India had early influence is touched upon in the *History*, v. 223 [Eng. trans. vi. 169]; the most powerful influences came from that quarter only in the times of early Christianity, vii. 178 ff.

in the second half of its history, Messianic, *i.e.* Christian, anticipations in due time reinvigorated it again; until finally, when most violently threatened and well-nigh wholly eclipsed, Christianity itself raised this grand fundamental thought to perfect conquest over all heathenism from without or within, carrying it forward into the Christian community energized by higher power and transfigured in more effulgent light.

Special Indications of the Opposition to Heathenism.

§ 79. Meanwhile, in surveying this obstinate struggle between heathenism and true religion in Israel, it may very well be perceived, by a few specially strong and conspicuous indications, how mighty was the original impulse, how effectual the vehicle of true religion, notwithstanding all the dangers that menaced it from the spirit of heathenism. The struggle through more than fifteen centuries was indeed always of such a kind that heathenism, with all its long, powerful, and continually-changing assaults, was never able to touch the life-veins of the true religion that flowed with vital energy from the time of Moses, and were so well concealed and so firmly protected from the beginning by the living structure of the community. Apart from the proof its finished history gives, many an involuntary expression of its inextinguishable vitality manifests that this community itself could never be utterly destroyed. When, for example, after the first serious relapse into heathenism the whole community is threatened with extinction, and it is proposed to form a new community from Moses alone as the sole survivor, and instead of desiring this honour Moses pleads against it, and becomes still more urgent as intercessor for the existing community, what is there in this sublime narrative [1] but the breaking forth of the feeling that the community, when once established, has from the beginning, by virtue of the higher divine energy working in it, an indestructible life? When afterwards, at the

[1] Ex. xxxii. 7-9 ff.

commencement of the declining day of the old community, the gathering clouds, forecasting the overthrow of the kingdom of the Ten Tribes, threaten the overthrow of the whole community, and it is said that yet seven thousand loyal worshippers, untouched by heathenism, remain,[1] what does this indicate but the deep consciousness that the community, once built on the true foundations, can never subsequently fall into utter and irrevocable ruin? And when at last, as the declining day drew to its end, and all the great prophets from Joel and Amos[2] onwards so surely and constantly anticipate that, after the great inevitable blow had descended, a nucleus or remnant will survive as the beginning of the transfigured community which by divine necessity will come, what do we see in this but that the fundamental thought of the indestructibility of the community has now found standing figurative expression,—a figurative expression representing with the historical growth of the community the growth of the certainty of this fundamental thought and hope? But unconnected with the fluctuations of this great conflict, an obvious witness of this inner energy is found in indications more and more settled in the course of this history, showing only the deep feeling calmly dwelling in the life of the community, that cannot be otherwise than it is, and that again and again breaks out announcing its signal and abiding presence. The outward palpable marks of opposition to heathenism that find embodiment in law, such as that connected with material images of God, are not intended here; for they are not vital in themselves, and do but imperfectly correspond to the truth they aim to express; but rather are meant such marks as spontaneously show themselves in language and thought, as well as in the principles, manners, and usages of the community. Now it is

1. A well-known indication of heathen life that in common speech and in the prevailing intuition, much more in the freer picturing of poetic imagination and in imitative art, the divine is lowered too much to the level of the human, and

---

[1] 1 Kings xix. 18.   [2] Joel iii. 5; Amos ix. 8 ff.

confused with it. How far the ordinary custom in this community was from such a confusion is clear from this, that in their language the ideas of God and man are always very definitely and sharply separated, and in the delineation of the human there was never such a mingling of the divine in pernicious flattery as was always usual in heathenism, and ultimately became an ineradicable custom. Nothing is more common in heathenism than to speak of divine men; in the Bible, however, "men of God" is a phrase not employed, although sometimes an individual is called "a man of God;" but this is rare and exceptional, and occurs only in relation to one who merits the highest distinction for service in the advancement of divine things in humanity; and, moreover, it is used strictly not till long after his death, and with free retrospect upon his whole completed life,[1] and in ordinary discourse in the case of a prophet only in the early time during the purer theocracy and for temporary reasons.[2] Still more strictly, as if by the mere force of a fine feeling, it was never customary to call a man, even if he were the lawful king, "son of God," although the possibility of some such phrase was conceded;[3] but the term itself, with its combination of ideas, was reserved for one unique personage. Even with the use of the name of honour, "servant of God," the language was sparing, so far as it might apply to an historical

[1] Moses is spoken of as simply as possible in the Pentateuch. He is called "the man of God" in Josh. xiv. 6 in solemn discourse, but in the Pentateuch only by the last editor in a superscription (Deut. xxxiii. 1), and later in Ps. xc. 1; Ezra iii. 2.

[2] This is evident from 1 Sam. ix. 6; 1 Kings xiii. 1-31, xvii. 18, 24, xx. 28; 2 Kings i. 9-12, iv. 9-40, v. 8-vi. 11, viii. 4, xiii. 19 (xxiii. 17); Jer. xxxv. 4; and the explanation is found in the meaning of the word אֱלֹהִים, God, gradually received in certain phrases during the theocracy, and which obtained till the first times of the kingdom of the Ten Tribes; cf. *History*, ii. 443 f., 581 [Eng. trans. ii. 313 f., 412]; concerning Chanan, mentioned Jer. xxxv. 4, cf. *History*, iii. 22 [Eng. trans. iii. 14, n.]. The frequent use of this name, "man of God," is found only in the narratives of Elijah and Elisha. David is so called only Neh. xii. 24, 36. On the other hand, plain words are employed in the proper prophetic books of the Bible.

[3] But only so freely, with such little ambiguity and flattery as in Ps. ii. 7, Deut. xiv. 1, and the few similar passages.

man; when the dead were distinguished by it, the simple honour was therefore the greater.

2. Similarly heathenism is readily prone to elevate man as such above what is human, and to give divine honours to the living and especially to the dead. How far Israel was from doing this in all the centuries of its history, under the influence of an ineradicable feeling, cannot be made too conspicuous. Even the most respected prophets, who might readily be in danger of being worshipped as gods, and powerful kings, who in heathenism least of all withstood such temptation, were in this community constantly regarded only as purely human; and if any of them had basely desired deification, they would at once have seen such desire summarily extinguished. It was simply by the heathen, according to the Book of Origins, that Abraham was addressed as "Prince of God."[1] As a matter of fact, however, the disposition to attribute divine prerogatives to certain men on account of their position or their descent, and, what is essentially the same, to concede to them immunities to which in themselves there is no true claim, does obtain far more widely than is usually supposed. Thus, as this community in the course of its earliest centuries became more firmly established amid a thousand severe struggles from within and without, the priesthood was at last, it is true, made hereditary in the house of Aaron and the whole tribe of Levi; but although this house, even in the Pentateuch, was invested with full legal authority, and although, in the earlier times of the community of true revelation and religion, its sacerdotal prerogative, in a certain respect rightly considered divine, might easily become dangerous, and at a later period also there was always a danger of relapsing in so far into a heathen way of things, yet in point of fact the other spiritual forces in this community contributed so powerfully and so salutarily to prevent the possible worst consequences, that the longer its priesthood existed the more it shaped itself after a wholly different type than among the

[1] Gen. xxiii. 6.

heathen. The hereditary high priest in his unique pre-eminent distinction as the medium of the oracle might have degenerated with the greatest facility; but he always stood far removed from any divine reverence, and in the times of Christ belief in his gift of divination existed only among the common people as the colourless remnant of an antique reminiscence.[1] But the chief thing was, that so certainly as, according to the Pentateuch, true religion in this community always contemplated the prerogative that fell to the lot of the priestly tribe as not purely inherent, but only given by God under special historical circumstances, and therefore under similar circumstances revocable, so certainly might it at once cease in Christianity; as in fact it actually did cease without its being felt that any real contradiction was thereby involved. Now it is, it is true,

3. Not to be ignored that the rigid opposition in which the community at its founding was at once placed, not merely against all the perverse inner impulses of heathenism, but also against all previously made attempts to represent the divine to the senses by means of art, called forth a sudden breach with such attempts, and led to a new simplification in human thought and discourse and imagery, which, persisted in too obstinately, and conceived in a spirit of such one-sided anxiety as obtained during the last of the three great changes in its history, would have caused early the same irreparable injury to all the efforts of the human mind as we may see clearly apparent in Islamism. But every earnest and irreconcilable breach with perversities and errors deeply implanted in the mind, and every new tendency of mind arising, as in the primitive time of the founding of this community, under the overpowering constraint of law, involves this danger. But we have already seen how little this danger occasioned mischief for any length of time. A new freedom in discourse and imagery, corresponding to the requirements of true revelation and religion, must here break for itself a way; and it

[1] As is very strikingly apparent from the incidental remark in John xi. 51.

did this so completely and so well during the middle and finest period of this whole development, that, after the new rigidity that prevailed in the last period, Christianity perfected everything that had thus been begun. Side by side with the highest revelation and religion, no greater and more creative freedom of the faculty of imagination exists than that found in the New Testament, which combines in itself all that the Old Testament contains of such freedom, and all that the new Christian freedom further matures. Thus everything in which this community, as against heathenism, appeared to be at a disadvantage at last turns out rather for its benefit.

III.—THE RISE OF THE POWER OF THE HOLY SPIRIT.[1]

1. *Its Significance and its Possibility.*

§ 80. Necessary for the community of true religion, when once founded, as was that whole long conflict against heathenism, it was not competent to form the last aim of the community itself, nor to satisfy the main essential idea upon which it was based. When a living organism has to defend itself against the obstructions which from any quarter attack its very life, every conflict finds its necessity; and if what may be called the inner power of this life succeeds in such conflict in overcoming all the obstructions which throw themselves in long succession one after another against it, this power and this life, from their first violent breaking forth, that is, from their birth, grow more and more within the bodily limits the life itself gives, grow, indeed, as long as the outward body with its hidden life can grow and thrive, until the fruit of this life can no longer be kept in its bodily limits, but breaks forth from them by a violent final effort corresponding to its commencement. Thus it was that the life-impulse of true religion, as soon as it had become incarnate in this

---

[1] Explained below, § 132 *a*, as "the entrance of the Holy Spirit as a conscious power into humanity."—Tr.

community, turned itself against its foe in a first mighty movement. The rupture with heathenism accomplished under Moses, and made the law of the community, could not have been more violent or, if one may so say, more convulsive than it was;[1] so the conflict began precisely as it was continued through the long series of changing centuries and against ever new obstructions, until the fruit of this impulse of life, fully ripened at length amid uninterrupted struggles, broke the hard, strong, ancient limits of the community by a last all-powerful conflict under Christ, in order from its midst to form a new body corresponding to its spirit. If, therefore, the conflict itself from that first violent beginning to this still more violent end was necessary, it yet had its aim never in itself alone, but rather was initiated and inspired by a principle standing high above it, which found for itself in this community a new invigorating sphere of activity, and when this was dissolved continued its work in a new and transfigured sphere with larger designs and still greater vigour. And if the contemplation of that conflict through all its varied changes is instructive enough, nay, absolutely indispensable in order to trace distinctly the onward historical development of all that is at last preserved, not only as the highest but also as the purely immortal element in the life of the old nation of the true religion, yet we cannot stop with this, but must ultimately contemplate more directly what stands high above it, and yet, because it is not the purely divine, but the humanly-divine, finds advancement likewise with all the pains and labour of this long conflict.

This is nothing, however, but the impulse of the life of true religion itself. True religion alone was the continually uniform immortal life of the community founded by the forces of the spirit of it; and only because this life had from the beginning ever inspired the community all too purely and

---

[1] Apart from outward conflicts, the second, not the first commandment is here meant, with all other laws similar to it; cf. *History*, ii. 177 ff., 219 ff. [Eng. trans. ii. 124 ff., 154 ff.].

energetically, was there kindled in it that conflict against all hindrance and opposition seeking to limit and even stifle and suppress a life that in its purity and inborn divine energy is nevertheless immortal. If, now, in the struggle and conflict with obstructive errors, the human spirit, by the impulse and also by the light of revelation, approaches the divine, which always waits the favourable moment and the true point of communion in this approach (§ 17), and if both persistently and arduously co-operate permanently to win and successfully to maintain the truth and active energy which check the growth of human corruption and advance the interests of human wellbeing (§ 21–25), there arises thus a new humanly-divine spirit, which, as it has once worked effectively to this end, may work again more and more in a similar way and under similar circumstances. This same spirit may revisit the man it has once animated and possessed, guide him anew in every new complication of affairs, become the unvarying and predominant motive-power of his activity, nay, the very life of his life and spirit of his spirit, making its home within him, and filling with its own fulness his whole moral being. Nay more, an entire community may be decisively and powerfully influenced by it, and as an attendant spirit it may ever afterwards hover near, to inform it again in moments of conflict and trial, and renew its impelling power when new energy and inspiration are especially desired. Very appropriately may it be designated "holy," since it is no longer the merely human spirit, declining more and more in its indifference and alienation from the divine, a spirit that some definite historical period, with its earlier spoil of spiritual wealth, but also its new errors and darkness, infuses spontaneously into individual men, but it is the spirit long familiarly known as co-operating with the divine and therefore Holy Spirit, the spirit that is replenished with purely divine energies and inviolable by human corruption.

§ 81. If it is maintained, therefore, that what thus gradually grew in efficacy more and more in the community of Israel during its mighty conflict, standing high above it and directing its cause, was the holy spirit, the new power that in such a way and in such efficacy could arise only in this community, there is nothing inadmissible in the statement. For when the Spirit or the Holy Spirit is in question, as a purely divine power, it would be altogether inadmissible to speak of it as growing in efficacy or arising; the Spirit is, with God Himself, primordial and ever the same. It is otherwise, however, when we speak of this spirit in human history. For this history is in itself nothing but a certain co-operation of the spirit dwelling in man by his very creation (§ 11 f., 14) with the spirit acting upon it and influencing it from without by virtue of the entire creation and the divine forces dwelling therein; and this co-operation may by man's fault become so obscured and enfeebled that it is gradually more and more repressed, and then disappears altogether. But though such interaction may become in thousandfold gradation so dull and languid that it scarcely seems to exist at all, yet it does exist always, and always may one speak therefore of a spirit which, in a definite position of things and a definite age, arises or is formed historically, as with the individual man in actual life, so also in the pursuits and ways of human fellowships of all kinds, or even possibly in the whole of humanity. Moreover, if in a certain condition and age of human history an unholy spirit can arise, constituted of several mingled elements, as the Bible manifoldly shows,[1] so also a holy spirit can arise historically, as we maintain it has arisen in the community of Israel as the power of the Highest and Divinest that was possible in it.

But further considerations will enable us to understand this possibility more surely and in detail. What is termed spirit can be thought of as the impelling force of a life, especially of a higher, *i.e.* a rational life. Every force seeks to maintain

---

[1] One takes such delineations of the רוּחַ and πνεῦμα as Isa. xxix. 10, xix. 3; 1 Sam. xvi. 14 ff., xviii. 10; 1 Kings xxii. 22 f.; 2 Kings xix. 7; Hos. iv. 12, v. 4; Zech. xiii. 2; Rev. xviii. 2; 1 John iv. 1, 6; Eph. ii. 2; 2 Tim. i. 7. The different ways in which, according to the Bible, the Spirit can be Lord over men, and how God sends the Spirit upon men, will be subsequently considered.

itself and to continue in operation in its own province. Now if we speak in this sense of the humanly-divine spirit, we well comprehend that such a spirit, because it is historical, may suddenly be strongly moved and powerfully excited by a special conjuncture of circumstances; we comprehend just as well, that to become so powerful it must be cherished for a length of time and grow, and that it always seeks, nevertheless, to maintain itself in that force and form in which it has once arisen; even as it takes its name from the incessant, unremitting, ever-recurring expiration and inspiration as from a hidden depth. Thus arises among men that historical spirit of which we speak; it does not come from mere thinking and discoursing, or from occasional, detached acts of mere external necessity. Only as the spirit of man is consecutively and continuously moved by the Divine Spirit, moved more or less and with greater or feebler impulse, and chiefly in the great conflicts of life which violently stir and call forth its activity, does this historical spirit assume a definite existence, standing above man in this definite form and efficacy as a special spirit, and seeking to react upon him. For whatever has spiritual contents and force, and has once passed through the mind of man and taken more definite shape as it comes forth out of it, confronts him again as a spiritual entity from without, and seeks to determine his spirit still further where and how it can.[1] The spirit that flashes from the word can ever again present itself to the mind as a more or less distinct form; every completed act of man, the outcome of his mind, may, in the determinate intellectual shape it has taken over against the mind which has impelled it forth or beheld it, react upon the mind; word and deed can react upon the same mind from which they issued, or upon innumerable other minds which hear or see representations of them made clear by

---

[1] How the best thought and counsel lie chiefly as deep water in the wellspring of the soul, and become clear only as discreetly drawn forth, *i.e.* only as brought into clear words that perfectly exhaust the whole question in hand, the proverb (Prov. xx. 5) strikingly expresses.

conspicuous expression; if once, then also innumerable times, in a good or bad sense, according as the mind in its activity in speech and action may be impelled by the Divine Spirit or not; and all this in incalculable gradation. But by this reaction is already formed historically a definite spirit standing above the individual man or a whole human society, a spirit which, however powerful it may be, can yet, by every new excitation and elevation, be newly determined in character or force.

But where true revelation and religion are once in proper activity, according to § 21–25, there, on the part of those whose spirit is in suchwise most purely touched by the Divine Spirit and whose discourse and action place them before the world, words and deeds more perfectly agree, succeed each other more uniformly, and react more powerfully and emphatically upon themselves and upon all whose spirit is thus loyally guided. If, now, for this end those upon whom a spirit that is becoming historically more and more distinct and stedfast reacts, are enclosed by the firm native walls of the same community, the reactions and the further creations of this spirit will alike follow one another the more closely, and will maintain themselves the more firmly in a higher uniformity. And the same spirit which has established the community by its own mighty efforts will more stedfastly maintain itself in it, and continue to fashion itself more fruitfully in its own way.

It is thus clearly conceivable what the result must be when there worked in the community such men as Moses and as the rest of the founders of this community of whose labours, alas! reminiscence has left to us but scanty memorials, though along with Moses they certainly put forth for this object the highest exertions;[1] when subsequently to Moses similarly inspired men similarly worked in long, often slender, but never wholly interrupted series; when in the later changes

---

[1] Reference is once made to them outside the Pentateuch and the Book of Joshua in an old writing, 2 Sam. xx. 18 f., according to the better reading.

of the history of the community the more complicated and confused the conflicts of the time became, the more aims of a higher kind were striven after and obtained by ever new men of essentially the same spirit; and even the entire nation of the community was by this same spirit more and more informed. The new power that here arose is a power fully unknown, nay, impossible in all heathenism,—the power of the Holy Ghost resting in the community and at the same time sustaining it and leading it onward with an energy unattainable and inviolable by all the world. This power could be secured only along with and by that incessant conflict against heathenism already described, but it is something wholly different from that conflict,—a purely elevating and inspiring energy, ever as in a luminous cloud hovering about the community, available for all who sought to be elevated and sustained by it, uplifting and informing first of all and pre-eminently the sublimest and purest prophets, then with increasing influence others — poets, rulers, and incalculably many of the nation besides. And this alone was the power that could raise this community high above its extremest perils; and finally, when it had become in its whole divine strength and purity more and more palpably conspicuous, transfigured in itself in the highest degree, it could similarly transfigure the community also.

2. *Its Realization.*

§ 82. For what is most noticeable here is that this power of the Holy Spirit was actually enjoyed before the community itself was conscious of it; and indeed it was not possible that it should be otherwise. That which is purely spiritual (and there is nothing in humanity that could be so purely and definitely spiritual as the Holy Spirit) cannot come by human arrangement and institution, still less be manifest at the caprice of man. It either never makes itself felt among men at all, or it is in their midst before they are aware of it; and it is then a blessing of eternal and wonderful efficacy, never again to be withdrawn.

Indeed, the wonderful operations of the spirit in general, so far as it became, in the sense explained above, a humanly-divine power in this community as nowhere else, could very well be recognised early enough, as in fact they are recognisable. The power of revelation and religion was nowhere so intensely quickened and so often kindled to an all-irradiating and effulgent glow as in this community; and this is always a manifestation of this spirit as it should be active in humanity. It was active first of all most vigorously and persistently through the prophets (§ 29), and became at length pictured by Ezekiel in the midst of the exile as the inspiring energy which caught up and carried away the prophets whither it would; for Ezekiel with his vivid imagination readily represents such spiritual powers in sensuous figures, and lends to them definite shape and bearing. No power, however, was so purely Israelitish as this; and in the midst of the exile and of foreign surroundings it could on this account occur to the prophet as such a special power, high and long holy to Israel, far earlier than to the prophets who lived in great numbers in the old fatherland itself. Yet from the unique character of this community it could never be seriously supposed that the spirit in its wonderful manifestation and power necessarily belongs to the prophets alone, and could not influence other citizens of the community with its peculiar force and impulse perhaps suddenly, and fill them with its whole energy; as indeed the possibility of this was early enough admitted.[1] But it must not be overlooked that here the reference is throughout simply to the spirit in this special signification; of the "Holy Spirit of God," or more briefly, the "Holy Spirit," there is as yet no mention, although this spirit alone gives the wholly special conception and contains the full, true, all-comprehending energy here implied. In our immediate discussion the holy spirit is that which can

[1] Num. xi. 25-29; cf. above, p. 88; Joel iii. 1 f.

take possession of man, and strengthen him wonderfully with its power, withdrawing him from all contact with the unholy world, so far as the world might estrange him from the sanctity of the will of God and a holy course of life; or in other words, is the ultimate and at the same time highest protecting power of the holy God, which stands continually as a luminous cloud above and beside the individual man and the entire community to render aid and support when the danger is greatest.

According to all indications, it was not until the time of extremest peril, when the continuance of the community with its thousand years of high development was once more threatened, that this thought of a holy spirit penetrated it, a spirit for the community itself and the most isolated members of it inalienable, whose wonderful energy would forsake no one who once appropriated it and was earnestly desirous to follow its impulse in everything. When the old national realm of Israel sank to its decline and was soon to be overthrown, when consequently the protecting wall, that stood ready during the continuance of the old strong community to guard every member of it, seemed to be utterly demolished, and innumerable devout souls saw themselves wholly isolated in the midst of the heathen and exposed to thousands of unexpected and severe temptations testing their loyalty to the true religion; then for the first time the thought flashed forth clearly and attained its irrefragable certainty, that a power of holy spirit had long existed in Israel, and would forsake no one who in the deepest need of life should cherish it firmly, or in complete moral declension wrestle profoundly to win it back from God.[1] It must have been perceived, moreover, on glancing freely back into the whole past of the community, that this same holy spirit was already active from

[1] Ps. li. 13-15, cxliii. 11; Ezek. xviii. 31. This historical connection entirely agrees with the otherwise recognisable indications of the true period of Ps. li.; if in any far earlier psalm holy spirit must have been mentioned, it would be Ps. xxxii.; but in vain is this mention sought in that song whose Davidic origin is historically established.

the first founding of the community, and never since had there been a time when it had completely abandoned the primary sphere of its operation on earth.[1] In like manner, in the outlook into the whole future the thought was now suggested that the holy spirit could never again be actually taken from the community in its dispersion and contrition, much less in its return and renewal of strength.[2]

§ 83. The idea of the Holy Spirit and its consolation was afterwards firmly established in the renovated community assembling together again about Jerusalem's ruins. Yet it did not receive its full transfiguration until in Christ Himself in everything He spoke and did without exception the power of the Holy Spirit was manifested upon earth in its immediate presence and perfect and transparent operation, as never before, and possible only in Him. Under the assumption and claim that He spoke by the Holy Spirit, He, indeed, said nothing; still less did He, under such assumption and claim, perform even the smallest, most special and peculiar of His works. Yet never from mortal man flowed words and acts which came so clearly, so mightily, and in so direct and unbroken a stream from the purest impulse of the Holy Spirit as did His. In full historical light we see this, and the New Testament attempts in some passages to express it by general images and sayings drawn from undoubted experience. Here, then, was the ultimate issue as it must come. If, as remarked before, everything spiritual, having passed through human discourse and action, creates an image of itself more or less clear and of definite form, that will react upon the spirit of man and does more or less react upon it,

---

[1] Isa. lxiii. 11. The brief mention of this so important subject suggests that the prophet quotes from an earlier fragment, in which it was more copiously presented. The Book of Wisdom ix. 17 f. certainly pushes back the sending forth of the Holy Spirit beyond Moses to the beginning of human history. Cf. ix. 2; the division of the chapter in recent editions is still unfortunate.

[2] Ezek. xi. 19, xxxvi. 17-28; cf. xviii. 31; also especially briefly and emphatically at the end of a long description, Isa. lix. 21, where the "Spirit of God," according to lxiii. 11, is essentially one and the same with the Holy Spirit, but the simpler name suffices.

and if since the early dawn of the community this was an essential basis for the development of the power of the Holy Spirit; then, after our Lord's departure, the collected image of His discourses and deeds, and all that befell Him, must so influence those who believed in Him, that the same power of the Holy Spirit that working secretly and on separate occasions in the mortal Man had flowed from Him into the world, would now from the glorified Lord, united as into one intense energy, lay hold upon them with far greater and more irresistible force; and this power aroused anew by new circumstances and needs could, in the course of its operation, become still mightier.[1] Thus the Holy Spirit won its full significance and efficacy; and if, in the entire Old Testament, it is but seldom mentioned, and in the Apocrypha or intermediate books yet more seldom,[2] because in these last intermediate times everything which had been won before in the community sank back again into the most serious peril of derangement and dissolution, nevertheless the whole of the New Testament is full of its power and its wonderful fruits.

§ 84. Meanwhile there is a special idea which can come into consideration with this great chief all-embracing idea of the Holy Spirit only as collateral, but which nevertheless may prove to demonstration that the important agency which is here alone ultimately in question was active in its proper principle and elements long before it entered in perfected power and form into the history of the community of the Old Testament and then into that of the New. It is not surprising that, in a nation that at an early period must have reflected much and keenly as to what revelation is and should be for men, inquiry should just as early arise as to what it

---

[1] John xiv. 12-14. A passage important but obscure, perfectly clear, however, in this connection; repeated because of its importance, xvi. 23 f.; a principle not so definitely stated as in John's Gospel, yet essentially conspicuous in the synoptics, as is clear from Mark xi. 22-25.

[2] Wisdom of Sol. ix. 17 f., and Sus. 45, where the "holy spirit of young Daniel" is spoken of. The Apocrypha of the New Testament is a late and loose appendage, that of the Old an "intermediate" and transitional literature.

cannot be if it would be accepted as a true revelation at all; for, according to a known law of human thought, truth is recognised most distinctly by its direct opposite. It can now clearly enough be seen how easily and how certainly the right answer was found to this question, and with what sharp brevity it was expressed. He who will know whether he actually possesses a revelation from the true God or not, inquires whether what he regards as such has not been derived merely from his own heart, and from what is simply pleasing to himself.[1] Every one, if he will be candid with himself, may institute such an inquiry in his own case; but others may also perceive whether what is regarded as revelation is actually revelation or not, since the mind of man in its deepest ground and eternal essence is everywhere the same. What is to have authority as revelation must therefore be derived, not from man, but from the mind and heart of God, and must correspond to His inmost will and nature as well-pleasing to Him; but what is in this respect the truth to the distinct apprehension of one man only, he may be sure, must be current as truth among all men equally. Nevertheless, since the word of God and His will to men cannot be externally published like a human command and a human word, self-deception concerning what is God's word and will is always possible, and every one must therefore verify what he regards as God's word and will by acting in accordance with it in all strictness and integrity. Only what in this way at every step by practice and experience verifies itself as right and well-pleasing to God can be ultimately accepted as the word of God. Thus, then, a circle of necessary movement opens so far to every man; he must (1) withdraw himself from himself, not regarding his own capricious fancies, and such opinions as are simply well-pleasing to himself, as right

---

[1] The oldest relevant passage is from the Book of Origins, Num. xvi. 28; another old passage is found in Prov. xviii. 2; but Jeremiah presents the fundamental conception most clearly, xxiii. 16, cf. xvii. 9; and similarly Christ discourses, Matt. xvi. 17. Cf. also Ps. xxxvi. 2, according to the right reading.

and therefore divine; he must (2) be always on the alert to attend to every actual word of God, come to him whence it may, whether immediately from God or indirectly from tradition and instruction;—and with every individual and all men there are times when to learn the true will and counsel of God is most urgent and most earnestly desired;[1] but he must also (3) test by his own conduct and ascertain by experience whether what he regards as God's word and will be so actually, that he may not deceive himself.

This, then, is the outline of all true procedure in this community from the earliest times in inquiry after revelation when the starting-point is the idea of the revelation of one's own heart. And no one expresses it in every way and in all brevity more definitely and clearly than Christ Himself, when He says, according to the reminiscences of His beloved disciple, that faith is to be placed in Him, because He knows certainly that His will and His word agree with the will of the Father; if that is refused, however, one may seek to do the will of God itself earnestly, or, what is still more easy for every one, believe in Christ "on account of the divine works themselves" which He does and which every one may do after Him, and in the doing of them learn by experience that they bring salvation. It is therefore self-evident that no one may first demand of Christ outward signs and wonders for what he is to believe, since already such signs and wonders are abundantly manifest if one will see them; and no one is excusable who will not see the great divine work itself which is accomplished in Christ as revealer of the word of God.[2] If, however, all the better members of the nation of this community, all through so long a series of centuries, continually acted according to these clear principles, as in the plainest manner Christ Himself ultimately disclosed them, and most

---

[1] Amos viii. 11; Deut. viii. 3 (cited Matt. iv. 4).

[2] This is the sum of what is said on this subject in John's Gospel, especially cf. John vii. 16-18, xiv. 11 f., with ii. 18 f., iv. 48, vi. 30 ff., and xii. 37; and it does not in the least contradict Matt. xii. 39, xvi. 4.

fruitfully too, because He could point to His own lofty example, then the explanation is thus given what superabundance of a new spirit, such as no single heathen nation ever experienced, and for which there is no more appropriate name than that of the Holy Spirit, could at length firmly upbuild its power in this community.

§ 85. It is just such a residue[1] of spirit and life, accumulated in a nation from past ages of splendour as an inexhaustible treasure, that can lead it happily through the darkest periods of distress and dissolution, repeating themselves anew and with increasing gravity. What would have become of this community, grown grey as it were before old age, in the times of the dissolution of its old kingdom, had not the power of the Holy Spirit already been so efficacious as to be able, even out of this dispersion and gloom, to bring it together again for its final development? And what would have resulted from the last and permanent dispersion of the nation, had not the power of the Holy Spirit before its commencement become incomparably purer and mightier still through Christ and His disciples, and with sure hand saved from destruction at least all that was immediately essential for the building of a transfigured community? No single heathen nation, how much less one of so moderate an extent, ever experienced, in the midst of its gradual decay, such a history of new resurrection to nobler and immortal life! In short, as Christianity brought the true consummation of this whole incomparable history on the side of revelation and of the community (§ 42-48), so also it brought the same consummation on the side that is most wonderful and sublime, the power of the Holy Spirit.

3. *The Holy Nation.*

§ 86. If it is not until the last period of the history of Israel that the name and idea of the Holy Spirit are perfectly realized, there is another name that from the earliest age of

---

[1] *Ueberschuss, i.e.* superabundance, surplusage.—Tr.

the community was employed to designate the destiny to which this nation, as possessing the true religion, was to feel itself, and in its noblest elements did feel itself appointed, as its history ran its course in the midst of that of all other nations. Under the prophetic leadership of Moses, and amid a movement that affected the destinies of the whole existing world of humanity,[1] this nation had been made familiar, and in a most impressive and memorable way, with the knowledge and fear of the true God, and it had learned that it could find salvation and peace upon earth under His holy guardianship as it listened to His word. It must now also remain continually in this attitude of mind, and know also distinctly what eternal obligation, what security of trust, what inexhaustible hope such loyalty of mind to its calling involved. Every permanent relation into which an individual man enters, and every system of things under which a whole nation places itself, must necessarily have its clear ground of expectation, and if it should proceed from a message of divine assurance as here from the prophetic message of Moses, it may well be called a gospel. And this gospel of the Old Testament corresponding to the gospel of the New, yet having the colour and form of the ancient oracles of Israel, runs thus:—

> So shalt thou say to Jacob's house and tell to Israel's sons;—
> You yourselves saw what I did to the Egyptians,
> And how I bore you on eagles' wings, and brought you home to me;
> Therefore, if only you listen to my voice and keep my covenant,
> So shall you become my peculiar inheritance,[2] above all the nations!
> For mine, indeed, is the whole earth and the circle of all the nations;

---

[1] Ex. xix.; cf. Judg. v. 4 f.

[2] *I.e.* immediate property and eternal and favourite possession. The old German word *allod* is, alas! obsolete, but expresses as nearly as possible the meaning of the word סְגֻלָּה preserved in its fresh signification in this ancient oracle. Deut. vii. 6, xiv. 2, xxvi. 18 f. repeat it; Ps. cxxxv. 4, Mal. iii. 17 imitate it; Eccles. ii. 8, 1 Chron. xxiii. 9 give a new, freer, and late use of it. The old German word comes from the feudal age, and contains precisely the image here employed; for the distinction between an allodial estate (*i.e.* an estate held of no one, a free and independent property) and an estate held of a superior, was known in the early Persian, Assyrian, and Egyptian empires, and is not first found in the German feudal age. The word סְגֻלָּה is derived from סגל = שָׂכַל, *to look at, behold*, as ἴδιος from εἶδος.

But you shall be to me a kingdom of priests and a holy nation :
These are the words that thou shalt declare to the sons of Israel.[1]

Here, then, are the mutual terms which must ever be found in a covenant between two free spiritual beings, viz. promise and the fulfilment of conditions, privilege conceded and obligation imposed, each binding on each side in a sort of reciprocal interest as the special case requires; for here, of course, the agreement is not between two parties in every respect equal, the one being, so to speak, the self-mighty lord, the other the servant whose happiness depends on his intimate association with his lord. If, therefore, the true God, who as such is Almighty, may be compared to a great lord who in his wide domain has a number of larger or smaller well-appointed estates, all of which, however, he cedes to lower lords, retaining and cultivating one only as his true allodium and treasure, his special and favourite immediate possession; then in such comparison God here undertakes to deliver over the rest of the nations as estates in fee to other gods,[2] feeble and subordinate, and to retain Israel alone as His immediate most cherished possession, to care for it as property specially dear to Him, and to consider the advancement of its higher salvation as His own peculiar solicitude,—if only Israel on its part will always diligently hearken to His voice, and keep in all faithful submission the covenant thus set forth. That is to say, more particularly and in other forms of expression, this one nation shall not stand at a distance from Him as the other nations, *i.e.* the heathen do, having long since gone astray, and shall not be separated from the immediate knowledge of Him, and from His love and grace, by any insurmountable barrier; but as priests, according to an ancient and invariable custom, immediately surround their God, listen to His voice, and perform His works, *i.e.* offer sacrifices well-

---

[1] Ex. xix. 3-6; cf. *Hist.* ii. 195 [Eng. trans. ii. 142 f.]. From the form of the oracle, the fifth verse requires "and the circle of all the nations," or some such words, to complete the sense.

[2] The same image subsequently expressed in passages like Isa. xix. 1, Deut. xxxii. 8 f., with the peculiar, Deut. iv. 19, and many others.

pleasing to Him, so shall this whole nation be a kingdom whose King is the true God, and whose citizens are all priests; or in one brief and now clear expression shall be a holy nation, a nation in which not merely a few, as priests and kings, are holy, but all the members of which shall be alike invested with divine sanctity, and because so near to that which is holy, and so like-natured with it, shall be covered and protected by its own inviolability. Such, then, is the reciprocal relation between the true God who expects such obedience from the nation, received into His love and holiness, and promises protection on His part, and this nation which promises obedience and may expect protection in return. Nevertheless, this reciprocal relation, henceforth to be permanently obligatory, that is, a "covenant," has not casually arisen, and is not purely arbitrarily entered upon; it is rather the outcome of the lofty earnestness of that history through which already the nation itself has passed,—as indeed the first couplet of the oracle points out by lofty expressions that sound[1] as from the very sanctuary of Jahveh Himself.

This, therefore, was the fundamental thought upon which the community was based, which filled and sustained the spirit of the nation with just pride, illumined it with hope, and by its claims and discipline was the formative principle of its life. The whole passage is as the high clear note in which at length is summed up sharply and pointedly all the impressions and all the teaching of a mighty and decisive age just past; and indeed there is no lack of incisive expressions in it.[2] As the sublime oracle closes with the phrase "a holy nation," so in this name the whole fundamental conception

---

[1] This lies clearly in the word וָאָבִא, which from its essential signification and its connection may here be translated: "I brought home" to my house my sanctuary, as similarly in the ancient song, Ex. xv. 17. The first half of the whole image only is followed further by the later poet, Deut. xxxiii. 11 f.

[2] What an ὀξύμωρόν lies in that one phrase "a kingdom" (i.e. properly ממלכת) "of priests;" nothing can be more creative and at the same time more incisive; and in that primitive time!

had its firmest root, and by means of it retained its lasting hold upon the memory of every one. Not that in the life of the ancient nation this name was of common and everyday use; it would soon have lost its original elevation and full significance if it had been; on the contrary, it is never employed in ordinary speech. Only late poets, about the time when the idea of the Holy Spirit (§ 82) more and more strongly penetrated, venture to designate the members of the nation generally as "holy" where it appears suitable thus to distinguish them from the heathen.[1] But neither the name nor the entire fundamental thought could ever be forgotten in the community; and as soon as in apostolic Christianity everything that for a millennium and a half had been struggled after in the old community found its consummation, and the Holy Spirit was operative as never before, this foundation thought in the same words, now newly vivified, is applied, by no less a person than Peter, to the new community,[2] and Christians are now "holy" with a reality, an emphasis, and a just right such as never before had been known. In other respects, however, this idea of the Holy Nation is so extremely fruitful in its application to Israel by prophets and poets in the Old Testament, that many similar names and ideas are created after its likeness, which reappear in the New Testament with similar renewed freshness.

§ 87. For here it must be said further, that there is no nation, ancient or modern, that is not nourished upon some fundamental thought peculiar to it, as upon its imperishable life-bread, and that does not gather about some sanctuary which appears to it indestructible. But in investigating more closely the nature of that immortal element which, as an inspiring thought and a sure hope, was the soul of any ancient nation except Israel, not to speak now of modern nations, nothing will be found that can compare with what is observed here. In that grand august fundamental thought which in

[1] Ps. xvi. 3, xxxiv. 10 ; Dan. viii. 24, xii. 7 (not, however, Deut. xxxiii. 3).
[2] 1 Pet. ii. 9 ; but also Rev. i. 6.

its youth had fallen to its lot, as the true light and life of the spirit, Israel had everything that could serve as undying reminiscence, as all-pervasive discipline, as lofty sublime hope, and which, even if what is perishable in a nation does at length fall into corruption, should survive the mortal community in order, transfigured in purer light, to serve the same end in a new and immortal community.

1. No energetic and noble nation ever lived in antiquity without looking back to an elevating past, and without possessing in the remembrance of its ancestors and ancient heroes a perennial spring of fresh inspiration. But what nation could look back, as Israel could, upon a lofty primitive age, when it was itself born again into a genuine nation by means of the purest impulse and forces of true revelation and religion alone? Only implicit loyalty and confidence in the firm holding of divine truths once known, only unbending stedfastness in long deep sorrows, and self-denying and courageous turning back from error and stumbling to ever greater divine truths, and ever surer conviction of eternal human duties,—only qualities such as these in the highest measure possible to any nation of antiquity, together with the prophetic power of a Moses amid one of the most energetic national movements, and the very shaking of heaven and earth,[1] were the true founders of this community; and when, also, at length the recollection of this grand age firmly imprinted itself upon the mind in brief luminous pictures or in longer stories, certainly no other nation could look back as this could to such a period of its own great origin. The retrospect extended, moreover, beyond the special age of its origin to forefathers, as to distant and therefore purer exemplars, in whom already the first germs of all true religion began to appear; and upon what a brilliant array of mighty prophets, national leaders, and men otherwise worthy of honour, did the eye rest the wider the extent of the long succeeding ages of

[1] According to the ancient lofty figures in the song of Deborah, Judg. v. 4 f., and other older reminiscences; cf. *History*, ii. 306 f. [Eng. tr. ii. 217 f.]

changeful destiny through which the nation lived! But the chief thing was the very rigour of its religion had long since taught this nation to conceive and to retain in the memory every historical event with greater simplicity, sharpness, and truth than was easily possible among heathen nations, whilst in the survey of all divine and human things its lofty sweep and range of mind, in purity and energy impossible to the heathen, and possible to Israel only through true religion, sufficiently saved its historical intuitions and reminiscences from too prosaic and frigid a severity. And whilst a keener perception of what was historically elevated was native to this people, without at all accustoming them to overlook human weaknesses[1] in their own history, or even in the remembrance of their remotest forefathers and the noblest of their leaders, the penetrating backward glance into their whole changeful past must thereby be the more richly inspiring and instructive. But when at length the purest, and in all its apparent insignificance, nay, humiliation and dishonour, sublimest kingly life that could possibly enter into human history was yet, during the continuance of the limitation of this community, beheld in Christ, and threw back its soft but widely-illuminating rays upon all that was once resplendent in the whole past of this community, an historical light was shed over all the truths of revelation and religion such as nowhere else in all antiquity could be found, nay, rather such as must soon penetrate even this antiquity everywhere by its own excess of radiance.

2. Thus, then, was that fundamental thought historically attested and transfigured. If the nation that possessed it and bore its name was ever at any stage of its changeful life and

---

[1] It is remarkable that, according to the Pentateuch, even Moses standing already in the full sunshine of his whole historical elevation is overtaken, although only by a moment of unbelief, and Abraham alone appears as perfectly faultless. In the third division of the history greater anxiety and one-sidedness prevail, as in departments of the spiritual life, so in historical narratives and reminiscences, as the Chronicles compared with the corresponding older historical books shows; but how it is surmounted again by the first Book of Maccabees, and then far more by the Gospels and the Acts of the Apostles!

EWALD I. T

endeavour, transiently or more permanently, easily or with more difficulty, hurried away by caprice, or arrogance, or any other mistaken feeling, the same thought was an irresistible means of correction and discipline, because it would then become a question whether it still deserved the name under whose radiant lustre it once became a nation. Just then, therefore, the genuine prophets and other men like them arose to make clear to the mind the glaring contradiction in which the nation found itself with its own better destiny and its sublime past, nay, with its own fundamental laws and vows, old and yet ever new and ever binding. The idea of the covenant relation as the most evident and obligatory in which the relation between God and man can be conceived, or more strictly speaking, between the true God and the nation that had promised fidelity to Him, becomes then a luminous argument against obvious aberrations and disloyalty; the prophet becomes the advocate of the violated true God and the accuser of the nation, and the discussion of the most complicated situations and most grievous offences, whether of the whole nation or of some of its most powerful leaders, becomes an open plain transaction in the light of that divine truth which the audience itself acknowledges. Because the voice of the prophets, or of any one who will express his thought in prophet-like way, must now be heard without let or hindrance, according to the essential constitution of the community, the way was ever legitimately free upon which the inexhaustible fulness and clear light of divine truth could more and more be manifest, and could accomplish whatever might yet be possible within the community as the change of the times and continually new necessities permitted. And thus it was, above all, the lofty straightforwardness and frankness of the prophetic reproof, as it ever maintained itself subsequently in this community amid altered circumstances, and at length through Christ was transformed to gospel utterances in the mouth of a Peter, a Stephen, or a Paul, which so powerfully contributed to its further progress.

THE RISE OF THE POWER OF THE HOLY SPIRIT. 291

Now, in the different tendencies and movements possible to human freedom, the law of contradiction involves that just where the simplest, plainest, and therefore apparently the heaviest demands are made upon the human will, there opposition may assume the strongest form; where such demands, in the presence of open and mischievous resistance, must consequently rise higher and higher, there the opposition becomes most obstinate; and the more unreservedly and consistently the fundamental truth advancing unceasingly in its direct course unfolds itself to its supreme point of development, there all such resistance may also show its boldest possible front. And thus errors and offences against true revelation and religion, whether in public life or in writings of all kinds,[1] are nowhere so apparent as in this nation, and lamentations over the obstinacy of the people are nowhere so increasingly loud,[2] and against divine truths, as they became more manifest, complete, and conspicuous, nowhere did so decided and powerful a resistance show itself as here; and towards the end of each of the three great turning-points of this entire long national history, this resistance grew from stage to stage to the highest possible degree of force.[3] But that upon all these stages the divine truth was, on the other hand, the more perseveringly maintained and the more consistently promoted; that the increasing stiffneckedness was gradually broken and overcome, even amid the direst temptations and distresses, owing to the high measure of flexibility

[1] The Pentateuch shows clear traces of manifold refractoriness, transparent by their inner truth, *History*, ii. 239 ff. [Eng. trans. ii. 169 ff.]. So the New Testament. Where, indeed, do doubts, refractorinesses, stiffneckednesses against the truth already known, show themselves conspicuously in more or less artistic discourse in the whole of ancient heathenism so strongly and openly as in Job, in Ps. lxxiii., in Malachi, Ecclesiastes, and still more in the New Testament?

[2] Only writers from the time of the divided kingdom onwards discourse frequently of Israel's stiffneckedness, from Prov. xxix. 1; Ex. xxxii. 9 ff.; Deut. ix. 6, 13, x. 16, xxxi. 17, to Jeremiah, with the yet stronger words, Isa. xlviii. 4, and others later.

[3] At the end of the first turning-point such incidents as Judg. xvii.-xxi. are not so properly thought of (they are from an earlier age) as of 1 Sam. ii. 22-25; at the end of the second, Ezek. xvi. 22, where he speaks summarily; at the end of the third, the New Testament.

and pliantness of spirit induced by contemplation of the clearly-known divine will; and that thus there was added a brilliant and numerous succession of witnesses of divine truth revealing itself to the world, witnesses or martyrs equally great in misfortune as in triumph, till, as the greatest witness [1] of all, Christ with His disciples closed the series,—all this was only a further consequence of that fundamental thought.

3. Now it is the essential nature of every true fundamental thought, that even wholly apart from the special historical occasion which first called it into being, it retains its inner truth and fruitful influence wherever it is applicable. But where there is no point of connection for it, it remains as certainly always dead, although elsewhere it might long since live; and that in no heathen nation in antiquity, the longer human affairs developed themselves, was there a place for such a thought where it could have sprung forth with equal original energy, and have prepared a sphere for its own evolution, is evident from all that has previously been said (§ 52 ff.). According to the difficult course which all human movements take, when once set on foot for the highest task of all human history, only in Israel and during the existence of its national community could such thought at last completely work itself out; but the true possibility for it was already given in Israel's more definite constitution as it was fixed (p. 284) from the beginning of the community. For it was never said that every individual member of the nation, although he should sink down into an unholy life, should in any case belong to this "holy nation;" for excommunication was known and practised even in the oldest period of the community.[2] In this way it was understood for all time that in its ultimate fulness the promise of blessing in this as in every other divine utterance practically falls to the lot of those members of the community only who fulfil its conditions. Since, therefore, in the course

---

[1] Christ Himself is distinguished from all others as "the true witness," Rev. i. 5; cf. *Johan. Schrift*. ii. 105 f.

[2] *Antiquities*, 101 ff. [Eng. trans. 75 ff.].

of time, amid all the never-failing trials and afflictions, it was more and more clearly shown how few at all perfectly fulfilled these conditions, a threefold conviction established itself from an early period in this community, viz. (1) that inasmuch as in no God but Jahveh Himself, so also in no other community is that salvation to be found which is the one ultimate aim and the indispensable hope of all true revelation and religion;[1] (2) this salvation is never lost in this community, but rather out of all its temporal imperfection will ever arise again still more powerfully to its last great perfection; but (3) just as well in its efficacy as in the hope of it, this salvation belongs to the approved fragment or "remnant"[2] only of the actual people of this community, and therefore also to all men who fulfil its already established and eternally necessary conditions, for with the distinction of the spiritual Israel from its contrary, mere nationality with its outward limitations is already in point of fact broken.

Accordingly it was the Messianic hopes, with their new wonderful leverage for consummating everything that is yet incomplete in the ultimate vocation of this community, and for reforming everything that has become defective and perverse in its historical situation, which as a remote result sprang forth out of its fundamental thought. And thus, after the sultriness of the high mid-day of its history had made perceptible enough how much that was necessary was yet wanting to constitute it more emphatically and more surely, and not merely in name, a holy nation, the great prophets arose in long and varied series, rivalling with each other, and yet essentially agreeing in pointing out in luminous imagery and in demanding in struggles of soul, as it were, from the future the perfected salvation of this community and the Perfecter Himself; until in the sluggish course of the last period of this history, when these Messianic hopes gradually threatened

---

[1] A double-thought, by no writer so profoundly apprehended and so impressively set forth as by the great Unnamed, Isa. xl.–lxvi.

[2] P. 265 f.

to languish, Christ with His disciples at last fulfilled them most completely so far as in their time they were to be fulfilled, vigorously recalling the fundamental thought of the community, creating out of it for the entire body of mankind a holy nation, and leaving its further growth to that power, not till then wholly conspicuous (§ 83), the power of the Holy Spirit, which alone, as it must work in Christianity, can maintain and perpetuate a holy nation.

§ 88. In all this there is continuity, a single great history in spite of all deviations and entanglements ever returning afresh and finally perfecting itself upon its chief fundamental lines. This nation, in its first entrance into the great history of the world, had too truly experienced wherein lie the energy and work and the salvation of a true revelation and religion; it had accustomed itself since its first firm consolidation as an organized and well-ordered community, with too much difficulty at the outset, too deeply afterwards, to the laws and institutions of such a religion and to the rights and duties of its community; it had subsequently in a long and changeful history, by all its new offences and their issues, and by all the gains and losses of its earthly state, ever at last recognised anew the sole fundamental thought of its spiritual life as too well-grounded and too conformable with truth, to be able in its inner feeling and clearest perception ever to abandon it again. From a shepherd tribe it had become a settled nation; from a simple, thoroughly warlike people it had become an eager sharer in scientific and sceptical wisdom, and all the finest arts and practices of a tranquil and peaceful life, even finding at times its highest joy therein; from cleaving to its native clod it had been thrown into all the world, and had accustomed itself to the widest intercourse, and yet had assembled again on its old sacred soil as the dearest spot of earth; and from regarding the heathen with dread, it had become from various motives more and more familiar with the great heathen world; and yet in all these transmutations it was ever the same revealed word of God which formed its bond of union, the same fundamental thought which sustained and supported it, the same true God who was held to be its highest good of life and its inalienable heirloom;[1] whom it sang in its martial youth as its sole God of war and giver of victory;[2] whom it found again in the age of its wisdom as the spring of all knowledge and the light of all life,[3] whom it cherished continually in its deepest sorrows with new and wonderful fervour, and celebrated to all the heathen at the commencement of its great dispersion with even greater courage as the only true God,[4] and whom it would never really forsake in the darkest labyrinths of its latest life.[5] So completely did the highest truths of all revelation and religion, as well as the related problems of all knowledge, penetrate deeper and deeper into the whole life of this nation. What Moses and the great prophets first published as the sure word of God was immortalized in the actual life of the whole nation in home and kingdom, in charming reminiscence and sweetest refrain, by the flowing song of innumerable singers; was investigated, sifted, deepened by the schools of wisdom, and transfigured by the rare art of sublimest poets and practised writers of all kinds. All higher life of the spirit concentrated itself, therefore, with this people more and more upon the one endeavour, to protect and to maintain the more carefully that which it had perceived to be the highest good of its life, and whereby it found itself placed, with an ever clearer consciousness, high above all the heathen; and also to search into it, and in its

---

[1] According to the fine but originally purely poetic figures, Ps. xvi. 5 f., cxlii. 6; Jer. x. 16 (li. 19).

[2] Ex. xv. 1-18, xvii. 16; Judg. v.; Ps. xviii. and the rest of the Davidic Psalms; also 1 Sam. ii. 1-10.

[3] According to Prov. xiv. 27; cf. with Ps. xxxvi. 10; Jer. ii. 13, xvii. 13; Prov. xx. 27; Ps. xxvii. 1, xxxvi. 10; cf. with Isa. x. 16; Micah vii. 8; Bar. iii. 24-iv. 3.

[4] As is evident not merely from Isa. xl.-lxvi., but also from many psalms of those days; among them, however, are some much older than that long prophetic book.

[5] Taking all the three great Roman wars, that after Herod's death, that under Titus, that under Hadrian, and also that against Christ and His disciples, and the truth of these words will be found.

truth defend it against all doubts whencesoever they might come. Thus its glance and its judgment were on this side sharpened more and more in the long lapse of centuries, as if it were to be among all nations the only properly God-taught or theological nation. And the more the external power of the nation sank at last into gradual and irrevocable decline, not solely because of, yet indisputably side by side with this eager direction of its energy to, so to speak, divine life-questions, and the all-absorbing heated internal controversies about them, the more profoundly and exclusively it felt itself charged and summoned to maintain the spiritual boon, for such it certainly believed it, which had fallen to its lot from the hand of God.

§ 89. Yet the plainest proof of all this is that this nation was very early, with sufficient clearness and certainty to itself, impelled by its own true God to recognise as the highest and last aim of its life the maintenance of this very blessing and its diffusion among the nations. The inner fulness of knowledge of the true God, and the readiness to live according to His word alone, grown stronger and more concentrated during so many centuries, at length, in the time of the ripening fruit, pressed toward the world without; and when this nation in the Assyrian-Babylonish dispersion had so deeply experienced the corruption of the heathen, and the danger of losing entirely under their yoke its own better knowledge and activity, it felt itself for the first time summoned by its God, as with the loudest voice, to serve Him as an instrument in spreading His name and His honour among all the heathen. It was, as may truly be said, the first and most mighty stirring of the Holy Spirit itself, entering as it did at that time into the consciousness of this nation, which impelled it to recognise this vocation as the last and highest aim of its whole life;[1] and if this, the divinest

---

[1] Nothing can arise more creatively than this new thought as it came to the great Unnamed, Isa. xl.-lxvi., who at the close, lxi. 1, cf. with xlviii. 16, not in vain appeals to the Spirit of God as no older prophet had done.

aspiration of its whole earthly existence and every other that waited for consummation, could not be adequately and certainly fulfilled until Christ Himself, in the limits of this community, had brought the inner perfecting, it found its fulfilment at once the more irresistibly in order spontaneously to seal the dissolution of the perishing old community, and its transition to that which was new and imperishable. Indeed, about those times, when the whole ancient world was in a state of dissolution, great numbers of priests of Isis, of advocates of the heathenism of Asia Minor and other old and celebrated systems, and of Chaldæan mathematicians, forced their way from the East to the West, which was eager for such innovations; but a pure energy of the spirit impelled those only who had received the divine call into the West as into the whole heathen world.

The question is therefore no longer asked, why only in this ancient nation true revelation and religion moved on to their proper goal, and rounded the course marked out for them in antiquity? It is no longer asked why Christ and His disciples could go forth only from this nation—at once its greatest and most immortal glory, and its last and deepest divine humiliation? The nobler and more distinguished of the other nations of antiquity, each allowed some other high endeavour and task to be dearest to its heart, and to absorb its most earnest efforts; no one of them applied itself to the problem which filled the whole being of Israel with increasing purity and strength. By pursuing the end which appeared the highest, each attained fruits of imperishable value; but no one of them attained, as did this, a fruit of such indispensable and eternal value in relation to all other nobler human aims.

§ 90. But as we must here close, not so much with the perishable nation of Israel as with the growth of the wonder-working power of the Holy Spirit, whose high significance we shall still further consider in the discussion of Holy Scripture, just as definitely must we make it conspicuous that this power, even where it enters into history in its highest manifestation, as in Christianity, is never active without conflict against heathenism, indispensable everywhere (§ 61), as heathenism is explained above. This marvellous power is the freest and most mighty, but also the purest spring and impetus of the force with which this irremissible conflict is to be waged; so that whether it is as free, powerful, and pure in its impetus as it must be if it is really the power of the Holy Spirit, can clearly be perceived by this,—does it actually direct itself against heathenism, or have heathen errors and impulses possibly intermixed themselves with it? For this sacred power in man, like everything spiritual that moves him, may be again obscured and confused.

Here then is the most important fact to be noted, viz. that Christianity as soon as it appeared became deeply and seriously involved in the conflict against the principle of heathenism; so little did it originate in part from heathenism, according to the grave error of some modern scholars (§ 77 f.), that at once in its freshest youth, as we see it in the New Testament, it struggled most profoundly and sincerely against it. What was the whole wide aberration of scribes and Pharisees against which Christ and His disciples had unremittingly to contend, but a most dangerous outbreak of an element of heathenism, not, however, coming from without? But in those centuries, when the old community by its own error deeply declined, various heathen superstitions pressed in from without; and the whole demonism which Christ combated as no one before Him had done was essentially nothing else.[1] Moreover, the endeavour to amalgamate isolated propositions and truths of the true religion which at that time sought to penetrate the great heathen world so powerfully from the old community, with propositions of heathen school-wisdom, or indeed with the allurements of the more subtle arts of superstition described above (§ 68 f.), was

---

[1] To what is said in the *History*, v. 292 f. [Eng. trans. vi. 221 f.], may be added, Philostratus' *Life of Apollonius*, iii. 38–40, iv. 20, 45; and Plotinus' *Enneads*, II. ix. 14.

quite a common occurrence in those times. These attempts rapidly increased as the new knowledge of Christianity, deeply agitating and putting to so high a strain the minds of men, overran the world, and the first germs of gnostic false doctrine of every complexion appeared. We know how much the apostle had to contend against manifold species of this newly tricked-out heathenism.[1] The wonderful power of the Holy Spirit was active at that time as the genuinely Christian power, and its genuineness might be recognised perfectly as it directed itself against everything heathen, and did not allow itself to be obscured by it.

[1] The cases in Acts viii. 9-24, xiii. 6-12, xix. 11-19, may be taken. If that Syrian magician Barjesus (p. 229) sought to fascinate his victim with a glance, the apostle's threatening him with divine blindness is explained. What is the strife against Gnosticism, beginning in apostolic times and showing its elements in the New Testament, and subsequently rising higher and higher, but the powerful conflict of youthful Christianity, breaking away from everything heathen which would take possession of it because of the great essential freedom native to it!

PART III.

REVELATION IN THE BIBLE.

§ 91. THAT the revelation of the way in which the perfect true religion must exist among men could only be won in the ancient nation of Israel, stands now historically established, as previously explained. Just as undeniable is it, that in the higher historical connection in which all members of humanity and, as the chief members, the nations stand to one another, no true spiritual good obtained by one people is to remain useless and unfruitful to others. The greater such a good is, and the more inexhaustible its value, the more is it destined to pass over to all nations, and to serve for incalculable ages as the means of advancement and salvation. But of what significance this boon is, and how, when once surely obtained in one nation, it is to serve to all for the same firm basis of eternal ever-progressive salvation, is shown above at the end of the first principal sections (§ 48–50). Now in the right use of such a boon, the longer it is properly employed the more is it indifferent from what men or nation it has been transmitted to later times; just as we use the fine completeness of the arithmetical notation, unknown to the Greeks and Romans, without thinking very much that we owe this advantage to Arabians at present so deeply degraded, and more remotely to the ingenuity of the Hindoos. But if such a boon in its whole historical significance and its true nature and extent is recognisable perfectly by modern nations only from the carefully preserved writings of an ancient nation, it is indispensable to investigate and to understand those writings thoroughly; indispensable first of all for those who are regarded as the special administrators of this boon for the rest, and who take upon themselves in so far special duties, and further, for such also as seek by their own investigation to be assured how the boon is rightly administered, and whether it is so by those who are specially called to administer it.

This is the case here, since according to § 2 we have had for a long time no other historical means than the Bible by which to satisfy ourselves of the nature and content of true religion as it has been revealed. And the investigation must here turn specifically upon three questions carefully to be considered;—

First, upon the question what the Bible is in itself, contemplated as a collection of different writings; how it arose, and what actually belongs to it. In this special science we nevertheless do not desire to teach how the Scripture of the old Israelitish nation is to be explained in language and substance; how it has grown from time to time as a whole and in special parts, and what contents in particular it comprehends; nor how the smaller part now called the Bible has separated itself at length from its wide circumference, and has been preserved up to our times; these are three very comprehensive subjects of inquiry and knowledge, properly included under the science called at present with good reason "Introduction." Everything belonging to that department of inquiry we presuppose here. Nevertheless we must here touch upon as much in the wide circuit of this science as is indispensable from the intimate connection of everything that is to be said on this subject.

Secondly, however, a wholly different question arises which belongs entirely to the science here under consideration, since it refers immediately to the nature of revelation. Everything we rightly call revelation consists as to its contents, (*a*) of words concerning God and the relation as well of the universe as of men to Him and His will, words which were spoken or written down by men whom we briefly designate revealers; and (*b*) of the deeds and fortunes first of these revealers who standing in closest connection with such divine words, must be regarded as clear witnesses to the world of their truth; and then also (c) of the deeds and fortunes of the whole people in whose community and for whom they worked. For only in the full accord of these three elements lies the full and certain witness that the divine truths of which we here speak, as of that which is obligatory on men, in those human ages and relations were actually manifest in such a manner that we have not still to expect what is higher and truer as the guide of conduct. What we call revelation is therefore the divine truth as it reveals itself to men with its own peculiar force in the first instance, and by consequence also operates in a purely creative manner in the course of human affairs; nay, it is as a force and impulse, the most independent and powerful that can lay hold of the human spirit and determine it to corresponding action. But the Bible as it has come down to us, contemplated as a whole, does not give this original and immediate stream of revelation; it contains portions too various and at first sight too little in agreement with each other; many portions, moreover, which only remotely from that highest aim serve to impart to us pure divine truth, and finally it stands as literature far away from the original activity and first marked occurrence of revelation, which is the chief and most important point. For revelation permits those nearest to it in place and time to hear in their original clear sentences the words which flow forth from the lips of the revealers, and enables them to behold immediately in those revealers, and in the whole nation in which they worked, correspondent deeds and destinies. All literature which discourses of revelation is, on the contrary, somewhat more remote and mediate, with respect to which we ask only how far it is adequate as a mere means of giving to us the pure and perfect image of the original revelation. Therefore we cannot evade the question, how far the Bible, taken for what it is and must be, answers its aim as a means of representing to us the original truth and splendour of revelation.

Thirdly, the reply to the question why just these books retained in this collection we now call the Bible are recognised as sacred, belongs to this place, in conjunction with the other question how in that case we are to understand and employ more particularly the idea of sanctity.

In answering these three questions the whole subject here to be handled will be compassed. But since our present concern is rather with the many proper points of view from which the Bible has to be contemplated and employed in relation to revelation and religion, we most easily arrange everything relevant here concerning the historical development of the Scripture, and at the same time correspondingly to the nature of the subject, according to the following considerations successively :—

I. 1. *What preceded all Holy Scripture.*

§ 92. Now it is especially clear that revelation itself in its entire movement and in its highest effort is prior to all that is sacred, and also to Scripture itself. Revelation is the original force which in this domain first puts everything in motion; it existed already in the most distant primitive ages before Moses, when yet very little or nothing at all was written; it existed also after Moses, when writing was employed in the community with increasing frequency; it determined for a long time its whole spiritual life originally and creatively; and to it, as the starting-point, everything ultimately returns. Indeed, it may be said that at first between revelation and Scripture no connection was found, no link necessarily uniting both. It may be compared in this aspect of it with poetry as another original faculty of the human spirit, whose similarity has already been pointed out (p. 10 f.).

But so far as revelation in the old community from the time of its founding occurred chiefly in prophecy, and prophecy had the principal share in the public guidance of the nation, it stepped forth into the wide publicity of the whole national life from the first. The highest affairs of the community as they took shape in the changes of the times became the great permanent sphere of its activity; an abundance of great prophets worked, vieing with each other with their purely spiritual power; and as the market-places of Athens or Rome echoed with the public discourses of great orators, so in this community the public places by the sanctuary and elsewhere were resonant with the voices of the prophets;[1] only with this difference, the prophets spoke in a kingdom that was laid under obligation to remain ever faithful to the true God, and they always entered upon the scene chiefly as His public advocates. Had revelation at any time degenerated as deeply in this community as the oracle did among the heathen, it would just as little have borne the freest publicity as the oracle; but it was plainly distinguished from all heathenism in that, as the pure truth, it demanded as well as bore the greatest publicity. The great Unnamed among the prophets, glancing back, however, to all older prophetic revelation in Israel, expresses this briefly and expressively from the mouth of Jahveh Himself in the words,[2]—

"Not in secret discoursed I, in a corner of a dark land."

We no longer know exactly how Moses himself made his appearance as a prophet among the people. His mode of presenting himself changed, indeed, with the times. From the Pentateuch[3] it is evident that when he had become the great recognised national leader, and spoke to the people as such, or rather Aaron for him, there was such change of manner. But in those centuries when revelation worked most

[1] The form of such discourses of the great prophets as Joel i. 12, Hos. iv., Isa. i., ii., v., Micah i. and vi. 1, 9, Jer. vii. 2 ff., is significant; the poet, Prov. i. 20, viii. 1, borrows his lofty images from this source; and, moreover, Amos vii. f., Isa. xxix. 21, Jer. vii.–xliv., speak sufficiently of their public discourses.
[2] Isa. xlv. 19.
[3] *History*, ii. 250-255, 315 f. [Eng. trans. ii. 177-181, 223 f.]; *Antiquities*, 421 f. [Eng. trans. 318]. The reminiscences of the Pentateuch clearly indicate that in his appearing Moses was a wholly different prophet from the later ones.

perfectly, and the life of the old nation was yet wholly independent, it was in the way just described that revelation developed itself, that is, amid the freest publicity of the entire national life; and this would not have been possible had it not taken such a position in the community from the first. But in this, as in everything else, the end corresponded to so high a beginning and so luminous a middle period, surpassing, however, in its inner perfection everything that had preceded it. For what can be more public and open than the whole work of Christ, notwithstanding that in His day the old independence and freedom of the nation had long since disappeared? The double rule of the Romans and Herod oppressed the land, and in addition the scribes and Pharisees put their ban upon conscience. But men like the Baptist, and afterwards Christ with His disciples, made use once more of the original freedom and publicity existing in this community by the fundamental law of revelation and religion.

Ever since its leadership by Moses, this nation, not merely in politics, as was the case with many other Semitic and with Græco-Italian nations, but also in religion, had allowed itself great openness, freedom, and frankness of life, and it could not live otherwise. The whole first thousand years of its existence passes away while it is engaged in the highest task which could be committed to the mind and heart of a nation in antiquity, viz. by profound inquiry, free knowledge, open self-determination to bring its politics and its religion into perfect harmony; and when at length, during the long last centuries of its life, it lost its political freedom more and more irrevocably, it at least held fast with much tenacity, within the protecting limits of its community, freedom and publicity in all matters of religion. In this the nation stood alone in antiquity; and if peculiar dangers and ills were occasioned by such openness, there was in this, as in every similar case, the compensation of still higher blessing in that, once for all, in the highest affairs of human life, it had the courage not to shun the light, and it could not again depart from this settled constitution of its public life.

A clear and vivid conception of this whole relation of all revelation in Israel to public activity is most essential. Nowhere during the earlier centuries is there anything said of Scripture, or at least of Holy Scripture. Even the Ten Commandments were first received by the whole people purely by word of mouth, and by word of mouth were approved by them; their committal to writing, as the oldest reminiscences clearly attest,[1] was of later occurrence. From the nature and designation of Scripture it is thus very manifest that no greater, no more irreconcilable contrariety is to be conceived than that between the true revelation, as the Bible shows it to us, and Islamism, which from the first is based upon its sacred writings as its foundation. Whence this sharp distinction arises will be considered more particularly below; here, however, it is necessary to make the distinction itself conspicuous in its full importance.

2. *The General Relation of Scripture to the National Life.*

§ 93. Now the question the Bible raises is not at all a question of a mere manuscript, or of some special sacred fragments of a manuscript, as in the case of the Koran, but rather of such a vast multitude of books, diversified in character, yet all regarded as sacred, and handed down to us as sacred, that when we speak of it we can speak at once of a whole body of literature. If we consider, therefore, according to our previous remarks, the relation of the literature of a nation to the entire movement and development of its life, we find everywhere, both among ancient and modern nations, that it may be an exceedingly potent lever, incomparable of its kind, for the advancement and culture of the spiritual life of a people, but only with the coincidence of many other circumstances favourable to it. It is idle to expect from the best

[1] Ex. xix., cf. with xxiv.

writing much influence with a nation little familiar with letters or practised in their use; idle, too, to commend a composition to it as sacred and authenticated, if it knows nothing of sacred writings or desires to know nothing of them. One of the vain fancies and delusions of our journal writers to-day is that public opinion, or at least such a public opinion as shall be of real use and steady continuance, can be created by mere books and newspapers. All literature is rather only one of the many intellectual forces which contribute to the guidance and culture as well of the individual man as of an entire nation and age; it is never once an original power laying hold of the spirit with direct energy, but it arises slowly, is late in coming to perfection, and impresses men in different ways, not by itself, but by its good or bad contents, since, indeed, all literature is in itself only a means for attaining other ends. As a single and not at all primary spiritual power, literature only follows the far more potent and originally energetic aspirations and efforts of the human mind as they appear chiefly and specially in different stages of the life and aim of a nation, and ultimately also in periods when a higher impulse of universal humanity as it stands above them is fully pursued by separate nations. All this may be recognised the more surely among the oldest and earliest-cultured nations, the more everything is developed in their midst from its original sources. We may trace it also in the ancient nation of the true revelation and religion as plainly as possible, if we only follow exactly the historical indications which may with sufficient certainty be discovered.

1. Has a nation experienced something great and noble in its history, has it won and victoriously maintained its freedom, or better still, has it proved itself to possess the persistent courage to break the old inward bonds of its spiritual life, and subject itself to a legal constitution in which restraint is placed on base impulses and passions, literature will then acquire in its midst a new significance and authority; and should it have had up to that time little practice in letters,

and little pleasure therein, independent and creative minds at once readily rise up to make use of this agency for the nation's permanent elevation and instruction. Individual inclination and necessity co-operate happily to this end. The new laws and organization of public life must be perpetuated for constant use, and this is best done by writing. The overflowing stream of memorials of great experiences of life is collected from the wide flood of national songs and oral narratives into the firm channel of written composition for enduring remembrance; even for admonition and instruction in new dangers of the national life, the living word begins now gradually to avail itself also of the more widely-reaching literary publication.

That writing was known among the people of Israel before the time of Moses, and was applied to manifold needs, we now know with sufficient certainty; but their literature, rightly so called, without doubt commenced with the sublime age of Moses, and in the immediately succeeding centuries was further developed in various ways. It is self-evident, however, that since the spiritual life of this nation, after the founding under Moses of its religious community, began directly to take a direction quite peculiar to itself, and soared to a height unknown to the rest of the nations of those days; its literature also, from its first rise onward, could not but be wholly different from that common in the world of the nations up to that time, alike in contents, in import, and in spirit; and that it was so is fully attested by the few but genuine fragments of the literature of Israel that have come down to us from those earliest centuries, and are found in various parts of the Old Testament. Just as we have here a nation, wholly different from any other anywhere else upon earth, securing its formation and culture in this remote antiquity, so we have also a literature shaped and fashioned under a spirit, and thence also with results wholly different from those of foreign or of other Semitic nations, although in external literary forms Israel followed the old models of earlier Semitic culture. Where do we find in all the literature of those ages a fragment comparable in contents with the Ten Commandments, and at the same time in such good preservation? Where is there a composition like the responsive song of Deborah, swelling with such inward force and magnificence notwithstanding all ancient severity? Or like the oldest prophetic warning of Israel, still preserved?[1]

§ 94. 2. Meanwhile, in no ancient nation possessing a peculiar literature known to us to-day in its whole range, do we see the different possible branches and arts of literature developing themselves perfectly in the earliest age, even should this age extend through many centuries: the germs capable of highest growth lying in every literature once vigorously flourishing are too numerous to ripen all of them in one outburst. We see this in the case of Chinese, Indian, and Greek literature, and we see it also in the case of Hebrew literature. When the people of Israel towards the end of the time of the judges, half broken up as they were, learned to reconcile the greatness and strength of a lawful human government with the purely divine to which they had been accustomed; when under the kingly rule they felt themselves transformed to a wholly new energetic nation, reached in national power, in prosperity, and in aptness for government the highest point attainable in their mortal state, acquired a taste for the more exact knowledge of all nations and kingdoms and treasures and peculiarities of the broad earth, for universal science and for all kinds of higher art, and entered upon a competition in these pursuits with the most cultured of the older nations; and when by this wholly new elevation of their earthly life they became exposed to the new grave danger of losing altogether the foundation of all divine life already won,—then it was that their literature renewed, uplifted, and broadened itself with a surprising rapidity and marvellous power, and unfolded its wealth in the succeeding three or four centuries to the highest perfection which, so to

[1] Ex. xxiii. 20-33.

speak, was within its reach. In all this it followed only the new wonderful impulse which at the beginning of this whole historical period energetically seized the better minds of this people, and which, allying itself and blending with the eternal and divine elements already historically possessed, brought as the result this double glory. If this glory could not be unfolded, however, but as that new impulse seized the whole nation more and more deeply, yet it must be remembered that after all it is only spiritual incitements and powers which form the basis and entire structure of a literature, and upon whose special character its special value depends. But here these incitements and powers were the creative thoughts and pure energies of true revelation and religion which, inherited unenfeebled from the previous age of the community, passed over into the new state of things and into the new impulse of their literature, and sought and found in that literature the finest and most perfect expression possible.

Springing immediately from the warm glow of this new inspiration were the immortal songs of David and his imitators, which diffused the charm of a sublimity and dignity and a deep fervour and tenderness, with the polish of a perfected art, over all the Hebrew lyric poetry, so that it remains unsurpassed by the lyric poetry of all ancient nations. All other kinds of poetry also flourished at this time with an inward exuberant fulness of power and splendour. Didactic poetry transfigured the selectest fruits of independent wisdom or philosophy; dramatic poetry, in its lower form as comedy, sharply castigated the follies of the day in playful mood, in its higher form as tragedy addressed itself to high earnest problems of the relation of man to God and God to man; and the drama of Job, notwithstanding its simplicity, surpasses all the later Greek tragedies in sublimity of conception and depth of feeling, just as the true revelation and religion of this nation are superior to those of the Greeks. Moreover, historical composition displayed its strength early in every direction to satisfy the higher needs as they arose. In the

Book of Origins it attempted about the beginning of this time to fill up the outline of all old histories of men and of nations, of customs and laws, from the creation downwards, and the result was so complete, so luminous, so worthy of the high theme, that neither a Herodotus nor a Livy can be put in the scale against it. In later times it undertook to call back into remembrance in graphic narrative the gigantic conflict between the new kingly and the old prophetic power in Israel. These were only two of the principal directions it followed. The knowledge of the separate objects of creation found its literature also, but owing to causes mentioned below we are not now adequately informed of the more particular contents of it. Indeed, it is the nature of all literature, once carried forward to a higher stage of cultivation, and sustained in further progress by the expanding capacity of a nation nourished upon its fruits, to endeavour to bring within its scope everything in which the desire of knowledge can find interest.

In the meantime, whilst literature advanced thus on all sides with such creative force and originality to its purest perfection, there sprang forth in the nation a wholly new offshoot, which had nowhere its like in the works of any other ancient people, and which in Israel itself was destined to overshadow all other achievements of its literary activity. This was prophecy. In the age when the new kingly power, after it had won its highest merit and brightest glory as deliverer of a nation almost disorganized, was already succumbing to the danger of abusing its authority thus gained, prophecy developed rapidly and to high excellence; and the entire conflict between these two chief independent powers—a conflict possible in the midst of this community in the mid-day of its history—attained its sultry height. If the prophets of Israel, and most of all those of these centuries (§ 26-33), are unique in character, it is easily understood that the literature which sprang from this lofty conflict has nowhere its equal in all antiquity. And the more the conflict concerning the perfecting of all true religion became gradually the deepest and most vital thought of which this people was conscious as of the best part of its life,—a conflict whose mightiest lever the prophets always were,—the more highly significant must this new branch of literature become. For it sprang as no other did from the conflict of the hour, from the pressing momentary needs of the higher life of man, and may be compared with the daily stream of pamphlets of our time, or with those wonderful Epistles which ardent toil changing every day wrung from the Apostle Paul. From prophecy, therefore, all Hebrew literature first received its peculiar impress and acquired its inestimable worth; it was not earliest in the field, but it could not but become the firm substantial centre from which all the brightest radiations of Hebrew thought streamed forth.

§ 95. 3. But this whole literature must assume, in many respects, a very different attitude and form when the nation itself, from the ninth century before Christ, was gradually and unremittingly with violence and completeness torn from its native soil, just after its happiest condition had come to it there, and was scattered in the midst of the heathen. Its literature, cultivated to its perfection through so many centuries, was now too dear and too much a part of its life not to be found a priceless treasure and source of consolation in the Captivity; and the most pious were always, to be sure, the most assiduous in the preservation and in the study of the best of these books. In the thoughts and prayers and songs of the Exiles many of the old tones are heard again in new strains; and that a great number of the songs then collected in the psalter were composed in those times, earlier or later, and in those regions outside Palestine, we know to-day, after close inquiry, with sufficient certainty. But the same investigation has taught us that even apart from Ezekiel's great book not a small number of prophetic writings originated in the "strange land," called forth as it were by the powerful after-working of the genuinely Hebrew literature of the earlier prophets with all its imperishable richness and high culture, and yet were sufficiently independent and original to obtain equal estimation with many of the best works of the former period.¹ Indeed, we are able to mark a new feature which is important in relation to the history and significance of this whole literature of the ancient nation. Members of the community who felt themselves prophetically inspired in the strange land, if they delivered their divine utterances in the old way, could find few hearers or none at all; but they felt themselves irresistibly impelled nevertheless to put their words in circulation, and they therefore wrote them down at once, perhaps as whole pieces and books, and sent them forth into the world as shorter or longer pamphlets (the name is not to be feared), certain that they would find consideration enough from all who were sufficiently prepared to understand them. And the result shows us to-day what a rare influence must have proceeded from many of them.² For the first time in the history of this literature we have here therefore clear and evident examples how words and speech, without having been spoken in public, as was formerly the case, at least in their chief purport, and even without bearing the name of the author, can nevertheless purely by their own beauty and truth at once exert a rare influence. This is possible; but it can occur only when literature has long since become one of the first needs of a nation. But if such wholly special circumstances are present as in this case, it finds in its explanation its defence as well.

For many reasons it is best carefully to separate this whole powerful new stream of writings as it must have poured itself once into the wide lands; all the most important of them must naturally have found their way into Palestine sufficiently early, and increased the already broad volume of the rest as,

---

¹ The Book of Nahum is the first clear example of this. Cf. *Proph. of A. T.*

² The Book of the great Unnamed affords the chief example of this, Isa. xl.-lxvi.; it was evidently first compiled from several pamphlets by the same author.

indeed, they were preserved along with them ; but historically they can be again understood with sufficient certainty, and rightly estimated only as they are thus separated. They represent a first great powerful echo of the loftiest notes of that earlier genuinely Hebrew literature without which they could not have originated. But in other respects they are fully inspired by the breath of the most genuine revelation and religion peculiar to this people ; and some portions of them are of equal rank with the earliest in creative originality and power.

§ 96. 4. As soon as the remnants of a larger community of the old nation found themselves firmly settled in the ancient home again, the activity of its literature, so peculiarly cultivated for a thousand years, reawoke also in its old way ; and the first elements of the community chiefly that, sustained by august Messianic hopes, gathered about the new temple in Jerusalem, raised this literature once more in all its branches to its ancient elevation. Nevertheless, the new literary impulse was but as the fine evening-glow of a bright day in which the purest and mightiest forces of the true revelation and religion had produced their master-works. In the succeeding centuries, as the old spirit of the community declined from stage to stage, and the original power of revelation was more and more enfeebled while religion became proportionately formal and dull, the characteristic literature of the people could less and less retain its old pure elevation ; and during the prophetless time a literary spirit prevailed in which a lofty creative originality was conspicuously wanting. For a long time, indeed, the inherent energy of all true revelation and deeper religion reacted salutarily, forming as it did the indestructible constituent principle of this community, and ever breaking forth afresh, vitalized anew by the old literature whose more important parts were now collected and pondered with growing zeal ; only very slowly did the spirit that had vivified it earlier disappear from the national literature, which nevertheless lived and according to the needs and expedients of the age became extremely fruitful again; and in the declining stream of these centuries there still emerged many a composition as if newly created by the purest impulse and inspiration of the ancient time.[1] But in the main the wide and varied literature of these later days was but an aftergrowth of the best literature of the community, more and more feeble in conception and degenerate in spirit.

Influences from without are closely connected with this declension within. As these last centuries came to their close, and the life of the community was thrown into greater confusion, the disposition increased to give precedence to the literature of the foreign nations who swayed the destinies of the time, and the wider the diffusion among the heathen the greater was the blending of the style and manner of heathen models. When the resuscitation which the Maccabæan age brought both to the whole nation and its literature was attended with no results of permanent advantage; when also the most ambitious poetic authorship of the time assumed the dress of the Sibylline oracles, and a man like Philo in Alexandria knew only how to flavour the old native wisdom of Israel with the Greek in order to make it palatable,—then death itself, one may well imagine, must have already cut the lengthened life-thread of this literature once so wonderfully proud, and for so long a period running its mighty course.

§ 97. 5. But when Christianity appeared, at once the inner and immortal life of this people, grown grey with years, rose again in literature also, and the risen Christ wrought this marvel. Indeed, it may be truly said that Christianity, bringing, as was shown above, the fitting conclusion in the development of revelation and religion, gave also to this literature the true perfection. It is of no moment that in the new literature which streamed forth from its inmost heart in the early years, the Greek tongue was soon exclusively

---

[1] The Book of Daniel, the oldest contents of the Book of Enoch, the first Book of Maccabees, and the Book of Wisdom may be mentioned; but, alas! many that must have had a quickening influence were subsequently lost.

prevalent; the spirit from which it flowed is the most genuine and at the same time the dearest and mightiest that ever breathed in the literature of this people. It is of no moment also, in this most important aspect of it, that through the new stream of writings there ran two clearly distinguishable colours of thought, indicating the two different provincial springs from which it flowed; for the earliest portions of the Gospels, even as the Apocalypse, the Epistle of James, and the four writings of John, bear the most genuine Hebrew impress, whilst Paul's Epistles, with others dependent upon them, come from a Hellenistic source; in Luke's writings, however, there is a kind of mingling of both colours, and the rest of the later writers more and more divest themselves of the Hebrew dress; but such different peculiarities are lost and vanish in the mighty homogeneous spirit that penetrates them all. It is the spirit of true revelation and religion that moves in these writings in the richest and most varied way that it can move in any mere writings; and when the stream of thoughts, reminiscences, and intuitions it originated flowed in the fullest and purest force, the pages of Christian literature gave them an imperishable record, the noblest and brightest possible.

It is idle to suppose, then, with respect to the spirit that inspires the literature of this nation, that the latest and noblest expressions of it now blended in the New Testament are different in their origin and source from those immortalized in the Old Testament. The truth is rather that in all kinds of literary art, in narrative, song, prophecy, admonition, and doctrine, the same spirit which dominates in the Old Testament once more revives in the New in all creative ardour and power, in order that there may be a fitting receptacle for the highest truth and knowledge which on the basis of the old true revelation and religion could come at last to decisive clearness and eternal certainty. Where a branch of literature like the prophecy of the Old Testament, so wholly special and possible only under special historical conditions, had lost its fitting place (§ 38) in the progressive life of revelation, it could flourish once more only as it was artificially resuscitated, as the Apocalypse shows. Nor is a perfect work of art like the Book of Job to be expected; in this time of dissolution of all the main conditions of the old national life, the peaceful happy moment for its creation was wanting. But, nevertheless, each of these writings is conceived with a literary skill with respect to which one does not know which most to admire, its simplicity or firm and certain execution. Yet most of all to call forth our wonder is the fact that writings like these, composed principally by new authors in the most changeful and transient moments of an age which oppressed them severely and persecuted them with hostile hate, are yet characterized by so great an inward and outward perfection, and form the eternally eloquent and noble witnesses of the loftiest and purest thoughts of all true revelation and religion.

§ 98. These, then, are the five distinctly-marked periods in which the long history of this literature falls. If we see now how in its general unfolding it always follows essentially the great impulses and needs of the history itself, we can clearly observe also it has one special tendency. If we cease to look exclusively at the mere length and temporal change of this literature, and consider its breadth or the compass of the different great subjects which with special zeal it drew, as it proceeded, into its circle, it is not to be mistaken that only in the second of these five periods did it unfold itself most copiously. The different kinds of poetic art flourished at that time, but the memoirs of all the objects in the universe exercised its powers also, as well as the free wisdom of the world; and scarcely among the Egyptians, Phœnicians, or Greeks was the circle of the departments of all literature ever so widely extended as it was then among the people of Israel. In the following three periods, on the contrary, this circle became increasingly contracted, whilst writings on the questions of revelation and religion continually multiply, and not only in number, but above all in contents and significance also far surpass just as certainly those of all the rest of the nations.

Even in this the literature follows only the powerful course of the general development of the nation. As it was more than all others (according to p. 295 f.) a theological nation, so its literature became with growing exclusiveness and completeness a literature that can very well be characterized in one word as truly theological; and in this it stands alone in all antiquity, as will more particularly be shown below. Thus was perfected on the side of literature what (§ 86–90) was specially significant in the growth of this nation. With every people of antiquity its highest and most perfect aspiration and its noblest wealth always found corresponding expression in its literature: so was it with Israel, and hence it became possible that a literature was formed in its midst which has not elsewhere its equal. Nevertheless, before we consider this more at large in its more particular significance and issues, we must direct our attention to another of its features.

3. *Natural Simplicity and Artificiality in Literature.*

§ 99. An immediate consequence of this relation to public life is that the literature of the nation of Israel arose and continued to shape itself just as freely as that of all other ancient nations. To this its essential naturalness and simplicity belongs also the circumstance that the prevailing form in which the writings appear publicly is in the highest degree simple. Public documents, such as the Ten Commandments, always bear in themselves their own authentication. But a book of history was issued in this nation, pursuant to a standing custom, without any indication of its authorship; indeed we can trace this custom down from the oldest to the latest book of history, so long at least as the genuine Hebrew usage was faithfully retained. The superscriptions of the books, according to the same old custom, continued to be very simple, very different from the ornate and over-ornate style of the superscriptions in books of the later Semitic peoples;

of prologue or epilogue there is in the later books scarcely the first rudimentary forms, as will soon be noted more at large. Even collections of songs appear without the names of the particular poets being indicated in them; and indeed to such splendid old artistic poetry as the Song of Songs or the Book of Job their authors did not subscribe their names, although the artistic poets gradually became fond of superadding their names. At a subsequent period, when it seemed necessary or useful to distinguish the names of authors in historical books or collections of songs, it was done with all antique simplicity.

The single branch of literature in which from the first, and as an invariable custom, the names of the authors were specified was prophecy; not, however, from literary vanity, but from quite another cause. The writings of the prophets, far more than all others, excepting public documents, proceeded from the public life of the nation itself; and as the prophet must answer for all he said in public, so it was only a corollary of this that he should publish nothing in writing without his name. Moreover, what he published of the winged words of his discourses was intended to remain as a permanent witness of the truth of his prophecy, and on this account his name could not be omitted. Thus it is sufficiently remarkable, that just in that branch of literature that was most important and characteristic, and by which Israel was distinguished so highly above all other nations, the exact indication of its authorship was in earliest times a necessity. Still more easily is it understood that each of the Epistles, more and more numerous as they were in the times immediately succeeding Christ, must bear at the top the designation of the author; the two exceptions, the Epistle to the Hebrews and the First Epistle of John, are explained from special causes which in each case were decisive.

It is this grand simplicity and naturalness, visible everywhere by a thousand signs, which distinguishes the Biblical writings so pre-eminently. It is seen even in the only two prologues and epilogues which are found, one in one of the latest books of the Old and the other in one of the latest books of the New Testament, for each is a model of its kind in brevity and modesty.[1] Certainly it is not the high antiquity alone into which a great part of these writings runs back which explains this simplicity, for all kinds of rhetorical art flourished among this people, even to over-refinement and fastidiousness, long before there is any mention of them among the Greeks.[2] Only the dominant power of a true religion could have preserved simplicity and simple vigour for a longer period, as well in the entire life as in the literature of this nation.

§ 100. But nevertheless in this literature we must distinguish from this predominant simplicity some kinds of artificiality which occasionally prevailed in it, and at a later period increased. We mean simply the artificiality in relation to what at the moment of hearing an address or reading a document is most decisive and effective, viz. the way in which the author introduces what he has to say. If a man speaks or writes not in his own name, but in another's name, we may generally designate that an artificial way of introducing a subject, because it is always the most simple for the ego of the speaker to coincide with the ego of the writer; whilst in the opposite case the hearer or reader has to reflect who this ego is, and also the speaker or writer himself must take care that he carries out consistently the discourse of the foreign ego he introduces, and does not, according to the common expression, depart from the *rôle*. Meanwhile the widely different cases here possible must be well distinguished; and as we look at them more closely, everything pertaining to this subject resolves itself into one of the following possibilities:—

1. That a man should speak in the name of another is generally in actual life of very frequent occurrence. How many messages, for example, are delivered wholly in the words of the sender, namely, those of persons in authority and kings; and in antiquity this was so much the more common the

[1] Ecclesiastes and Luke's Gospel. [2] Cf. *Poets of Old Test.* ii. 352, 2nd ed.

simpler the times were; if, therefore, such a discourse is only introduced perspicuously, and the speaker pointed out beforehand or even at the end, the foreign ego is self-evident. But this takes place often and much more artificially in the epic poem, and still more in the drama; for no artistic poet has the least hesitation in introducing the men whose fortunes and deeds he seeks to represent with new vividness, each speaking from his own ego, whether to the mere hearer as in narrative, *i.e.* epic poetry, or still more vividly in full impersonation in acted, *i.e.* dramatic poetry. Nor is this at all simply an invention of the Greeks, but it was employed previously in the far older and more primitive literature of other nations. If modern readers ascribe the Book of Job to Job and the Canticles to Solomon, the authors of those poems are quite innocent of the mistake, indeed the more innocent the more clearly the discourses of their heroes are introduced with great fitness in the proper place just as the plan of the poem requires.

Now it is certain that even historians of antiquity readily took the liberty to represent the words and discourses of the personages, whose advent and fortunes they related, more vividly and completely than they had received them by mere reminiscence. In the earlier ages this easily happened, as history was based in great part upon traditional materials; in later times, too, it easily happened the more history learned to pursue still higher and still wider aims than are necessarily associated with the mere rehearsal of past deeds,—for example, the aim to call back the events of the higher antiquity into the recollection with the greater vividness the more remote they were, and consequently the less intelligible to contemporary times, or to teach by a new representation of the past what was of importance for the immediate present. How far this complete freedom was carried by Greek and Roman historians is well known; in this as in other things, however, the Hebrew felt himself restrained by the more rigid religion prevailing in the community, and is therefore generally much more limited to sober fact. Where, indeed, is a more faithful mirror and model of all true history given than in the discourses of the men the history of David presents in the great Book of Kings in the Old Testament, or than the discourses of Christ and the apostles in the Gospels and the Acts? Even John's Gospel carries this freedom of presentation in no way beyond the limits which antiquity regarded as allowable, since an exact reproduction, wholly documental, from notes made at the moment, of discourses of living men, was in the entire condition of antiquity very rare. But when the historians of this nation would revivify the phenomena of far more distant times, such a freer mode of representation and rehearsal readily and spontaneously began to intrude; as may always be clearly recognised in proportion as the history goes back to those times. And the employment of this complete freedom was modified, it is true, conformably with the special spirit which prevailed in particular ages, as well with respect to the endeavours of men as in the style of narration and historical composition; as is proved in the Old Testament principally by comparing the Chronicles with the older historical books, and in the so-called Apocrypha by comparing the later with the first Book of Maccabees.

2. The most conspicuous example of the way in which a speaker and author can discourse in the name of another is given in the Bible by the prophets themselves when they introduce that Ego which, to be sure, should be present in all vividness to every man without exception as the true Ego. But since they introduce this Ego, speaking always so as to be clearly recognisable, or its import, where it enters into their discourse here and there suddenly and frequently, is always perfectly apparent from the connection, no one can ever seriously have taken offence at it unless he was disposed to deny everything divine in whatever way a man may feel and express it.

But long before this august "word of Jahveh" first resounded in the world in imperishable tones through Moses, there was in the nation of Israel, as it existed in the oldest times, another immortal spirit, which it was the task and function of its oldest prophets, in moments of deep need and despair, or even of other higher moods of feeling, to bring to living utterance. This was the spirit of the patriarchs of the nation, long since dead, and yet regarded as immortal; and the higher the repute among the Egyptians of the oracle of the dead (according to p. 225 f.), already in the most ancient times, the more must the ancestors of the nation of the community of the true religion have preferred, at least in those early days, to listen to the voice of their patriarchs as it found expression in the mouth of their prophets. A complete and instructive example of this we still possess in the voice of Jacob concerning Joseph,[1] which, according to all indications, goes back to the times before Moses, and belongs to the very few small fragments of the oldest Hebrew discourse which have been preserved till to-day. But as the first early veneration of the patriarchs, and with it many a sacred custom from those most ancient days, was, according to p. 215 ff., very tenaciously retained long after Moses, this old custom also did not die out for a long time; and in the days of the later judges, when the new prophecy, after the creative precedent of Moses, together with the whole condition of the nation in its oldest form, had become weak again, he who did not venture to discourse publicly in the name of Jahveh sought to revive this most ancient type of genuinely Hebrew prophecy. The great fragment of Jacob's blessing[2] is of this type, and it has come down to us having incorporated into itself the far older utterance concerning Joseph. But if, in the conviction of the nation, the patriarchs were regarded as such immortal spirits, ever newly living and calling forth new life, the freedom with which the narrators of the primitive history continually reanimated them and their words, as we see this now in the Book of Genesis, is thereby the more readily explained.

[1] Gen. xlix. 22-26. [2] Gen. xlix. 1-27.

Meanwhile the memory of Moses also had long since been surrounded with a halo of glory. Supposing, then, an old custom existed in this nation of eliciting from the immortal and exalted dead of previous glorious days new living words in the darkness of the present, a prophetic spirit, not wishing in the clouded time of those early centuries openly to discourse to the nation as a prophet of Jahveh, might cause a Jahveh-voice to sound forth artistically from Moses' time at least, and as it were from his mouth. From that time onward this is the new artificial type of prophecy in the name of Jahveh. Of this we possess still a very old fragment, which, for an already less vigorous age, scarcely a century after Moses, lifts up the voice of Jahveh as Moses would have lifted it up had he been then alive.[1] But we see also how readily such a type of prophetic discourse, once formed, could continue in existence in this nation the more persistently, and rise higher and higher, the more it accustomed itself, by its whole culture, to understand and relish also such noble, copious, clear, and determinate divine utterances. Yet we do not find that this artificial kind of prophecy, with all similar literature, was continued in special writings during the splendid times of the ascending kingly power in Israel. It is not to be overlooked that, like all artificial discourse and indirect literature, it is only specially necessary in such junctures when the entire national life is in sad obscuration and deep decline. Such times in the early periods of history were more and more quickly survived.

3. But in the long series of centuries in which the old national life of Israel fell completely into weakness and decline, from which it never sufficiently recovered itself for any length of time, there were many intervals when the recollection of the old high personages, who once had ruled in this community, scattering benediction for all eternity, could revive the noblest courage, and when many supposed they could speak to their contemporaries most effectively if

[1] Ex. xxiii. 20-33.

they spoke as from their mind and lips. These were just the times, as we can still plainly recognise, when the activity of the great prophets, after the first half of the seventh century before Christ, suffered gradual and severe paralysis, and at length wholly stopped; and it seems as if the never-resting spirit of the higher revelation and religion, the more these times were destitute of prophets, had the more diligently laid hold of this device to advance its own work. Add to this that all literature had then been cultivated in the nation most faithfully in all its capabilities and possibilities, and had attained the unusually high attractive power which marks a literature that has succeeded in forming permanently the spirit of a nation. The energy and resources of such a literature are not exhausted for a long time after it has achieved the finest and noblest development that appeared possible, and always new paths are opened in each new age to suit the changing need. Accordingly, an artificial literature sprang up the more luxuriantly in many of these later periods that seemed favourable to it, yet only as a supplemental growth on the old fruitful soil, though bearing many noble blossoms and fruits. But however widely this literature extended itself, and however distant its remove from its origin back in the oldest times, it is ultimately nevertheless faith in the immortality of the earlier spirits of these exalted figures which calls it again into life; and thus the latest and amplest creations of this artistic authorship are closely connected again with the ancient brief discourse from the mouth of the dead. As the last moments before death appear to open to the mind the freest outlook into all the past and all the future, it was always at the moment before his death that this artistic writing delighted to make some one of the august ancients discourse. Works of art of this kind were not only increasingly numerous, but for the most part increasingly perfect in their grand and delicate finish.[1]

The special importance which this kind of authorship has

[1] So the Book of Jubilees, the now recovered Book of the Ascension of Moses.

in connection with our present subject necessitates our regarding it still further in detail. It was pre-eminently the lofty spirit of Moses whose irresistible heroic power was desired in vain for the maintenance and advancement of all true revelation and religion, and of the community he founded. Many, therefore, had recourse to him and his time most earnestly in order to speak to the present in his spirit. The Deuteronomist is one of the earliest examples, and at the same time the greatest in the extent and importance of his work. But similar attempts also occur before him and immediately after him; indeed, down to the last days of the existence of the old community the endeavour is made again and again to influence contemporary thought and life from the lofty age and the hallowed lips of Moses by the charm of an extremely artificial literature, partly narrative and partly prophetic.

But to pass from Moses, who might already appear as a patriarch, by a direct transition to later prophets, was a very great leap in this form of authorship. The leap was taken, so far as we know to-day, just after the powerful reinvigoration of mind which the dispersion of the nation and its unexpectedly speedy and happy close produced; and the immediate occasion was the work of a prophet who, like Jeremiah, had fallen as a last among many martyrs, and whose works at this period of change enjoyed the highest honour. It was, however, only a fragment which an unnamed younger prophet, when a new edition of Jeremiah's great book was issued, appended to it, charmed, as it were, by the vehement longing with which the book closes to attempt to discourse as Jeremiah would have done had he been still alive.[1] And so in this case it was also the spirit of the great dead which filled with its immortal power the mind of the younger prophet. But in the course of the following centuries the age and the discourse of many other prophets were soon made to live anew,—those of Baruch, for instance, with a new edition of Jeremiah and likewise in the appendix

---

[1] Jer. l.

to it, of Daniel in the book still preserved, further on of Elijah, and at the end, of Ezra also, as if he had been a prophet, and of many others.

The boldest attempt that was made in the old community was that of venturing back beyond all the patriarchs of Israel into the early dawn of all human history in order to give narrative and prophecy from the times of Enoch, of Seth, and even of Adam himself.[1] Such book appeared after the impulse which the Maccabæan wars and victories imparted to the spirit of the nation; and the Hellenists were soon just as quick to discourse similarly in their own tongue, or indeed in the new style borrowed from the Greeks. But such books as the Book of Tobit or the Book of Judith and the later Maccabæan books —half narrative, half poetic or prophetic—were the outcome of the increasingly prevalent literary freedom with which in those times subjects connected with the religion of a country were celebrated. Or where the aim was to teach something of higher importance, the attention was confined to an old renowned personality, the reader was transplanted into the old better times of the nation, and taught and addressed from famous lips; as the Book of Koheleth under this name introduces the old wise great king in Jerusalem whom every one recognised as Solomon. Such books as Koheleth, Enoch, are, as it were, rude fragments of plays (dramas), which the authors could have easily remodelled into perfect dramas had they not found it better to leave them as they were, Koheleth as a portion of a drama to be recited, Enoch a portion of a drama merely to be read; since, indeed, in the flourishing times of the nation, the drama proper had once been the adornment of this literature, but was now no longer cultivated.

But the literature of this altogether special art flourished in these later times more and more. The nation, whose better soul now lived only by the inspiring memory of its earlier glories and by all the varied contents of the Pentateuch long

[1] Josephus speaks of a work from the history of Adam and Seth; *Arch.* i. 2, 3. Dillmann's Æthiopic version of the Book of Adam is wholly different.

since become sacred, felt itself in this literature transported into the midst of sublime eras and subjects affording the richest nourishment to its spirit; and how fruitful this whole series of after-growths from the old independent literature of Israel was, we can scarcely picture to ourselves with sufficient vividness to-day. Yet as the imitation of the voices of the great dead was the beginning, after the early times of the nation, of the whole system of artificial discourse and writing, as we said above, so in the first Christian age this highly-cultured artistic activity was abandoned again for the simplest style; so that Christianity in its youth, though surrounded by an over-wrought artificial age and condition of things, may be said to have returned to the utmost simplicity possible. Nothing can be simpler, nothing more touching and impressive, than the way in which certain gifted authors, towards the close of the first century after Christ, recall the tones of the great Apostles Paul and Peter, then so painfully missed and so urgently needed by the wants and requirements of the time. The voices of the dead, thus speaking again as memory suggested they would have spoken in such a conjuncture of affairs had they been still alive, were the voices of leaders, of powerful mind, but recently lost; and that the immortal spirits of such men were perceptibly near to the beloved brethren they had left, if only they could but realize it, was a prevalent belief not without its justification; but since the age was apt and experienced in literary work, unlike that distant early age of the nation, it is seen at once that in the department of epistolary composition only such spirits were likely to be recalled whose actual Epistles were already known. Four such Epistles written in the name of Paul and one in the name of Peter have been admitted into the New Testament;—the only five portions of this artificial literature which enjoy this distinction.[1]

---

[1] The Epistle to the Ephesians; the three pastoral Epistles (1 and 2 Tim. and Titus), and 2 Peter. Cf. *The Seven Epistles of the New Testament*, Göttingen 1870.

A similar example is seen in the Epistles of Ignatius from the second century;[1] and thus a wholly similar artificial after-authorship, so to speak, which followed the beaten track of the language of Holy Scripture, came into existence in Christianity, and at certain times and in certain localities was much in request and much read; and such authorship continued, in Christianity as in Judaism and Samaritanism that had broken off from it, until far into the Middle Ages.

§ 101. Such is in short this artificial literature. It indicates the end as well of the nation as of the literature of the old nation whose first bright light it follows at last as a shadow. As it was ultimately cultivated in many different branches, and in each in a special way and for the most part with delicate taste, it is evident that its peculiar qualities of skill and cleverness increased with its growth, and that its more simple forms of presentation are to be distinguished from the highly artificial. The like ending, the like after-growths, are found in connection with every highly-developed literature among the ancient nations, but nowhere did so rich an after-bloom find so luxuriously fruitful a field as here, where the highest aspirations and the most difficult problems of man's spiritual life invited ever to new efforts, and a Holy Scripture long since accepted offered for use its stimulating language and its high forms of thought and imagination.

If such were the circumstances in which this peculiar and vigorous branch of the literature of this nation flourished, it is clear that we must hesitate to speak of it with reproach and distrust as the work of intentional misrepresentation and falsehood. We have before us here a special and increasingly extended deviation and deflection from direct discourse and authorship, innocent enough in its first beginnings, perfectly excusable and justifiable by the historical situation of great affairs, and in its time doing really good service; but afterwards as it reached high artistic cultivation and authority, degenerating more and more in rank exuber-

[1] Cf. *History*, vii. 318.

ance, as everything does which from the first is not wholly direct and pure, till at length it is utterly dissolved and lost. But there is no falsification; and if we must in general be on our guard against lightly branding anything with the mark of "counterfeit and fictitious," so it would be a great injustice to the varied fruits of this literature if we were to speak of it in the mass as pseudo-Scripture. It should be considered, too, that misrepresentations and forgeries, in the proper sense of the words, occur only in the case of historical books and documents, or with respect to the superscription and signature of old favourite works much in request, and when discovered to be absolute frauds may also be suitably dealt with; but here we have in question writings whose sole aim was instruction and admonition, and which would in no wise be regarded as historical; although, to be sure, this whole literature if cultivated one-sidedly may deteriorate more and more completely, and if it mingled with the more direct literature and gradually displaced it, would be pernicious in its influence and result.

4. *The Advantages and the Deficiencies of all Literature.*

§ 102. If we look now once more upon this literature as a whole, not upon its manifoldness and diversity as in the two previous sections, we shall see that the great advantages which all literature afforded to the ancient nations are not to be mistaken, and that to the Israelitish nation its literature was a special boon.

What influence and effect the introduction and growing use of writing had in this nation, we possess now too little detailed information from the earliest centuries of its history to enable us clearly to trace. But, in truth, it is the same with respect to all nations of antiquity, and the use of writing in these nations is much older than many scholars fifty years ago would allow. That long before Moses Semitic writing was in use in the nation of Israel, and that Moses availed himself of it for the service of the nation, is now scientifically established ; moreover, our exacter investigations leave us in no doubt to-day that subsequently, in the first centuries of the existence of the community, writing was handled with considerable versatility, and all the beginnings of the peculiar literature of the nation, diffusing itself so widely at a later period, reach back into these centuries. But that condition of things in the Persian age, when Koheleth complained of the rank exuberance of all literature and the mischief it occasioned too frequently, lay far distant then from those oldest centuries of the community ; and we can confidently assume that only what was necessary or what appeared worthy of everlasting remembrance was in the oldest times of the community carefully committed to writing. That the Bible contains no observation at all concerning the origin of writing and its first notable employment, and does not even trace back its discovery and introduction in any way to Moses, is at bottom a very plain proof that, according to all reminiscences of this nation, it was known in very ancient times ; for in other respects the Bible contains many traditions and much information about the origin of memorable things, and writing is highly enough regarded in it.

But already the committing to writing of the new fundamental laws of this community, begun under Moses as all indications show, and carried on eagerly after him, principally in connection with the old divine oracles bearing directly upon the law, was a great advantage to the spiritual life of this nation. The first, and at the same time the most permanent service of writing is, that it seeks directly to immortalize thoughts and words, to form an exact and trustworthy record of them, and preserve it. The diffusion of human discourse is not its original aim, however increasingly important this became at a later period, but its certain preservation for immediate use, whether in the home or in the larger sphere of public life. If the laws by which a nation desires to be ruled were indeed elsewhere in antiquity a first and most important subject for activity in the use of writing, among this people it was the principles and the eternal conditions of all true religion that were so perpetuated. When, thus, the remembrance of the great events of history and the utterances of their heroes were by this means firmly retained; when so many a noble song, sung in the community on high festivals or composed by a singer distinguished in his lifetime, was in this way rendered immortal; when subsequently the prophets, who arose in the earlier and later times, in such numbers and splendour in this nation as in no other, sought by this agency to work for all the future, and the whole literature of the nation acquired an ever readier use and aptitude, and learned to embrace an ever wider range of materials of all kinds,— what an incalculable multitude of subjects worthy of everlasting remembrance and regard were then rescued from the danger of gradually vanishing again more and more irrevocably from the mere memory of man!

The second advantage which writing offers — united inseparably with the first—is this, it preserves all the different discourses and thoughts in smaller or greater sections with the most absolute exactitude and authenticity. Nothing is more important, however, for a thousandfold application of them, than that there should be a possibility of preserving such sayings, thoughts, and reminiscences as in general seem worthy of preservation, just as correctly and as definitely as they were originally expressed. There can be no period, however remote, when their original import may not shine forth again with the same clear radiance, inspire the hearts of men with the same warmth, and kindle the same enthusiasm as when they first entered the world with their fresh creative power. The human spirit in its deepest ground is always the same, and centuries and millenniums may thus shake hands. All this, however, is the more important and the richer in results, the more such original literature itself is replete in its contents with eternally significant and eternally vivifying thoughts and truths; and where, among the literatures of the ancient nations bearing upon revelation and religion, is this the case more completely than here?

In proportion as a nation developed its literature a long time with persistence, giving it a peculiar form and filling it with creative force, the more happily and helpfully there grew up for it, in the longer life its inherited literature gave it, a second, a higher and immortal life out of its own past, that in the darker days of its present especially might be an inextinguishable lamp, and for all its future a support and stay; a bright world of its own past in which it could ever again find a home, and which in new and difficult questions of life served as a guide just as well as, and often still more than, its traditional usages and institutions. Usages and institutions of life are, to be sure, very tenacious threads upon which the life of a nation may continue to hold, but they may gradually and imperceptibly pass through great changes, while a writing, and so a whole comprehensive literature faithfully preserved by a nation or community as the best treasure of its antiquity, remains unchanged, and may serve indeed as a mirror and a shield for the best of its old institutions and customs. Without referring at large to Islamism, which preserves itself tenaciously by nothing so much as its Koran and its ancient literature closely connected with it, we see how such communities as those of the Parsees of India and Yezd, long since fallen through the disfavour of the times from their old grandeur and glory, those of the Mandæans or Sabæans, and those of the Samaritans, preserve themselves even till to-day by writings inherited from antiquity.

Now an inherited literature is best understood chiefly by those who still speak its language, and who know from their ancestors more intimately the matters described in it. But, nevertheless, owing to the eternal similarity of all human feeling and perception, the special language, with all other peculiarities of an old literature, forms no hindrance at all to strangers, and does not prevent them from deriving from such literature all the benefits it affords. Moreover, if there is a long interval of time between the origin of an old literature and the life of the subsequent, much-changed descendants of the nation in which it arose, every national distinction or excellence will have long since vanished on this side, and strangers may well better recognise and more correctly apply the true original import of such old writings than the still living but intellectually altered representatives of the original people.

§ 103. But all literature has its deficiencies and imperfection. In the case of the literature we have here principally to consider, the most lamentable imperfection seems to be just this: of those minds which must rightly be held by us as the greatest in the great affairs of revelation and religion, we find few or no writings at all which we can trace back to their hand, or even to their suggestion and approval. Of Moses we possess only little that we can refer immediately to him, though what we have is in the highest degree important. That the most powerful of the prophets of the elder race after him, Samuel and Elijah, used the pen, and wrote what was most worthy of remembrance, admits of no doubt; but not even a single composition, however small, has been preserved which we can now refer to their hand by sufficiently certain proofs. But what is here of far the greatest importance is that Christ has left nothing written by His own hand, because perhaps His earthly life was occupied too seriously and too closely with other things, themselves too immediately necessary, to allow the possibility in His case of leisure or desire for literary labour. With the Twelve it is, however, essentially the same; there is only one Epistle of Peter's which we can, if not on account of its verbal structure, yet on account of its contents, ascribe with full certainty to him; and we should possess nothing from John's hand had not wholly special circumstances impelled him in his extreme old age to labour as a writer. All this seems now indeed very much to be regretted, and yet, more particularly considered, is neither so surprising nor so irreparably detrimental as it at first sight appears. It may serve us rather as a first and most emphatic sign that all writing and all literature, so incomparably useful as it is in itself, yet like everything external and sensuous has always its deficiencies ; and just the deficiencies here most perceptible we can in other ways so completely supply, that in the end, so far at least as the great interests of revelation and religion are concerned, on which everything here turns, there remains no very serious deficiency after all. What those lofty minds that availed themselves of writing, but whose works have suffered greatly from the ravages of time, desired and accomplished in their whole life, we can supply, if their own existent writings, whatever they may be, are insufficient, from other literary reminiscences, at least to such an extent that we are in no doubt about its principal features. This is a distinguishing excellence of the literature we are more especially considering, of which by and by more is to be said. With respect to Christ Himself, His whole purpose and work upon earth were too extraordinary and too wonderful, and accompanied immediately by consequences too mighty, for men not to be found early enough who, in spite of all opposing difficulties, nevertheless recorded what appeared generally and for all time most memorable in His discourses, His deeds, and His lot. That this actually is the case we can satisfy ourselves to-day with adequate sufficiency.

§ 104. But there are deficiencies which belong inherently to literature from the first, and can never be altogether avoided, only in antiquity, as it is sharply distinguished from our own times, they arise most readily and with the least hindrance, and make headway through many centuries without becoming very perceptible and without being painfully enough felt. They have not spared the literature now specially in question, and the somewhat more precise discussion of this matter is here unavoidable. There are two principal deficiencies arising from very different sources.

1. Every literature which continues to develop itself more and more richly and even luxuriantly for a long time and in

manifold new deposits and transmutations, suffers at last from its own ever-increasing extent, its prolixity and bulk, and on this account from the separation and dismemberment which then takes place, as well as from the change in the needs and (what is specially influential) in the tastes of men. The new writings, increasing in ever greater redundancy, displace the old, and the more readily if, in the meantime, literary activity continually seeks out and works up further material, or if practice in composition develops new arts and graces of style, or the language of the older works becomes more or less obsolete. The older books are then less sought after, and perhaps at length gradually disappear; while another and yet more powerful reason for their withdrawal from notice is that the most important contents of the older writings are by degrees more and more transferred or artificially worked up into the newer, so that the former seem superfluous and very easily get lost. Such causes are at work very little to-day, since the art of printing and the desire to arrange numerous collections of books on definite scientific principles has grown to so high a degree; but in the antiquity of all nations they had most important consequences in proportion as all literature developed itself without artificial restraint; and imperceptibly the most varied losses occurred. Severe shocks of ill-fortune befalling a nation or recurring frequently had besides a specially disastrous effect; chiefly on this account, that as every literature has its origin and growth in its own nation so as to become its treasure, its pride, its stay and consolation in misfortune, foreign nations therefore neither heeded nor spared it, or if they recognised its significance for the vanquished people, burned in wild fury against it. How did the Greeks rage against the sacred writings of the Persians! How did the Romans recklessly throw away the very celebrated works of conquered Carthage; and how, subsequently, did they vent their fury, at first in occasional outbreaks, and at length in systematic hostility, against the Jewish Scriptures!

So common a fate the special literature now particularly under notice did not escape ; and our investigations in the present day afford the means for correctly estimating, at least generally, the losses it thus sustained. Taking the five chief parts and periods into which according to § 93–97 this literature is best divided, the whole matter stands thus: From the centuries comprising the oldest period up to the time (to give a definite date) of the first destruction of Jerusalem and the years immediately succeeding it, the portions of literature saved were few and of small extent although highly significant and in a measure indestructible, and even these were saved only as they floated into the rich literary stream of the following century, and were taken up by it. On the other hand, those saved from the *second* period, the period of the broadest and at the same time the finest unfolding of this literature, constitute still the main body of the existing Old Testament (§ 94). From the *third* period, that of the first great dispersion of the nation, not many writings have been preserved, but some that in their significance are important. From the *fourth* period, when once more this literature gradually streamed forth in rare amplitude, at least as far as the number of its productions is concerned, many a work has been taken up into the Old Testament, and from that stream as it spread in the old community up to the age of Hadrian, and at last more and more appeared in the most different languages, we should certainly have possessed a great number of books, small and large, had not the violent destructions of the Romans and the overanxiety of the Jews unfortunately co-operated to occasion the loss of most of them ; so that from these long centuries we have preserved, apart from such as have been admitted into the Old Testament, scarcely anything save the Apocrypha, understanding that word in the broader sense to be explained below. Of Christian writings many of the earliest were evidently lost in the devastations which mark the course of the wars of Vespasian and Titus.

2. If the greatest pains are bestowed upon a written com-

position, it is possible to execute it entirely without mistakes; and it was customary in antiquity to bestow such care upon public documents and inscriptions, although our investigations in the present day with respect to inscriptions in all possible languages have shown that even here mistakes have crept in, and were not always avoided. But in the making of ordinary manuscripts such care was not always taken; and through the caprice of readers or of subsequent new editors many readings found place which were not the original readings. This was known well enough in ancient times, and many artificial contrivances were employed to protect an author's exact phraseology against misapprehensions, and to maintain it subsequently with the greatest possible accuracy. It is not to be supposed that such a scholarly carefulness arose first among the Greeks through the zeal of the Alexandrian grammarians; it was cultivated, as we are now able fully to establish, among the ancient Israelites, and most of their works were published all along with the highest verbal accuracy, although with some of them, particularly in a degenerate age, this might not be the case. But, nevertheless, writings at first published with the greatest care were never wholly exempt from the inadvertencies or indeed the arbitrariness of subsequent transcribers, whilst the original copies were readily altogether lost; and of no single work now preserved in the Bible can we maintain that it is faithfully preserved exactly in conformity with the original. Whether, however, there might possibly be any alteration in this respect, or whether there actually was such alteration after the compositions preserved in the Bible were regarded as sacred, will be touched upon below.

Similarly in the repeated remodellings of a work, or even in the multiplication of copies, the original superscriptions and divisions and subdivisions were often omitted for the sake of brevity. The oldest Hebrew writings, as all our most careful researches teach us to-day, were at first exact in such external particulars; but transcribers did not afterwards always keep rigidly to these original guides to the correct acceptation of a work; or with repeated new editions, new superscriptions and divisions were also arbitrarily introduced.

But all such observations only confirm the truth otherwise known, viz. that written composition, whatever its inestimable advantages for the promotion of our whole spiritual life and also for the interests of true revelation and religion, nevertheless has its imperfections and deficiencies; so that we understand at once how it is that we cannot rely upon it alone, although it cannot but serve us as a mighty aid and an indispensable support in all our higher aims and efforts.

II. 5. *The Origin of Holy Scripture.*

§ 105. If the case stands as we have represented it, not only with literature in general, but with that of the people of Israel in particular, it is difficult to explain, at first sight, how in this nation a Holy Scripture could ever have been formed. In point of fact, a break is here recognisable separating this wholly new development of things from that which is primary and all-essential according to our previous representation. That is to say, in other words, something special and substantially new must be added if upon this basis a Holy Scripture is to be formed and to win for itself the unbounded respect which it secured, and which, according to § 73 ff., ultimately exercised so deep an influence upon the entire view of revelation and religion in this community, and indeed upon the final destiny of the community itself. It is desirable, therefore, at once this new additional element properly to understand.

Only God Himself and His revealed word can be in like manner intrinsically and eternally holy. Now it is certain that in that sublime moment in the incomparably instructive history of this people, when they submitted themselves for ever of their own free will to guidance by means of the true revelation and religion, a pure recognition of that which is alone and for ever alike holy, and a deep overpowering awe before it, must have penetrated the heart of the whole nation (§ 58 f., 86). Nor is it doubtful that such moments, whose irresistible energy can illumine the mind of a whole nation as with a sudden lightning flash, were repeated subsequently at different times in the long and changeful history of this community.[1] But in ordinary times such a rare exaltation and tension of the mind of a whole nation is not maintained with equal loftiness and force;[2] and under the pressure of new events and experiences, new distractions and complications easily follow, leading the eyes and hearts of the people in a totally different direction. But if ever such seasons returned when the nation was arrested anew and more widely and intensely than before by the truth of the divine word, which, in the pride and aberration or the languishing and embarrassment of its better life, it had long mistaken and despised, then the light and splendour of that which is eternally holy was involuntarily transferred to the divine utterances previously heard and brought nigh to its heart, and the old record of them, itself suffused with a divine sanctity, shone forth in holy radiance as never before. To a nation in which the light of God's oracles shines with purest splendour and deepest truth, the record which fixes them in firm stedfast limits for all succeeding ages will also shine with a wholly different light from any other record; awe in the presence of its contents will blend easily with the venerable character of its age and origin, and even what in itself as a sensuous object cannot be holy, in the acceptation true religion gives to the word, may become holy in this way in the common estimation. But as this nation in its long history was destined to pass through everything which a nation of antiquity could pass through in order, under the impulse of all true revelation and religion, to rise up to perfection, this deepest experience of life was repeated in it in

---

[1] 1 Chron. xxviii.; 2 Chron. xv., xviii.–xx., xxiii., xxix.–xxxi., xxxiv. f.; Ezra i., iii.; cf. Judg. v.; Ps. xviii., xlvi., xlviii., lxxv. f., xlv., and others.
[2] Ex. xx. 18–21 in its permanent import.

ever stronger alternations and greater results; and when once, even with a small work, a real beginning was made in the way of regarding a writing as holy, this basis of a new power in the community would extend with every great succeeding accession, as often as the higher truth and significance of writings became manifest by the clear light of history with the most evident certainty and in ever wider extent. Thus in process of time was formed in this community, where alone it was possible, and with increasing determinateness and permanency, a very comprehensive Holy Scripture, which amid all the old nations is just as peculiar and as elevated as the revelation and religion itself of which it was to become the safest possible outward haven. We must, however, first of all distinguish the different gradations and stages that have marked the process of its formation.

§ 106. (I.) 1. The first foundation of Holy Scripture is to be discovered in the Ten Commandments, upon which rested the whole original constitution of the community after its inauguration at Sinai; and it was of the highest importance that this foundation, though inconsiderable in extent, yet great and indestructible in its significance, should actually remain the undisturbed foundation through all the long and changing ages that followed. No wonder, then, that with this wholly incomparable written memorial should be connected in later literature a diversified reminiscence, and in the Pentateuch manifold sacred traditions. Already in the Book of Origins it was held that these two tables of stone were inscribed as with the finger of God; and since they had been deposited from the times of Moses in the ark of the covenant, instead of images of deity with which the heathen usually filled their sacred chests, it was quite in harmony with the tradition of their divine inscription that along with the ark, the most venerable and, next to them, the most sacred of relics, they should form anew, as it were, when the temple of Solomon was built, the consecrated basis of the earthly sanctuary,[1] and

[1] 1 Kings viii. 9.

as it would then be thought, for perpetual generations. A community accustomed to no free and lavish employment of divine names and attributes could scarcely form a higher conception than this,—that these two tables of stone were inscribed with the finger of God; of not a single memorial beside this is such language used in the whole Bible. Nevertheless, the oldest narrators in the Pentateuch do not hesitate to represent the sanctity of the Ten Commandments as much more immediately conferred. Before the assembled nation, God Himself is said to have uttered aloud the words of the commandments, while every heart trembled with fear. According to this account, Moses is still regarded as the divine amanuensis. But according to another old reminiscence, the first original record was lost; the tables of stone received directly from God, before men could see them, were thrown down to the ground and broken in pieces by Moses in his first deep anger at the unexpected defection of the people; the covenant of the nation with the true God, almost before it was concluded, was demolished as its contents had been; and Jahveh was obliged with His own hand to write another copy of the commandments upon other tables of stone which Moses prepared. This the fourth narrator mentions in a representation conspicuous on account of its deeper truths, but easily misunderstood, as is everything so transcendent. The Deuteronomist, however, still proceeds from the same Ten Commandments as the groundwork of all the rest of the laws.

From these manifold and inextinguishable reminiscences it is not possible to doubt that the Ten Commandments were the first and firmest ground of all Holy Scripture in Israel. Whether other ancient systems of law, obvious remnants and traces of which of all kinds we discover principally in the Pentateuch, were so early regarded as sacred, is extremely doubtful: they might serve to judges and princes as the groundwork for the administration of justice, and on this account be held as sacred, but not in the same way as the

Ten Commandments. For Hosea's bitter complaint from the mouth of Jahveh—

" I write for him a myriad of my precepts
As something foreign he esteems them "[1]—

opens to us a manifold glimpse into the true condition of those times in which prophetic oracles that might be current as laws in far greater numbers than are now extant, of more ancient origin and preserved in a fair literature, might lay claim to popular respect, and yet were esteemed as something foreign, *i.e.* of indifferent value ; but the complaint refers especially only to the kingdom of the Ten Tribes, in which the original Decalogue so far as it forbade images of deity was despised, not because it was not then known, but because all kinds of misinterpretation and evasion of the plainest commands were then resorted to. But we cannot prove, even in the case of the kingdom of Judah, that in the earlier times the rest of the laws were held as equally sacred with the Ten Commandments.

If, however, we observe the great commotions and disquietude occasioned in the community in the earliest times by the question whether and in what way the laws of the true revelation and religion were to be regarded, commotions distinctly reflected in the Pentateuch, particularly in the narrative just mentioned concerning the broken and replaced tables of the original Decalogue, it admits of no doubt that this first firm basis of Holy Scripture was secured only after a long and severe conflict. The sanctity, too, that is, the inviolability of this first basis of Scripture, must be contested ; and not till the contest was won did it shine with that inextinguishable divine light of which the Bible is now the witness for all time. According to all the clearest evidence this took place, however,

§ 107. (II.) 2. In the first further progress which ensued, but not till a much later age, and which for that reason introduces us at once to wholly different conditions of the

[1] Hos. viii. 12.

community. In the days after Josiah, when in the kingdom of Judah a dissolution was on the point of occurring similar to that in which the kingdom of the Ten Tribes was destroyed almost so as to obliterate every trace of it; when the very existence of the true religion in this kingdom was severely threatened, no longer as so frequently before merely by the follies of contending factions, but by the kingly power, and when the prophetic word itself, till then continually esteemed as the living spring of all progressive revelation, was violently interrupted: at that time an admirer of Moses, influenced and moved by a prophetic impulse, though prevented from oral utterance, felt himself constrained to revivify in one great connected work the divine truths and corresponding regulations for the life held in regard in the community since the time of Moses, and to revivify them in such a way that they should sound forth to the nation as a last striking and impressive word of admonition from the mouth of the dying Moses himself, and also so as to be exactly adapted to his own later age. It was as if this second Moses felt most profoundly the need of a sacred book in compass, and in power to captivate, far exceeding those Ten Commandments, and that he could satisfy this need only as he, following the precedent of the oracle of the dead long sacred in Israel (p. 225 f.), ventured upon the boldest experiment that had ever been made in the way of posthumous prophetic utterance, if such a phrase may be allowed. In such cases antiquity looked rather to the contents and influence of a writing than to its authorship or form, as was stated more at large, § 100 f.; special fortunes, too, might await such a work; and the unexpected turning of the kingdom to the higher aims which took place under the young Josiah, helped to secure for Deuteronomy the high position in the public esteem which it obtained. This great prophetic elaboration of the law, which surrounds the Ten Commandments, long since regarded as holy, just as a broad outstreaming circle of radiance surrounds a bright and luminous centre, appears to have arisen as by an imperative necessity, the necessity that a great book, invested with more than merely lawful dignity, might be elevated to the fundamental book of all life conformably with the purpose of the true revelation and religion: and indeed the work transports the spirit of the reader from the first to the sphere of that far-off freer and happier age in which is heard, not the voice of a contemporary little esteemed, but the voice of a holy man long since removed beyond all this perishing scene of things, and in which is felt the breath of an inspiration that moves with thousandfold power the men who receive it in faith.[1]

And yet the sanctity which this work soon won for itself in that very century in which it came into public notice was not so great as to prevent talented writers from attempting to connect it more closely with selected earlier works concerning Moses and the whole primitive history. Certainly it is the best of the comprehensive works on the primitive history which immediately after the foundation of the new Jerusalem appeared under the name of the Pentateuch as the permanent sacred book of the new-born community, and which secured ever afterwards the highest esteem. One great book had now happily overcome all hindrances and opposition that could prevent its attaining the highest respect in this community. Embracing the history of all primitive ages, and especially that of the sublime founding of the community of all true revelation and religion, there was comprised in it everything of eternal value that could serve as inspiring retrospect into the creative past, as doctrinal guidance for the present, or as comforting hope for the future; and if, almost a thousand years before, the Ten Commandments by their sanctity had become the firm basis of all higher life for the community, so now the whole glory of this great book which had such high influence and respect was ultimately traceable to those same Ten Commandments.

[1] Cf. how the law-book of the Hindoos, long venerated, is said to have been spoken by God in the primitive time to Manu.

§ 108. (III.) After the great advance from the sanctity of the Ten Commandments to that of the Pentateuch had in this way been made, and a foundation had thus been laid, as excellent as it was broad and firm, for a Holy Scripture which should consist of larger books, the extension of the foundation presented less difficulty. Indeed, if it is remembered that in the old community, as it existed from the time of Moses, all revelation and religion had a marked and powerful leaning towards the law, and that this leaning alone became more and more predominant from the beginning of the third great crisis in the history of this community, as is shown more at large in § 76, it will readily be understood that the Pentateuch, specially devoted as it was to the exact knowledge of the old law now become sacred, must always maintain a significant pre-eminence. Every subsequent and further development of this community shows that; and it is essentially appropriate that the law, as it is here given, should contain not merely prescriptions for common life in the home and the State, but also all the higher truths so far as they could find expression in a legal form: and what should have a greater sacredness for man than these? Nevertheless in succeeding centuries, at least when the spirit of all true revelation and religion prevailed over adverse prepossessions and errors, the right conception at the same moment penetrated the mind with victorious power, the conception, namely, that among the vast treasures of the entire literature which had accumulated in this community there were still other books beside the Pentateuch which, measured by the canon, that is, the standard of the Pentateuch, might be associated with it, and raised by their superior sacredness above common books. For the clear conviction had long been entertained, among the most experienced and ablest men of this community certainly, that there must be perhaps one among the unlimited number of books in circulation best suited to communicate the nature and contents of the revelation and religion, now recognised indeed as the right as well as the true; and the Pentateuch, already acknowledged to be such a book, might serve as a first considerable and evident portion of the presupposed standard, rule, or canon. This later expression, starting from the idea and word "canon," is simply of Hellenistic origin, for Alexandrine scholars set up similarly a canon of the best poets and authors in each branch of literature, and the question was then asked in particular cases, does this or that work belong to it? In Latin the corresponding idea is found in the term "classical." Because, however, in those books which were to be equally valued as corresponding to the presupposed standard, that which is holy and divine, and inspired by its spirit, must be found, the definite name "Holy Scriptures" most readily occurred as determinately distinguishing them from all other books. Of the rare occasions, however, when additions were made to the canon in this sense, the three following are instances, and we see from them exactly how from this time forward the progressive development of the canon, together with that of all true revelation, was uninterruptedly accomplished.

3. About the same time that the Pentateuch began to be fully accepted as the great canonical book of the community of the new Jerusalem, a very considerable effort was made, also, with a zeal wholly new, in collecting and diffusing afresh the best of the other writings which in the great interest of true revelation and religion might be of certain use and kindle in the mind a new and abiding enthusiasm. The severe sufferings in the destruction of Jerusalem, and the wide dispersion of the whole community, had occasioned a great winnowing of the minds of men, and also of the books of a literature continually accumulating during many centuries; and as the fidelity of the better spirits became wonderfully strengthened, and everything that affected the old fatherland, so often grievously despised before, was held in new honour, it happened also that the best ancient and modern books were carefully collected together, newly elaborated, and zealously circulated. More recent inquiries enable us to know that

this was done in the case of the prophetic books, the songs suitable for public use, the historical books, and also the Book of Job and the Proverbs. A new and extremely lively movement and interest in all literature that might have any higher religious significance had seized the mind, and out of it had grown the determination in Nehemiah's time to annex to the Pentateuch—(1) a great collection of the best prophetic pieces; (2) a great historic work which, dealing with the history of the progressive movement of true revelation and religion in the community, might embrace at the same time the history of the community itself from the death of Moses to the destruction of Jerusalem; (3) the psalter, especially for use in the new temple; and (4) a book of documents concerning the foundation and public relations of the new Jerusalem. This is the *Canon of Nehemiah*. The most important enlargement before the addition of the Christian literature was thus made; and the three great branches of the old literature being each distinct in itself, viz. prophecy, poetry, history, and all three being united as a whole much more completely than in the Pentateuch, here for the first time an unmistakeable selection from the whole of the ancient literature of this nation was compiled in such a way as the aim of the collection required.

4. Meanwhile an idea may be formed how the remainder of the best books, not yet admitted into the canon, but which had been preserved from antiquity, were collected together with increasing carefulness and more correctly estimated, whilst from the flood of new works many a better one would emerge. The aim which an enlarged edition of sacred books should have was fully decided by the previous enlargement; more particularly considered, it was a double aim, so far as that with the more general aim there was associated the special one, viz. to give the preference to writings which, regarding pre-eminently the interests of the true revelation and religion among men, yet dealt particularly with the history and privileges of Jerusalem. In the course of these

centuries there was a point of time in which an extraordinary enthusiasm for this twofold aim blended itself with a nobler courage; and this led to its successful issue the second enlargement of the canon, whereby the extent, and soon also the whole arrangement of the books, called afterwards by Christians the books of the Old Testament, were determined as they have since been preserved in the schools of Jerusalem and their successors. This was the *Canon of Judas Maccabæus.*

5. Already, however, by that first enlargement of the canon was it decided that this whole collection of Holy Scriptures, notwithstanding its essentially more general destination as the literary medium, sacred and venerable with years, for the preservation of the true revelation and religion, was nevertheless first of all and specially intended for the use of the community gathered about the new temple in Jerusalem. From that moment, accordingly, the Samaritans, with the Pentateuch alone as their Holy Scripture, just as decisively severed themselves from this community. The separation would have been very prejudicial to the happy forward development of all true revelation until it attained its perfection, as well as to that of the canon of Holy Scripture, if the greater aptitude to contend for true revelation and religion had actually remained always on the side of the Samaritans. But, in point of fact, notwithstanding the strict provisional limitation to the sanctuaries in Jerusalem, in which amidst the prevalent great darkness of the time the active spirit of all true revelation and religion must now be found, the thread of development was far more firmly held and more directly carried forward in Jerusalem than in Samaria. The proof of this shines forth most conspicuously, since directly after the Maccabæan age this revelation and religion were openly published and defended in heathen lands with a lofty confidence and boldness unknown before; attempts at exposition and commendation by means of the most polished forms of heathen wisdom increased, and the translation of the Holy Scriptures into

foreign tongues was more and more zealously prosecuted. Thus a greater freedom now spontaneously appeared in the contemplation and critical estimate of such writings as were best calculated to explain true religion and kindle its light in the hearts of men, and even in Jerusalem the number of such writings increased. For why should the attention be limited merely to writings approved by the schools of Jerusalem? Must Holy Scriptures, written in the old sacred language known at present only to a few, but now also to be read in Greek, the greater their number became, and the more zealously they were read and investigated, appear more and more exclusively the only fitting channels to dispense instruction and edification in holy things, the only source whence the spirit of all true revelation shot forth its living radiance? Why, in addition to them and along with them, should not other writings of a similar spirit be gladly read and admired? As the Greek language and the outward forms of Greek life overspread the world, many were fond of reading such additional writings in Greek or some easily intelligible form, and collected them together, and combined them with the older writings, sometimes even as interpolations. Translations from the ancient tongue were always the first to be added; but why not add also at length such works as were written in Greek in such increasing numbers, if only they did not contradict the spirit of the older writings already acknowledged?

Under the predominating influence of this new freer tendency a new canon was in reality to arise, which we may designate the *Hellenistic Canon*, and which remained for a long time flexible, as we can still very plainly trace by the most obvious signs, until at length it became fixed by reason of the sudden appearance of the lofty Christian impulse, and when it was fixed it may very properly be named the *Christian Canon*. For since the question here turns, as we have already seen, upon the ultimate prevalency of an opinion, conviction, and usage, flexibility may be predicated of the canon; and just because the opinion, conviction, or usage does gain ground, it tends also to form, and in the end may legitimately form a standard. In matters so essentially belonging to the sphere of mind as the opinions and views of men concerning the value of writings, a standard, by which the procedure in actual life may be readily regulated, can be formed in no other way than that of conviction and faith; and it is possible, should serious errors and pernicious preconceptions mingle from the first in the views that tend to prevail, that a very bad standard may be the result, a canon that becomes the law indeed, but is nevertheless pernicious. In this flexible canon, however, which we may designate the Hellenistic Canon, there had mingled from the very beginning no views and aims that had to be fully rejected, and consequently it became possible, without the serious difficulty that would otherwise have occurred, for Christian writings, with their wholly new and yet very similar spirit, to be taken up and become a part of it. In recent times this has been doubted. But, in the first place, there existed all along something which, in relation to books, could properly be called a canon; writings were to be judged and estimated by it, whether they might be worthily placed by the side of those long since recognised as sacred, therefore whether they might form part of the same standard or rule, or not. And secondly, no one acquainted with the subject can deny that in the course of the second century after Christ, or about the time when the whole wide circle of the full development of the true revelation and religion altogether closed, it was out of this flexible canon that the stationary Christian canon arose. Moreover, we see here much more definitely what we recognised above in all other matters as important and decisive, that with Christianity only did the true end of all development come, whilst with the adoption of a third and essentially Christian enlargement of what may be called the first greater canon, and not previously, could the whole canon of Holy Scripture be closed.

6. *The Settlement and Limitation of the Canon.*

§ 109. Such, in brief, is the history of the rise of a collection of books, which once formed was to be the firm foundation of all exact knowledge of the origin and the eternal essence of the perfect true religion. The conclusion of this history comes into the full light of facts best known to us; its beginning is more obscure, but may be traced with sufficient certainty if the few, but by so much the greater, facts which we can still discover to-day are taken in close and proper connection with the stages of the larger history, that of the community of this revelation and religion, in which this special history moves. For as it is one of the best features of this entire literature that it came forth out of the whole public life of the ancient nation, so the rare excellence of this choicest kernel of it is likewise guaranteed, because it was not selected and set apart arbitrarily according to the taste of a few unknown individual men, but it resulted from the deep living experience through which this whole nation had to pass in its conflicts for the true religion.

Very different, however, from the rise and growth of the canon of these books, hitherto contemplated, was its final settlement and limitation. For this canon of Holy Scriptures had been formed, as § 106-8 clearly showed, in direct relation with the five great periods which we must distinguish (§ 93-98) in the history of the growth of the entire literature of the ancient nation. Naturally the kernel, or choicest and most comprehensive abridgment, of an extensive literature is not rightly formed till the end of its full growth, and so the canon was formed in each case at the verge of one of those five great periods; and that just in these five ever-widening circles it developed itself onward to the close, is one of the plainest indications how little arbitrarily it arose. This kernel of sacred writings was at first the smallest and most exquisite that is conceivable; and just as many a nation of our modern centuries may rejoice if, out of the mighty strife of so-called political principles, it has rescued at the end, as inviolable by any further caprice, even the brief aphorisms of one constitution, so the much smaller and much more significant, and certainly much more contested, Ten Commandments on the verge of the first circle was the first portion of writing which had surmounted for ever all the testings and destructions of the time, and become in a sense a sacred writing, a sense, in this case, the most essential and strongest of all. For every pure divine truth, and every command grounded upon it, should be holy to man; it was so here; but this portion of writing became holy also, because at length it was elevated by the faith of the whole nation above all doubt and conflict, and for that reason was acknowledged as inviolable. About this small but solid and indestructible kernel were grouped at the verge of the four following periods, as in four ever-widening circles, a constantly increasing number of books, attracted as it were by this living centre, and resembling it in firm, unshaken, verified, indestructible contents, and sharing accordingly in its honour and splendour. Each of these four circles had in itself its own special claim to the glory radiating at length over the whole wide circumference. The first surrounded the original centre only to make it shine the more brightly, and to guard it the more securely; the second brought with it the fulness of the immortal oracles and songs, which, kindled at the glowing hearth of this well-founded sanctuary of all true religion, shone forth resplendent and threw back their bright light upon the shrine; the third diversified this splendour chiefly by the distant twilight gleam of artistic poetry and prophecy; the fourth brought the fitting close by the transfiguration of all earthly existence in the pure clear radiance that touched the skies. But with this ever w der extension a considerable change took place in the nature of the additions, so far at least as their literary character is concerned. It was no longer, as in the Ten Commandments, the simple brief principles of all life, according to the true religion, that this great increasing mass of writings presented; all of them were indeed penetrated with these principles in a thousand ways, but yet much besides is taught in them; much that merely shows historically how all the world and all history, especially that of the Israelitish nation, stood toward such foundations of all true religion; and much that, partly in its contents, partly in its form and presentation, goes far beyond those simple foundations. The original standard of the sanctity here in question had therefore been extended more and more, until all such writings were judged to meet its requirements that were already approved by time as of intrinsic worth in themselves, and might serve especially to ascertain the whole nature and demands of all true religion with such living force that the spirit of religion, deriving from them new vigour, should react upon hearers and readers. Wherefore, so long as Jerusalem and its temple seemed the surest Rock of the community of this religion, it was specially determined in addition to regard with special favour such writings as made reference to this sacred Rock, and to the community that more nearly or remotely sought its refuge.

If, now, the possible limits of the standard were thus extended, the question might arise at the close of each of the wider circles, what books, in particular cases, were to be permanently received into it. For as good as no contest at all could take place over the most important of them, because this whole matter was consummated in the great public life of the community. What books are the best, not for a single science investigated and studied as a favourite pursuit by a few specialists, but what are best for a whole nation or a great community, among such as are either destined for its use from the first or still suitable for it, this is never very doubtful in the full life of a nation or a community; or should a doubt exist in the outset about particular works in the minds of many members of the community, it is settled soon enough by experience or the severer conflict of different opinions within the precincts of the community itself, and specially urgent events may very well add their influence to make the decision the more certain and prompt. The originally true and powerful contents of a writing win by the clash of opinion, and by every new and deeper experience of life, new confirmation and force; and should there be disparagement at first, disparagement all the more extended and serious because of the evident intention of the writing to serve an immediately useful end, afterwards the universal respect for it will rise the higher. It may truly be said that time itself, not in so far as it consists of mere moments, but in so far as it receives in its progress through the progress of the human mind richer and nobler contents, brings with it the best sifting (critique) of everything perishable and transient; and if, nevertheless, many a true thought is lost that sought immortality in a writing, since all writing belongs to that which is material and may be destructible, yet, in the higher connection of all that is true, the higher possibility always remains, that the contents of such a lost writing may be supplied from the rest that have been preserved. But since writings of the contents indicated above were always placed before a whole community, and came into collision more sharply with the better feelings prevalent in it from old time for everything true and sound in revelation and religion, a double sifting would in that case be actually accomplished and a decision established, which on the great chief question could not go far and certainly not long astray. But here again everything ultimately turns upon the presence of the Holy Spirit (according to § 80 ff.), whose wonder-working power never fully died out, even in the most troubled times of the community; and indeed, if a writing had issued from the most palpable impulses of this Spirit, and was full of its life, would it not the more readily meet in this community the kindred spirit, and be made use of by it? It is just this quality in a writing that must be the commencement for every kind of eternalization of it reaching beyond the letter.

But it is to be remembered that in all bodies of literature the different books are not so co-ordinated that they fall simply into two divisions, the best and the worst, and the public judgment is thus easily formed in reference to every particular book. And if it is remembered further, how in reality the circles of the canon widened, it will be the more readily understood that there could be a feeling of doubt for a very long time about the admission of many particular writings. For the progress of the formation of the canon was not such that, upon any one of its stages some particular authority came suddenly to the conclusion to increase the already existing canon by this or that series of books; rather was it, that so long as the entire literature of the old nation, along with the nation itself, was in living and active movement, that is, up to the times of Hadrian, there pressed continually into the already existing circle of Holy Scriptures new writings which the more general judgment held to be suitable for it, forcing their way involuntarily, at first quite occasionally, always as here and there a work was held to be suitable for a place in the number of writings which, with respect to this community and its adherents, might be regarded as writings of a higher grade; but what must be the nature of such writings, in the judgment of the more devout, is indicated more particularly above. We see this progress most plainly, and as it is actually going on before the close of the last of the five circles; and according to all plain indications, it answers exactly to what occurred before the close of the two previous circles, although it is self-evident that this entire movement, the more the circles widened with the ever-widening development of the general literature itself, was increasingly extended and increasingly difficult to control. But if the movement became so difficult to deal with, and the number of books admitted here and there multiplied, and were too much mixed up with those till then held as of higher grade, to come to some decisive judgment about them would at last be urgently necessary. The community itself, for which and in which all such books were to have a higher value, had the right to come to such a decisive judgment, to counteract the caprice of individuals as much as possible, to separate the best of such books from the rest, but especially to single out those that were now well known to be wholly necessary. But for all this there would clearly be required an exact survey of the whole situation, and a mature judgment upon all the separate books; still more, a correct insight into the grave question itself, whether an actual extension of the earlier circle were at a definite time necessary or not for the true need of the community. For that such inevitable needs might arise, so long as the inner impulse of the true revelation and religion towards perfection continued in this community, is evident and is set forth more particularly above.

Now, if the voice of prominent individual men in the community does not readily command the spontaneous assent of all, the decisive judgment in question comes best from a representative body, since the members of a whole widely-scattered community are too widely scattered or too little prepared to give it. And accordingly in Jewish circles, if the thought went back in later days to the origin and formation of the canon, the details of which gradually became obscure in the recollection, it was always preferred to say, the great synagogue, *i.e.* the greater body representative of all the separate communities, fixed the canon of the Old Testament. We know more definitively that from the days when Hadrian wholly destroyed the ancient community, distinguished Christian scholars in part, and in part synods, sought to fix the canon as it appeared to them most just for Christians; and whether the suffrages of scholars or of synods had the greater weight is somewhat doubtful. But as to whether the decisions arrived at at that time and those arrived at afterwards in the heart of Christendom were adequate, and how it stands with all such decisions, we can best perceive if we consider the first question more particularly.

§ 110. After the war of Vespasian, and still more after

that of Hadrian, as soon as it felt itself completely severed from the old community, Christianity, then in its youth, had to decide whether it would recognise in general a Holy Scripture, and what; whether, if it recognised what had hitherto been received in the community, it would leave it as the scholars of the old community left it, or would enlarge the circle; and, in case of enlargement, how far it should be carried. These three or four very different questions presented themselves for determination at the same time, though not with the same degree of uncertainty; but a definite decision must be secured about them all, and in some respects this was difficult enough.

1. Christ had frequently taken occasion to discourse sharply against the scribes, whose perversions disfigured and dishonoured the very Scripture they sought to extol so highly. He had often appealed to the Scripture as a witness and proof, and He certainly understood by that word the Holy Scripture of the ancient community, even if He never expressly called it " holy," nor enumerated the separate books of which it was composed. Since, now, Christianity proposed to introduce something more and something better than the old community till then possessed, it was not outside the range of possibility that a new error would be committed, and Christians as such would prefer to reject the Old Testament altogether from the category of Holy Scripture; indeed, the gross misunderstandings about it, easily possible to gross eyes then as to-day, and especially with respect to the Pentateuch itself, might ultimately lead to this rejection. Moreover, since Christ had neither established any new Holy Scripture Himself, nor commanded it, and what Paul had said concerning " the letter killing" was well known, the rejection of all Holy Scripture might even be desired. But all the apostles and all the most intelligent Christians knew very well how little Christ had wished to set aside the Holy Scripture existing in the ancient community, and felt too clearly how, on the contrary, the whole of Christianity conspicuously and urgently

then exchanged their views on the whole question, scholars commented on difference of opinion, and finally synods sought to settle the controversies that arose.

§ 112. 3. But in the meantime Jewish scholars had judged a separation necessary between this Christian Bible, so wonderfully growing in bulk, and their own; consistently with this feeling, and influenced by increasing abhorrence of the Romaico-Greek kingdom, they soon thought necessary also a separation just as rigid between everything Hebrew and Greek; moreover, as a further result, they formed an estimate of all those writings that had found their way into the Hellenistic Canon already described. Thus, therefore, they returned purely to the limits of the fourth circle of the canon;[1] the twofold vehement opposition to everything Christian and everything Græco-Romaic at that time dominated with its whole first glow the minds of these Jewish schools, and in a little time they carried out in the whole sphere of their jurisdiction everything of this kind they wished to carry out. To Christians in their turn no manifest reason presented itself why they should follow this example, especially after the blending of their own Christian writings of the higher kind with those of the then current Greek Bible had been so unanimously and so quickly accomplished. To be sure, as soon as the now existing disproportion between the extent of the Old Testament, which alone was valid among the Jews, and that which passed current among Christians as belonging to the Old Testament, appeared more plainly and often glaringly enough conspicuous, there occurred a certain wavering in Christian circles; yet it proceeded at first only from some scholars who in part had somewhat closely investigated the disproportion between the Jewish and Christian canon, and in their learned controversies were the more deeply sensible of it, but in part also had not wholly mistaken the really less worth of single portions received into this wide canon of the Old Testament. But did one or another of these

[1] The Canon of Judas Maccabæus. See above, p. 348 f.

advise that the example of the Jews should be followed, he found no hearing; and that not without reason, since it was natural to hesitate to reject from the canon what the first Christians had admitted without scruple. Thus these Greek pieces, associated with the Septuagint, now become a Christian book, were retained; nevertheless they were not in all lands entirely equal in number, just as was the case with the Greek books of the New Testament.

If, therefore, it is not in itself possible that all books of any one department, and so also of this department, should be divisible only into purely good and purely bad, or into purely noble or purely base, absolutely necessary or fully superfluous, and if there will always be found standing side by side with the best, noblest, and most necessary some about which the judgment may waver, a smaller community will be tolerably well able to succeed in drawing the sharpest limit between those books which it ought to regard as sacred and all others, as we saw just now that Jewish scribes, in the time of Christianity's youth, managed to push back the canon to the fourth circle mentioned above. Matters of legal observance, by which in these later times the old community, according to § 76, allowed itself to be more and more powerfully influenced, were also in this respect of superior force in the community that, after the destruction of Jerusalem, still remained faithful to the old doctrine; and in the straits of the life in which this community, hard pressed alike by Christianity and heathenism, found itself, it was thought that there could be safety against the intrusion of books injurious to the faith only as a determinate number of such books as might be regarded as sources of true revelation and religion, clustering about the Pentateuch as the most sacred central book, should be publicly recognised and allowed; and as all the rest, which, according to their character and bearing or their title might raise a similar claim, should be held as apocryphal or secret, *i.e.* not publicly recognised and allowed, but rather as forbidden, or even open to censure, if, indeed, they were not also all of them to be considered straight away as completely impious or godless books.¹ It was therefore essentially outer constraint or proscription by which this community, faithful to the old doctrine, sought for safety against the inundating intrusion of the new Christian writings, and writings otherwise repugnant to it; and how much by such means it succeeded in falling back upon the Maccabæan Canon is well known; just as well known, however, is it how by this compulsory limitation it became itself in its whole spiritual life more and more limited and impoverished. Youthful Christianity also, as it was deluged from the second and third centuries onward more and more powerfully by writings which in character and bearing laid claim to higher respect as apostolic, or as going back to the old sacred times, thought it could do itself service by rigid prohibitions against them, expressed by means of synods. But since the Christian communities were already too widely diffused in the world, and their spiritual freedom was already from the beginning too great to allow compulsion in spiritual things, neither synodal decisions nor other means fully attained their aim. As the New Testament prescribes absolutely nothing concerning the canon which affects the mere number of the writings, during the long centuries of the Middle Ages there has never been a complete outward uniformity in reference to it in Christendom, nor has such uniformity ever been considered absolutely indispensable. Some books have always stood as if on the verge of the sacred circle, and have been held, here as in the highest degree worthy of all acceptance, there as less worthy and essential.

§ 113. Indeed, the wholly new zeal for everything genuinely sacred, and the earnest scorn of everything profane

---

¹ Jewish scholars from the second century after Christ, and similarly the older Christian scholars, distinguished rightly three divisions of βιβλία—(1) κανονικά, (2) ἀπόκρυφα, (3) ἄτοπα, whilst the ἀντιλεγόμενα are wavering, and ultimately might be installed in one of the three divisions. Josephus *against Apion*, 1, 8, does not know such divisions, but only the great opposition of the θεῖα to all others.

that obtruded itself into it, from which the great German ecclesiastical movement of the sixteenth century proceeded, attempted to fix the canon more firmly whilst it turned itself decisively against the Greek books of the Old Testament wanting in the Hebrew Bible, and separated them rigidly as "Apocrypha," renewing an agitation which in the old Church had scarcely ruffled even slightly the surface of its life. And it is not to be denied that these books, if compared as a whole with those retained in the Hebrew Bible, fall perceptibly enough far below them in pure worth for the highest things of revelation and religion. Nor is this to be wondered at, when it is remembered that they arose in an age of the old community, which just in relation to these highest things, notwithstanding the swiftly passing elevation of the Maccabees, declined more and more deeply up to the advent of the Baptist and of Christ. In such a time single pieces of writing might indeed attain a high mark, as the Book of Daniel, the oldest parts of the Book of Enoch, and a few others; but the greater part of the writings, although moving in the groove of the old sacred literature, could not keep the high level of the old prophets and best authors of the nation. Nay, as the declining spirit of a whole long period easily draws everything after it, so the morality in the religious life depicted or demanded in these books does not stand at that lofty height to which we are lifted by the older sacred books of the nation.[1] And perhaps there might be a disposition to agree with those who, in the sixteenth century or still to-day, would remove these books altogether from the Bible, if the result of our more exact investigations in the present day had not long since shown that the historical grounds upon which such exclusion would rest are untenable. For how weak the principal reason is, viz. that they are not found in the Hebrew Old Testament,

---

[1] The Book of Sirach is certainly one of the most excellent of these books; but its estimate of women, and its sharp summary counsel concerning divorce, place it far below the height of the Hebrew Bible. See Ecclesiasticus xxv. 13-26.

follows naturally from all that is said above (p. 349 ff.); the contraction of the Old Testament to the fourth circle of the canon already described, which Jewish scholars after the time of Christ first arbitrarily effected, has no binding force upon us. But just as weak is the other reason, viz. that in the New Testament books merely those Hebrew books which were retained by the decision of Jewish scholars are considered as writings of a higher kind, or as sacred, as I have elsewhere so manifoldly shown. In addition it is also to be remembered that these doubted books, when compared with those of the Hebrew Bible, fall below them only as a whole, and that conspicuously the Book of Esther forms a natural transition to them. If, now, all such reasons as are urged against these books that in point of language come between the Old and New Testaments fail, everything returns to the question how, on scientific principles, to decide in general concerning the conception of the sanctity of the whole Bible and the degree of it; and this must be taken into further consideration below.

Moreover, if these writings, which, according to all their characteristics, we designate best of all as intermediate writings, are once estimated in modern times as the Apocrypha of the Old Testament, such writings as are anywhere met with of similar character, and in actual age and dress falling back into the times of the Old Testament, must be relegated to a lower third gradation. To distinguish three gradations with respect to all writings which can at all come into consideration, because they here or there had been raised to a higher stage or laid claim to it, was entirely proper in those centuries in which the question of fixing the canon was a burning and necessary question, as above shown; such writings were therefore then called rather *pseudepigrapha*, because there was no wish to characterize them directly as impious or godless. But in this another mistake was made. For into this division must now be thrown such books as are introduced as Holy Scripture in the New Testament, as the Book of Enoch, which also among the oldest Christians without doubt were freely read as Holy Scripture of the higher kind, and have maintained themselves as such in different communities of Christendom far into the Middle Ages, or indeed until to-day, as the fourth Book of Ezra in most editions of the Armenian and Latin Bible, or the Book of Enoch and the Book of the Jubilees in the Æthiopian Church. In their inner worth, as well as in the respect once more commonly paid to them, and partly also in age, such writings stand not very far away from those intermediate writings, and for various reasons (for example, the Book of Enoch, because it is too prolix and contains much of a foreign nature) might in most Christian communities gradually be more and more driven into the background. But there is no sufficient ground on that account for removing them all into the third gradation, and thereby designating them as entirely unworthy. They are, indeed, productions of the somewhat artificial literature described more particularly above (§. 100 f.), which in the later centuries increased with increasing luxuriance, and sent forth its shoots long, indeed, after the close of the Christian canon even up to the Middle Ages; and that a strong growing aversion to them, prevailed in greater Christendom the more wantonly they multiplied and, the more widely they became known and read, is readily explained. But in such questions the Middle Ages could less and less hit upon a proper decision, and it is already more particularly proved above that the name of *pseudepigrapha* must be used very cautiously, since, should it be applied without care, it would cover far more than is included within the limits of the books here classed together as such.

However, in any case, the books which would thus be designated as apocryphal with respect to the Old Testament would stand far removed from the Apocrypha of the New Testament in ancient regard and worth, and the injustice would be done of being obliged to distinguish with respect to the Old Testament three gradations, but with respect to the New Testament only two. That these books in our modern times are designated so very commonly as apocryphal cannot prevent us, in science at least, from judging otherwise about them; rather is it apparent in this matter that to-day, in the so-called Reformed Church, there cleaves yet indeed many an imperfection arising from its origin, and that Luther in the choice of the new name he gave to these books was not happy. In the meantime good service could easily be done if these books, which are very useful in supplying somewhat to the customary reader the historical connection between both Testaments, were admitted for the national use in a somewhat smaller type or publication as intermediate books, omitting the third and fourth Maccabees, already wanting in the Vulgate, but adding the most important portions of the Book of Enoch and the whole fourth Book of Ezra. As intermediate books they might be rightly held in much respect.

7. *The Ante-canonical and Post-canonical Position of the Sacred Books.*

§ 114. Whether a book that became canonical descended from an earlier or later time, it would nevertheless be a great mistake to suppose it was received into the canon forthwith as soon as it was written. This would amount to the same thing as will be discussed further below, viz. the erroneous supposition that it was written of set purpose for the canon, or with a view to admission into it. Such mistaken presuppositions are at once dissipated when all that is relevant to this subject is more closely investigated. Now that more exact researches in the last centuries, and especially also at length in our own time, have penetrated this whole wide region more and more deeply, and we have discovered anew the true state of things with greater certainty, we can express sufficiently on this footing the sure results in the following positions:—

1. All the books which were ultimately received into the secure haven of the canon, and now lie in it as if certified for

eternity, came into existence as all those that have not been received, and in their origin show absolutely nothing recognisable by our eyes in which they had any advantage over the others. The whole literature of the people of Israel was already in early times uncommonly various and abundant, and amid the fluctuations and changes that were indicated more particularly above, § 92 ff., maintained itself all along through all the very diversified times of its life up to the era which led to the final close of the canon itself. Traces observable still in the canonical books themselves suggest this certainty with respect to the older times; with respect to the later we possess also, apart from the canonical books, testimonies which do not allow us to doubt of it; and as we follow out such traces properly, there arises before our eyes a wide superstructure of most wonderful activity and labour in the most different departments of literature. With these ever ascending waves of movement and the very different kinds of mental work that found its outlet in the literature, this activity itself was broken up again into different circles; and as in the earliest times there were authors busily occupying themselves principally with prophetic writings, others with poetic and artistic works, others again with books of history or with books of wisdom,[1] so there were still, in the last times of this entire wide literature, authors devoting their energies especially to the literature of the Gospels, and others to that of the Epistles; and as everywhere, so here, literary men, properly so called, followed when the great authors in the different departments had exercised their creative gifts.

2. The books that had now become canonical in the four circles described in § 107 f., and expanding at an ever-increasing distance round the Ten Commandments as a fixed centre, show themselves as little recognisable, according to all the most exact researches, as the oldest in their department, so that they must rather be considered generally as the most

[1] Num. xxi. 27 speaks of poets who wrote or sang small aphoristic or proverbial couplets.

recent but also the ripest and most perfect of their kind. The number of writings belonging to the same department was in the course of time too great, and the writings themselves, for the common reader, were too widely scattered and too difficult to get together not to induce men, expert in each department, to bestow labour and pains in connecting and combining them more closely in appropriate fashion; and we can still plainly mark a special art displayed in blending, more or less completely, the best productions of a department, the one with the other; whilst, on the other hand, some satisfied themselves with placing the best works merely in juxtaposition, because they considered that the better course. All this was a labour in the highest degree of diligence, of variety, and of well-nigh inexhaustible extent, begun in Israel in tolerably early times, repeating itself with every succeeding age, and, in particular conjunctures of circumstances, that called forth its activity with special vigour, prosecuted with exceptional zeal. Many of the most important pieces of the older literature have been preserved either entire or in longer or shorter fragments by means of this vigorous twofold work of collecting and blending documents and books; without it they might have been wholly lost. Our canonical books as a whole now consist only of such larger works as have partly resulted from manifold remodellings and interweaving of many older works, partly arisen from collections of all kinds. The old custom was to arrange together a series of similar writings under a name that was great in literature; whence the new custom gradually grew up of reckoning all these similar writings as belonging to the same name. In this way the two smaller books of Solomon have probably been preserved along with the larger Book of Proverbs; with which among the Hellenists the two other books of Wisdom were associated; and in the same canon were arranged under Jeremiah's name three (properly four) other small prophetic writings. A few smaller books stand as isolated as the Book of Esther in the Old Testament and the Apocalypse in the New, so that they were ultimately in the augmentations of the canon added to those regarded as on a par with them. But such as were books of extracts might also before they were received into the canon suffer many additions or go through other transformations; as in the Old Testament the Book of Proverbs and the twelve books of the prophets show. Only a few have passed into the canon just as they were originally composed; as in the New Testament the Apocalypse, the Epistle to the Hebrews, and the two writings of Luke; in the Old Testament, Koheleth and the Book of Esther.

3. On closer contemplation, a whole previous history, longer or shorter, of most of the books of the canon is disclosed to us, but this previous history gradually fell into oblivion the longer the now canonical books remained alone by themselves, and afterwards each one of them was infinitely more read and used than before. Among the ancient nations little exact inquiry was made into the history of the origin of the ancient books, and what was once known readily slipped away from memory in the course of centuries; it is not surprising, therefore, that with respect to the way in which many canonical books first came into existence and took their final form, certain new and distinct opinions, little in harmony with that previous history, should have firmly established themselves even before the close of the last circle of the canon. Thus not only was Moses now regarded as the author of the Pentateuch, David as the poet who wrote all the psalms of the canonical psalter, but to the latest of those just before called prophets were ascribed prophetic pieces that either have no superscription at all or one without the name of the author. If such universally prevalent opinions give indications of their existence in the language of the New Testament, this can have for us not the smallest significance from a purely historical point of view, since nothing is necessarily taught thereby that is of moment for the severer requirements of history, and since we know that what Christ and His disciples desired to teach,

and for which they demanded faith, lies in quite another province.

§ 115. Certain books having been placed by public acknowledgment upon a far higher stage than others, in the way described above, § 105 ff., it was difficult, in the circumstances affecting everything of the nature of books in antiquity, to prevent the entire loss more and more of those put in the background, unless some of them were guarded by specially favourable conditions. And in this way have been preserved, even outside the canon of the New Testament, a considerable number of that moiety of all the books which may be called Greek or even Christian, and belong in the widest sense to this literature, — a moiety which, as is clear from all previously said, embraces all outside the Hebrew Bible. But not a single book side by side with the books of the Hebrew Old Testament has survived from the old nation, partly because the greater number of those books go back to times so ancient that very many originally contemporaneous with them might already be lost when the third and fourth circles of the canon, as explained above, were closed, partly on account of the special rigour of the schools against all books not received into the fourth circle, a rigour which was ultimately superadded according to § 112.

The perishing of so many books, occasioned as it was, not by this sharp separation alone, but conjointly with it, may be properly regretted ; yet, on the other hand, it must be thankfully acknowledged that the books once elevated to the higher grade were afterwards the more securely guarded against all further danger of perishing or even of mutilation and abridgment. And this is in fact a great advantage gained by making such books sacred. Even from the earliest centuries of antiquity portions of literature have thereby been faithfully preserved which otherwise would have been almost certainly lost, or at best would have been saved in later epitomes and remodellings. If we now possess pieces of writing of the ancient nation of Israel which afford us manifest proof that the literature of this nation is not indeed the oldest in the earth, but yet proportionately one of the oldest and best preserved of all, we owe it simply to their being made sacred. But, to say nothing for brevity's sake of Chinese and Egyptian literature, it is very similar with the Indian Veda and the oldest portions of the Zend Avesta which, as the offspring of a wholly different world, would never have been saved out of their remote antiquity for later times and for our own days, though in the case of the Avesta in a very mutilated form, had not the special protection of an inviolable sanctity surrounded them. Even the anxiety which appears to us exaggerated with which the later generations often sought to preserve such holiest treasures of their antiquity from all alteration and disfigurement, and indeed from every touch of profane hands, and wherein the Hebrews were on a par with the ancient Hindoos and Zends, has had so far its advantage.

But what is of most importance for us is that this learned solicitude extended principally to the preservation of the right readings of such books, partly just on account of their sanctity, partly also, and still more so far as it was the case, because such books were publicly read in the assemblies of the community. In proportion as everything depended with respect to these books upon the most exact preservation of their original sense, must we estimate the more highly the solicitude which later scholars on their part so manifoldly and persistently displayed, and whose best good consequences we are still able always to make our own. The question for us is simply how far this specially active solicitude has, in particular instances, benefited us, and how we have to judge of it further. And since in connection with this whole subject of discussion the answer to this question cannot be evaded, we must at once distinguish carefully the two great halves of our Bible above mentioned, viz. the Hebrew and the Greek. It would be a great thing if, through the rare solicitude of ancient scholars, we were enabled to assume that everywhere in the Bible a wholly reliable text had been preserved;

nowhere is this so much to be desired as in the books of the law and other writings that are to be regarded as public documents. But in point of fact the whole case stands in detail thus:—

The Hebrew Bible has its Massôra, the object of which is to prevent its text being ever changed by the caprice of the scribe or the reader. This is an extremely carefully planned and well executed work of Jewish scholars, consisting partly of special books, partly of mere marginal readings, longer or shorter, to this Bible itself, and which, among other things it aimed at, was principally to prevent that what had been accepted as the right text should ever again be altered. The work has shown its great value in preserving this Bible the more completely in its purity and integrity all through the darkness of the Middle Ages to our own times; and if it is not wholly unique in its kind, since the Syrians have dealt similarly with their Bible, the Mussulmans with their Koran, the Hindoos with their Vedas, it nevertheless surpasses in extent and in thoroughness of execution everything of the like nature. Since, however, it was composed with so much labour and so much completeness at a time when the schools of Biblical learning exercised their sway over the whole of the still existing Jewish community, it is not surprising that the text of the Massôra was followed in all subsequent manuscripts of the Hebrew Bible, just as the rigid exclusion of all books seeking admittance into the fourth circle of the canon was repeated; and the question arises, Can we to-day anywhere in any corner of the earth find a copy of the Hebrew text free as a whole from the influence of the Massôra? But this whole work was entered upon only as the Biblical school with its one-sided anxiety was formed and took simply one single species of text as the right one for the scientific basis of the letter of the Bible; it has therefore preserved only the Biblical text once acknowledged by it to be infallibly correct, and with all its merit derived from the fidelity with which it has been preserved it cannot suffice for us, since we have long known for a certainty that in other old manuscripts readings altogether different and in part much more correct were once found. Moreover, even the text of the Massôra, prescribed as it was, did not maintain itself in the course of centuries in all manuscripts with complete uniformity.

With the text of the other half of the Bible the case is altogether different. Among Christians of the older centuries, conformably with the freer Christian spirit, a similar school of learned men was never formed who dealt with the Bible on the basis of narrow and one-sided views; and it would have been well-nigh impossible, on account of the wide dispersion of the communities in the most remote and different lands, to carry out with respect to them any kind of restraint or impose upon them a Massôra. On the contrary, from the oldest manuscripts of the Greek Bible, and pre-eminently of the New Testament, which have been collected and examined in our day with great zeal, rather do we recognise with certainty that a large freedom prevailed among copyists, though the best manuscripts were often repeatedly revised by learned correctors and restored to conformity with other manuscripts. In the more ancient manuscripts of the Greek Bible we note, therefore, the presence of the same old freedom—often, it is true, leading to errors—which unquestionably prevailed also in the Hebrew manuscripts in the centuries before the Massôra. Not till the Middle Ages were the Greek manuscripts of the Bible more and more assimilated, without doubt because the dangers of the older but too unrestrained freedom became increasingly perceptible and their avoidance was desired, although even then a school so rigorous as that of the Massôra was not in existence.

The exaggerated expectations, or, indeed, stereotyped fancies, concerning the Bible as Holy Scripture must therefore in this respect be abandoned. Neither in itself, according to § 104, nor by all such learned manipulations, can the mere letter of Holy Scripture be sufficiently guarded and as it were itself made holy. The means are put into our hands, especially in the modern centuries, obtained by persevering zeal of research, through which, even as by our own further reflection we may approximate more and more closely to the original text of the separate writings of the Bible; with respect to the New Testament and other parts of the Greek half of the Bible we can collate old manuscripts, which of no other book are so numerous; with respect to the Old Testament, for the times before the Massôra we can collate chiefly the old translations; and it is no small advantage that the sanctity and wide use of the Bible have secured that we can gather together to-day so many more manuscripts of it than of any other book so old, and can with these collate translations so ancient in the most different tongues. But that this sanctity, notwithstanding all solicitude exercised often so anxiously on this account, never sufficed for the complete protection of the mere letter of the Bible, is plain.

8. *The Sanctity of the Bible is neither arbitrarily determined, nor arbitrarily determinable.*

§ 116. If we cannot therefore rest the sanctity of the Bible, and retain the proper sense of the term, upon its letter, as if that letter had been preserved for us entirely without change, even if in the original text it was absolutely free from errors, nor yet upon the uniformity of its extent as if it had been everywhere the same which, according to § 112 f., it has not,—the question further arises, whether that sanctity is then the product of the will of the individual writers of the Bible, and so ultimately of the Bible itself? That is to say, whether it was of set purpose willed, since every earnest volition presupposes in the special case a purpose; we might, however, also say arbitrarily willed, since the will without its own free choice cannot act. But to state this question rightly, and to have an accurate acquaintance with the Bible, is already to give an answer in the negative. For everything is specially applicable to this point that was remarked in § 99 concerning the perfect ingenuousness and simplicity from which the Bible everywhere discourses. But the proper answer is found in the nature of all true religion itself; so that it may be said, only if the Bible had not arisen from the predominating true religion in it, would it pretend to be sacred by its own absolute will.

That the Bible grew out of writings and books that were written by men, it says everywhere itself. For the names of the authors of particular books are known in many instances from the books themselves; but where this does not occur in the case of a small or large work, it is accounted for by the old custom of authorship in this nation, discussed above in § 99; and yet even then, at least in the case of the four Gospels and the Acts of the Apostles, the name of the author is supplied by ancient hands. Only in a few cases are we otherwise unacquainted with the names of the authors, either on account of special circumstances which were caused by the time, as when once a prophet, contrary to all former usage of the old prophets, sent forth a mere fly-leaf into the world (p. 313); or when a later collector and editor of earlier writings added something of his own; for the old simplicity in the literary usage of this nation of Israel remained down to the latest times so far unchanged that mere compilers and new editors of old books did not regard it as necessary to append their names, as the Greeks did not learn to do till after the Alexandrian school of literary lore. That as a result of the factitious authorship, described further in § 100, or because the purely historical recollection became gradually obscured, according to p. 370 f., some books were traced back to authors who in the more rigid historical sense had either not written them at all themselves or not wholly, is of no moment here; for even this attests that some particular men were always thought of as authors of all these books. And thus in the end only the Ten Commandments themselves would be left as regarded by the narrators, according to the accounts in the Pentateuch, noted in § 106, as indeed written by the divine finger. But that this representation is not to be understood in any gross material sense, and with what justice it may nevertheless always bear for us its good sense, is explained above in § 106. And, indeed, were we to understand it in an entirely gross material way, we should not be entitled to transfer the representation to the whole Pentateuch, or indeed to the whole Bible.

If we take now at once even the greatest writers of such books as belong to this class, viz. the prophets and apostles, they were no different men in their writing than they were in their purest and (to express it so here) divinest life and effort; but just as they discoursed and worked publicly in the community, so also they composed these writings, although precisely with respect to this special occupation again with a wholly special collectedness and concentration of mind necessary for it, therefore in such a way that if the Holy Spirit moved them on other occasions, according to § 82, He would certainly not be wanting to them in such writing also. But such lofty things as holiness and godliness, like all similar perfections, are verily things that man is to strive after with all his might in accordance with the eternal law of all true religion, which he is never to suppose himself to have in perfection, nor to boast of them as if he possessed them; and though every one of its members may be and is said to be holy according to the most ancient sentiment of the true community (§ 86 ff.), whether he was so actually the total impression of all his conduct and effort can show, but not till after his death. Still all true religion, according to § 79. 1, the more purely it kept itself upon its own lofty height, was never from the beginning prodigal of the name "Man of God;" and if the author of the pastoral Epistles, at least in such connections of discourse as are not to be misinterpreted, calls Timothy so,[1] he nevertheless only seeks by it to make

---

[1] 1 Tim. vi. 11; 2 Tim. iv. 17. Paul himself does not love this coloured discourse; the expression is, however, very striking as coming from this, so to speak, later Paul.

conspicuous the lofty type of man which in his high position especially such a man as Timothy was to be, and in the retrospect of the author had also actually been. But if all this is so, it must be transferred also even to the writings of such men, and we must suppose that these could truly become sacred so far as anything like a writing may become in general sacred to man, but without itself intending to be so originally. And this all appearance confirms, as well if we take these writings as they are in themselves as if we look closely to their history before they became sacred.

For, contemplated from that side, no one of these writings declares anywhere of itself that its aim is to find acceptance as a sacred and divine writing. The prophets discoursed in the name of Jahveh, and, impelled by the same spirit which animated them in public discourse, they also work, whether in small or large pieces of writing, for the public; but nowhere do they put upon their writings as writings a further special divine value or the weight of a special sanctity. A younger prophet who newly edited for his contemporaries the noblest portions of Isaiah with a shorter piece of his own production, appears indeed once to designate the book, at the end of which he gave this addition of his own, a book of Jahveh,[1] therefore to be sure, it may be supposed, in this sense a sacred book; and he refers to it that the latest generations of men shall not fail to see the truth of the prophecy here pronounced; but this book was not at all to him the old Book of Isaiah which he simply edited afresh, and whose accomplished prophecies he had desired only to continue somewhat; the vivid feeling which is expressed in these words is rather that of the certainty of the divine judgment of the world at the conclusion of things when all this, just as it is here announced, it shall be possible to read off as from God's book of account. This is therefore simply a very characteristic image, for this later prophet, of the last judgment of the world, which he could think of the more readily the greater

[1] Isa. xxxiv. 16 f.

the judgment of the world had been which had just in reality been witnessed in the overthrow of the Chaldæan kingdom. Accordingly the expression has here no relevancy. The factitious authorship, described more particularly above in § 100, produced effect indeed to this extent, that among those who accepted such a literary device with little scruple or overlooked it, a special glory fell upon the writing, the book, and the words themselves by which an ancient man of God received a new transfiguration, as if it had been written in old time, or, as with the Book of Enoch, in a primitive age just as it had now been fulfilled. And it created or favoured entirely new conceptions concerning books that could then readily become more deeply established; just as it did not become gradually customary to think of Moses as the author of the whole Pentateuch till after the work of the Deuteronomist already mentioned. But we cannot depend upon such later opinions although at length they were coined into standing titles.[1] And if the Apocalyptist counts him blessed who reads his prophetic book and, which is the chief thing, makes its contents a truly individual possession, and if he threatens severely, after the fashion of the Deuteronomist, whoever should add anything to it or take anything away from it, by all that he simply expresses himself concerning its serious contents as he was obliged to express himself in his day without claiming for the writing as a writing an exceptional position. Moreover, Paul might in an Epistle once indeed exclaim that he thought also that he had the spirit of God, and on this account had not said anything in the Epistle that was unchristian; but that he assigned any higher importance otherwise to any one of his Epistles so far as it was a writing, is against all appearance.

If we regard now on the other side what is described

---

[1] Such as the "Pentateuch of Moses," the "Psalter of David." It is of no historical significance that such names, freely used for five hundred years, are found in the New Testament.

in § 114, viz. how all these writings before they got into the canon simply shared with all the rest the same fate in the stream of the entire literature of Israel, and how especially the New Testament writings, after they were received into the canon, were for a long time very freely handled (according to p. 374), everything is harmonized in the certain judgment that they became sacred indeed at the right time, but without professing to have been so originally. And if in the later of them the earlier are considered and honoured as sacred, it does not follow that the authors of these later writings deliberately and artificially aimed, as it were, to compose and send forth sacred writings or in any way to rival the old sacred writings; there is not the smallest indication of such an intention. Besides, who would expect this of a Paul, or of the authors of the Gospels, or of the apocalyptic John? But indeed not even the writers of the more factitious kind of works, frequently mentioned previously, so far as these works nevertheless found a place in the canon of the New or Old Testament, had ever the design by their writings to rival the old Sacred Scriptures or to displace them.

Wherefore the result arrived at above stands good, that it was only the deep and fervid feeling of the sacredness of all true revelation and religion in the successive stages of their progress, and the experience that just those writings enclosing the Ten Commandments in ever wider circles were most fitted to guard and promote that feeling, that brought about the conviction of the sacredness of the Scriptures. So that even here the universal truth is confirmed that everything divine and holy cannot be enforced among men and by them, and cannot be guarded by violent means, but exists and comes only where it can exist and come in its own proper freedom and in the fulness of its invisible power.

§ 117. As the sacredness of the Bible is not the product of the arbitrary will of the authors of the books of which it is composed, even so in its true signification it cannot be arbitrarily determined at a later period by the changing opinions of the time or of schools, without such opinion sooner or later operating very perniciously. Nevertheless, this happened before the final closing of the canon. In the centuries which elapsed between the last but one and the last making up of the canon, the conceptions and fancies concerning Holy Scripture, according to § 73, mounted higher and higher, even to the most giddy heights. Starting from the mere idea of a writing, it could be supposed that as all the old venerable relics, which had vanished before the ark of the covenant, at that time upon the earth, were regarded as in their true essence laid up mysteriously in heaven, so not merely the Ten Commandments, written according to the Pentateuch with the divine finger, were hidden there, but also all Holy Scripture bound up with the book of life of which poets and prophets had discoursed,[1] and expanded to the great reckoning book of God and the broad wall-tablets upon which all the destinies of humanity were already inscribed beforehand; just as in the Book of Enoch this conception of heavenly tablets is found everywhere. Yet this representation must more and more remain suitable only for the higher discourse. Starting, on the other hand, from the contents of Holy Scripture, whether of the Pentateuch chiefly as the sacred book of law as was the case with Philo, or even of other books depending upon the Pentateuch, the idea of sacredness might be exaggerated, and be supposed to lie in the letter as such; and since it cannot be allowed to distinguish arbitrarily between this or that letter, if it only stands in the text, acknowledged to be genuine, it is only proper to think that everything to be read in the Bible is equally the immediate word of God. And this conception could then be best followed out further by saying either that the Holy Spirit of God who impelled the prophets did the same for every writer of the Bible in the penning of every word, or that the whole Bible is only as it were one embodiment and manifestation of the Word or Logos of God.

[1] Ex. xxxii. 32; Isa. iv. 3; Ps. cxxxix. 16; cf. Mal. iii. 16.

Both conceptions are in effect the same; but the first is the more readily apprehended on account of the idea of the true prophet familiar to all; the other, proceeding from the mere idea of the word of God, makes everything more simple, universal, and uniform. According to the first, all writers of the Bible must necessarily have been prophets, which to be sure in those days was a view more and more prevalent with respect to the Old Testament, David himself being freely spoken of as such. According to the other, this would not be so necessary, as indeed it would occur to no one to designate the New Testament writers prophets, with the exception of the John of the Apocalypse. And since, indeed, the Old Testament books are constantly thought of in the New Testament as sacred even where they are not expressly so designated, but the New Testament books do not anywhere so speak of themselves, sacredness would rather be ascribed to the former than the latter, if after the complete close of the canon it had not been easy to transfer this idea to the whole body of the New Testament writings.

But if the sacredness of the Bible is thus to be assigned to letter and word, as if in relation to its highest aim everything in it had equal value, so that in some way it consisted, as the Alexandrian Philo would say, of as many oracles as sentences, words, or letters, at once on three sides the gravest mischiefs arise, and of these a detailed description must be given.

§ 118. 1. Whilst the highest aim of the Bible is unquestionably to publish to men the will of God for their spiritual life, very many of its sentences in their most obvious sense fall below this mark. Few men, it is true, have gone so far as to seek in every sentence an immediate divine command for man; but so much the more have they presupposed that every sentence must contain some higher truth, even if this at first glance were not very easy to find, and the solution of the riddle then propounded must be sought only by great pains. This led necessarily to figurative interpretation or allegory; and the whole business of exposition and application of the contents of the Bible was resolved into the arts of allegory, which it was sought to reduce to fixed principles in order that the course of procedure might not be purely arbitrary; an endeavour which might be speciously commended because some passages of the Bible it was impossible to understand in their strictly literal and obvious sense. But we have long since been convinced with sufficient certainty how fully arbitrary every figurative or secondary interpretation is, indeed, strictly taken, how it allows only a wrong instead of the true sense and original genuine meaning of the author. Wherefore these symbolic interpreters of the Bible never agree among themselves, since upon mere caprice no spontaneous harmonious judgment of all who are capable of judging can be based. And as a result of this whole method, it is regarded as possible to find divine mysteries in every word, nay, in every letter of the Bible, as indeed many have attempted to do.

But as soon as ever old writings already only partially intelligible are held sacred in a community, there slips in everywhere almost involuntarily this effort and art of allegory, as we know it to have been the case in like manner in the history of the Indian and Persian religions. And inasmuch as they found their point of departure in the Pentateuch, such attempts and endeavours could the more easily succeed the more this most sacred book went back into an antiquity which was encompassed by a sacred splendour, yet had otherwise for men of the later age already become very obscure. Indeed, it is possible still distinctly to trace how innocent such attempts are in their first origin, and how it was simply an actual pressure and need of the spiritual life that led to them. When the author of the Book of Daniel felt the deepest pain of mind in the thought that the seventy years of the wasting of the community foretold in Jeremiah's book, then held sacred, could not after four hundred years be at the end, and the coming of the Messiah could be so long delayed; when he, praying in his spirit to God about the solving of this very difficult problem, had found it at last in the suggestion of a freer symbolic interpretation of the number of years, a suggestion won as it were in conflict from God, for the letter of Holy Scripture had verily become clear to him in this new divine light, not by an already familiar freak of fancy, nor by a previously established art of allegory, and he himself was set free from his anguish of mind: we are able in this case, as in the most vivid example, the better to realize how indefatigably and conscientiously the anxious heart suffered itself to be agitated under the increasingly heavy yoke of a sacred letter, and the higher impulse not blindly to submit to it, until there opened between the two the possibility of a new view that might afford rest. Allegory, therefore, which may often be extremely apt, and bring to light ingenious thoughts, served to give exercise in the best sense to a freer movement of the mind, and to satisfy a higher need in the prevailing darkness of those times; and this alone explains also why it could obtain so much favour, and amidst hundreds of changes could yet itself in its deepest purport remain so long the same. Moreover, it is also easily understood that it by no means sprang up and reached a high degree of development in this or that place, as it were, merely casually; it shot forth in many places from seed everywhere sown, and only from special causes did it flourish conspicuously in Alexandria, which had already been prepared for it by kindred Greek pursuits.

If, now, Paul with his Hellenistic culture adorned by a few such flowers his words to readers in heathen lands very susceptible to arts of this kind, and subsequently the author of the Epistle to the Hebrews still more illustrates what he seeks to teach in grand new creative trains of thought from this province, it is only something quite usual in the literature of those times. In fact, it is simply a special mode of specially explaining and demonstrating some subject of difficulty in the realm of sacred things and sacred questions,—a method at that time much loved and resorted to by many persons which we should be obliged to look upon with anxiety and aversion if it were employed to demonstrate anything in itself erroneous; but how little this is the case, we know. If, therefore, the New Testament were far fuller than it is of such rather artificial passages and arguments, that would not lead us also on our part to make further use of the arts of allegory, any more than the instances given above (p. 370 f.) of views then prevailing concerning the authorship of some of the old sacred writings would induce us to discontinue more exact historical investigations. All such things are changing historical phenomena which have a significance for us of a transient kind, but not one immediately determining our faith and our religion; and there being very many ways in which something right in itself may be proved is no justification for rejecting what is right in itself because it is pressed home upon the momentary conviction of the world merely in this form or that. But the consideration truly important, and for us in this case most immediately decisive, is, that according to our New Testament books, yet quite distinctly and positively, we may know that neither Christ Himself nor His disciples who once stood in closest connection with Him made use of such arts of allegory, as all the Gospels, with the writings of John, of James, and of Jude, as well as the First Epistle of Peter, show. The pure simplicity, plain directness, and inwardly sure confidence of all truth mark also on this side all earthly steps of the Lord; and as we clearly realize how certainly Christ did not call to His aid this art, widely intrusive though it was at that time and unusually loved, nay more, how little He needed it for His highest aim, so certainly can we also to-day completely dispense with it.

§ 119. 2. If all the separate words and sentences of Holy Scripture, in every passage where they may be found, have directly this great importance, even for all public life in the community and in human society, then conclusions may be legitimately drawn from them of the most significant character, and affecting the life most profoundly, as precepts and legal awards for the public conduct of nations; and nothing can be more acceptable than to find in them such thoroughly decisive references to things that happen to be in dispute to-day or to-morrow in the community, or in national intercourse. Does this or that place, for example, seem to have, especially in matters of divine service, a superiority over every other, or does a great party feel itself obliged to defend some one of its favourite opinions against other opinions, nothing can be more desired than to find in the words of the Bible perfectly evident support and proofs. But in the wearisome obscure controversy, zeal may then become so deeply stirred, so one-sided and blind, that the one or the other may think himself able also to make the letter of Holy Scripture ultimately favour his own supposed sacred insight, by fixing upon this or that special reading, in this or that sentence or word of the Bible, as the only correct one, whether he has good ground for it or not, and by holding tenaciously to it, and sparing no exertions to induce his whole community to accept it. Thus the Samaritans sought to prove, from the Pentateuch, that their sacred Mount Garîzîm is the only legitimate place for all true divine worship; the Jews, from the same book, showed that the Samaritans are mistaken, and each accused the other of tampering with the sacred word; the Egyptian Jews, against vehement contradictions of the Jerusalem Jews, attempted to prove, from a passage of Isaiah, that they had a perfectly legitimate temple in an appointed place in Egypt;[1] and still further, late in the middle age, Jewish Massôra-scholars approved an unsuitable reading in the Psalter, in order thus to take away from Christians the ground of a favourite Messianic interpretation.[2]

§ 120. 3. After the diffusion of Christianity, when mutual accusations increased with increasing severity amidst the divergent tendencies of those who yet, properly speaking, acknowledged only the true religion, and therefore held a Holy Scripture in high esteem; when not merely Samaritans and Judæans, Jews and Christians disputed about the Holy

[1] Isa. xix.   [2] Ps. xxii. 17; cf. *Poets of Old Test. in loc.*

Scriptures, but Christians themselves had not everywhere the same Holy Scriptures; when, nevertheless, in their wearisome controversies, hard to be understood by simple minds, all appealed to a Holy Scripture, and each party charged the other with serious alterations and corruptions of the sacred text: then, indeed, is it explicable how the wholly new view could come into vogue, that all Holy Scripture, up to that time, is still not the true divine Scripture, and that something far more reliable must yet be hoped for. Among a people such as the Arabians at that time still were, in their great ancient chief tribe, hemmed in round about on three sides by powerful victorious kingdoms and loving still above everything their old freedom, hard pressed from the north and the south by Christians with their long-continued attempts at conversion and their very mischievous internal controversies, and yet being themselves too simple, and at the same time too shrewd, not to see the moral weakness and mistakes of these zealous neighbours—among such a people a view of this kind could easily and powerfully gain ground; and Mohammed was the peculiarly gifted man, at first pure as an angel, afterwards, when he stood on the giddy height of his worldly power, degenerating more and more profoundly, through whom such a view found its fullest realization, and became a force that shook with mighty energy the whole earthly universe to its centre, yet still is itself to-day tottering enough. Holy Scripture must come to the prophet in legible form, freshly and immediately from heaven, and if inscribed plainly for men, must be inscribed as it were by invisible hands, to be forthwith communicated to men, with the greatest certainty, as something to be read (Qor'an); only thus is it reliable as a divine work, and to be held as the infallible prescript of God for all men; moreover, it is not then composed in languages unknown and hard to be understood as the old Holy Scriptures, reported as divine, were composed, but in living, clear, eloquent speech, so that no living man can complain of its obscurity. Such is the entirely arbitrary conception of what a Holy Scripture must be, and this conception was the originator of a new Scripture; and the double charm that dwelt in it, as a Scripture of the highest eloquence in itself, and also especially ravishing through its heavenly mysteriousness, suggesting the real depths of all piety, was the more fascinating to the world of that period, since Mahommed proposed to reject neither the old sacred writings of the true religion nor the religion itself, but maintained only that through this more reliable Holy Scripture the imperfections of the former were to be removed. And, in fact, if it is once admitted that there must be Holy Scripture or the will of God cannot certainly be made known to man, and an arbitrary conception is formed in that case of what character it must be, it will readily be supposed that the Scripture which in itself as a composition to be read is perfectly clear to every man and reliable, and therefore in itself not to be contradicted, and comprehending nothing that is too prolix and apparently too multifarious and lying too remote, is the best. Moreover, the external restriction which it is then thought necessary to employ, in order to preserve it from every further addition and every various reading, such as was the law of the realm in Islam soon after Mahommed's death, is only a logical consequence.

But, in fact, the outcome is the contrary of all that Holy Scripture originally is (as is clear from what was said above), or indeed ought to be, if it is not to act perniciously upon the pure essence and beneficent influences of all true revelation and religion. What, as Scripture, can only be a means to a higher aim, and not at all something essentially and at all times wholly indispensable to it—this conception makes the most essential and indispensable chief thing; and whilst genuine Holy Scripture, according to § 116, can indeed become holy, but without asserting itself as such, here is said to be something in itself, yet only outwardly and materially holy from the first. This Holy Scripture, therefore, just as it is originally, steps, of set purpose for those who believe in it, into the place of God Himself, and its divine charm clings to the mere sounds of the language of it. Its contents, moreover, are then immediate and compulsory prescript for all men; and all religion, as all good morals, all science, and all civil law as well, must be tied to this rigid sacred letter; a result the more obstructive, the more limited and uniform that letter is. So mere fancy is content to possess in this writing for a short time, indeed, the genuine Holy Scripture in the limited circle in which it arose, and seems able to preserve it perhaps for ever, so long as good fortune attends it in the world; as was the case for so long with Islam, owing to the hollowness of the Byzantines of that day. But how terribly has at last just this Holy Scripture, and faith in it, devastated the world! Notwithstanding all its pretensions, the Qor'an is not without internal contradictions, as soon was apparent when it was collected together and much read; and just as soon was it perceived that its contents were far too meagre to direct in detail the whole life. So it was soon necessary that another class of men should seek to expound it and supplement it, and thus the caprice from which it had originally sprung took a further step; and since, nevertheless, the sacredness of the letter must be retained, even the allegories of it, by which some profounder spirits sought to soothe their better conscience, were finally, for good reasons, rejected again, and the Qor'an, by a narrowing and limitation the more severe of all the better intellect, brought over the world the long misery which still so visibly attends its steps.

If no one since Mohammed has succeeded, upon the basis of arbitrary conception as to what a Holy Scripture should be, in creating a new Scripture, which has found so much faith as the Qor'an, and brought so much misery over deceived humanity,[1] still from those old errors concerning the very idea of a Holy Scripture which led on the one side to Islamism, there has resulted on the other side principally in our more recent times, that misconception and contempt of all Holy Scripture

[1] A Mormon Bible was possible merely in North America, and even there will, it is to be hoped, soon vanish again.

which has already done amongst us almost as much mischief as Islamism. Since no confusion of thought about the most important things can ever, in the long run, be maintained, so is it with that concerning the very idea of the sacredness of Scripture; the exaggeration of the idea of this sacredness, so long as it will dominate the thought, either drifts to its last conceivable stage, as we see it with abhorrence enough in Mohammed, or veers round to its direct opposite—a disesteem of all Holy Scripture which, from another side than the Qor'an or any similar Scripture made perhaps in another way factitiously sacred, destroys the true significance and best uses of Holy Scripture that, rightly understood and employed, should remain to us in its incomparable dignity for all ages. But after all the preliminary observations made above, we can now the more certainly perceive

III. 9. *The Nature of the actual Sacredness of the Bible.*

§ 121. Scripture, even if we perhaps esteem it as holy, remains in its essence Scripture, and neither can be nor does it pretend to be holy in itself,—that Scripture at least of which we here speak, and which in so far as has been shown is the direct contrary of the Qor'an. We designate indeed many other things holy which are not in themselves either God or divine; as we speak of holy places and holy vessels. But such things as these are consecrated by us, and can just as well at our will be unconsecrated again and become common. But we do not speak of Scripture as holy in the same sense as we speak of these things; for though every Scripture is in itself likewise only a vessel, yet what it, if we will call it holy, has received into itself and holds, that we cannot and dare not, as in the case of other things, take away again at our will or as it were strip off and despise, if it is to be esteemed by us as holy; rather, if it becomes and is already actually holy to us, can it according to the expression be holy to us only through that which is actually in itself holy and once for all deposited in it and not to be cast forth arbitrarily. Now the holy for us is simply God and His will, His will being to us inseparable from Him, and when revealed one and the same with His word. If, therefore, we find this word in any writing more perfect and at the same time more original and fresh than in any other, it may be rightly regarded as holy to us above all other writings; that the word would still be regarded by us as just as certainly holy even if we heard it from the mouth of a living man and fully understood it—because we apprehended something serviceable for our salvation and so as well good in itself as inviolable rather than holy,—cannot be said. But if this writing contained something of this kind, of which we knew that it was long ago regarded by the best men as something holy (and this can occur historically with a Holy Scripture), it would fairly be obliged to be regarded as to us all the more sacred. Now no single writing and also no holy writing meets us in such a way that we should be compelled to regard it as holy, as in a human kingdom a law if we violate it can immediately and perceptibly compel us even against our will by means of punishment; for indeed God Himself does not meet man in such a way that man cannot for the moment reject and despise Him apparently with impunity. If, however, we not merely know that this writing was esteemed holy by innumerable of our best and foremost men in accordance with their own living experience and free conviction, but if we also have learned to hold it as such ourselves through our own free experience, then, to be sure, will it rightly appear to us so holy that we shall regard it, not indeed as fully equal in sanctity with God and His word, but next to them, as the most holy thing that can ever be holy.

Now it is with Holy Scripture as with all conceptions that are true not so much in themselves as in relation to some higher conception which they indicate,—we distinguish with respect to them that which is essential from that which is less essential yet contributive to completeness, and we are pleased if we meet with the former, though we should be still better pleased if we had the latter with it at the same time. For example, if we heard of some man, that he was a good man in rare wise, but ascertained about him only one isolated authentic actually good deed, we should yet be obliged to regard him as a really good man; but we should be more perfectly satisfied if we came to know for certain that his whole life stood in the closest connection with this single good deed of which we had heard, although no other good act of his was so conspicuous, because we know very well that in the life of a man each individual act stands in the closest connection with every other; and just so we know well enough that the idea of the good in its strictest signification belongs properly only to God, though under certain conditions it is predicable also of man. We must therefore now consider exactly just this essence of the actual sacredness of the Bible apart from the wider signification of the term. Above everything,

§ 122. 1. It is certain that the deepest and purest essence of all actual sacredness of the Scripture of the Old and New Testament is resolvable into this, that it contains the word of God in accordance with which we men should live. He to whom God and His word has no significance, still less a purely sacred significance, can desire to know nothing of Holy Scripture; of this we may subsequently speak in the proper place. But what in the deepest and most necessary sense is holy in Holy Scripture is immediately connected with the Holy Spirit as, according to § 80–81; it exercises its active influence in the community of the true revelation and religion, creating its manifold works. As the Holy Spirit moved with its most original and purest power in the prophets of the Old Testament, as it struggles in a thousand ways to manifest itself by word and deed to the world, so at the right time its revelation passes over into writing. Many of the greatest prophets sought gradually by writing to immortalize the most imperishable of their words and the most memorable of their deeds springing from the same Spirit; and what they themselves did not so immortalize was preserved in the community so far as it was worthy of immortality without their aid, by other written documents and the living memory, and passed over sooner or later into writing likewise. Afterwards, when this power of the Holy Spirit, so peculiarly old in Israel, had renewed itself in the whole manifestation of Christ (§ 83), and in such a way that in one mortal life it could not be manifested more powerfully and transcendently, alike in word and deed, then, immediately after His heavenly glorification, it is His Holy Spirit which, enkindled and made more strongly aglow through the fire of the same Holy Spirit still living in the already existing Holy Scripture, now expressed itself in the new community by word and deed; this community itself feels its working and its gentle or all-penetrating essence as its very life;[1] the apostles, and in rivalry with them Paul and others deeply influenced by it, suppose themselves, not vainly, to be swayed by its impulse and pressure if possible in a mightier degree, although always ready to submit their judgment to that of the whole community so far as this community on special questions was actually further enlightened by a yet purer illumination of the same Holy Spirit; the new prophets publish their words[2] no longer as those of the Old Testament in the name of God, but in that of this new Spirit raised to its full power and splendour, and there soon circulate in the wide community words which are regarded, if not as immediate words of Christ in His earthly manifestation,[3] yet as utterances " of the Spirit," viz. of just this genuinely Christian spirit, with which, however, the full life of youthful Christianity so overflowed that it passed already in more refined streams into its general literature, and at last in still more refined streams into the canon of Holy Scripture.

[1] Cf. 1 Cor. vii. 40 with Phil. iii. 15, Acts v. 32, viii. 29, x. 19, xi. 12, xv. 28.
[2] Rev. ii. 7 and often; cf. xix. 10; Acts xiii. 2, xxi. 11.
[3] As in 1 Thess. iv. 15; cf. v. 1, and 1 Cor. vii. 6, 10-12, and often.

For it is self-evident that the most loyal and pious members of the old community in their very different times, and then especially of the new community transfigured out of the old, readily perceived all along in what writings the stream of the Holy Spirit flowed most purely and richly, and what writings were best fitted to call forth its earliest life and impulse with the like original power; but it is here of great significance and wholly congruous that the first firmer beginnings of the canon (§ 107 f.) fell in exactly those periods when (§ 82), as it were, more palpably, and in the broader features with more perceptible vividness, a certain potency of the Holy Spirit presented itself to the view of the community; and its final close occurred when in the new community the same Spirit had already in its fullest development been just most powerfully active. Since now this power of the Holy Spirit produced the most manifold effects, one of the last effects, in periods of its stronger excitation, was ever a more enlightened retrospect upon all the portions of the whole allied and most fully corresponding literature, and a purer and more ardent desire to separate and immortalize the best of it, together with a superadded boldness sparing no pains and labour in the task, a creative boldness without which no great work of enduring significance can be called into existence. It was a higher inspiration which created these writings themselves; but another and still genuine inspiration akin to it well understood how to estimate their eternal significance for the community, and knew what on its part was proper to be done, and was strong enough to accomplish it. Moreover, considering what alone is the main quality in such a literature, this higher spirit could not doubt by what name this selection of writings should be designated. The word of God being the sole element which was actually sought and found therein, no name was more suitable by which to distinguish them from all others than Holy Scriptures, of which name "the Scriptures," or still shorter "Scripture," are only abbreviations; and these were the commonly prevailing names. But when the attention is directed rather to the Spirit of God, by whose vivifying breath the mind is ever again inspired as it is eagerly intent and absorbed in the reading of these books, they may be called "God-inspirited,"[1] although this clumsy designation was not usual, but is employed only once in one of the last writings of the New Testament as the special designation of the nature and true distinction of these books. The abbreviation of this name to "divine writings" is foreign to the Bible, though preferred by Josephus and many others after him.

§ 123. 2. Now the rays of the Holy Spirit which beamed forth from these writings did not by the writings themselves, even after they were distinguished from all other writings and regarded as holy, then first of all enlighten and warm the hearts of their readers or hearers. Moses led the nation in the primitive time with words, as they were at length eternalized in literature in the Decalogue, and with innumerable similar commands which we can now rather think of than enumerate, before he cared to trouble himself with writing down even a principal part of them; and of Christ's words and deeds nothing as yet was written down when the clear radiance of their holy spirit flashed across the minds of the Twelve and of so many others. But even the purely artistic writings, whether of the simply direct kind, as the Book of Job, or of the far more artificial kind, as the Book of Daniel or the Book of Enoch, did not first uplift the hearts of men after they were associated with other holy writings and irradiated by their splendour. But if such writings had already been for many thousands a means of enkindling the

---

[1] Θεόπνευστος only once, 1 Tim. iii. 16. When spoken of men it is well rendered "God-inspired," but of writings better "God-inspirited" (*Gottbegeistet*), *i.e.* full of divine spirit and as it were vivified by it; describing the condition and nature of the writing, not a transaction by which it was first created. The translation of the Vulgate—*Scriptura divinitus inspirata*—is borrowed from Josephus, *Against Apion*, i. 7, who speaks of the Old Testament histories and genealogical tables as learnt κατὰ τὴν ἐπίπνοιαν τὴν ἀπὸ τοῦ Θεοῦ. But such a conception would lead us much too far, and involve in some cases that the Holy Spirit corrected Himself.

more glowing or the milder rays of the Holy Spirit in the mind, and if there already fell upon these writings, many of them, the bright radiance of a venerable antiquity and of the memory of the high sacred forms of remote days or of the mysteries of all primitive time, then indeed must the splendour of a sacred glory,[1] which already surrounded them, rise higher and higher, and their sanctity be doubly increased. So was it completely in the time of Christ and the apostles with that Bible which we now call the Old Testament. In far shorter space of time could the selection of the new Christian writings re-illumine at length with the same splendour those already long canonized, now more and more firmly annexed, not as if the power of the Holy Spirit that radiated from them could not have been the same in an earlier day,—rather can we clearly enough recognise how much this was the case in the earlier day,—but only so far as fire grows by fire, and the splendour of the one heightens that of the other.

§ 124. 3. And yet in this highest signification which, according to a last clear judgment, supported by a good passage of the New Testament, Holy Scripture can attain, it is not regarded as a means which *must* compel man to the recognition of God and his duty, as a penal law in the human kingdom must compel him who is amenable to punishment to render the required obedience. For it is as if just on the last verge of the whole Christian Bible a declaration must be added which teaches this with special clearness, although from all indications it would be otherwise certain as is shown above. The author of the three pastoral Epistles,[2] having in Timothy set forth how a man must act as a simple Christian and at the same time a prominent leader of the Churches and a pattern of all Christians, makes conspicuous towards the end as specially significant that "from a child he knew the Holy Scripture in its original sources," that is to say, the Old Testa-

---

[1] Cf. Ex. xxxiv. 29-35.

[2] 2 Tim. iii. 15-17. θιόπνευστος here designates more particularly γραφή, and the assertion of the sentence begins with καὶ ὠφίλιμος.

ment; writings which are "able to make man wise unto salvation," in which dwells the power to afford to the man who is sufficiently conversant with them the appropriate wisdom and prudence for the attainment of salvation, although, to be sure, only through faith in Christ, without which even the most precious contents of the Old Testament are not to their fullest capacity vivifying and enlightening. Is it thus said that all Holy Scripture is *able* to make man, and so indeed a Timothy, wise unto salvation, not that it *must* make him wise as a penal law and compel him through fear; this is explained by the sentence that follows, which enters into everything relevant here, a sentence which may be called the resplendent evening star of the long day of the growth and formation of the Bible among men; "For every God-inspired writing;" there are many writings which deserve to be so indicated if their inner worth is rightly estimated; but take which you will of them, it must be said "every one" "is also useful for doctrine" in general, "for correcting" error in the special case where it is necessary; further, therefore, in consequence of this, "for rectifying oneself again," that after marking the mistake one may be established again in the better life through the divine promises of grace; and therefore finally "for discipline in righteousness," that one may be trained by the divine righteousness to be, after the years of childhood, a matured and vigorous "man of God," *i.e.* "equipped for every good work." The inner worth and best contents of Holy Scripture, together with its true profitableness in use, are thus both so perfectly placed on a par with each other, that if it has this full content of the divine spirit it must *also* be thus profitable, and that it has its worth and high estimation and value among men only just so far as it has this profitableness also; so that both are really one and the same, each implies the other, if one is present the other cannot be absent. Every one may thus test Scripture by using it, and so experience in himself whether it is full of the Spirit of God. He may do it with each of the writings regarded in the world as God-inspired, and do it as Timothy, who through the Old Testament alone as Holy Scripture was drawn to Christ.

That which is most important, however, for us here is that the last writings of the New Testament nowhere indicate our present sacred writings of the New Covenant expressly as holy, nor lay stress upon their right to bear this or a similar designation, still less do they say which of them individually is worthy to be associated with the venerable writings of the Old Covenant. The New Testament does not canonize itself; unquestionably the Old Testament did not before, in the order described and in the different circles, it formed the canon; but that we actually see under our eyes that such is not the case in the last circle is for us to-day very instructive, since it contributes to enable us likewise to form the right conceptions concerning everything that belongs to this subject. For early enough, even at the beginning of the second century of the Christian era, the need was felt in Christendom of selecting out of the many new Christian writings on all sides such as would satisfy the double want of that day; the first and most pressing being the great final settlement of the canon through the addition of the New Scriptures to the Old, *i.e.* the addition of such new Christian writings to the canon as were not higher but equally authorized, and which best of all could show that the new and perfect promised in the old canon now at last is actually present. But even here this first need of receiving the best writings as a rule for the further conduct of the true human life and endeavour now once begun, could not otherwise be satisfied than as such books only were esteemed suitable out of which vividly and certainly the same Holy Spirit was felt to shine forth which was already conspicuously present in the Old Testament, strongly enough in many parts, and which was after all the ultimate cause why all the Old Testament books were made use of and read with faith. And so is it with the whole Bible; it was ultimately the presence and power of the Holy Spirit alone which was sought in it, and which if sought rightly, not idly, could be found, that gave it its value ; and it is this which must oblige us still to regard it as holy, as is to be shown further below.

10. *The further Significance of the Bible and its Sanctity.*

§ 125. If there did not cleave to the Bible before everything else as essential to it this power of making us feel, as no other writing does, with such originality and primitive force and with ever new vividness, the presence and working of the Holy Spirit as it once manifested itself through the prophets and then through Christ and His disciples, and if it did not ever again call this Spirit into life in ourselves also, so far as in general a writing can do it, we should then have no cause to reverence it above all others as to us a great holy book. But, in point of fact, it contains far more than isolated passages out of which something of this Holy Spirit, as if spontaneously, confronts us and would lay hold upon us, supposing we were willing to allow ourselves to be swayed wholly and for ever by its sacred might alone. For this holy power indeed, as such an actual power in human affairs and collective history has from stage to stage only, as was shown § 80–85, so developed itself as it must develop itself if it was destined to influence in like manner every man without distinction, and as it may still always in like manner influence and lead us all. Only, then, from this history of its development among men can it be perfectly clear to us how it must in reality work if it is to lead us in entire conformity with its intent and impulse. But its development has taken place only in one nation,—a nation destined by this means, and after its first transformation into a true independent nation, to become, so to speak, the seat of its origin upon earth, in the sense in which the whole second division of this volume has already shown ; and this seat of origin, however, was not a special part of the nation or a single institution in it intended for special development, it was the whole nation, or, as we may say at once, according to the highest signification of the present subject, the nation as a well-ordered community of God, in which through all hindrances and obscurations that power grew at last to this perfect power we know, and in such a way as alone to be capable of influencing all men equally, and thereby bringing about the fulfilment more and more perfectly of their ultimate destiny, according to § 50. The history of this nation is thus for us the preparatory school to enable us to comprehend the more surely and perfectly what kind of a power it is which alone can ultimately lead us aright as the holy power of all human history, and so also of our own human-divine development. And however otherwise the issue of this long thousandfold, intricate, changeful history may be, at all events its highest and for ever most significant result is that at last, through the full earthly appearing of Christ Himself, it has become evident to all the world in what manner the perfect power of the Holy Ghost must ever rule among men, and how instead of being annihilated by His death it but spread itself from that moment with irresistible force into all the world, in order to become for this whole earthly sphere the sacred power alone pre-eminent and for ever unchangeable.

If, therefore, ultimately only that entire history can teach how this sacred power, become mighty and perfected among men, is for ever to lead them on, it is evident, indeed, that we cannot sufficiently avail ourselves of sure means in order to know this history exactly, especially in its last and highest significance. And this was manifestly also the feeling and the conviction which, in the different times in which the different circles of the canon arose, more clearly or obscurely guided the men in the community who chiefly helped to form it. Another course might have been adopted. From the writings that would serve this purpose the best passages might have been extracted, those most suited and most excellent for the edification of the faithful, or out of which the fire of the Holy Spirit appeared to shine forth most powerfully and clearly; and there might have been many then, as to-day, who would have preferred a Holy Scripture so compiled. But as good fortune for the thing itself would have it, such a view and such an aim did not prevail, and it is a splendid result of the healthy contemplation of things which always at last won its way in this community in critical times that it was so. Only the full light of history suffices to enable us rightly to recognise the origin and development of such purely spiritual powers, and properly to estimate their eternal significance and their fitting application for all future times. The light of history shows how necessarily they come, and must further develop themselves from stage to stage; but it shows also from their last perfection, attained in a determinate sphere, and according to all circumstances attainable only in it, most clearly and for all the future, how they must for ever continue to rule among us, if we do not hinder their free course nor occasion that by our own fault they do not promote the salvation which they are destined yet further to advance to a much higher goal. And so with the choice of the Pentateuch for the first great fundamental book of the community, it was likewise a chief aim by means of it, as the most appropriate instrument, clearly to pronounce how a holy nation arose upon the earth with those peculiar gifts and obligations and hopes whereby alone it could arise and can hope to be able ever to continue as a holy nation. If, now, to promote this further aim, which we may designate historical, was not, indeed, the first and sole but still an inevitable chief aim in the formation of the canon, an aim which repeated itself with equal propriety in the extension of the canon through all its wider circles, it is evident—

1. That the number of the writings held with right to be most suitable could, it is true, never in itself come into question, for of those actually most suitable too many could scarcely be admitted. When the first wider circle was closed about the Decalogue with the Pentateuch, this one work, itself divisible nevertheless into many large parts, sufficed, since the

question at that time was simply, and above everything, for all the future to know clearly and certainly how, amid the confusion of all the rest of the nations, a holy nation could arise upon the earth, and on the one hand what duties, on the other what rights and hopes, it had. But that sufficed only for this once; with every succeeding enlargement of the canon there were both several and very different kinds of books which it was held to be right to annex to that great firm centre. And so, finally, was completed this whole wide number of sacred writings, which afterwards, when with Christians as well as with Jews the canon was fully closed, were connected together in the form of a book in a single large but much-divided manuscript, whose bulk, however, was yet in itself so great, and whose primary application according to their different contents was so manifold, that they could afterwards, as it might seem desirable, be written out in single portions and contemplated as a veritable library. But just as properly did—

2. The wholly different feeling make itself influential, that in number and extent the books of the canon must not be too great. First of all, because only those already long since universally esteemed as the best of their kind should be selected and appointed for public use in the community. But then, again, also because all these books, without distinction, were to serve more and more for the instruction and edification of the whole of this large community; and this second reason is in itself of unusual importance. For it is an essential peculiarity of all these books that they were not destined for the use of a special part or smaller groups of men in the community,—for leaders merely, or for scholars, or for priests,—as was the case with the sacred books of other ancient nations, of which something more is to be said further on. As the Holy Spirit in this community was not destined for single members nor limited to them, so neither were these books, whose highest aim (§ 121–124) is to afford the possibility of deriving from them its own divine power and

hope. But what is to have so universal a significance and use in the nation that every one, without exception, is to be able freely and readily to avail himself of it, this should not, as a writing, have too wide an extent. Since, therefore, this feeling, though opposed to the first, was just as well authorized, it is—

3. Not surprising that in those times, when the canon was yet in course of formation from stage to stage, the question could properly arise with respect to this or the other book, whether it necessarily belonged to the canon, whether it was worthy of belonging to it or not. That no reasonable doubt could be entertained with respect to the principal books, but that some books should appear to many less necessary or less worthy, and stand, as it were, on the outer verge, the one or other being almost accidentally accepted in this part of Christendom and rejected in that, all this was said in § 109. There was once conflict in the communities everywhere over such details, and in many places it was vehement and persistent enough, and in the nature of the case this conflict waxed hottest just as the canon inclined to its ultimate and final close. Some persons, starting from various kinds of arbitrary conceptions, depicted § 117–20, concerning the nature and peculiarities of a Holy Scripture, would remove or put a ban upon books which did not harmonize with their erroneous presuppositions; others also, with one-sided tenacity, would retain books which, according to the feeling of most individual communities and the judgment of experts, were less worthy. But the closing of the canon could nowhere be for very long actually hindered on this account. The conclusion of it came in Christendom less through compulsion, which, even if attempted, can never in such purely spiritual things permanently avail, than through that double feeling which became dominant, and in its coincidence is decisive of the whole question, viz. first, that as wholly other times had now come since the days of the apostles and their nearest friends, it was matter of importance now for the first time to make

rightly prevalent in the whole world the truths then secured by conflict, and the forces in their perfection which had then in the smaller community been won; and, secondly, that these writings now in hand perfectly suffice for a right estimation, in its unchangeable and deepest ground, of what is relevant to this end, so far at least as it can be known and estimated by a writing. This state of things continues to the present day, and now that the controversy raised three centuries and a half ago over the Apocrypha has shown itself unimportant (§ 113), we can the more readily suffer those older contentions to rest, at least the more we guard ourselves against the various kinds of arbitrariness already mentioned (§ 117–20) in relation to the idea and the nature of the canon.

§ 126. For if we go more particularly into detail, and ask how far the canon suffices for this wider aim of a Holy Scripture, the question turns principally upon the following points :—

1. The supreme and pure words of God by which we are to live have not casually and abruptly become known as we can see them revealed in the Bible; they have ever, as may be said in one word, been wrung only from the obscurities and errors opposing them, and have dawned on the world from dark clouds, or, indeed, devastating storms, like serene and sunny days of fruitfulness. Indeed, the same thing occurs with respect to all insight and truth on the one hand, and all skill and art on the other; they have all been wrung by the entire human race from their direct opposites historically, and fought out in conflict with thousandfold ignorance and inaptitude, so that we can appreciate them in detail the more, the more clearly we recognise their origin and understand the many difficulties which obstructed their coming into existence and use. But what is learnt with the greatest difficulty is the perfect divinely-human life in its totality and its permanent progressiveness as the true revelation and religion demand it of us,—with the greatest difficulty

by individual men, with how much more difficulty by an entire nation, and now, indeed, by all mankind! In the coming forth and strengthening of this life, in its retrogressions and advancements, its stages and its last perfection, lies the whole history of humanity, because strictly taken it embraces everything which the individual man, an entire nation, and all mankind in all incalculable separate endeavours and toils should strive after and attain. The Bible has accordingly just this excellence, it gives us, as a whole and entirely, the clear image of all the stages of errors and perversities through which the genuine divinely-human life as it should be must move itself onward to its ever purer perfection; and as youthful Christianity is ultimately nothing but the consummation of this all-embracing historical progress of individual men, and of an individual nation, until the point is reached where what has been won in this narrower circle could pass over to the entire human race, so the Bible presents to us just this progress in its purest perfection. The great wide scene it brings before us most luminously and uninterruptedly is, indeed, only the history of this one nation, which alone among all the nations of antiquity had the courage to determine to be an actual nation of the true God; but since the true religion in whose spirit it arose very well knows how an individual nation stands in the great inter-connection of all humanity, the history stretches out in the proper places far beyond this one nation. It introduces us to the contemplation of all humanity as it was before the moment when one nation earnestly resolved to become the nation of the true God; and it lets the contemplative mind linger in those remotest spaces of all conceivable history, where we see not merely the origin of this one nation, but also in the simplest and clearest way how from all humanity the most divine but also the most undivine existence could arise; and if it does all this in simple narrative briefly, as was best, it still shows at the same time, in the conspicuous example of the Book of Job, what the higher art was competent to do just on this freer field of wide historical contemplation. From that moment of the whole history onward, when the one nation that alone can fill the wide historical scene here to be presented, enters into the development of the great world-history, the narrative, however, limits itself so little to this nation alone that we get in the Bible rather a universal history of nations, at least so far as this is closely connected with the history of the maintenance and progress of all true religion as its highest subject.

It is in this view that we tolerate the admission into the canon of the Book of Esther, and its sharing, in its incorporation in the great whole, the special distinction and honour which lies in the conception of the canon. For so long as the canon had not yet reached what may be called (§ 112) its true conclusion, but was yet in course of formation for the special use and service of the old community of all true religion, a little book could very well find place in it which brings before us a not unimportant change in the history of the relation of the community to heathen nations, and at the same time serves as a memorial of this relation in that, as a festival-book, it explains a yearly festival then coming into use. So far, however, as this book, in its conception of the true religion and the life that should harmonize with it, does not stand upon the elevation of the older historical books, it belongs to those that form the outer verge of the canon, and fits exactly into the intermediate books of whose nature and worth we have already spoken (§ 112). These intermediate books, as was shown, very properly take a place in the Bible, because as historical memorials they illustrate for us in the best and truest sense what movements occupied the old community in the ever darkening centuries of its last great changes. That every man, not merely the learned, may be able to form a more perfect judgment concerning the entire course of the great development of all true religion up to its highest consummation, these books have properly their place in the Bible; and if in intrinsic value for true religion they stand lower than the rest, in their attitude and ultimate aim they are equal to the rest; whilst the writings of Philo and Josephus, for example, are far removed as in special aim mere learned elaborations. But it is not directly necessary, it is true, that the Bible should give a complete and connected history of these last centuries from the building of the second temple to the time of Christ, should suitable books for this purpose not be found; yet the filling up of this gap as far as possible is certainly to be desired.

The Bible is thus through and through of historical nature and spirit. Standing conspicuous amid all the efforts of all antiquity, the most profound as a work of mind, the loftiest in elevation and sweep of thought, a product of noble pains, compact in itself and finished, it bears upon its face, looked at as a whole, the clearest impress of historicality; it promotes therefore all sound historical views of things, and proves itself the mightiest lever in all our world-historical contemplation and research. In this respect it is the direct opposite of the Qor'an. Islamism, as the last and most powerful offshoot of Gnostic errors that could strike firm root in youthful Christianity upon its transition into the great heathen world, proceeds from an arbitrary assumption as to what true religion and Holy Scripture must be, and in its own arbitrarily produced Holy Scripture it thinks it has the only proper type of it. All actual connection between itself and all older national histories it therefore severs, just as it does all connection between the earlier Holy Scripture and its own. Owing to this original impulse, and in spite of many deviations in the attempt to establish in its midst juster and more fundamental religious ideas, it can only move on in the same lines without being able to overcome the unhistorical character native to it. Strictly speaking, it knows only the splendid side of its own history from Mohammed downwards, and neither of the remote spaces of all antiquity nor of the deficiencies and mistakes of its own historical movement has it a clear apprehension or a sufficiently deep desire of knowledge. In the Bible, on the contrary, all the rich and marvellously varied contents it embraces, even outside its narrative parts, serve ultimately to fill out for us the more completely and instructively the whole wide framework of the historical picture portraying the life and movement and final perfection of all true revelation and religion. And since, as already shown, the Bible does not profess to be holy in itself, but everything which it presents to us it presents only as luminous pictures of the life and development of all true religion, it is the more important therefore that it should give pictures which strike us by their fulness and their graphic power.

§ 127. 2. It is not indeed necessary that of all the different historical periods and conjunctures there should be the like graphic and complete pictures illustrating the course of events. For from a few brief outlines, if they are only authentic and vivid, the whole picture may be drawn, as the entire body of a living creature from a few bones; and further, in that whole period within which the canon was formed, the possibility was not afforded of giving such complete historical sketches of all the longer or shorter eras of the long history the Bible presents to us; indeed, just the most extended, but also the remotest spaces of all human history, are of such a kind that neither writing nor even mere dim reminiscences offer means sufficient for drafting as good a picture as of other times. Yet, nevertheless, it may be shown that for all the great periods and phenomena of the time which the Bible must embrace, it furnishes just such living and complete records as suffice for its highest aim. For as to—

1. The remotest periods of human history which, according to the Pentateuch, are rightly designated the first two ages of the world,[1] it is not to be denied that the pictures of them found in the Bible have been derived neither from contemporary records nor purely historical reminiscences, however many and important the traces of such reminiscences that may be discovered in them. They give in their present form

[1] Gen. i.-xi. 26.

merely outlines, partly of higher conceptions concerning the origin of all visible things, partly the most memorable fragments of primitive reminiscences, materials of both kinds blended closely together and in diversified setting, older or newer, but always in the highest degree charming. But we have long since recognised that another possibility could not have place here, and that there were portions of narrative of the higher kind and colour which must not be confounded with those of the ordinary parentage, and which yet may contain by implication the purest historical truths. Such are some Biblical pieces of narrative and history; and just this, that so few of them are found in the Bible, and yet so sufficient a number for all true revelation and religion, whose literary treasures the Bible seeks to give, is one of its excellencies. What are all the histories of creation and primitive times in heathen nations in comparison—histories so similar in mere material, but, since no such breath of true revelation and religion inspires them, so dissimilar in spirit! Here, however,—

2. May be separated with fitness those periods of time which are most appropriately designated periods of the primitive history, standing in closest connection with the special nation Israel, viz. those of the three patriarchs and the periods down to the time of Moses and the next generation after him.[1] When the Pentateuch was sketched out in its original form, or rather, with the Book of Joshua, the Hexateuch, a considerable number of literary records existed, going back to earlier times, although only a few that reached up to the patriarchal era; and these were accompanied with the most graphic reminiscences of the principal features of that time as they were preserved in the community. But the entire literature of the earliest centuries vanished (§ 104) before the vigorous tide of a new and mightier literature that already flowed in; and the more the original fulness and living freshness of the earliest reminscences was gradually lost, the more

[1] From Gen. xi. 27 to the conclusion of the Book of Joshua.

was it sought in the living onward development of all the loftier spiritual activities of the community, to transform their eternal contents into new shapes of luminous splendour. What occurred almost entirely with the patriarchal history extended also in part to the Mosaic. And yet out of all these so highly different periods, the more important they are individually, the more imperishable literary memorials, along with the most ineffaceable reminiscences, have been preserved. The number of the documents and fragments of oldest historical records that have been saved is not a matter of moment; but what have been so rescued stand out the more conspicuously in the wide deep sea of those times, and none of them higher than those originating from Moses himself and his time.

3. From thence onward the sources the Bible presents to us of historical knowledge of the circumstances under which the truths of the genuine revelation and religion step forth into the light of day, are more and more copious and extensive. Not, indeed, equally for all periods, but especially for those in which religious conflict and victory had most significance. How the eternal principles of true religion should sway the entire life of a whole nation, even as of the most isolated man, we can now see most vividly on all sides; and there is scarcely a conceivable circumstance in human effort upon which some clearer ray of light is not thrown from the luminous pictures of those times. We see the prophets in the severest conflicts of human life and national destiny maintaining eternal truths with the greater stedfastness and the more prudence and eloquence the more keenly they suffer from the errors of their time; and we are profoundly impressed as we mark the sharpness of noble rebuke, the clearness of the vision of the future, the certainty of eternal hope. We see human folly veil itself in the proud garb of subtle wisdom, and spread out the nets into whose toils the unwary may be misled; and we hear the more distinctly the voices of the higher wisdom reveal her wonderful secrets and offer her sure counsels to guide the feet in the eternal ways

of human happiness. We catch the most manifold tones of lofty joy and deep pain in human souls and the whole community as they sing and worship before the true God; and our own spirits join in the strains as if they were part of our own immediate experience. We behold in the Book of Job, in Solomon's Song, and in a hundred other occasional artistic pictures, the most remote and yet the most sublime truths, as if they stood in living forms before our eyes; and we feel how we must keep them with the same vividness for ever before our minds. Even the narrative introduces us into the whole breadth and many-sided light of full life; the more readily do we mark when it seeks to lift us up exceptionally into the heights of the spiritual life unattainable by the common eye, and yet only too real, and see that they are just such heights of historical experience no common narrative can reach, just such depths no common narrative can reveal. Thus we no longer meet everywhere with the few simple outlines of all knowledge and all reminiscence which we found in the first of the three strata of the historical contents of the Bible; nor do we any longer meet with the remote prototypes of human life and the lofty legislative height of Moses as in the second stratum; but only so much the more have we before us full actual life revolving round the high truths and engaged in the difficult tasks of all genuine revelation and religion, and feel that there is here enough of the transcendent and eternally typical, nay, that we must first appropriate to ourselves completely all that touches us most intimately in the later portion before we can estimate surely what lies further away in the earliest.

§ 128. 3. With this writing, as with every other, whether sacred or not, everything turns ultimately upon the question whether, so far as it is to serve as an historical witness, it is authentic or not. This question with respect to the Bible we must raise here, and we can answer it the more certainly and briefly to-day at this point the more accurately now everything that belongs to it has been already investigated, and the more opportune it is to put together in a summary the results of those investigations.

Throughout long centuries the question about the historical authenticity of the Bible was regarded as superfluous, or as easy of solution. What was held to be holy must naturally, it was thought, be authentic. But such a belief is without reasonable foundation, and is the more groundless since it has been shown in § 116 that the Bible does not claim for itself to be holy; we should therefore in this case be referred simply to the faith of the ancient Church, which was right indeed in holding the Bible sacred, but yet felt itself on this side too confident, and was thence too little active and expert in investigating more thoroughly purely historical questions with respect, that is, to the Old Testament. In our modern days, when such purely historical researches have become both more necessary and more difficult because of the dense clouds of many wholly different eras that have intervened, prevailing doubt could the more easily reject everything formerly believed, and occasion a desolation of mind which operates to-day so perniciously in many less enlightened circles; some would place the books of the Old Testament from the Pentateuch downwards with their entire contents in very late times, and would prove that Moses could not have written at all, or indeed that he could not have ever lived as a real historical person; others in like manner would transfer the books of the New Testament into the dark times of the second century after Christ. It accords well with the sinister purpose that fears the light, to prefer to becloud, disparage, and finally reject everything great and elevated in history, because it is either despised or not understood. Nevertheless, when we have submitted this whole province to the most exact researches, a new universal certainty arises which is just as far removed from these hazy and dark innovations as from that old security which was not at all secure against the gradual entrance of grave errors, and whilst an incalculable number of old prejudices once so perniciously prevalent has been irrevocably destroyed, the historical trustworthiness of the Bible has come forth with new certainty out of the fires of the keenest investigation. Since, now, all this can be taken for granted, we limit ourselves to the following observations, of importance at this point :—

1. It cannot be disputed that it would be an irremediable loss if, concerning Moses and his time and concerning Christ, the two poles upon which the whole history of the community of the true religion turns, we possessed in the Bible sources of information only late in origin, and half or wholly untrustworthy. If we had no authentic guidance on the first of these great subjects, we could not trace aright from the beginning this whole history of all development of true religion in its community, whilst it is a first need to mark aright the genuine commencement and fundamental impulse of all the great movements in human history; and if our knowledge of Christ came only from sources much too late, the uncertain end would correspond to the uncertain beginning, and the shadows of both would so overspread the long and wide intermediate time, that even of that we could know nothing with sufficient certainty. But it is now shown clearly enough how widely all those scholars erred who held it to be the best task of their lives to make uncertain either the true beginning or the grand close of this whole long history, or perhaps we should say the endings of both parts of it. For that we no longer possess such copious and numerous reminiscences of every kind of Moses and his whole time as from the nature of the case we could wish, is explained by the great antiquity of the time and the course of the entire literature of the ancient nation indicated in § 104, 1. It is sufficient, however, with respect to a remote period of beginnings, if we know with perfect certainty the few firm warps that cannot be broken which sustain the whole subsequent fabric of the history that is woven by means of them; and that we can know with certainty who Moses was, what constituted his life-work, and what were its immovable

foundations, is fully established. But with respect to Christ, merely as much as this would not be sufficient, because with Him the point in question is not the founding of the first certain beginnings of a people of God in their legal condition, or a new Decalogue of stone, but chiefly the proper spirit in which all human things, even the things of law, are to find the element of their life and power. Consequently the more His teaching and work were purely spiritual, and therefore transcendent and definitive, the more it is important that our historical knowledge of His words and deeds should be exact even to minutest detail; so that Christians would be entirely in a state of uncertainty if they had not accurate information of all that He taught and did. But we may now be convinced that they are thus informed.

2. Now, according to § 93 ff., the Bible is but the compact deposit of a literature once in all its departments and in every important era much greater and much more extensive, and this deposit was, according to 105 ff., determined by one definite principle of selection, the tendency to conserve the true revelation and religion; but if this must be understood to mean that all the oldest literature from each of the great eras, and in each department, has been lost entirely, and only some late fragments saved in the canon, that would be a sad fate. But in point of fact the case stands quite otherwise. It is true, indeed, that when we properly ascertain at what period of time every portion of the Bible great or small has its true place, we see that many portions are not so old as was supposed according to opinions formerly prevalent, and finding currency from mere uncertainty. The Book of Ecclesiastes, for example, as well as Solomon's Song, were not written by Solomon nor in Solomon's time; the Book of Daniel also was not written by Daniel, nor in Daniel's time; Moses did not write the Pentateuch in its entirety; the majority of the songs in the Psalter were not of David's composition, and many later productions are inwoven with the Book of Isaiah, or annexed to it. But yet the Song of

Solomon is much older than is commonly conceded in modern days; some portions of the Pentateuch, as we now have it, are beyond dispute by Moses and from his time, and others, and these both copious and numerous, are from earlier times; a fine number of songs of David, which show us sufficiently who David as a lyric poet actually was, are without doubt scattered up and down in the Psalms and elsewhere in the Old Testament. Conversely, some older pieces are assigned by a mistake of later readers to a much later time than they really belong to, as portions of the Book of Zechariah (ix.–xiv.); and in the midst of various principal portions of the present Book of Isaiah much older pieces are occasionally found. Similarly, indeed, the oldest evangelical records in their original books have been lost, but they have been preserved in the existing first three Gospels so completely and authentically that we could well-nigh restore them as they were originally. Furthermore, we do not now possess in the Bible everything a Solomon, an Isaiah, or a Paul wrote; but yet in the existing Book of Proverbs the main part goes back into very ancient times, and certainly portions of it to Solomon himself; of Isaiah's own writings a considerable part has been saved, and most of them in their original arrangement by the hand of the great prophet; and of Paul's Epistles, so many have unquestionably come into the canon, that by them we can estimate certainly enough the peculiar greatness of this apostle.

If we now put together all the cases thus cited by way of example in which, according to our present knowledge, we can restore the original relations of the writings, we see even here that the Bible has in it far more of historical completeness and trustworthiness than the common opinion to-day supposes, or the perverse will likes to allow. And, indeed, the circumstance mentioned in § 104, 1, that most of the great comprehensive books of the Bible, the Pentateuch with the Book of Joshua, the great Book of Kings, the Book of Chronicles, the Book of Isaiah, the twelve prophetic books, and in a certain sense also the Book of Jeremiah, the Psalter, the Book of

Proverbs, the Book of Job, the commonplace books of the first three Gospels, are each properly speaking but the deposit of a whole branch of literature originally very extensive and very rich,—this circumstance can serve as an evidence how much of purely historical life is everywhere hidden in the Bible, if only we know how to discover and appreciate it as we should.

3. Some books of the more artificial kind in composition, described in § 100, are associated in the Bible with the rest; and it is not to be denied that if such writings constituted its chief element, they would give to it a less purely historical aspect, and indeed a smaller historical value. For however superior such writings may be of their kind, they are yet only as it were second-hand compositions; whence it happens that if they were not known and carefully distinguished according to their nature, they would easily disturb the historical consciousness of the readers. But in point of fact the chief part of the Bible consists of writings of the simple style of composition: of such are all the prophetic books of the Old Testament and the New, with the single exception of the Book of Daniel and some appendixes to the Book of Jeremiah; all the historical books of both Testaments, with the exception of some additions in Ezra the first,[1] and of the second Book of Maccabees; also all the poetic books, with the exception of the Book of Ecclesiastes and the Wisdom of Solomon; furthermore, all the Epistles of the New Testament, with the exception of the Epistle to the Ephesians, the three pastoral Epistles, and the Second Epistle of Peter. But where a writing of a more artificial character is united with others of the simpler kind, as Deuteronomy is united with the older portions of the Pentateuch, it is only just to restore to the latter their original essential character; smaller portions of a species of primeval oracle of the dead, such as the blessing of Jacob, of Moses, and the like, are only the first essays of a literary art more and more extensively cultivated. Counting up all such pieces of a more artificial literature, it is clearly

[1] Cf. *History*, iv. 163 ff. [Eng. trans. v. 126 ff.].

seen how little they affect the general character of the contents of the Bible; and if it is considered that the literary art creating such writings is only a special art among many others, caution will be exercised in applying freely the designation pseudo-books, as remarked already. When, however, a book of this more artificial character has such a vast influence upon the history of its time as was manifestly the case with the Book of Daniel, it may properly be called in this sense a book of historical significance, and may reasonably be thought worthy of a place in the canon.

4. Common justice demands that to such portions of the Bible as have been assigned, by later collectors or readers merely, to other names than those which according to their real authorship belong to them, their original right should be restored; as already has been observed with respect to the most important cases. It would indicate only that there was no true understanding at all of the way in which the great Book of Psalms originated, or the Book of Isaiah, if every psalm that names David in its superscription were on that account referred to him as historically its composer, or the portion of the Book of Isaiah from xiii. 2 to xiv. 23 were ascribed to Isaiah as the actual prophetic author on account of the superscription, xiii. 1; or, in like manner, the long and anonymous portion from xl. to lxvi. were ascribed to him merely on account of the name the whole book received at a later date. Historically what is significant for us in this whole matter is that evidently the Psalms and the Book of Isaiah were eagerly read in early times and circulated in repeated new editions.

§ 129. If, now, we sum up what has been said in detail in § 126–128 together with what was maintained in § 125, we see at once wherein lies the high significance of the Bible, viz. that it gives us through writings, which whether in the strictest or in a remoter sense must be held as genuinely historical, a perfectly authentic picture of the origin and development of all true revelation and religion in humanity.

In this aspect of it, and so far as everything it contains may instruct us historically in one way or another concerning its main great subject, it can never be too copious and comprehensive. In fact, the Bible contains nothing which cannot serve, in a nearer or remoter connection, although that might not be its immediate aim, to set before our eyes with a fuller and more graphic completeness what is really its one sole subject. If, therefore, two or more narratives, or other presentations of the same thing, occur in it, this is not a superfluity; it is only of higher service for the end in view. For the same song, prophecy, or narrative is either repeated in several places without alteration of words, and then the repetition establishes clearly the right tradition or reading; or it is repeated with deviations, and then the deviations themselves, well understood and collated, may be usefully employed for the more certain recognition of the original form of such song, prophecy, or narrative. Exceptionally useful is the repetition of portions of purely historical matter; and specially noteworthy is it that it occurs just with the principal elements of the Biblical history. Indeed, it is precisely as if the last historians of the old nation at the verge of every decisive epoch of the great national history, and in each main department of historical reminiscence, had a clear anticipation of what would be needed. The Pentateuch and the great Book of Kings were purposely compiled from the most varied sources just as they have been preserved, the former wholly, the latter in great part. That so much is repeated in the Chronicles and older books of history, and in the first and second of Maccabees, has its advantage. But at last the compilers of the canon of the New Testament present the most conspicuous example, knowing as they would not fewer than four Gospels as forming the authorized group.

If, now, the Bible is sacred to us, according to § 121-4, because true revelation and religion, whose most original and inexhaustible interpreter it is, is sacred to us; more remotely it is sacred to us also because the wonderful entrance of all true revelation and religion into the world, and their whole historical development to perfection, which it so exhaustively and sufficiently teaches, must have for us some measure of sacredness. The greatest wonder possible after the creation of the universe and of man, viz. the creation and progress of all spiritual life in mankind, in its highest effort and struggle towards that consummation in which we ourselves must find all further impulse and movement, we can here directly and fully contemplate, and also learn from it many a lesson which may conduce to the elevation and sanctification of our life. The New Testament we will not sunder from the Old, nor unthankfully overlook or mistake anything significant for the last great aim, here manifest to us, of this inner human spiritual creation of God,—anything which meets us upon any one of the stages leading to the goal here at length attained, and never more to be allowed to drop again out of sight.

And nevertheless, this sacredness, so recognised and apprehended, we must not suffer to fetter and dazzle us to such an extent that we shall hold as the highest and most lasting that historical element which meets us here or there in the whole literature, since indeed the best part of it presented to us in the Bible always points beyond itself to a yet loftier future and to the purely Eternal; still less, to the extent that we shall estimate anything of historical significance mentioned in the Bible at a higher value than it really has in the great connection of things the Bible itself seeks to disclose. If, in a long changeful historical development, a firm goal of importance is once gained, and so far a consummation realized, this brings also the great advantage of enabling us the more correctly to judge of what preceded it; and we see how Christ and His disciples judge freely, in accordance with the perfection now attained, such historical regulations as the Sabbath and the like, made sacred principally by the Scriptures of the Old Testament, and in themselves worthy of perpetual observance. But this precedent is now for ever and for everything to remain valid, since we saw above that the New Testament as literature claims for itself no superiority over the Old. And this precedent we can apply to single portions of the Bible itself, and, for example, can assert as freely as we have ascertained legitimately, that most of the books that arose in the declining centuries of the public life of the ancient nation do not stand in intellectual and spiritual force so high as the earlier. Yet it is ultimately only as a particular contribution that this precedent belongs to the entire great history whose significance indeed is so great, and whose living image it is so increasingly important to have familiarly before us, that we can never recognise and retain with too great exactitude and correctness all its details.

11. *The Sacredness of the Bible in its Manifoldness and Unity.*

§ 130. Moreover, however widely and carefully we search in all human literature, nowhere do we find a work of the same extent containing so extraordinary a manifoldness in materials and forms of discourse as the Bible. Considering only its wealth and variety in matter and contents, it may be truly said the Bible is a whole world of itself. And as in the great world around us the most different things are seen to exist side by side, and it is supposed they have some connection one with another, although it is not immediately traceable, so in the little world of the Bible, compositions large and small, of the most different character in matter and contents, and in great abundance, are unexpectedly seen standing closely together and even compacted and wrought into one another,—particularly if we look with close and minute observation. Just as varied are the forms of discourse in which the different subjects live and move. We find the simplest and the most artificial species of narrative, each again in very different subordinate forms; information is given in the baldest and the most fascinating manner; we are introduced to that which is most elevated in divine and human affairs, and to that which is very base in human conduct, this last, it is true, only by way of warning.[1] In the prevailing lofty earnestness of the narrative there mingles at times most appropriately an outburst of noble scorn and keen satire;[2] and whilst commonly the remembrance and the name of God occur so significantly and constantly in connection with every incident that there is no difficulty in perceiving the purpose for which the record is given, yet in the Book of Esther these characteristics are wholly wanting, for its whole colour and form are more after the style of the "Thousand and One Nights" than that which is elsewhere usual in the Bible. Prophetic discourse appears less varied in colour and complexion; and yet the more carefully it is contemplated the more is it seen to change and to assume all conceivable hues, sometimes in the same prophet, still more in different prophets and different periods; there can hardly be a wider contrast than between the short, sharp, incisive oracle of the earliest times, and the full stream of discourse in Isaiah,[3] and between both and the style of the Book of Daniel and the Apocalypse; and what an interval there is between the high teaching of the prophet, coming down from above in sonorous and resounding phrase, and the not less certain but so deeply human and kindly familiar words of Christ and His apostles! In the poetry of the Bible of all kinds and species this manifoldness is also seen very conspicuously, and indeed with reason, partly in the special books of poetry, and partly as passages of poetry occur more or less in other books. Moreover, in addition to all this must be mentioned the extremely varied kinds of the more artificial prophecy and professional authorship already spoken of, increasing more and more in the later centuries, but in their beginnings appearing also in the older literature. There are often, too, examples of a

---

[1] Gen. ix. 18-24, xix. 30-38, xxv. 30-34, xxxviii. 9 ff.
[2] Num. xxii.-xxiv.
[3] Ex. xvii. 16; and Isa. xxi. 11 f., 13 f., for example.

special kind of artistic discourse, but they are few and brief.

The possibility of so rare a fulness and manifoldness of small and extensive writings in so narrow a space results, in great part, from the peculiarity (p. 92 f.) of expression which speech assumed more and more in the ancient nation of Israel. Not in vain were they nurtured through so many centuries by the ever watchful power of living revelation; as their opinions and convictions received thereby a deeper impress, and their manners were the more determinately shaped, so the expression of their thoughts also was characterized more and more by the sharp brevity and pithy conciseness peculiar to the speech of genuine revelation, and this passed over from the prophets to the poets, and so to the historians. With brief words, as if from above, forcible and striking, to give prominence to what is most weighty; to get the truth and depth of thought to shine in the bright light of clear intuition, and with every movement of the discourse to let its innermost certainty and confidence display itself: such is the marked peculiarity of Biblical language. Indeed, the whole Bible, from its first sentence onwards to that remarkable conclusion which the writings of the Apostle John form, who as a writer was a most genuine disciple of Christ, consists rather of short luminous sayings than of diffuse discourse and long wordy periods. To be sure, upon a nearer view a difference in this respect is observable between the different writers of the Bible; Ezekiel does not write like Jeremiah, in simple words, here and there strongly touched with emotion; and the Second Epistle of Peter has, in its style, far more of artificially involved structure than the First. But, as a whole, the language of the Bible is remarkably distinguished by its conciseness from that of the other ancient nations. The more artificial kind of authorship, often mentioned before, may trick out with adornments this incisive simplicity, and lead in many later writers to the preference for expressing the manifoldness of discourse more pointedly and sharply than formerly by successions of rounded periods; but even this adornment does not change the chief feature of the discourse. But what was not secured by this entire peculiarity of style, coming from early times, was effected by the repeated sifting of this whole literature, which took place (§ 104) in the great decisive eras of the history of the nation; and in this winnowing the full and ripe grains, few though they were, yet more compact, finer, and heavier, fell upon the ground and remained as the substance of the new collection; these were the best books which the canon selected and set apart, as above is further described.

§ 131. In this way, indeed, the possibility of so extraordinary a variety and diversity in the compositions crowded together in the Bible is explained. Nevertheless, in the form they had at length before their collection, they were not all thrown together accidentally; manifestly they were put together to serve a single lofty purpose; and this purpose is equally apparent in all successive enlargements of the canon. To carry out this highest aim, an ultimate unity must therefore dominate over all diversity; and the manifoldness spoken of has its uses, as is shown in § 129; the unity standing above it must never, with respect to the Bible, be overlooked, but must rather be more and more carefully sought for and kept in view. We may rightly suppose, no doubt, that the regulators of the canon were convinced that they were about to place here, in close connection, nothing absolutely incongruous, nothing that was irreconcilably self-contradictory; and certainly it would have to be proved, by the most irrefutable arguments, that they admitted just what glaringly contradicted the very highest aim they proposed in the collection. It is certain, however, that this ultimate unity of the whole contents and aim of the Bible is often very erroneously sought, and has been even somewhat violently forced, with respect to the Old Testament, especially before the canon of the New Testament was settled. For the whole art of allegorizing Biblical discourse, which once (§ 118) so widely prevailed, arose principally on this account, that certain words and sentences of Holy Scripture were thought to correspond too little in elevation and sacredness with others, and so must contain some hidden sense which had to be disclosed. Since, however, we all reject allegorizing, notwithstanding that (p. 384) it insinuates itself, from such times, into some portions of the writings of the New Testament, there returns upon us the more urgently the question what the unity really is which stands conspicuous above all the diversity of the Bible.

A conception arbitrarily formed can help us neither in this nor in any other question; here, however, such a conception is altogether unnecessary. For the ultimate unity of the whole contents of Holy Scripture, from which the founders of the canon might proceed, is given in the thing itself, so far at least as the question is not concerning a Holy Scripture conceived to one's pleasure, but just concerning this actually known to us. According to the intention of the founders of the canon, Holy Scripture is to be the right means of placing before the eyes the contents and purpose of true revelation and religion, so far as a writing can do it; and the great manifoldness and multiplicity of the separate portions of Scripture, if it has any meaning, is ultimately to serve the same aim, according to the intention of the founders of the canon; for how can it be thought that everything in the Bible was meant, like the words of the Decalogue and similar words, to be regarded immediately as mere prescription and law? Rather must they have intended that certain portions were to be held as an immediate divine summons to our will, but other portions were to impel us, indeed, ultimately to the hearing and doing of the divine will concerning us, but only by reasonable conclusions which we ourselves must draw from what is heard or read. Such compositions as admit of the drawing of no such inferences, but which by their presentation of sin would incite us to sin should we entrust our soul's health to them; or such as offer no contribution to the better understanding of the great, and as we may say, according to § 125-9, sacred history of the whole development of the true religion,—only such would be foreign in this case, and the former, indeed, directly pernicious and to be condemned. This aim of the canon is clear in its beginning as in its final close; and if there were any writing found in the Bible which did not accord with what must be the real intention of a canon, we should have a right to suppose there had been an error in framing it. It might, indeed, be thought that the authors of the canon had at least left one and another smaller writing, just in the place where they found it, merely because they did not wish to break the connection of a set of writings; for example, the Book of Ecclesiastes and Solomon's Song, merely because found in connection with the Book of Proverbs, as writings of Solomon, and Solomon himself appeared to them even then as an almost sacred king; or, the marriage-song of Ps. xlv. and the imprecatory song of Ps. cix., because both stood in the Psalter. But of such smaller compositions, every one of which forms an essential whole, should there be one not proceeding as a whole from the innermost life and impulse of true revelation and religion, we should then with right take exception, and we might doubt whether the Bible does really correspond to the aim which, as a whole, in its unity it seeks to have. Always should we have to call to mind in this matter that, according to § 109, many a composition may stand only upon the verge of the canon; but whether it may stand there even, without occasioning mischief in the sense above observed, would have to be considered.

If, then, we survey from this point the actual purport of every writing, it appears—

1. That even such accounts in the Bible as stand in themselves in no direct connection with the question of revelation and religion, like the many accounts of history, the statements concerning the once existing Books of Solomon as found in the Book of Kings,[1]—even those serve to complete our view

[1] 1 Kings v. 12 f.

of the great history within which revelation and religion ripened to their final perfection. How important this whole history is, and how precious to us every contribution to it must be, is shown in § 125-9. More important is it—

2. That the Bible contains nothing that commends an ungodly life. For the bad deeds it informs us of in the course of its narratives are intended, by the very drift of them, to serve as warnings, even where a special admonition against such deeds is not added; for this is self-evident from everything the Bible elsewhere contains, and which, in its true import, is calculated to instruct or admonish. Still less does any whole work recommend what is ungodly; he who actually comprehends Solomon's Song or Ps. xlv. will not suppose that they seek to excite the sensuous passion of love; he who reads the curses as they are found especially accumulated in Ps. cix., and more occasionally elsewhere in the Bible, will feel that there is in them another kind of sentiment than that which prevails in the superstitious curses of the heathen their poets were so accustomed to sing. . . . Moreover, the Bible contains also nothing merely suitable for entertainment and diversion, nothing that does not remind us of the divine and the duties of life. Since now—

3. The manifest aim of the Bible is not to teach us various arts or useful knowledge pertaining to the lower life, but definitely to show and remind us how we are to think and act in harmony with true revelation and religion, it is clear that what it says of other things, or what it incidentally mentions, may serve incidentally for further instruction, but is not to be confused or mistaken as if it were its one great chief subject. It may be instructive to us to know from the Bible incidentally how in this or that period of its long development the old nation of Israel contemplated the different phenomena of heaven, the different countries of the world, and the origin of the foreign nations, what arts and aptitudes in this or that age flourished or were neglected in it; but that we are to accept its casual teachings on these subjects as

absolutely decisive it nowhere prescribes, and they are only of special moment to us in so far as the spirit of all true religion, as it prevailed in this nation, may have impressed itself upon the form these conceptions assumed. But since the Bible also—

4. In the historical sequence of its great constituent parts demonstrates as clearly as possible that true revelation and religion, the one great chief subject it seeks to teach, went through very different stages in the course of their development to that final consummation by which alone we are firmly to stand, it follows therefore that everything which the Bible contains in its different books and its different ages of time bearing on this subject of revelation and religion, we are laid under obligation to compare and adjust with the ultimate consummation itself, and to judge also of the pure or permanent value of it all by the rule that consummation affords. But if there is no single book of the Bible written with a mere desire to amuse, as thousands of works are in other literatures, and if nothing, when properly understood, is conceived to have proceeded from a spirit that could actually instil into the reader an inclination or desire to base conduct, it may be said with justice that none of them is alien to the spirit of true revelation and religion. In like manner, if one composition is uplifted by this spirit more than another, and uplifts the reader to it more conspicuously, we shall nevertheless finally hold that all portions are essentially of the same spirit, which is emphatically good, and are equal among themselves in the matter here chiefly and ultimately decisive. Even that which is less remarkable in its elevation may give us a contribution to the better understanding of this one chief subject by at least illumining one or other of its many sides, and fulness and manifoldness of detail has its uses. Along with this rare fulness and manifoldness, the diversity of the stages of the development of true religion, often spoken of above, furnishes indeed peculiar advantages, similar as it is to the diversity of the circles of life out of which individuals

arise. The Bible has, accordingly, something for everybody, for the less cultured and the more highly cultured, for the simplest and the wisest, for the warrior and for the quiet in the land, for youth [1] and for grey hairs, nay, for those of such different callings in life that we cannot enumerate all of them, but can only say that in this respect it is the universal book, and is of inexhaustible fulness and unfading freshness. But since it presents to our view, as we have already said and set forth at large, the highest perfection of all revelation and religion, it is evident—

5. That all the apparently unlimited manifoldness, nay, even diversity of its contents, of importance with respect to that one great chief subject, may nevertheless be traced back to unity. For the perfect, when it is come, throws back its full rays upon all that is less perfect, so that in its light we justly appraise even the least earlier fragment of the like good spirit according to its eternal worth, and we can rejoice in it without placing it too high or too low; and on this account, too, the closest union of the New Testament with the Old has its unavoidable necessity. If, therefore, the Bible has for us otherwise, according to § 121-4, its well-understood sanctity, it has it also as the result of our present considerations, since all perfection of divine forces and operations is sacred to us, and therefore this is; but we make good our reverence for Holy Scripture chiefly by holding fast that which is most perfect in its teaching, and measuring all the rest of the like spirit by it, without despising even the least considerable portion of it.

§ 132. If, now, the question is directly asked, in conclusion, how the Bible can have a unity including and comprehending in itself all the manifoldness and diversity of its varied contents, a unity which transcends the mere outward similarity of a common origin of all its parts from one and the same nation, and is capable of giving to us the feeling of actual affinity in mind and heart, this is essentially the same question

---

[1] As Proverbs and Ecclesiastes.

as whether it is possible that all true revelation and religion have really attained their evolution from the earliest times to their highest perfection. This possibility we established in the first part, § 8–50; and in the second, § 51–90, was set forth how, in the Israelitish nation, it has actually been realized from its commencement in primitive times onward. Literature, according to § 92, but follows even in this highest subject, as a whole and in the main, the general life and aspiration of the people. If, therefore, we consider the question of the ultimate unity of the Bible historically from above, that is, from the first beginnings and the subsequent development dependent upon them, we must speak here somewhat in this fashion :—Since the forces of true revelation and religion were, in this nation, from the commencement after the founding of its community on this basis, set in motion too perfectly and regularly not to attain, conformably to that divine series of consequences originally lying in them, and through all the stages of human development, the ultimate perfection possible to them in this nation, therefore its entire literature so fashioned itself that every portion of it, the empty chaff and whatever lay remote from its main purpose being separated in the making of the canon, was touched and inspired by these forces, so that we can clearly recognise of what description they were, and how they there exercised their sway, although some portions show this more particularly and at large than others. When the attention is directed, therefore, to these purely spiritual forces themselves, and it is perceived beforehand how historically they here shaped themselves from the beginning so determinately, set themselves in motion and sought to accomplish their development provisionally in this more limited part of all humanity; then may also be recognised how the separate portions of Scripture stand related to these forces, what portions were held to be partly the ripest, partly the most necessary, for a place in this woven garland of sacred literature, and it will be seen how a higher unity and similarity sustains them from the first, and how the one proportionately more than the other contributes to set these forces vividly before our eyes as alone in the last issue sovereign and paramount. The whole body of Scripture, as collected and fixed by the canon, is thus but the fruit of that whole long history, so far and in such sort as writing has immortalized it; and as there is only one continuous history of all development of the true revelation and religion from the beginning of humanity onward, and as in this history there is only one instance of their direct and ripe development to perfection, and that in this nation, where alone in all antiquity perfection was attainable, therefore corresponding to this, and as one of its finest and most enduring fruits, there can be but one Bible, and, indeed, but this we are now considering. Other similarly imperishable and similarly perfected fruits of the same greatest of all spiritual movements and aspirations of antiquity have their place beside it,—the entrance of the Holy Spirit as a conscious power into humanity (§ 80-90), Christ Himself as the glorious Lord of all spiritual movement and impulse in humanity, the Church as it was transformed by Him from the old community. But whilst these fruits for ever advance and increase in power, the Bible, as the glorious treasury of all genuine remembrance of that development, and of those truths which, as the ground of all corresponding further development, must remain sacred, stands in its own dignity and complete repose as already uplifted far beyond all the storms of an age shaken by new errors,—stands abiding unchangeably as it is, and proffering its inexhaustible resources only to good and wise use, shunning, as everything perfected does, no investigation and no critical inquiry, not even the sharpest, suffering much through man's want of understanding and bad passions, and yet ever making itself felt again as henceforth and for ever indispensable.

If, however, we consider that question, not as we have just done from the beginning of that whole spiritual movement of which the Bible in its outer and inner unity is one of the many fruits, but from the end of this movement, it will be seen at once that no one but Christ Himself is the unity whose light shines back from the New Testament upon all the earlier books, at least as soon as it is seen and apprehended that, in the narrower circle of the New Testament itself, Christ alone is the light that penetrates every part of it with His radiance. If that whole special spiritual movement in the midst of the old humanity aimed to make possible the coming and working of Christ just as at last it happened, and if He also is the sole true unity of all His first disciples as they are known to us in the New Testament, it is evident that neither in the wide and very diversified expanse of the Old Testament, nor in the nearer and narrower regions of the New, indeed nowhere in the Bible, can there be anything important in relation to the one great chief thing for which Christ appeared, which we are not obliged to consider in His light, and to estimate it as it stands more nearly or remotely related to Him. Moreover, it will ever be found that all the noblest efforts of the old nation of the true revelation and religion as the Old Testament has preserved them in writing for ever, already in the moments of their purest elevation and boldest flight, bordered closely upon that which we at last find attained in its time through Christ, although they could not have reached their goal had not Christ appeared. That we are able from the point of view of this clear unity to put together so compactly, and to vivify so freshly in our higher thought and conception all that is most diverse and manifold in the contents of the Bible, this it is that constitutes in this case so great a charm, affords us one of the most fruitful sources of instruction we could desire, and gives to us all the more complete an idea of the unity of the Bible. For that which casts light upon all parts and yet enables us to see at the same time the gradations of this light in the separate parts, appears to us resplendent with double radiance and preciousness.

12. *Conclusion. Comparison with other Sacred Books.*

§ 133. It is then essentially the same with the Bible as in the second division of this volume we showed it to be with the Israelitish nation, the Bible is a remnant, although of the highest kind and unalterable in character. As that nation was the original and remains the pattern nation of the true revelation and religion, inasmuch as by its inquiry and discernment it traced out divine truths most profoundly, and with consistency and fearlessness allowed these truths to work in its midst in its enterprise and its suffering; so the Bible has its incomparable significance and its whole sacredness, because it brings these truths before us in clear decisive utterances and profoundly suggestive images of every kind as a light for our thought and understanding, and because it presents them also as admonitory examples for our whole life and behaviour in the earnestness of its great authentic history, if, indeed, we are not ready to treat with disdain what should ever be sacred to us. Just this complete harmony and exact correspondence between knowledge and deed is in this case everything. And to him who holds Christ Himself as sacred, the Bible will occupy the second place.

We can recognise, however, the true dignity and inner glory of the Bible in yet another way, if we compare it, as Holy Scripture, with the sacred books of other nations and communities, old and new. These are divided, if we consider all of them, into two very different kinds which we must carefully distinguish in the outset.

On the side stand such writings as can only be characterized as late, degenerate after-growths of the Bible, and which therefore cannot be at all compared with the Bible as works of a like original and creative power. They are essentially the product of the conceptions and efforts of men who sought to improve youthful Christianity and with it the Bible, which as yet had scarcely reached its close, but who ill understood either Christianity or the Bible itself,—men who may be designated generally by the historical name of Gnostics. Two courses were followed; either they manufactured a special Bible out of that already in existence, one that answered better to their caprice, and about which they attempted to throw the same sacred splendour; or they went further, creating at once a wholly new Bible, and gathering a community upon its basis. He who first cherished such a thought found ready to hand very much help in the inclination to the more artificial authorship described in § 100, which also afforded a good opportunity to trick out anew the mysteries of all religion that easily touch and move the heart. To such a work of sacred Scripture songs for the new community were then readily added, and similar writings corresponding to the spirit of it, so that in this case also a tolerably manifold and comprehensive Bible was possible. Of this kind, in the midst of its community, has been preserved (after the holy scripture of the Manichæans had perished with the sect itself) the Bible of the Sabæans or Mandæans, which only in our days has become wholly accessible to us, but which at least in its then condition Mohammed knew as extant long before his time, and regarded as a third holy scripture of equal dignity with the Bible of the Christians and the Bible of the Jews. As soon as this Bible, which may be called with a certain propriety that of the Johannean-Christians, is fully known to us and trustworthily translated, it will be seen how little it sustains a comparison with the old genuine entire Bible. At the end, however, of this whole period of youthful Christianity, when Christendom itself, especially in the Eastern nations, was already guilty, alas! of new and grave aberrations enough, Mohammed was in so far more honest as that he sought to give quite openly, on his own responsibility, such selections for reading (Qor'âne) as should be immediately acknowledged as brought to him from heaven, and, when secured in literary form, as holy scripture. But how little also this holy scripture, in its origin so utterly and manifestly unhistorical, could suffice in any way for a true revelation and religion, has already been considered at length in § 120. The Qor'an, instead of giving, as it proposes, a final and necessary work advancing beyond the three other earlier Bibles which it acknowledges, is only a lamentable retrogression on the great path of the development of all divinely-human things; and it would be liable to still more severe criticism had it not been occasioned, as indeed was the case with Islamism throughout, by the serious mistakes by which Christianity, just in the wide regions of its first appearance, had allowed itself to be carried away, so that Islamism itself may be regarded more suitably as a righteous divine punishment of them.[1]

Turning away from these sad divergences from the great spiritual movement which is the subject of discourse, there are only (since the sacred books of the Sibyls and the Druids are now lost) the Egyptian, Zoroastrian, and Indian Scriptures which can be taken into account. These are all of them not merely independent of the Bible, but also in their main elements derived from a primitive age which alone might make them sacred, supposing mere age could make anything sacred which is of human origin. They are accordingly the groundwork of religions of a primitive type, which nurtured and trained in a culture of thousands of years the greatest nations of antiquity, and which even yet in some parts exercise an unbroken and powerful sway over the most widely diffused and prolific of the peoples of Asia. Since, however, we are not yet able to form an adequate judgment of the Egyptian religion, and of the Zoroastrian only a small selection of writings has been preserved, there are only the two branches of the Indian religious books which we can make use of in more exact comparison, viz. the Brahminical, whose close affinity in their original elements with the Zoroastrian has in our day become further manifest, and the Buddhistic. Now it is certainly of great importance that the

---

[1] And if the present wanton and unpardonable mistakes of Christendom are not speedily removed, may not the advent of another Mohammed be near?

most ancient and fundamental portion of the Brahminical and Zoroastrian sacred scriptures consists in an abundance of hymns to deities and sacrificial chants which have been saved from a very early time of high spiritual elevation in that nation, and which still show traces in themselves of that time of humanity's youth by a simplicity so peculiar, a sincerity so childlike, and a naïveté so touching that men of more recent days, formed under a wholly different culture, think they can regard them as sacred only by manifold allegorizing interpretations; many other writings, partly for the elucidation of these divine hymns and sacrificial songs, and also of sacrificial usages, partly for the expression of the views and presages of more ancient seers concerning the nature of religion and of the gods, have subsequently been added, but nevertheless the original groundwork of hymns has remained inviolate, and, in so far as it consisted of most sacred materials, has kept its high honour. It appears thus that the Brahminical and Zoroastrian sacred writings are of purely priestly origin, as indeed they also in later times were especially reserved for the priestly caste alone, and were accessible, if at all to others, only to the ruling class in the nation. If, now, there is found in the wide extent of this whole sacred scripture much that carries with it an inexpressible charm, coming down as it does from humanity's apparently purest age of innocence, and other things also which are worthy of the highest regard as containing in themselves profound anticipations of divine truths, it is yet easily evident how far it stands below the Bible. Moreover, as under Brahminical rule a genuine national community was never possible, and all Indian life continued to be very one-sided, so also this sacred scripture, notwithstanding its great extent, is of very limited aim and contents; and as it has not in the least proceeded out of the whole great continuous history of the nation, so it has never been of very great use to the whole nation, and, indeed, since the vehement conflict against Buddhism Brahminism has become only more and more one-sided. . . .

On the other hand, the Buddhist sacred books may be compared with the New Testament; first, because Buddhism did not desire to enter into an entirely hostile relation towards the older Brahminical culture; and secondly, because the basis of the older books consists of reminiscences of Buddha's life, words, and deeds, as the Gospels do of Christ's. But Buddhism was so far from realizing a true consummation of the old Indian revelation and religion, and was so little able to supply with any fitness the want of it, that it fell away only into a series of further limitations and deficiencies, both in its conceptions of the relation between God and man and in its regulation of human society. It was unable to create a genuine community (p. 178 f.); in its one-sided development only a community of holy monks was formed; and throughout it possessed only a narrow and limited spirit, and had an unhistorical significance. Since, however, it arose in a time learned, fond of controversy, and given to book-making, its literature, out of which subsequently the attempt was repeatedly made to form a genuine Buddhist canon, multiplied to such an enormous extent, that it is difficult to collect all its sacred writings, and only in camel-loads can they be carried away; but what is this huge bulk in spirit compared with the Bible! A library for the cloister is what it has ever remained.

The Chinese books of higher grade, by which everything is determined, are not, however, according to p. 244 f., to be called sacred so much as classical, that is, generally pre-eminent, for they are indeed inviolable, and as such seek to lay the basis of a salvation for the nation; this salvation, however, they do not know how to find where alone it is to be found unalterably the same for every nation for ever, in a real and thence for man sacred Deity.

IV. 13. *Consequences. Growing Worth of the Bible.*

§ 134. To us, however, as we saw, and as our Bible itself teaches, the holy can only be God Himself and His pure word.

We know that the Bible proposes to be for us, and can only be to us a means to lead us to the knowledge of the true God and His eternal word as both become clear to us in the whole history of His to Him specially sacred nation and by means of it, if we seek rightly to contemplate and firmly to grasp this historical clearness as it is actually and wholly. Our judgment therefore is that the Bible—to express it in the shortest and most incisive way—may be sacred to us on many sides and for many reasons, but at last, and with perfect determinateness, it is so only because it is to us an authentic means by which we recognise with certainty the true God in His whole nature, and His word to us in its whole significance and its entire sacredness.

Moreover, we cannot to-day fix the canon of the Bible essentially otherwise than it was already fixed at the end of the period of Christianity's youth, and there is no necessity to do so, if we think with correctness, according to § 105 ff., how it arose and what aim it had from the beginning and subsequently in its whole wider development. The truth is, the canon as it was ultimately determined proceeded from the great necessities and needs of the true revelation and religion, as these transcendent blessings sought their own preservation in humanity, as they must. We may know exactly everything upon which the canon depends, and by our present investigations and experiences we can more particularly determine some things which in the time of its final close remained somewhat indeterminate. And besides this, we must at last wholly abandon the immense number of misunderstandings and prejudices which in the course of time have become established in relation to the sacredness and canon of the Bible.

But the more unavoidable is it here at the close to ask precisely how it stands with our later day in reference to the worth of Holy Scripture as against all earlier times, and especially those in which the sacredness just of this very Bible celebrated its first great victory in the world and in connection with which its canon was finally fixed. Is its value the same to-day? Has it grown less? Or has it become greater, so that we can estimate it more highly to-day than they did in the time when its canon was settled? In order to give the true answer to this question we must discuss, as carefully as the high importance of the matter demands, the two further questions which are bound up with it, so to speak, at each end.

For, on the one side, this question at once presupposes another, viz. does the worth of all revelation and religion, and especially of that to which the Bible, with its whole peculiar contents, seeks to guide us, stand to-day as high as it did in the long series of centuries in which (§ 105 ff.) the canon by degrees was constituted? There are among us to-day people who no longer wish to know anything of any revelation or religion; they therefore deny God Himself; yet what grave, self-destructive folly this is, is shown above in § 13 ff., and will be shown more determinately in a subsequent volume. Others in most recent times are ashamed of absolutely denying God's existence, as, twenty or thirty years ago, was becoming customary in Germany, but they do not wish to know anything of this definite Deity as the Bible presents Him to us, and still less of the revelation of this Deity and of a true religion. But these are sufficiently refuted by the fact that neither they nor their predecessors, as has long since been shown, and as in the nature of the case cannot be otherwise, have ever been able to set up and teach anything better, still less to show by their own lives that there is anything better; and that all the details they adduce in opposition to the truth of this revelation and the necessity of this religion rest on more or less serious errors, is shown even in the present work. Moreover, if the thing itself did not show it, the history of humanity up to this time would prove sufficiently that in the course of events it is never loyalty to the contents and claims of this revelation and religion that is punished, but disloyalty and ignorance of them. Yet why dwell further upon this subject here, when it is the aim of this whole work to show it in detail?

On the other side it might be said, although it is not to be denied that this revelation and religion are alone capable of laying the foundation of a true salvation alike of every individual man and of all nations of the earth, yet there are to-day other means than the Bible, and altogether different from it, whereby they may be accurately known. They might, for instance, be ascertained from the doctrine of the Church and the entire uninterrupted continuance of its ordinances and organization, or from what, in one word, is called tradition; and so much the more could this be done in that the Church, both of the Old and New Testaments, existed earlier than the Bible, and only by its consent has the Bible itself been elevated to its high position; moreover, it could embrace very properly much also which quite accidentally has not been recorded in Holy Scripture. But how little this means would suffice in the great chief subjects on which in this case everything depends, is obvious, and need not here be discussed. Precisely the questions and doubts which may arise as to whether everything conformable to eternal divine truths exists and is in use in the Church, and whether in all its efforts, in thought and judgment as in action and in particular usages, something may not have crept in or sought to creep in which contradicts those truths,—precisely such questions can be decided only by those testimonies which have been preserved for all time unalterable in the Bible, and to which the Church has pledged itself to the determination to stand for ever, by recognising these books as sacred to her once for all. Furthermore, it is altogether wrong to maintain that the Bible has been created only by the Church, and on this account, as the creation of the Church, may be dealt with as the Church pleases, expounded as it may choose, and wholly or partially hidden or interdicted as it may think well. For the divine truths which form the essential contents of the Bible stand elevated far above everything which is called "Church," have been first of all active and further developed in humanity in their own significance and power, nay, have themselves made any community or Church even possible (§ 48–60); a canon of Holy Scripture has been created by the Church only because she felt it was best to secure possession of those truths by written records, and so for all future time to preserve authentic documents, and for such an aim just these special books that had long been held in high and deserved estimation were the most suitable. However high, therefore, the sacred community or Church may be placed, and however certain it is that these divine truths find in the community itself, which they and their appropriate human instruments have founded, the mightiest and most permanent of their spheres of work and culture, yet it would mean the destruction of these most ample and resplendent spheres themselves where the truth works, and thereby the weakening of the best influence of the truth among men, to allow that the Church might deal arbitrarily with the Bible and supply its place of honour in her midst by anything else, by a confession of faith or some other verbal utterance, by another book or a multitude of other books, by a Council or a Pope.

§ 135. As a means by which the true revelation and religion may be known to-day there is only one thing that is at all equal to the Bible, and to be placed on a level with it in dignity and impressiveness. If all true religion has only been made manifest to us that we may the more surely walk in it, and if also the Bible ultimately seeks to serve no other end than to present to us the bright mirror of this true religion, and to incite us by the knowledge of it to walk in accordance with it, as far as a book can do this; it is possible then that every man living may appropriate it to himself as it is to be known from the Bible, and so find in actual experience the better life of the soul which it promises to him. What was first mere letter and perishable writing becomes then for him spirit and life, and if one short sentence out of the whole wide volume can serve as a most wonderful and permanent impulse to induce him to persevere in that way of his better self which he has here found, he will do this with yet further constancy and enlightenment, if he has appropriated to himself the whole import and spirit of the Bible in the full light and purest energy of both. Thus the truth of the religion contained in the Bible, and the divinity of its revelation, are attested to the individual man, and he believes in the letter as such no longer, and no longer is swayed by it; what once moved the greatest prophets and saints, what issues as truth from all the higher history of the joint working of the divine and human spirit, works now also in him; and the Holy Spirit Himself, from whom the eternal element that lives in the Bible has proceeded, may also in this way take possession of him. In point of fact, it is only in this manner that the Bible can attest its divine truth to man; it has attested it thus to innumerable men in all times; and the influences which have passed over from the Bible into the great history of all humanity, come to the heart of the individual as the thousand-fold confirmation of this testimony. But this second means of knowledge is absolutely necessary, for the whole question is ultimately a question of the salvation of our own spirit, and only by self-knowledge is this attested.

If therefore the Bible has on account of its unique contents a value which nothing can replace, whereby it is the only means of conveying to us with perfect certainty the knowledge of that true religion in which every man should live,—a means which receives complete confirmation by our own living experience as the necessary counter means of knowledge (the counter proof),—it follows further that its worth cannot be diminished, but can only increase with the course of centuries and millenniums. This is the case in the main, indeed, with all real gains once actually won in human history, because their employment in the course of all human development advances in importance and is more and more widely extended. The various possessions of permanent value which the old Egyptians, Chinese, Indians, Greeks and Romans attained, and which we have received from them, we do not prize less to-day than they were once prized, but rather since they have secured a wider certification we prize them more. But especially does this happen with the Bible, so far as it can happen with what is a means to a higher end. For the purely spiritual life and endeavour of man, because it is man's supreme aim, and leads to holiness of character, is also most difficult, and is pre-eminently exposed to the power of the most delusive errors and the most destructive fluctuations; and the more widely the truth has already revealed its signification and purpose in this realm, where with the mind itself only the mind's free resolve and self-determination can have authority, the more freely do old errors, as well as the evil intent of innumerable men, exert their influence here. So there spread easily more and more widely prevailing and powerful errors and corruptions; and indeed, since in Christ the highest divinely-human life, which can develop itself in one man, first appeared, and with this appearing, the Bible, as historical witness of that whole highest spiritual movement of antiquity ending in Him, itself also came to an end, these powerful errors and corruptions have repeatedly been diffused with the greatest energy. But the Bible serves, even against all these repeated and more and more powerful aberrations, as a clear and ever adequate monitor of those eternal truths, which, as they have created this whole New World in opposition to the Old, so also are alone able to conduct it to its true divine goal. The more widely the new errors gain ground and the more perniciously they at length work, the more freshly and mightily can shine forth again in ever new splendour the eternal truths which alone possess saving efficacy, and which are preserved in the Bible with unalterable lineaments for the whole future of man; and since this Bible in well-nigh innumerable copies, in its original languages and in almost all possible tongues of the world, is in our day to be found in almost every cottage and every corner, no tyrant can ever succeed in wresting it from the hands or indeed the minds of men, as once a Chinese emperor (Tsche-hwang-ti, B.C. 240) sought to annihilate all books out of mere hatred of all free activity of thought, when he had by force consolidated anew the old Chinese Empire. As the Bible ever authenticates itself afresh as the very means of knowledge and enlightenment it professes to be and alone can be, its value just on this account rises higher and higher with the course of time.

14. *The Right Use of the Bible.*

§ 136. But as every means of good has the influence it ought to have only as it is properly used, so it happens with the Bible,—the noblest means of good in literature antiquity could bequeath to us. How single passages of the Bible whose sense is clear in themselves may be taken out of their connection and applied with advantage for the elevation and improvement of our spirit, we would not now discuss; the question is simply as to the right employment of the Bible as a whole, although to be sure upon this to every conscientious man the right use of even the smallest parts of it should depend, if there is a desire to proceed safely and neither seriously to deceive ourselves or others. But on the threshold of our subject there lies the question, whether it gives us itself general laws and proper examples of its use. Every sentence of the Bible that can be turned to account in this direction, nay, every suggestion it offers as to its own proper use, must at least be eminently worthy of our consideration.

As much as this nevertheless may at once be seen; it would be idle to seek in the older portions of the Bible a prescription how it is to be explained and applied. It must be an ill sort of writing that has first to tell every man how it is to be expounded and used. Some of the earliest as well as the latest prophets allowed themselves to give hints and admonitions to the effect that their writings were to be well considered and not abused; but that the reader could understand the words and sentences of his work, every prophet and other writer presupposes as in itself certain. If the Deuteronomist sharply admonishes us not to add to or take away from God's word, we saw above what that means;[1] and if towards the end of his work he declares how it is to be read annually in public before the assembled nation, that is connected with the more artificial aim and plan of his work which has already been spoken of.[2]

When, however, after the close of the seventh century B.C., a canon of Holy Scripture was gradually established, and the Pentateuch had won for itself its high regard in the community, it is one of the latest psalmists who, in a long discourse, very artificially arranged and connected together,[3] yet flowing forth from the deepest thought of a heart at rest in God and His word, and courageous in the midst of suffering on account of its free confession,—a discourse which celebrates the glory and consolation of Holy Scripture, and especially its luminous clearness for the guidance of every step of man,—breaks out into the prayer to God,

> "Open Thou mine eyes, that I may behold
> Much of wonder out of Thy law!"

and into the like utterance,—

> "The way of Thy commands teach me,
> That I may meditate upon Thy wonders!"[4]

And it is evident from the connection that these divine wonders are such as the poet found in the Pentateuch, the whole of which it was not easy for him to understand; for what he calls the "teaching" of God is, according to the well-known Hebrew expression (Thôra), just the Pentateuch, that true Bible in miniature. For it is a peculiarity of Scripture when it is already old, that it contains much that to later readers is very obscure and difficult to decipher, in which

[1] P. 249.   [2] P. 326.
[3] The aged poet was perhaps cast into prison and sweetened his involuntary leisure by his task.   [4] Ps. cxix. 18, 27.

because of its connection with the contents of the rest of the Scriptures they expect to find, not without reason, wonderful divine secrets, which they would be glad by deeper meditation to penetrate into, in order that they might follow more confidently the clear prescriptions of Holy Scripture relating to the life and work of man;—secrets which, quite in accordance with the divine greatness and glory, it is difficult for them to understand. It is indeed remarkable enough that here already we find so clear an indication how difficult the full comprehension and joyful application of the entire contents of Holy Scripture can become even to the most pious intelligence. After our poet's time, the days came soon enough, when, with respect to such wonderful or divinely mysterious things of Holy Scripture as there was no hope of understanding otherwise, or of harmonizing with the rest of Scripture, the art of allegory was applied; pains were taken to read the riddle in this way, and it was thought to be possible to advance more and more with entire safety upon this path in expounding and applying Holy Scripture. But that our poet approves such art, or even knows it, he does not say; and indeed there lie as yet some centuries between him and the first serious attempt to make use of allegory in interpreting Holy Scripture. That long psalm is, however, the most copious and notable witness within the Hebrew Old Testament of the feeling and spirit in which the pious contemplated Holy Scripture during the earliest centuries of its common acceptance; although we know also from other sources by a short narrative what care and pains were taken to give a profitable exposition and application of it to the assembled community.[1]

§ 137. Meanwhile, the time now actually arrived when it became more and more necessary not merely to explain Holy Scripture in the public assembly of the community, but to investigate also its great fundamental truths and wider relations, to group together more fully the doctrines and precepts to be drawn from it so as to exhibit them according

[1] Neh. viii. 8, 12.

to their foundations, and thus to lead back to first principles all exposition and application of the truth. Different schools of Scripture exposition flourished; some found their joy in the refinements and subtlety of allegory; others held themselves with more reserve towards it; but all were accustomed with increasing frequency to prove all their opinions by passages of Holy Scripture, or at least to sustain and adorn them with such passages. The scribes became the spiritual lords of the time;[1] all this had completely developed itself in this way already before the age of the appearing of Christ and His disciples. The strongest indications of it are shown in the New Testament; and the question arises whether the New Testament undertakes, by means of passages and oracular utterances, in this matter very important, to give us prescriptions for the exposition of the Old Testament. How little this is the case we may infer from the fact that all passages of this kind in the New Testament of any significance for the matter in hand occur only incidentally, and nowhere seek to teach anything really new, although some of their suggestions are worthy of grave consideration. But as the subject is of the greatest importance, we must go more into detail and ponder well what is of special weight. We see now—

1. That Christ holds the Holy Scripture of His days in all the high honour it can demand, quotes readily its examples and proofs for the truth and rectitude of what He teaches and does, refers with all impressiveness to its short sharp divine oracles as decisive, nay, contemplates it as the treasury— great and ample, but for the common mind somewhat obscure and little precisely known—whose contents regarded as sacred need only be examined in order to lead to the conviction that He is the true Christ. Just as little does He reject the Biblical scholarship and science which are everywhere indispensable where Holy Scripture is accepted. But the scribes who were then predominant He wholly rejects as

[1] Ecclus. xxxviii. 24–xxxix. 11; 1 Macc. vii. 12; 2 Macc. vi. 18 ff.

a matter of principle, and demands that the Christian scribe shall know how to draw from that treasury, now supplemented by the gospel, not merely old things, but also and especially new;[1] these are the truths and forces of the perfect true revelation and religion which for every new age renew themselves, as necessity requires, without losing their connection with what has been long since given in the Old Testament. For the more particular meaning of Christ's saying, in this case, is seen partly from the connection of the discourse which He closes with this intimation;—He is discoursing, however, there of the progress of the development of the perfect kingdom of God as He had just established it in humanity;— partly also from the spiritual freedom with which elsewhere in every instance He deals with the contents of the Old Testament without attenuating what is of eternal significance and worth. Consider now more particularly—

2. The way in which the Old Testament is used in the whole of the New, and we shall then see that a twofold use of it is open to us. The Apostle Paul is the most important author who stands as an example of the first method. He is fond of proving everything he expressly touches upon in the way of doctrine by means of passages of the Old Testament definitely introduced and, should he think it expedient, abundantly accumulated. He makes use also of these proofs in the proper place very skilfully by comparison of two or more Old Testament passages, or by setting them over against each other, giving thus a double inference; and he even resorts to the aid of the art of allegory; while the writer of the Epistle to the Hebrews follows him, only with still greater ingenuity, in all these three aptitudes of citation. All this was the outcome of the apostle's special training in the culture of the schools, to which as a Hellenist he was accustomed in his early years, and which as a Christian and apostle he thought he was necessitated to retain, since it promised good service in learned contention with his

---

[1] Matt. xiii. 52.

opponents; the more so as, in his time, Christianity had gone forth into the great heathen world, and there the Jewish scribes delighted by such learned arts to prove everything. The favourite disciple John stands as an example of the second method, and pre-eminently Christ Himself. In all the three directions before mentioned the greatest simplicity is here shown, and especially is there no use whatever made of the art of allegory. But the fact that these two methods of proving a truth of Christianity stand peacefully side by side in the New Testament, itself attests how little depends in Christianity, as against the pure truths themselves, upon such distinctions in the procedure of proof; and how this procedure might change with time and place as the purpose and aim of the matter of discourse changed, if only what was artificial did not deviate too far from simplicity and directness in knowledge and speech. And in reality we see how Paul himself, in Epistles[1] less elaborately planned, refrains from such more learned arts of proof; whilst inversely James, Peter, and Jude, in their Epistles, do not indeed resort to allegory, but nevertheless like to inweave Old Testament proofs, because their writings were intended to be instructive. A similar variation may be seen also in the first three Gospels, since Mark nowhere has a special regard to the Old Testament, and only the last editor of Matthew, conformably to the special aim of his work, intentionally interpolates all the Old Testament passages that appear to him competent to afford the very best proof that Jesus is the Christ. The Epistle to the Colossians occupies a very peculiar position, for notwithstanding the literary art that is conspicuous in the longest passages, it cites no Old Testament texts; whilst the Epistle to the Ephesians, and the author of the three pastoral letters, attach themselves wholly to Paul, the former even in love of allegory. Accordingly in the whole of the New Testament nothing is seen but how a sound Christian freedom in this matter rules everywhere, and how little of intention there is to give us a

[1] 1 and 2 Thessalonians, Philippians, and Philemon.

one-sided prescription concerning the exposition and use of the Old Testament, apart from the view, which prevails throughout, of that higher unity that (§ 131 f.) stands over everything in the Old Testament and in Christianity. . . . Indeed, it could—

3. Not well be otherwise than that of the various principles of the whole contemplation and exposition of the Old Testament at that time accepted and long since laid down in the learned schools, many of which penetrated into the nation far beyond the pale of the schools themselves, some at least should be mentioned in the New Testament; and they are at once of great importance to us. But so far as they are approved, or not altogether rejected, in the New Testament, there is valuable truth in them; and they give to us, besides, a noteworthy evidence of the scientific conscientiousness and care with which, in earlier times, the inquiry was prosecuted in the old community into all questions here relevant, and the effort was made to trace back everything to its firm basis. "The Scripture cannot be broken,"[1] as it might be were it a common writing whose words might be true or not, firmly accepted or rejected; as holy it must be of solid worth and contain truth, so that no sentence of it is to be made weak and perishable as an untrue or unmeaning sentence; this is one of these principles, borrowed from language of legal complexion as if the Old Testament were a book of legal maxims. And if this is referred, as it may fairly be, to the contents of the Bible, which have an immediate significance for practical religion, the principle serves properly to show that we are not to estimate too lightly such words as belong to the Scriptures, even if they appear hard to be understood, and might on that account rather be laid aside as unmeaning or indeed empty. "Not above what is written,"[2] or what the Scripture says, is a kindred principle which admonishes that we are not to hold ourselves as wiser than Scripture,

---

[1] John x. 35, cf. vii. 23; Matt. v. 19, xvi. 19, xviii. 18.
[2] 1 Cor. iv. 6, cf. iii. 19 f.

even if it says something we do not like, and which, yielding to human vanity, we might wish to discard. "Whatsoever the law says, it says to those under the law;"[1] that is, to those who belong to the sacred community; is also a very similar principle, teaching that the members of this community are not to consider the denunciations and words of earnest displeasure the Scriptures contain as having no reference to them; or "everything which was written aforetime," *i.e.* long since, in the sacred Scriptures, "was written for our instruction!"[2] And if Christ exclaimed to the Jews, "You think in the Scripture to have eternal life,"[3] He does not mean to deny thereby that the Old Testament could contain such life, although He does not mean to say it is contained only in it, according to the exaggerated opinion of the scribes, and could not also be obtained by another means; but so far as such is their opinion, they condemn themselves only the more severely if they do not so search and apply the Scripture as they are bound to do. So correct are these principles that Christ as well as Paul repeats them, although the latter, in opposition to perverse scribes and stiffnecked contenders for the letter, says, "The letter killeth, but the spirit giveth life."[4]

In the youth of Christianity this principle, that everything the Old Testament contains was written for the instruction and admonition, or for the hope and comfort of posterity, was soon applied with the greatest possible fervour and glow of feeling. The consciousness awoke that now at length in the Christ who had just appeared, in accordance with Old Testament promises, there had been attained the consummation of the past, and, in sure and certain hope in Him as its accomplisher, the consummation also of the whole future of human destiny. This consciousness worked so wonderfully, irradiating the whole field of vision with its new splendour, that every detail of the Old Testament became invested with new freshness and life; and after Old Testament hopes had been so mani-

[1] Rom. iii. 19. [2] Rom. xv. 4; 1 Cor. x. 11, possibly a traditional saying.
[3] John v. 39. [4] 2 Cor. iii. 6, cf. 15.

festly fulfilled in a matter of chief moment, it was not difficult to find the Old Testament everywhere full of emblems and types of Christ and His disciples. If the art of allegory subsequently came to be employed, it was easy to explain the most remote and unrelated passages as referring to Christ and Christians, and finding its fulfilment in them. When now Paul, and soon after, and in a far greater degree, the Epistle to the Hebrews, had breathed, as it were, the breath of a new Christian life over the Old Testament, its historical sense would in the end have been more and more explained away if there had been much further advance made one-sidedly in this direction. But it was not so, and there remained, as if ingrained in the white marble of the New Testament books, a few motley stripes of wholly distinct methods of thought and speech, more as a memorial of the thorough flexibility of the spirit of that last Biblical age, and in so far for our instruction, than as furnishing to us authoritative precepts and universal rules of procedure in the exposition of the Old Testament.

§ 138. The Bible therefore gives us no prescription specially to show us how it is to be interpreted and used. In short historical accounts of the procedure in later times it admonishes us, by the examples it brings forward, to the diligent investigation and use of Holy Scripture;[1] it gives to us occasionally, from the same periods of time, some very useful suggestions as to its use; it lays down in one of its latest writings the principle that every actually God-inspired writing has also its corresponding uses for the spiritual life; but prescriptions how we ought to interpret it, it does not give us. In fact, it is unworthy of a writing that with the best right is to be called holy to be obliged first to state how it is to be interpreted and used. Truth, and most of all divine truth, is its own proof and its own expositor, and it would be to represent itself as something ambiguous and obscure if it must first give an exposition of itself. It indicates, indeed, in scattered

[1] Deut. xxxi. 9–13; Dan. ix.; 2 Tim. iii. 16; Neh. viii. 8 f.; Luke iv. 16–21.

passages of its later books, that certain portions of its entire contents were at that time already regarded as somewhat difficult to understand,[1] for whose correct interpretation special and even unusual pains are requisite; but for all that, it contains no prescription how we are to understand it. It is therefore quite otherwise with these Scriptures than with, for example, the Brahminical, the latest issues of which are books intended to explain the older, but to be held as sacred as well.

Care must be taken here not to confound two things which are specially to be distinguished: the mere application of the contents of a passage in the Bible and its exposition in the strictest sense of the word. The application of a passage may be infinite; nor can it be denied, indeed, that the sense of a passage in its application to a new case may flash up with new vividness. When Christianity in its youth observed how many passages of the Old Testament shone forth with a new living meaning if they were contemplated in the light of the just glorified Christ and His history, as well as of His Church, it turned with a wholly new fervour and confidence to search for such passages; and the more profoundly it felt the obligation laid upon it, since it was misjudged in the world, to authenticate first of all its right to recognition in the circle of the sanctity of the old true religion, the higher did its fervour rise in finding and establishing how Christ and everything truly Christian already shone forth in the Old Testament; and in this effort help was found in the old custom, already prevalent in the existing community, of fondness for proving everything by Biblical texts, as well as in the certainty that Christ is the promised One of the Old Testament. Thus a new resplendent light seemed to be suffused over the entire Old Testament; even if the art of allegory had not then been known at all, this enthusiasm in discovering what is Christian in the Old Testament would have been the same, and in point of fact the art of allegory came into use in this way in the apostolic period

[1] 2 Pet. iii. 16.

only by degrees; the many passages of this kind, however, which are now to be found in the New Testament appear in it only as it were incidentally, for we know that the Christians of those times dealt with the Old Testament throughout after this fashion. But all these are mere applications of Old Testament passages; and although the tendency to vivify anew the Old Testament in such wise did not readily return in equal fervency, yet the same passages at different times were even wholly differently applied; and indeed in the New Testament the same passage finds wholly distinct references.[1] Quite otherwise is it with what must be called exposition in the stricter sense. This aims solely at the discovery and establishment of the original meaning of the author; and in our times, indeed, it has become indispensable first of all to lay ourselves under the obligation to find this original meaning accurately in every passage, that we may escape from the many earlier misuses, and attain an irrefragably certain historical contemplation of things; and since Christ Himself has furnished the example of this prudent reserve (p. 419 f.), we can the less doubt that in every case where it is necessary our chief business is accurately to ascertain the original meaning of the contents of the Bible. Not till this has been done can we on this basis calmly consider how manifoldly the words may be otherwise related and applied; and only as the Bible forbade us from accurately knowing this meaning as it is, should we be justified in entertaining a low opinion of it, and treating it as unworthy of its own proper respect.

§ 139. If, now, the exposition and right use of the Bible itself have been assigned to us, we must first of all rightly understand it, that thus we may find the sure basis for all profitable use of it. Whatever has been in earlier times overlooked and neglected, or even has occurred through mistake, cannot fetter us as soon as we have recovered the true meaning which in the case of every author of a greater or smaller

---

[1] As Gen. ii. 24 in 1 Cor. vi. 16; Eph. v. 31 f.; cf. Matt. xix. 5 f. So Isa. liii. 6 in Matt. ix. 36; 1 Pet. ii. 25.

portion of Scripture was indisputably connected with his words. Most of the sentences of the Bible are of themselves readily intelligible to any one who knows the original tongues or compares reliable translations; but this is not the place to discuss the universal laws of all correct hermeneutics. Two things, however, are here relevant.

First, that all those words, sentences, sections, and smaller or larger books of the Bible whose meaning from any cause whatever has been more and more, in the long course of intervening centuries and millenniums, pushed into the background, and thence become more or less obscure, are in that case to be the more carefully considered and the more accurately applied. We can accomplish this the more confidently to-day, the more certainly our whole science, after frequent attempts, immature or indeed wholly mistaken, has arrived at this point, viz. to be able to proceed with sure footing everywhere, and nowhere altogether to miss our way where words or parts of the Bible are in question which have most vital significance in connection with our present purpose. So long as we had not yet returned to the position of seeking to understand all the great and small parts of the Bible, each in the full sense of the original author and of his time; of looking into the face of every age out of which any flower has been woven into the wonderful garland of the Bible, and of marking the very soil where only it could have grown up as it is, and at the same time of distinguishing, where possible, each author in whose garden it has grown from others in whose gardens other, although similar flowers grew: so long everything remained imperfect and constantly exposed to a thousand errors. The simple reader could then at best but overlook such flowers as were for him half-hidden, half-disfigured, and hasten on to others that pleased him; moreover, he who among readers and expositors would not hastily pass by such passages, but linger over them intentionally, fell into the danger of mingling continually a thousand arbitrary thoughts in the exposition of them, of attempting every device of allegory, and of making ultimately both his own labour and that of his readers altogether fruitless. To-day we may, on the contrary, avoid all such vain toil, if only we seek to direct our labour aright. This, however, is, to be sure, the more necessary, since we are—

Secondly, under obligation not to pass over even the least portion of the entire contents of the Bible that falls within the circle of the complete discharge of our task, if our task be to give a summary of the whole contents of the Bible, in order to see clearly what it announces to us concerning God and His will. Every tittle of the Bible is in that case important, and in the end not merely every sentence, even the smallest, but every word; and not seldom the minute particulars in the Bible, hitherto least of all correctly understood or wholly overlooked, and indeed concealed to the common eye, render us the best service. In short, a new certain apprehension of the entire wide contents of the Bible, such as our present knowledge can give us, indispensable as it is for incalculably many other aims in our day, especially belongs in its widest extension to the science to which the present volume is introductory.

The Bible does not forbid us, nay, rather it summons us in the most urgent way, by the highly manifold, nay, at first sight apparently wholly diverse, contents of its separate parts, to seek, just in relation to the highest aim for which it is to be of service to us, the right connection of its contents and the unity of all the truths it offers us. In point of fact, the attempt to bring the entire body of divine truths, vast and extensive as it is, and the corresponding human duties which genuine revelation gradually discloses, into one comprehensive summary, that is, into a firmly connected series, and therefore into a new unity, is as old as true religion and its community; already the Ten Commandments, that granite substratum of the whole Bible, proceeded from such an endeavour; Christ Himself shows no aversion to the attempts made in His time by learned scribes to establish in new form such a unity, to call the first commandment that which according to its nature is to be placed foremost as most important, and to reduce to a few main duties and truths the immense manifoldness of Old Testament teaching; all the books of instruction in the Old Testament designed for handy use are full of such attempts; indeed, in his new exposition of the law the Deuteronomist allows such an endeavour to influence him; and if the New Testament is somewhat free from such examples, this arises from the fact that Christianity was then only in its first beginnings, but even here there is an instructive commencement of this kind of summarizing. But considering the great manifoldness of the contents of the Bible as well as the task itself, if we would rightly summarize Biblical teaching, we must take into view the following observations, always presupposing the right principles of exposition already mentioned, and solicitude for the most certain verbal accuracy:—

1. If we look at the inner nature and development of all true revelation, and if we know from our first section that everything which is here of decisive importance goes back to the original energy and original activity of revelation, then it is evident that we should everywhere proceed specially from such portions of the Bible which set forth before our view the fundamental truths as they flow forth from this their purest and mightiest spring. It is the voices of the prophets, and, still higher, that of Christ Himself echoing in those of His disciples, that we have to seek before everything else, and to discover as accurately as possible. Whether these utterances stand in special prophetic books or have been interpolated in narrative pieces, in every case we must start specially from them. Whether principally only the shortest utterances that have become laws of life have survived as the results of once higher prophetic activity,—as in the case of the Ten Commandments and other short legal compositions from the primitive times of the community under Moses,—or whether the fundamental truths of all genuine religion pour forth in full, clear, transparent stream, as in the case of the prophets of the flourishing time of Old Testament literature, and also of Christ; and whether the glow of discourse in them flames

only from above, as in the Old Testament, or veiled under the most human condescension penetrates everything, as with Christ and in the Epistles of His disciples; throughout we must start first of all from them. And even if only a little, and that here and there, may be rescued from individual prophets and apostles, still we must specially everywhere take heed to these remnants, and observe how the great stream of all development of true revelation has swelled to its copious fulness by means of such influxes.

But over and above these utterances of the most immediate and mighty power of all revelation there stand in the Bible, on the one side, a multifarious stream of songs for the most part animated by the deepest feeling and the noblest sentiments which the life and sufferings of the true religion called forth in its community in a thousand ways, but also giving expression to new upspringing incitements of the energy of revelation in the same true religion, and these partly in free spontaneous overflowings of poetic excitation, partly at a later period in artificial creations when the public activity of the prophets gradually relaxed. Thus all these songs which are found in the Psalter and elswhere, partly as lofty witnesses of the sentiments actively present in the community of the true religion, partly as further outworkings of genuine religion's force and faculty of revelation once so strongly excited in this community, may offer the most important contributions to the knowledge of which we are here in quest.

On the other side, there stand in the Bible the books of instruction, partly those of the first kind, as almost the whole of the Book of Proverbs and the Book of Sirach, partly those which are creations of poetic art of manifold gradation and dress, the Song of Songs, the Book of Job, many Psalms, Proverbs xxx. 1 to xxxi. 9, the Book of Ecclesiastes, the Wisdom of Solomon, and even such books as Tobit and Judith. They show how true religion shaped itself on all sides, or struggled to adjust itself with all the forces in the actual life of the community, and contain in themselves in so far a wide varied wealth. But many of the highest thoughts also of this religion's power of revelation, long so inexhaustible,—thoughts which were too elevated or too difficult to grasp, and therefore could not at once appear in the ordinary discourse of the people and in the common teaching,—sought a presentation in the manifold departments of didactic poetry which could be found only there in such vivid and luminous clearness.

And these three groups are surrounded by narrative pieces as by their indispensable, broad, easy setting, so that only the New Testament closes with a book of prophecy pointing into all the Christian future. But these historical pieces, sometimes very short, sometimes very copious, are also themselves in their matter so necessary, that without them everything else would be on the one side quite dark, on the other incomplete. Above all, they attest the great chief point, that this whole progressively-arisen revelation of all true religion has so little come into the world accidentally and arbitrarily, that it is rather inseparably connected with the huge weight of all history itself, and forms nothing less than the most brilliant and best part of it, the most consoling too for all the future. But they admonish us still of something else just as important. If we did not know it, or rather if we men of modern times should not already spontaneously know it from the experience of all millenniums, these historical settings admonish us of it, viz. that every prophet, nay, even Christ Himself, discourses for his time under the power of the historical connection standing high over all humanity; that even what is spoken for eternity is yet in its manifestation and first setting historically conditioned; and that therefore we must rightly apprehend whatever is temporal in order to find in it the more certainly that which is eternal. But the highest suggestion offered by this historical setting of contents of eternal value which alone we are in quest of, we can understand only as we observe that among the narrative pieces of the Old and New Testaments there are not a few which by their contents as well as by their bearing lift us up far above what otherwise passes as customary narrative in the Bible itself, which relate to us in such human form purely divine thoughts and divine incidents, and not by prophetic or poetic but simple narrative words transplant us into heaven itself. In such pieces the power of revelation in all true religion prosecutes its task in point of fact only as it can prosecute it in simple narrative; but they admonish us of this also, that all the ten thousand customary narratives do not suffice to place just as clearly before the eyes the working of the divine powers which yet are ever active in history; and that there is behind all human history a divine history also visible only in its effects. If, now, such narratives of the higher kind were alone prevalent in the Bible, we should lose in their presence all actual visible history; but appearing only in moderate frequency, and always where the higher contemplation and knowledge of all divinely-human history urgently presses into notice,—that is, in the right place,—the finest intermingling is formed, whilst we are ever admonished to combine both kinds of narrative indeed in a higher sense, but in other respects rightly to apprehend each kind only according to its own nature, and to be satisfied with the sense it will yield to us. Thus then is it seen that the Bible, placing as it does that which is most prosaic and common-place in narrative side by side with the most elevated and inspired, is also in this respect a true book of the world.

All these many kinds of material we must closely combine, and ascertain what truths result from them as a whole. Only the most accurate and complete combination of these materials, so different in themselves, can conduct us to authentic results. And, moreover, we must be on our guard against overlooking anything because it does not lie immediately at our feet; as, for instance, we are not to deduce from the Book of Job isolated thoughts merely that find verbal expression, while the great thoughts and truths, which alone in the final issue it seeks to place clearly before our view, are unnoticed. Nothing indeed is more hazardous than to draw wide and perverse conclusions from words and sentences broken off from their context, as we have already seen in the case of the word and thought with respect to that which is "God-inspirited" in the Scripture (p. 395). But nothing also is more unfair and mischievous than to overlook or to wish indeed wholly to obscure the indications of a truth, less strongly conspicuous at first sight, as for example the traces of the belief in immortality in the Old Testament. And thus, here as everywhere, the true task is, neither to put into the Bible nor twist out of it anything foreign to it, but rather its own wealth, and its certainty also, fully to exhaust.

§ 140. 2. In the meantime the truths belonging to the circle of religious doctrine do not appear in the Bible, all of them or always, upon the same stage of clearness and certainty; and the Bible, unaffected and simple as it is, and as its compilers without additions of their own happily left it, is honest enough to leave this variation in condition just as it really was to the men whom we may now contemplate as spokesmen and writers of divinely-human things. Starting as we may fairly start from the idea of revelation and its development, we can distinguish three stages of clearness and certainty, namely,—

1. There are names and ideas which meet us in the Bible as fossils from an earlier age in which they must have been still living, fresh, impressive. These plainly should indicate high truths in the circle of revelation. On a closer contemplation we can yet plainly enough perceive the different times from which they descend; but their original living force has vanished as behind a veil. As examples illustrative of this may be mentioned such names as "Cherub," "Seraph," which appear in certain passages of the Bible so closely connected with the divine, yet only as reminiscences from the remote primitive age of the nation of Israel,—august forms which confront us only as names divested of their original essential life. Similarly the name "Jahveh, Lord of Hosts"

unexpectedly and obscurely comes before us from the older centuries of the community; the name "Satan" occurs too, first as it seems in the Book of Job,—from earlier books we do not know him, and cannot properly say who he is. All this must we recognise as it is, in its abruptness and even in the relative darkness which for us arises from it. But in point of fact this twofold result thus appears, viz. the revelation and religion which the Bible seeks to set before our eyes with their earliest origins and beginnings, go back into the most remote ages and regions of the earth, a matter which, taken purely historically, may yet be of great significance; and, further, very many portions of the entire literature of the ancient nation are lost to us, as, moreover, we cannot doubt, according to § 93 ff. And thus, all that belongs to such subjects we may characterize as lying as it were at the back of the Bible, and to be regarded by us rather as once actually existent in greater livingness and primitive power.

2. In the sunny centre, on the other hand, there lie in the Bible everywhere the great truths concerning God Himself, concerning the divine kingdom and the sacred community, concerning the goodness and love of God as His highest relations to the universe, and a hundred like them; such truths also as those concerning the Holy Spirit and the Messiah or Christ, although penetrating only the comparatively speaking later portions of the Bible, yet are everywhere clear as sunlight, if only we know how rightly to understand them in their true sense. Nevertheless, just as we see some important names and ideas of the Bible withdraw themselves behind these its sunny parts into an obscure realm, as if into the first morning-glow of that whole day that dawns in it, so it bids us look again—

3. Into other realms which lie darkly before its future, and where it discourses of mysteries, into which one may indeed gaze from a distance and by anticipation penetrate, but which are not by any means to be placed on the same level as those certainties already clear as sunshine. Here, to be sure, we

must in the outset well distinguish such mysteries as bear this name only in accordance with the artistic plan of certain writings. If one of Job's three friends suggests to him that there are mysteries of divine wisdom which neither he nor any man can know, this is perfectly right in Job's case at the moment when he says it; but the mysteries here meant in Job's affairs the readers of the book already know in part from the introduction, and Job himself with all his contemporaries learns at last at the close of his bravely-endured trial. The mysteries to which the Apocalypse refers, with the exception of the one great mystery, are similarly purely artistic; but even this great unique mystery to which it refers frequently is at the end solved, so far as prophecy can solve it. The mysteries to which the New Testament in all earnestness alludes are rather new difficult questions of the future, which did not arise till the completed earthly manifestation of Christ, and into which indeed the inspired glance of a Paul and of others like him might cast a first ray of light, but which, penetrated though he was by the spirit of Christ, could only float before him at that time as riddles which the future had to solve. For with every great advance in the human-divine destiny of all creation, and with every beginning thereby won of a new and better life, new enigmas at once arise for all the further future; and if since the origin of the whole human creation there had been no advance so great as that which Christ brought, so also there had never risen to the view of a new future such deep and comprehensive new problems of the whole divine government of the universe as at that time. And yet there was also never a period more competent to cast the first sure glance into such mysteries of the whole infinite future as just then, when Christ's spirit still touched most immediately His own disciples. Upon the directly opposite side of all conceivable history it was, to be sure, the things of the remotest past, or the origin of the universe and of man, into which the power of revelation in the old sages had directed its gaze, and which nevertheless at this present time might properly appear as mysteries still to the common mind. And if a thousand passages in the entire Old Testament appeared as mysteries in the apostolic time (p. 384 f.), this is for us to-day only so much the more an impulse to seek their true solution.

For our duty is to put together these three stages, and to bring everything they contain into a higher unity. In every case we must set out towards our aim from the sunny centre; but we must follow also those traces lying further back, so far as it is at all possible, and consider as well what is the nature of these many kinds of mysteries, and whether they have for us to-day wholly the same significance. Only as we grasp thus from the sure centre the two extremes upon which we can look, shall we exhaust the great whole which in its extent the Bible presents to us.

§ 141. 3. Finally, it should be self-evident that every error prevalent in earlier times or to-day, affecting any subject relevant to our inquiry, however powerful that error may have been, cannot be allowed to disturb us. If the Jews, for example, have rejected rigorously since the wars of extermination under Titus and Hadrian all Hellenistic writings, and consequently Christianity, how should that constrain us not to see great historical truth? But if, on the contrary, so many Christian scholars in more modern times desire to retain firmly only the New Testament, and as good as reject the Old, that is in point of fact a much more mischievous error still, and leads by direct consequence very soon only to throwing away the New after the mistaken and despised Old Testament; a course of procedure which is a main source of the unhappy confusion of all ideas and all endeavours in the midst of which we now live. Thus, only in other fashion than it happened among the Jews of those times, misconception arises as to the necessary connection, as wonderful as it is real, of the entire great history whose eternally beneficent fruits are now in question; nay, we are compelled to maintain that this error that is so powerful among us to-day is not only far less pardonable, but is far more pernicious than that. The truth is, the Old Testament contains a multitude of fundamental truths in such certainty and completeness that they cannot be more deeply grounded or better defended in the New Testament, but are everywhere presupposed as standing firm and inviolate since the old times. If it does not in other things attain the highest perfection, it yet not merely contains in itself the most active endeavours after it, but even touches upon it closely enough at least in some of its loftier points and elevations. And precisely because in it, or rather in the great whole which stands behind it, the ultimate perfection at which the entire movement, once so mightily active, aimed, was so surely anticipated, so clearly recognised, and so stedfastly pursued,—precisely this is not only the element of interest and instruction, but also the indispensable condition without which the consummation itself could never have come. There is no greater praise for the Old Testament than this, that without it the New Testament with all the fruits it brings home to us had not been possible.

V. 15. *The Transition by means of the Bible to Revelation and Religion.*

§ 142. If, now, the Bible is used by us in such a way in thousandfold application, it helps us as it alone aims to do and can do, as the means, unique of its kind and fully indispensable to-day, whereby we reach the goal to which it seeks to lead us, viz. the knowledge of the true revelation and religion, and loving obedience to the word of God in everything. It is not the only means which serves the men of our day to this end; beside it stand two other means, each of which may be powerful enough in itself. The one is the religious community itself in which we live, and which surrounds us from our earliest existence or from our entrance into it, with all its immortal blessings and all its admonitions and demands; essentially the same community in which for almost four thousand years the same revelation and religion has found its home, enlightening and blessing innumerable people of our race, and in which our life's best aim can also be recognised and attained. This community reveres the Bible as its sole, immutable, and sacred literary document, and being itself the living seat of the piety the Bible demands, it is a boon as great as if wholly different from the written word. The other means is (§ 135) the exercise and experience of this religion in the individual life, by which alone we appropriate it to ourselves and live in it independently, and which just on this account is also an indispensable means to the knowledge of it. But over and above these two means, the Bible is the sole invariably clear mirror of this revelation and religion, which alone enables us now to see whether error has slipped in or is slipping in to the great wide knowledge and practice of the Church or to our own intuition and practical life, and whether these two other means are as pure as they should be.

But, nevertheless, however high the Bible stands as the means to this higher aim, altogether unique and irreplaceable, and however carefully we must take pains to apply it as such rightly and perfectly, yet we may never forget that it is only a means for what is far above it, and should ever be held as alone our highest aim. It is only a passage or gate by which we arrive at the point whither alone we should come; let us not mistake the nature and value of the entrance, and regard it as itself the realm to which our way should ever lead us; and let us not think that we hear in this or that word of the Bible, the word of God Himself, without reflecting what the word of God actually is which we have implicitly to follow! Moreover, let us not hesitate and stumble in the way at this or that word of the Bible, so that what should elevate and save us becomes our offence and snare. As we may not be offended that it was only this single and apparently insignificant nation of antiquity in whose human incidents this sublime gift perfected itself which is to serve us for ever for our elevation and instruction, even so what is temporally imperfect in the Bible should not hinder us from rightly recognising and fruitfully appropriating the eternal truth in it, since we know that all that is visible is imperfect, yet that which is eternal can consummate itself in it; and thus let the Bible be sacred to us, but in such a way that we never forget that there is yet a higher sanctity whence whatever is immortal in it has been derived, and to which alone it seeks itself to raise us. Or does that fire shine forth from the letter without whose active energy the best and the most enduring element in the Bible could not have been—the Holy Spirit; let us not forget that this fire should result in something quite other than this, the mere glimmering forth upon us in single and isolated rays!

But what the still higher sanctity just mentioned is, and what its word demands of us, that must be more particularly elucidated subsequently, together with the question whether this word, as the Bible makes us acquainted with it, can be held to-day as the sole rule of our spiritual life.

INDEX OF SUBJECTS.

AARON, spokesman or prophet of Moses, 87 ; honour of house of, 268.
Abraham, as national leader, 184 ; as example of obedience to God, 34 ; where called "Prince of God," 268 ; his character in the Pentateuch, 289 n.
Acts of the Apostles, discourses in, 322 ; added to canon, 360.
Adam and Seth, apocryphal book of, 327 n.
Æschylus, 214 n.
Æsculapius, 227 n.
Ahaz, his conflict with Isaiah, 239 n.
Allegory, why art of, applied to Scripture, 382 ff., 424 ; employed by Paul, 384, but not in Epistles less elaborately planned, 448 ; never employed by Christ or His immediate disciples, 385, 448 ; employed by early Christians, 453.
Allodial estate, figurative reference to, in Old Covenant, 284 n.
Ammon, oracle of, 169.
Amos, the prophet, 52, 72 ; first to speak of wonders of skies, 231.
Angels, adoration of, vanishes before solitary grandeur of Christ, 130.
Antiquity, why revelation perfected in, 154 ff. ; remotest periods of, 158, 213 ; succession in problems of, 159 ; its earliest task, language, 159 f. ; dispersion of nations in, 161.
Apocalypse, see Revelation, Book of.
Apocrypha, described, 280 n., 364 ff. ; Old Testament, books of, when originated, 327 ; preservation of, 337.
Arabians, the religion of, 205.
Aramæans, the religion of, 205.
Aristophanes, favours high estimation of prophet, 233 n.
Ark of covenant, reverence for, checked, 217 ; tables of stone deposited in, 341.

Asia, Eastern, shows highest type of heathenism, 207, 212.
Assyrians, religion of, as influencing Israel, 264.
Astrological science in antiquity, 230.
Atheism, its possibility in Israel, 242 ; not characteristic of Chinese, 17, 180 f.
Authorship, how regarded in antiquity, 344 ; questions as to, of books of Scripture, 414 f.
Avesta, age of, 17 ; its preservation, 372.

BABEL, sanctuary at, 174.
Balaam, narrative of, 93, 167 ; prophecy of, 197, 201 ; heathen practices of, 213, 214 n., 215.
Barbarism, its historical appearance, 163.
Barjesus, why threatened with blindness, 299 n.
Baruch, Book of, 97, 295.
Birds, watching flight of, in augury, 219.
Books, sacred, Egyptian and Asiatic, 17, 247, 434 ff.
Brahminism, its characteristics, 178 f., 226 n., 435 ; transformed by Buddhism, 207 ; its sacred books, of priestly origin, 435.
Brahmins, a priestly race, 174.
Buddha, his rise and power, 178 ; his life the basis of older Buddhist literature, 436.
Buddhism, its deficiencies, 178 ; accurate knowledge of, desirable, 179 n. ; its community-founding, 204 ; its transformation of Brahminism, 207 ; its serpent-taming, 226 n. ; its books, a library for the cloister, 436.

CANON of Scripture, its formation, 347, 352 ; its aim, 424 f. ; its kernel, the

INDEX OF SUBJECTS.

Decalogue, 353 ; the ruling principles of its settlement, 354 ff., 403 f. ; prophetic books, etc., added, 348 ; the canon of the Pentateuch, 345 f., of Judas Maccabæus, 349 ; the Hellenistic canon, 350, the Christian, 350, 358 ff. ; the Jewish, after the time of Christ, 361 ff. ; relation of, to the great synagogue and to synods and Christian scholars, 357 ; founded upon the necessities and needs of revelation and religion, 437, 440.

Canticles, its anonymous character, 319, 321, 414 ; its value, 457.

Capacities, human, 10 f. ; the law of their development, 11 ; their fruits, 12.

Carthage, ancient works of, destroyed by Romans, 336.

Celts, the religion of, 205.

Cherub, original significance of, lost, 460.

Chinese, not atheists, 17, 180 f. ; their emperor seeks destruction of all literature, 443.

Christ, not simply a prophet, 45 ; the consummation of revelation, 111, 116, 251 ; is conscious of His Messiahship, 108 ; His idea of kinghood, 108 f., of the Perfect, 109 ; founds anew the kingdom of God, 110 ; possibilities realized by Him, 111 f. ; does not first seek truth, but has it always, 115 ; His perfect purity and repose, 117 ; His revelation not perfected till He is glorified, 119, 257 ; conditions of the perfecting of His revelation, 120 f. ; His peaceful glance into the future, 133 ; His final victory over everything heathen, 251 ff. ; distinguishes hagiocracy from previous era, 252 ; His death and resurrection break the yoke of the law, 255, and open the community of God to all nations, 256 ; His life throws back light on all the past, 289 ; His relation to the national life, 305 ; His discourses in the Gospels, 322 ; His references to ancient Scripture, 358, 445 ; Himself the true unity of Scripture, 431 ; His teaching historically conditioned, 458 ; not averse to summaries of truth, 455.

Christianity, its youthful energy, 179 n. ; the possibility of its falling into Buddhist error, 179 n. ; the essential question of, 254 ; perpetuates the commonwealth of Israel, 257 ; not a mixture of heathenism and Judaism, 258 f. ; impresses its own spirit on everything Greek, 259 ; inherits all the rich possessions of the past, 259 ; not to be wrested from its historical connection, 261 ; its conflict with heathenism, 298 f. ; brings consummation of Israel's literature, 315 f.

Chronicles, Book of, character of historical narrative in, 322.

Church, another name for community of God, 147 ; not the source of Scripture, 439 ; may not deal arbitrarily with Scripture, 440 ; a means of knowledge of truth, 464 f.

Cicero, 219 n.

Communities, Christian, commence collection of Christian Scriptures, 360.

Community, religious, in what its fellowship consists, 140 ff. ; its relation to national life, 156 ; feeling of the need of, in antiquity, 157 f. ; imperfect forms of (prophetic), 166-170 ; (prophetico-priestly), 170-174 ; (Zoroastrian), 176 f. ; (Buddhist), 177-179 ; (Confucian), 179-182 ; perfect form of, its pre-conditions (true conception of God), 183 f. ; (conflict with false), 184 f. ; (God-sent leader), 186 ; founding of Moses' great work, 186 f. ; advantage of the true, 190 ff. ; overleaps national limits, 201 ; limits of, broken by Christ, 256 ; consummation of, in Christian Church, 258 f. ; its life-impulse and characteristic, the Holy Spirit, 272-76, 277 ; the power of the fundamental thought of, 293 ff. ; a means of attaining knowledge of the truth, 464 f.

Confucianism, its ethical system, 180 ; its defects, 181 f., 436 ; the liability of civilised nations to, 180, 182 n.

Confucius, his age, 17 ; his writings classical rather than sacred, 245.

Conscience, not the source of revelation, 9.

Creation, narrative of, 153, 263 n. ; its excellence, 409.

DANIEL, Book of, its pictures of heathenism, 210 ; the period of its origin, 315 n., 364, 414 ; refers to wonders of the skies, 231 n. ; its example of deliverance from yoke of letter, 384 ; its place in canon, 417.

David, prophecy in time of, 51 ; called "man of God," 267 ; his lyric poetry, 310 ; not the author of the whole Psalter, 414.

Deification of man, not known in Israel, 267 ff.

INDEX OF SUBJECTS. 469

Delphi, oracle of, 169.
Deterioration possible in case of all activities of mind, 193.
Deuteronomy, Book of, its laws concerning prophets, 91 n.; its influence, 96; its spiritualization of the old law, 104; its admonitions against worship of the heavenly host, 231, and against the prophet who works by miracle, 240; rebukes offences against contents and spirit of revelation, 249, 444; anticipates second Moses, 249; speaks in the spirit of Moses, 326, 344 f.; its origin, 344; its value and worth, 345.
Divination, gift of, as belonging to the high priest, 269.
Divining cup, Egyptian usage of, 221; Persian usage of, 221 n.
Dodona, oracle of, 169.
Dreams, revelation by, 227 f.

ECCLESIASTES, Book of, its prologue and epilogue, 319 f.; the form of its composition, 327; its addition to the canon, 370; not written by Solomon, 414; its value, 457.
Egyptian kingdom, 167; its military power, 174; its different gods, 173; its seductive charm, 185; the antithesis of a true national community, 185 f.
Egyptian religion characterized, 204, 207; its religion of the dead, 225; its serpent-taming, 226; its sacred books, 17, 247 n.; how far Israel under Moses was influenced by it, 262 f.
Elijah, 167; his prophetic power, 90, 95, 235; called a "man of God," 267.
Elisha, 167; his recourse to music, 229; called a "man of God," 267.
Enoch, Book of, 107, 315, 327, 364 ff., 379.
Essenes, their origin, 178.
Esther, Book of, a transition to the Apocrypha, 365; stands alone in the Old Testament, 369; its addition to the canon, 370; why accepted, 406; its colour and form, 421.
European kingdoms, their danger of sinking into a Chinese condition of things, 182 n.
Experience, religious, the test of truth, 441; a means to knowledge of truth, 465.
Ezekiel. gives the doctrine of prophecy, 74, 94.
Ezra, Book of 416; fourth Book of, 366.

FAITH, in Moses, 232; in Christ, 232; in Scripture, its possible tendency to heathenism, 243; its origin, 244; not compelled by Scripture, 396 f.
Fear of God, its importance, 30; its nature, 31; associated with knowledge, 33; its transfiguration into love of God, 32, 35.
Franciscans, their origin, 178.
Freedom, of prophecy, 89; in public affairs, 91.

GERMANS, their relation to Christianity, 198, 205; feudal age of, 284.
Gnosticism, strife of Christianity against, 299 n.; relation of, to Islamism, 407; its treatment of Scripture, 433.
God, elevated idea of, in Israel, 267; an ancient designation of, 461.
Gospel of the Old Testament, 284.
Greek writings added to ancient Scripture, 350.
Greeks, the religion of, 205; the prophets of, 232.

HAGIOCRACY, significance of the time of, 103, 105 f.; explanation of heathen tendency of, 252 ff.
Heathen, the, 201; reverence for Old Testament among, 247 n.; Paul's view of, 260; Christ's relation to, 260.
Heathenism, defined, 200 f., 207 f.; its degenerate revelation, 193, 202; its arrested development, 203; its entrance into Israel, 197 f., 214, 223; its distinction from true religion, 202 f., 204; its better elements, 203 f.; its varieties, 205 f., 212; its failure, 206, 208; Israel's conflict with, 208 ff., 211; all types of, dealt with in Scripture, 212; its faith, superstition, 212; John's opposition to, 260; rise of power of Holy Spirit impossible in, 276; Christianity's conflict with, 298.
Heavenly bodies, references to, in Bible, 183, 231.
Hebrews, Epistle to, follows Paul at a wide interval, 128; anonymous authorship of, 319; added to canon, 370.
Hegelian school, its injurious influence, 250 n.
Heights, or high places, 229.
Hellenism, not predominant in Christianity, 259.
Hermes Trismegistos, age and character of his writings, 247 n.
Herodotus, reference to oracles in, 168.
Heroes, age of, 164; characteristics of, 45 f.

Hexateuch, its name and period, 409.
Hieroglyphics, Egyptian, 50 n.
High priest, oracle of, 102 n. ; never deified in Israel, 269.
Hindoos, the religion of, 205, 207 ; law-book of, 345 n.
Hippocrates, 228 n., 244.
History, as interaction of human and divine spirit, 273, 459 ; freely represented by Greeks and Romans, 321 ; fidelity of Biblical, 322 ; value of Biblical, 458 f.
Holy Spirit, the life-impulse of the community in Israel, 270 f. ; as not purely divine but humanly divine, 271 f. ; as a purely divine power, 273, 277 ; as historical, 274, and historically developed, 275 ; impossible in heathenism, 276 ; its power enjoyed before consciously realized, 276 ; pre-eminently characteristic in Israel, 277 ; realized in time of peril, 278, 283 ; inalienable in the community, 279 ; firmly established on the return from exile, 279 ; conception of, transfigured by Christ, 279 ; New Testament full of its power, 280 ; witness to the reality of revelation, 281 f. ; its relation to Scripture, 355, 359, 393 ff., 398 f. ; its power spreads in all nations, 400 ; its ultimate end more than revelation of truth, 466. See also Spirit of God.
Homer, 131 ; his poetry, 205, 244.
Hosea, 235 ; does not picture the ideal prophet, 53 ; warns against formality and ritualism, 249 ; form of discourse in, significant, 304.
Household gods, 220.
Hyrcanus I. revives the oracle of the high priest, 102 n.

Ignatius, Epistles of, 329.
Imagination, must apprehend things spiritual and divine, 240 ; value of, for true revelation and religion, 241 ; its power not repressed by spiritual religion, 269.
Immortality, faith in, inspires artificial literature of Old Testament, 325 ; traces of belief in, in Old Testament, 460.
Incantations, 229.
India, its Buddhists, 178, 217 ; its Brahmins, 174 ; its sacred books, 434 ; its cultured life, 177 ; distinction of its ancient people, 178 ; reverence for springs and rivers in, 216.
Introduction, what properly belongs to the science of, 301.

Isaac, his expedient to induce the prophetic mood, 229.
Isaiah, the prophet, 53, 90, 93, 94 ; occupied with subordinate service, 76 ; complains of formalism, 105, 249 ; his resistance of evil counsel, 235 ; his relation to miracle, 239 ; warns against mere repetition of God's word, 249 ; the calm and secure repose of his style, 94 n. ; the second or younger, 378, 414.
Isis, priests of, 225 n., 233 ; dignity of prophet of, 233 n.
Islamism, its mixed character, 10 ; its idea of religion, 34 ; its doctrine of the divine unity, 202 ; its wide diffusion, 208 ; its relation to Gnosticism, 407.
Israel, its early prophets, 50 ; its peculiar glory in its prophets, 51 ; its prosperity in the time of David, 60 ; kingly power in, struggles with prophecy, 70 f. ; its transformation, 151 ; its early superstitions, 218 f. ; the only possible seat of true revelation, 154, 292, 297 ; born again by its new religion, 194 ; need of true community of God satisfied in, 182 ff. ; its power of self-regulation, 191 ; entrance of heathenism into, 197 f., 214 ; its distinction from the nations, 201 ; the conflict with heathenism, the sum and glory of its history, 209, 251, 261, 264 ff. ; decline of prophetism in, 233, 236 ; problems of faith early discussed in, 239 n. ; atheism in, 242 ; its perverse faith, 243 ; its new kind of heathenism, 250 ; its place among the nations, 261 f. ; its indebtedness to heathen nations, 262 ff. ; its loyalty to its high calling, 264 ; its indestructible life, 265 f. ; objects to lowering the divine to the level of the human, 266 f. ; or giving divine honours to the living or dead, 268 f. ; designated a holy nation, 284 f. ; God's covenant with, 285 ; its inspiring retrospect, 288 ; influence of its regarding itself as holy, 290 ; advantage of its openness and freedom of life, 290, 304 f. ; its obstinacy subdued and overcome, 291 f. ; its promised blessings conditional, 293 ; its limitations broken by selection of remnant, 293 ; grand continuity of its history, 294 ff. ; its last aim, world-wide diffusion of truth, 296 ; growth and influence of its literature, 308 ff. ; decline of originality in its literature, 314 f. ; variety and excellence of its literature, 317 f., 368 ;

INDEX OF SUBJECTS. 471

its artificial literature, 325; its entire history shows to the world the power of the Holy Spirit, 400 f.
Italians, the religion of the ancient, 205.

JACOB, the blessing of, 323.
James, Hebrew stamp of Epistle of, 316.
Jeremiah, the prophet, 53, 74; his doctrine of prophecy, 94; desires new covenant, 105; rejects the dream-oracle, 228; regards observance of signs of heaven as heathenism, 231; resists false prophets, 235; seeks no proof from miracle, 240; warns against perverse religion, 249; laments Israel's stiff-neckedness, 291; his style, 422.
Jewish scholars, their division of the Bible, 363 n.; limit the canon, 361, 365, 463; approve unsuitable reading against Christianity, 386; modern, misstatements of, about Sadducees and Pharisees, 250 n.
Jews, Egyptian, contend about temple in Egypt, 386.
Job, an example of the reciprocal action of revelation and religion, 39 ff.
Job, Book of, its character, 310; added to the canon, 348; period when its composition became possible, 92; "fear" used by Eliphaz as brief expression for religion, 34; artistically depicts the higher antiquity, 213; its author well versed in history, 214 n.; its fine discrimination in character, 228 n.; reference to wonders of skies in, 231; its anonymous authorship, 319, 321; its wide historical contemplation, 405 f.; its value, 459; its mysteries solved at the close, 462.
John, the Apostle, his repose of mind, 133; his style, 128, 316, 422, 448; aim of his Gospel, 132; his attitude to Jew and Gentile, 260 f.; freedom of his Gospel, 322.
John the Baptist, his advent, 107.
Jonah, Book of, reveals some of the experiences of prophets, 67.
Joseph, his life shows power of resistance to evil, 37.
Josephus, his distinction with respect to the Bible, 363 n., 395; his view of inspiration, 395 n.
Joshua, period of his leadership of Israel, 100; significance of his name, 146 n.
Joshua, Book of, 409.
Jubilees, Book of, 325, 366.
Jude, Epistle of, parallel with 2 Peter, 128.

Judith, Book of, 107, 327; its value, 457.
Justin Martyr, 214 n.
Justinus, 228 n.

KINGDOM of God, not consummated by prophecy, 99; starting-point of the Baptist's ministry, 107; established by Christ, 110, 115, 121. See also Community, religious.
Kingdom of Judah, its continuance secured by Isaiah, 235.
Kingdom of the ten tribes, early degeneracy of its prophets, 234; peculiar style of its prophets, 237.
Kingship, Christ's idea of, 108 f.
Knowledge, religious, the basis of true piety, 32 f.; grows by experience, 35.
Koheleth, see Ecclesiastes, Book of.
Koran (Qor'an), how it arose, 387; effect of exaggerated reverence for, 389; its style, poetic, 50 n.; its superstitious use, 246; the preservation of its text, 373; its unhistorical character, 407; its retrogression on the path of development, 434.

LAMENTATIONS, Book of, anonymous, 97.
Language, its origin, 161 f.; Renan's view of, inadequate, 161 n.; its insufficiency as basis of community, 162.
Literature, its uses, 245; invests authors with its glory, 244; sacred, strange use of, 246; its relation to national life, 307 f.; gradually developed, 309; impersonation in, 321; artificial, speaks in name of old prophets, 326: returns to simplicity in Christianity, 328; artificial, in New Testament, 328; artificial, not to be characterized as fictitious or counterfeit, 330, 417; its higher service, 333; causes of destruction of, 336.
Livingstone, 227, 233.
Logos, idea of, not borrowed from Greek philosophy, 259.
Lord of Hosts, origin of designation, obscure, 461.
Lot, the, practice of, late, 222.
Luke, though Gentile Christian cleaves to Israel, 260.
Luke's Gospel, its style, 316; its prologue, 320; found early almost everywhere in the Church, 360; added to canon, 370.

MACCABÆAN age, brings no permanent gain to Israel, 315.

INDEX OF SUBJECTS.

Maccabees, Books of, reference to, 9, 98, 107, 315, 327; character of their historical narrative, 322.
Maccabees, time of, prophetless, 98 f.
Magic, arts of, 228 f.
Man, his purpose and destiny, 211.
Man of God, a designation exceptionally used in Israel, 267; its significance in the pastoral Epistles, 377.
Manasseh, 96.
Mandæans, their Scripture, 433.
Manichæan heresy rejected by early Christianity, 179 n.
Mankind, without knowledge of God inconceivable, 13; division of, into nations and languages, 161; relapse of, to barbarism, 163.
Mark's Gospel does not specially refer to Old Testament, 448.
Massôra, the, its character and aim, 373.
Matthew's Gospel, Old Testament passages in, inserted by last editor, 448.
Mediæval Christianity, its division into saintly and secular, 179 n.
Melampopides, hereditary prophets, 233 n.
Memphis, sanctuary at, 174.
Messiah, Christ's consciousness of His office, 108; the perfect kingdom of, 110; power of expectation of, in Israel, 293, 314.
Micah stands forth against false prophets, 93, 234; announces no doctrine of prophecy, 94.
Miracles, their rationale, 238; may hinder spiritual faith, 239; not relied upon by Deuteronomist and prophets, 240.
Mohammed, deterioration of his character, 387; his arbitrary conception of what a Holy Scripture must be, 387 f.; his aim in the Koran, 433; possibility of advent of another, 434 n.
Moloch oracle, condemned in Deuteronomy, 214 n.
Monogamy, favoured by spirit of true religion, 153.
Mormon Bible, possible only in North America, 389 n.
Mosaic revelation and community, deficiencies of, 195, 253 f.; how far influenced by Egyptian religion, 262 f.
Moses, not simply a prophet, 45, 50 f., 77, 83 f.; unique among heroes of the spirit, 46 f.; reveals afresh a known Deity, 77, 79; opens anew intercommunion between man and God, 78; founds a new community, 78, 82 f.; starts from true conception of God, 79; finds life in the knowledge of the true God, 80; his sublime self-abnegation, 80 f.; his pre-eminence among prophets (as national leader), 84 f., (as seer), 85, (as chief servant or friend of Jahveh), 86; spokesman of God to Egyptians, 87; favours free prophecy, 89; stands at head of a line of prophets, 90; fulfils pre-conditions of founding true religious community, 183 ff.; the community, the sum and crown of his work, 186; deficiencies of his revelation, 195 f.; his conflict with Egyptian priests and magicians, 87, 207, 239 n., 263; his setting up a brazen serpent, 227; intercedes for Israel, 265; overtaken by momentary unbelief, 289 n.; mode of action changes with the times, 304; subsequent revival of voice of, 324; breaks the first copy of Decalogue, 342; his name attached to the Pentateuch, 379.
Moses, grandson of, debases revelation, 169.
Music, inspiration of, in prophecy, 229.
Mystery, in revelation, 27; in religion, 36; different significance and uses of the word, 461 ff.
Mythology, tradition in Israel different from, 241.

Nahum, an example of after-working of the earlier prophetic spirit, 313.
National life, its relation to revelation, 162, 201; always nourished on some fundamental thought, 287; its relation to literature, 307.
Nations, the, 200 f.; dispersion of, 162; their struggles for territory, 163 f.; absorbed by other questions than revelation, 297.
Nazarites, their origin, 178.
Necromancy, condemned in Deuteronomy, 214 n.; connected with ventriloquism, 225 n., 227.
New Testament, character of its literature, 316 f.; no historical significance in its references to Old Testament authorship, 370, 379 n.; does not canonize itself, 398; not to be sundered from the Old, 419; claims no superiority over the Old, 420; its citation and use of the Old, 447; principles implied in, affecting our view of Scripture, 449 f.; bears traces of different modes of thought and speech, 451; had not existed without the Old, 464; its mysteries, 462.
Nineveh, sanctuary at, 174.

INDEX OF SUBJECTS. 473

OLD TESTAMENT, revelation of, contrasted with that of the New, 3, 32, 128, 138 ; its prophecy revived in the New, 131, 316 ; regarded as full of emblems and types, 450 f. ; illumined afresh by the New, 452 f. ; summaries of truth in, 455 f. ; folly of rejecting it, 463 ; its greatest praise, 464.

Oracle, word for, found in oldest languages, 24 ; seats of, in antiquity, 162, 167 f. ; prophetic, as centre of influence, 166 ; artificial means of obtaining, 168 f. ; combined with the sanctuary, 171 ; at Dodona, Delphi, Ammon, 169 ; lays foundation of communities of men, 49 ; the visible, 219 f. ; the audible, 217 f. ; priestly not so esteemed as prophetic, 221 ; causes of decline of heathen, 235 ff. ; difference of heathen and Hebrew, 237 ; difficulty of belief in, how met, 238 ; of the dead, 225, 323 ; revival of high-priestly, 102 n.

Origen, 214 n.

Origins, Book of, characterized, 311 ; referred to, 221 n., 281. See *History of Israel*, Eng. tr. i. 74-96.

PANINI, the celebrity of, 244.

Pastoral Epistles, the, colourless, 128.

Patriarchs, revelation in age of, 213 f. ; their free glance to starry heavens, 183 ; their reverence for place, 215 ; voices of, revived, 323.

Paul, an example of the reciprocal action of revelation and religion, 39 ; his individual or private revelation, 43 f. ; his style, 128 ; his eschatological revelation, and doctrine concerning, 134 f. ; his view of Christianity, 254 f. ; shows the constraint of the law is abolished, 255 ; his resort to allegory, 384 ; his familiar Epistles free from allegory, 448.

Paul, Epistles of, Hellenistic influence in, 316 ; peculiar character of Colossians, 448 ; Ephesians written for Gentile Christians, 257, and artificial in its style, 128 ; freedom from law shown in Galatians, 2 Corinthians, Romans, 255 ; no allegory in 1 and 2 Thessalonians, Philippians, and Philemon, 448 ; Ephesians, 1 and 2 Timothy, and Titus written in his name and spirit, 328, 448.

Penates, reverence for, in Israel, 220.

Pentateuch, its formation, 345 f. ; becomes standard for canon, 347 ; not written throughout by Moses, 414.

Persia, character of ancient nation, 176 f. : its religion, 205, 207, 216, 264.

Peter, his style, 128, 422.

Peter, Second Epistle of, written in Peter's name and spirit, 228.

Pharisees represent heathen element in Israel, 263.

Philo, flavours Hebrew wisdom with Greek, 315.

Philostratus, 298 n.

Phœnicians, the religion of, 205, 214 ; influence of, upon Israel, 263.

Piety, right attitude of mind, 152 ; transfigures all life and pursuits, 153.

Plotinus, 298 n.

Poetry, its special faculty, 11 ; its wide range and possible reproductiveness, 40 ; compared with prophecy, 90 ; is earlier than revelation, 50.

Porphyry, 214 n., 219 n., 228 n.

Priesthood, in Israel different from heathen, 268 f.

Priests, elders or leaders of the community, 149.

Prophecy, compared with poetry, 90 ; effects of, upon Israel, 91 f. ; its cultivation to highest perfection, 93, 311 ; doctrine of, late in origin, 94 ; works itself out, 94 f. ; causes of its end, 96 f. ; resistance to corruption of, 234 f. ; publication of, as pamphlet literature, 312 f. ; not anonymous, 319 ; artificial, 324 ; true, its power of recovery, 236.

Prophet, the, ideal pictures of, 52 ; as pupil, 53 ; as man of the spirit, 54 f. ; as messenger, 55 ; as servant of God, 55 ; as outlooker or scout, 56 f. ; as seer, 57 ff. ; limits of his prophecy, 60 f. ; his self-collectedness in ecstasy, 63 f., 130, 232 : as spokesman of God, 65 ff., 322 ; his Hebrew and Greek names, 68 ; the under-prophet, 69, 232 ; as popular orator, 71, 304 ; his life is to harmonize with his word, 72 f. ; not violently to attempt fulfilment of his own prophecy, 73 f. ; as interpreter of the true God, 75 ; as advocate, 290 ; mediator and intercessor, 76 ; his dress, 97 ; his energy and violence, 105 ; degeneracy of heathen, 232 ; hereditary, 233 ; his resort to miracle, 238.

Prophetesses, exceptional in Israel, 233.

Prophetism, causes of its decline in Israel, 233.

Prophetless time, the, 98.

Prophets, schools of, 233.

Proverbs, Book of, when collected, 348 ; receives additions before placed in the canon, 370 ; value of, 457.

Qor'an, see Koran.

Rabbinical literature and teaching, 102, 103.
Rachel, her household god, 172 n.
Rebecca, her household god, 172 n.
Rechabites, their origin, 178.
Reformation, in sixteenth century, 179 n.
Religion, or the fear of God, the aim of revelation, 29 f. ; distinct from superstition, 31 ; transfigured into love of God, 31 f. ; associated with knowledge of God, 33 ff. ; not mere sentiment, 36 f. ; tests and verifies revelation, 37 f.
Reminiscence, of times of patriarchs by Moses, 79 ; of times of Moses by prophets, 99 ff. ; of prophetic period by subsequent age, 101 f.
Remnant, in Israel, 266 ; doctrine of, breaks national limitation, 293.
Renan, criticised, 159 n. ; reference to errors of, 205 n.
Revelation, immediate and mediate compared, 5–7 ; mediate contrasted with poetry, 7, 40, 50, with science and doctrine, 7, 8 ; its special faculty, 8, 9, 12 ; an accomplished fact, 24 ; typical example of, 25 ; eager search for, 26 ; its mysterious origin, but practical nature, 27 ; involved in existence of God and man's capacity to know Him, 27 f. ; gradually perfected, 28 f. ; of the individual, its strength and weakness, 42 ff. ; of the prophets, from a definite deity, 47 f., and shared and verified by others, 49, 51 ; not consummated by prophecy, 105 f. ; not consummated in Christ's earthly life, 118 f. : conditions of its perfecting, 120 f. ; meaning of its perfecting (no previously-revealed truth lost), 123 ff. ; (direct presence of God with men), 127 f. ; (revival and perfecting of spirit of prophecy), 129 ff. ; special marks of its consummation—(simple divine certainty), 136 f. ; (agreement with immediate revelation), 137 f. ; (universal application), 139 ; its results—(1) fellowship of (light), 142, (truth), 143 f., (life), 145 ; (2) Priesthood, 148 ; (3) Spiritualization of humanity in itself and its laws, science, and industry, 150 ff. ; in heathenism and in Israel (compared), 154-192 ; (in conflict) 193 ; deficiencies of Mosaic, 195 f., 253 f. ; its development in Israel, 199 ; deterioration in, possible, 193 f. ; energies of, overtopped by science and art, 206 ; earliest means of obtaining, 213 f. ; perverse means to obtain, 211 ff. ; associated with (sacred places), 215-217 ; (objects of nature), 217–220 ; (images and works of art), 220 f. ; (the lot), 222 ; (sacrifices), 224 ; reality of, attested by Holy Spirit, 281 f. ; intended for all nations, 300 ; its priority to Scripture, 395 ; of what it consists, 301 f. ; its relation to national life, 304 ; is to be sought in its first sources, 456.
Revelation, Book of, its authorship, 131 ; the time of its composition, 133 ; shows purity and anti-heathen character of Christian community, 258 n. ; its Hebrew impress, 316 ; stands alone in the New Testament, 369 ; added without change to canon, 370 ; its last verses, 379 ; its mysteries artistic, 462.
Ridicule of prophecy, mark of its security, 93.
Romans, their idea of religion, 33 ; introduce foreign faiths, 206 ; destroy literature of Carthage, 336 ; hostility of, to Jewish and Christian Scriptures, 336 f.

Sabæan heresy rejected by early Christianity, 179 n.
Sabbath, free treatment of, by Christ, 419.
Sadducees, their atheistic tendency, 242.
Samaritans, separate from Jewish community, 349 ; contend about Mount Garizim, 386.
Samson and degeneracy of revelation, 47.
Sanchoniathon, work of, 205 n.
Sanctuary, as national centre, 170, 173.
Sanscrit, its name for serpent of abyss, 227 n.
Satan, first mention of, in Book of Job, 461.
Schools, learned, their origin, 103 ; their danger, 104 f.
Schools of prophets, not founded by Moses, 89 ; their uses, 233.
Science, its province, 8 ; possibly exhaustible, 40 ; involves special faculty in man, 11 ; astrological, in antiquity, 230.
Scripture, revelation prior to, 395 ; perverse faith in, tends to heathenism, 243, 250 ; origin of faith in, 244 ; reverence for, how it arose, 246 ff. ;

INDEX OF SUBJECTS. 475

known and admired by heathen, 247 ; becomes superstitiously regarded, 248, 381 ; prophetic warnings against misuse of, 249 ; proof of excellence of, 249, 309, 405 ; fidelity of its narrative, 289 n. ; not the original revelation itself, 302 f. ; not spoken of in earlier centuries, 306 ; its influence on the national life, 306 ff. ; its gradual development, 309 f. ; its variety, 317, 420 f. ; anonymous books of, 318 f. ; simplicity of, 319, 416 ; its conciseness of expression, 422 ; preservation of books of, 337 f., 371 f. ; the Ten Commandments the first foundation of, 341, 352 f. ; its direct relation to national life, 306 ff., 352 ; its first four circles, 353 ; union of New and Old facilitated by LXX., 360 ; compilation of its books, 369 ; history of some books of, forgotten, 370 ; confessedly written by men, 376 ; does not itself claim to be sacred, 378, 398 ; how it becomes sacred, 391 ; nature of its sanctity, 392, 437 ; misuse of, by Samaritans and Jews, 386 ; contempt of, arises from exaggerated view of its sacredness, 390 ; disputes about, among Christians, 386 f. ; its relation to the Holy Spirit, 393 ff., 398 f. ; its value seen in its use, 397 ; not destined for special orders of men but for all, 402, 408 ; its thorough historical character, 407 ff. ; its wide historical range, 405, 408 ff. ; its wealth of human experience, 410 f. ; sceptical criticism and treatment of, 412, 438 ; the sufficiency of its historical element, 413 ff., 418, 458 f. ; its high significance, 417 ; questions as to authorship of, 414 f. ; its unity in its contents and aim, 423–428 ; its unity often erroneously sought, 423 f. ; its unity in Christ, 431 ; its high moral elevation, 426 f. ; its inviolability, 430 ; itself the fruit of a long history, 430 ; its imperishable worth, 442 ; does not prescribe how it is to be used, 443, 451 ; different schools of interpretation of, 446 ; difference between exposition and application of, 452 f. ; historical method of interpretation essential, 454 ; minute particulars in words and sentences important, 453 ; its great truths clear as sunlight, 461 ; its mysteries, various in significance, 462 ; early errors respecting, not to mislead us, 463 ; is our way of entrance to truth, not the whole realm itself, 465.

Seer, oldest name for prophet, 65 ; parallel with prophet, 85.
Semitic nations, the religion of, 205 f., 214 ; writing known in, before Moses, 330 f.
Septuagint, renderings of, 10, 34, 218 f., 220, 225 ff., 229, 263.
Seraph, original significance of, lost, 460.
Serpent-oracle, an oracle of the dead, 227.
Shamans, their prophecy, 225 n.
Shiloh and its ark, 216.
Sibyl, derivation of the word, 216 n.
Sibylline books, superstitious use of, 246.
Sibyl-oracle, its early practice, 216 ; imitation of, in Jewish literature, 315.
Sirach, Book of, estimated, 364 n.
Sodom, tradition of, 263 n.
Solomon, prophecy in time of, 51 ; books of, united with Proverbs, 369, 425.
Son of God, a designation reserved in Israel for one unique personage, 267.
Song of Songs, see Canticles.
Speech, human, never without a word for God, 17 ; compared with revelation, 135 ; its formation in antiquity, 160. See Language.
Spence Hardy, reference to, 225 n.
Spirit, definition of, 273 f. ; ideal impersonalization of, 274, 279.
Spirit of God, contrasted with word of God, 2 ; the sum of forces underlying the universe, 19 ; how said to come upon men, 46, 54 ; the free wide action of, 88 f. ; with God Himself essentially one, 273.
Spirit of man, its capacities, 10 ; historic development of, 11 ; fruits of, 12 ; its earliest activity, 13 ; law of its exercise, 14, 15 ; its first knowledge of God, 15, 16, 19, 20, 21, and desire to know His will, 17, 18, 25, and to know Him, 22 ; accessible to the Divine Spirit, 272.
Spirit, unholy, possibility of, in Israel, 273.
Spiritual life, more than truth needful for, 171.
Stars, worship of, condemned, 231 ; conspicuous to Eastern shepherd-tribes, 183.
Strabo, reference to oracles in, 168.
Superstitious practices, classified in Deuteronomy, 214 n. ; block up the way to God, 223 ; resisted by patriarchs, 214 n. ; with respect to place (hills, caverns, springs, streams),

215 f. ; to observation of trees, 217 ; of birds, 219 ; the divining cup, 220 f. ; images, 220 ; the lot, 222 ; serpent-taming, 226 ; dreams, 227 ; sacred books, 246.
Susannah, Book of, 280 n.

TATIAN, 214, 217, 228 n.
Temple, reverence for, checked, 217.
Ten Commandments, foundation of the Old Testament, 341 ; granite substratum of the whole Bible, 455 ; their incomparable excellence, 309 ; are their own authentication, 318 ; inscribed with finger of God, 342 ; second copy of, 342.
Text of Scripture, exactitude sought in, 372 ; original, how recoverable, 374 f. See Massôra.
Thebes, sanctuary at, 174.
Theology, comparative, why needed, 1.
Timothy, drawn to Christ by Old Testament, 397.
Tobit, Book of, 327 ; its value, 457.
Truth, of things, 19 ; definition of, 28 ; always won from its opposite, 404 ; is its own evidence, 451.

UNBELIEF in Israel, 240.
Under-prophets, 232.
Urim and Thummim, 220 n., 221.

VAMBERY, 225 n.
Veda, the, 17 ; its preservation, 372 : guarding of its text, 373.
Vedic songs, 203.
Ventriloquism, practised by necromancers and others, 225 n., 227.
Voices, divine, 7, 103. See Oracle.
Vulgate, 395.

WAY, the, Christianity so called, 144 n.
Wisdom of Solomon, Book of, 9 n., 107, 279 n., 280, 315, 369 ; its value, 457.
Women, sensuous arts abandoned to, in Israel, 229 ; could not officiate as priests, 230 ; exceptionally tolerated as prophetesses in Israel, 233.
Word of God, its broader sense, 1, 2 ; its reality, 20 ; in the Bible, 3 ; moment of first experience of, 21 ; difficulties respecting, 3 ; its peculiarity as authoritative command, 23.
Writing, known and practised very early, 331 ; its first service, 331 ; its further use, 332.

ZOROASTER, his celebrity, 176 ; unsettled questions concerning, 177 n.
Zoroastrianism, 204 ; its scanty literature, 434.

INDEX OF SCRIPTURE REFERENCES.

GENESIS.

CHAP.	PAGE
i.,	262
i. 28–30,	25
i.–xi. 26,	408
ii. 5–25,	25
ii. 18–23,	160
ii. 24,	453
iii.,	25
iii. 1,	226
iii. 20,	263
iv. 1,	263
iv. 6,	25
vi. 4 f.,	25
vii. 13,	23
ix. 18–24,	421
x. 5,	201
x. 32,	201
xi. 27–end,	409
xv.,	213
xv.,	227
xv. 5,	183
xvi. 13,	33
xvi. 14,	23
xix. 30–38,	421
xx. 7,	50
xx. 8,	32
xx. 11,	34
xxii. 1–18,	34
xxii. 17,	183
xxii. 1–19,	225
xxv. 22,	50, 172
xxv. 30–34,	421
xxvi. 24,	227
xxvii. 3 ff.,	229
xxviii. 10–22,	227
xxviii. 16 f.,	33
xxxi. 10 f.,	227
xxxi. 19 f.,	172
xxxv. 2–4,	172
xxxv. 5,	34
xxxvii. 6 ff.,	227
xxxviii. 9 ff.,	421
xli. 40, 44,	75
xlix. 1–27,	323
xlix. 17,	226
xlix. 22–26,	323

EXODUS.

CHAP.	PAGE
i. 8–xv. 21,	163
ii. 23–25,	186
iii. 11–xv. 27,	84
iii. 15,	77
iii. 17 ff.,	79
iv. 2–9,	239
iv. 10, 17,	70
iv. 10–20,	87
iv. 16,	75
vi. 29–xv. 21,	36
vii. 1 f.,	70, 75, 87
vii. 3 ff.,	79
vii. 8–12,	239
xi. 3,	110
xiii. 19–22,	186
xiv. 30 f.,	186
xv. 1–18,	295
xv. 11,	33
xv. 17,	286
xv. 18,	146
xvii. 1–7,	239
xvii. 16,	237, 295, 421
xix.,	284, 306
xix.–xxi.,	189
xix.–xxv.,	100
xix. 3–6,	285
xix. 4–6,	237
xix. 9,	232
xx. 4,	214
xx. 6,	32
xx. 7,	214
xxii. 18,	230
xxiii. 20–33,	69, 209, 309, 324
xxiv.,	306
xxviii. 15–30,	221
xxxii. 7–9 ff.,	265
xxxii. 9 ff.,	291
xxxiii. 7–11,	82
xxxiii. 19,	237
xxxiv. 6 f.,	237
xxxiv. 29 f.,	33
xxxiv. 29–35,	82, 88, 396
xxxv. 11,	85

LEVITICUS.

CHAP.	PAGE
viii. 8,	221
x. 3,	237
xviii.,	237
xviii. 24,	201
xix.,	237
xix. 31,	214, 226
xx. 6, 27,	227
xxvi. 1 f.,	214

NUMBERS.

CHAP.	PAGE
xi. 24–29,	89, 277
xii. 3,	110
xii. 6,	228
xii. 6–8,	62
xii. 16,	146
xiv. 18,	237
xvi. 28,	281
xvii. 1–10,	217
xx. 1–13,	239
xxi. 27,	368
xxii.–xxiv.,	48, 93, 421
xxii. 24,	213
xxii. 31,	22
xxii. 31–33,	23
xxii. 41,	220
xxiii. 3,	219
xxiii. 4,	220
xxiii. 9,	197, 201
xxiii. 14–16,	220
xxiii. 23,	219
xxiii. 28,	220
xxiv. 1,	219 f.

DEUTERONOMY.

CHAP.	PAGE
iv. 2,	249
iv. 5,	95
iv. 7,	162
iv. 19,	231, 285
v. 10,	32
v. 29 f.,	249
vi. 5,	32
vii. 6,	284
viii. 3,	282
viii. 24,	287
ix. 6 13,	291

INDEX OF SCRIPTURE REFERENCES.

DEUTERONOMY—contin'd.
CHAP.	PAGE
x. 13,	32
x. 16,	291
xi. 1,	32
xi. 26–28,	105
xii. 7,	287
xii. 31,	214
xiii. 1,	249
xiii. 1–5,	91
xiii. 2–6,	228
xiii. 2–7,	240
xiii. 5,	30
xiv. 1,	267
xiv. 2,	284
xvii. 3,	231
xvii. 11,	249
xviii. 9–22,	91
xviii. 10 f.,	214, 225
xviii. 15,	78, 107
xviii. 15–22,	98
xviii. 18,	249
xxvi. 18,	284
xxviii. 14,	249
xxx. 11–20,	105
xxxi. 9–13,	451
xxxi. 17,	291
xxxii. 8 f.,	285
xxxiii. 1,	267
xxxiii. 3,	287 f.
xxxiii. 11 f.,	286
xxxiii. 28,	197
xxxiv. 10–12,	249
xxxiv. 11,	78

JOSHUA.
i. 7,	249
xxiii. 6,	249

JUDGES.
iii. 10,	46
iii. 15,	46
v.,	295
v. 4 f.,	100, 284, 288
vi. 34,	46
vii. 13,	227
ix. 37,	218
xi. 29,	46
xiii. 25,	47
xiv. 6,	46
xiv. 19,	46
xv. 14,	46
xvii. f.,	169
xvii.–xxi.,	291

1 SAMUEL.
ii. 1–10,	295
ii. 22–25,	291
iii. 1,	156
iii. 7,	6
ix. f.,	235 f.
ix. 6,	267

1 SAMUEL—continued.
CHAP.	PAGE
ix. 9,	65
x. 6, 10,	46
xv. 16,	46
xvi. 14,	273
xviii. 10,	46
xxviii. 3, 9,	227, 230
xxviii. 6, 15,	220
xxviii. 7 ff.,	225

2 SAMUEL.
v. 23 f.,	217 f.
vii. 27,	22
xx. 18 f.,	275

1 KINGS.
iii. 5 ff.,	228
v. 12 f.,	425
ix. 22,	229
xvii.,	236
xvii. 1, 20 f.,	95
xix. 2–15,	66
xix. 18,	266
xxii. 5–28,	235
xxii. 21–23,	54
xxii. 22 f.,	273

2 KINGS.
i.,	236
iii. 27,	225
iv.–viii.,	236
ix. 11,	67
xvi. 3 f.,	214
xix. 7,	273
xxi. 6,	227
xxxiii. 24,	227

1 CHRONICLES.
xii. 18,	46, 54
xxiii. 9,	284

2 CHRONICLES.
xxiv. 20,	46
xxxiii. 6,	214

EZRA.
iii. 2,	267

NEHEMIAH.
viii. 8, 12,	445, 451
xii. 24, 36,	267

JOB.
iv. 6,	34
iv. 12–17,	43
iv. 12–21,	228
xiii. 23,	39
xv. 3,	36
xv. 4,	34
xv. 8,	43
xxii. 4,	34

JOB—continued.
CHAP.	PAGE
xxvii. 3,	39
xxxi. 26 f.,	214
xxxiii. 15–17,	228
xxxiii. 23,	75
xxxviii. 1–xlii. 6,	35, 43
xlii.,	39
xlii. 2–6,	23
xlii. 4, 5,	22

PSALMS.
ii. 6,	112
ii. 7,	267
v. 8,	144
xvi. 3,	287
xviii.,	295
xxii. 17,	386
xxv. 4,	36, 144
xxvii. 1,	295
xxvii. 11,	144
xxxii.,	278
xxxii. 8,	144
xxxiv. 10,	287
xxxvi. 2,	281
xxxvi. 9,	142, 146
xxxvi. 10,	295
xl. 6,	43 f.
xl. 7,	22
xlv.,	425
xlvii.,	189
xlix. 8 ff.,	112
l.,	261
li. 13–15,	278
lviii. 6,	229
lxiii.,	261
lxvii.,	189
lxviii.,	189
lxxiii.,	291
lxxiv. 9,	156
lxxvi. 8–12,	32
lxxxv.,	97
lxxxvi. 11,	144
lxxxvii.,	189
xc. 1,	267
cix.,	425
cxix. 18,	22
cxix. 18–27,	444
cxix. 27–32,	144
cxix. 105,	142
cxix. 142–160,	144
cxix. 142, 151, 160,	143
cxxii.,	189
cxxiv.–cxxvi.,	189
cxxxv. 4,	284
cxxxix. 17, 23,	64
cxliii. 11,	278
cl.,	278

PROVERBS.
i. 20,	304
ii. 32,	36

INDEX OF SCRIPTURE REFERENCES. 479

PROVERBS—continued.		ISAIAH—continued.		JEREMIAH—continued.	
CHAP.	PAGE	CHAP.	PAGE	CHAP.	PAGE
viii. 1,	304	xxix. 13,	249	vii. 22 f.,	249
ix. 13,	36	xxix. 13, 18,	105	viii. 8 f.,	243, 249
xvi. 27,	295	xxix. 19,	68	ix. 23 f.,	243, 249
xv. 22,	36	xxix. 21,	304	ix. 24 f.,	138
xvi. 10,	220	xxix. 23–29,	138	ix. 24–x. 16,	261
xviii. 2,	281	xxx. 1,	234	x. 1–10,	231
xx. 5,	274	xxx. 10,	65	x. 10,	143
xx. 19,	36	xxx. 19–22,	36, 105	x. 12–16,	138
xx. 27,	295	xxx. 21,	26, 144	xiv. 1–xvii. 8,	235
xxv. 9,	36	xxx. 22–32,	261	xv. 15–21,	67
xxv. 14,	36	xxxiv. 16 f.,	378	xvii. 9,	281
xxviii. 4, 5, 7,	243	xxxviii. 7,	239	xvii. 13,	295
xxix. 1,	291	xxxviii. 21,	76	xviii. 18,	156
xxix. 18,	156	xl.–lxvi.,	293, 295 f., 313	xxiii. 9–24,	67
xxx. 1–14,	242	xl. 12 ff.,	138	xxiii. 16,	48, 281
		xl. 60,	183	xxiii. 18,	23 f.
ECCLESIASTES.		xli. 5,	52	xxiii. 18–22,	75
ii. 18,	284	xlii. 1–4,	86	xxiii. 21,	48
iii. 14,	31	xliii. 1–4,	56	xxiii. 25–32,	228
x. 20,	9 f.	xliii. 27,	75	xxiii. 25–40,	128
		xliv. 26 ff.,	56	xxiii. 29,	70
ISAIAH.		xlv. 19,	304	xxiii. 30–40,	249
i. 2,	162	xlvii. 9, 12,	229	xxiii. 32,	48
i. 3,	138	xlvii. 11, 15,	227	xxvii. 9,	228
i. 10–17,	249	xlvii. 13,	231	xxviii.,	235
i. 10–20,	105	xlviii. 4,	296	xxix. 26,	67
i. 24–31,	261	xlviii. 16,	296	xxxi. 31–34,	249
ii. 3,	156	l. 4,	53	xxxi. 33 f.,	96, 106
ii. 5,	142	l. 4–9,	22, 56	xxxi. 34,	34
ii. 6,	93, 221	l. 5,	22	xxxii.,	150
iii. 3,	229	l. 10,	52	xxxiii. 19–22,	150
v. 1–7,	75	lii. 8,	57	xxxiv. 34 ff.,	53
vi.,	54	liii. 6,	453	xxxv. 4,	267
vii. 1–17,	239	liv. 13,	34, 53, 106	xlii. 1–7,	156
vii. 11,	239	lvi. 10,	57	xliv.,	235
vii. 19 f.,	95	lvii. 3,	230		
viii. 1–4,	239	lvii. 9 f.,	197	LAMENTATIONS.	
viii. 11,	64	lvii. 21,	95	ii. 9,	156
viii. 11–13,	30	lix. 10,	52		
viii. 19,	214	lix. 21,	279	EZEKIEL.	
ix. 4,	93	lxi. 1,	296	i.–iii.,	54
x. 24–xi. 14,	64	lxiii. 7–lxvi.,	76	ii. 2,	54
xi. 2,	34	lxiii. 11,	279	iii. 12, 24,	54
xiv. 4–23,	63	lxvi. 7–9,	189	iii. 14,	64, 67
xviii. 4–6,	57	lxvi. 9,	162	iii. 16–21,	94
xix.,	202, 386			iii. 17,	57
xix. 1,	285	JEREMIAH.		vii. 26,	156
xix. 3,	273	i.,	54	viii. 3,	54
xx. 7,	218	i. 4–19,	59, 67	xi. 5,	54
xxi. 6–10,	57	i. 10,	167	xi. 19,	279
xxi. 11,	57, 167, 237	ii. 11,	162	xii. 21–xiv. 11,	94, 249
xxi. 13,	237	ii. 13,	295	xiii. 2 ff.,	48
xxii. 4,	6	ii. 18,	197	xiii. 5,	76
xxii. 14,	95	ii. 31,	138	xiii. 17–23,	220
xxviii.–xxxii.,	93	ii. 36,	197	xvii. 2,	63
xxviii. 7 ff.,	67	iii. 8,	32	xviii. 31,	278
xxviii. 7, 15,	234	vi. 17,	217	xxi. 3,	63
xxix.,	93	vii. f.,	217	xxi. 21,	225
xxix. 9 ff.,	67	vii.–xliv.,	304	xxiv. 3,	63
xxix. 10,	273	vii. 2 f.,	304	xxxii. 9 ff.,	291

EZEKIEL—continued.

CHAP.	PAGE
xxxiii. 1-9,	94
xxxiii. 27,	57, 59
xxxvi. 17-28,	279
xliii. 5,	54

DANIEL.

CHAP.	PAGE
viii. 24,	287
ix.,	451
x. 1,	6
x. 4-10,	130
x. 8 ff.,	66
xii. 7,	287
xii. 11,	132

HOSEA.

CHAP.	PAGE
iii. 4,	220
iv.,	304
iv. 1,	34
iv. 12,	220, 273
v. 4,	273
v. 15,	26
viii. 12,	343
ix. 7,	54, 67
xii. 10,	51
xii. 13,	50

JOEL.

CHAP.	PAGE
i. 12,	304
ii. 19-iv. 21,	64, 228, 277
ii. 28,	65
iii. 5,	266

AMOS.

CHAP.	PAGE
i. 2-ii. 16,	56
iii. 3-8,	67
iii. 7,	24, 36, 75
v. 25,	249
vi. 2,	138
vii. f.,	304
vii. 1-9,	63
vii. 12,	65
vii. 12-14,	85
viii. 11 f.,	26, 282
ix. 7,	138
ix. 8 ff.,	266

OBADIAH.

CHAP.	PAGE
i.,	68

MICAH.

CHAP.	PAGE
i.,	304
ii.-iii.,	93
ii. 11,	70, 93
iii. 8,	70, 93
iv. f.,	64
iv. 1-4,	202
iv. 5,	144, 162
v. 11,	229
vi. 1, 9,	304

MICAH—continued.

CHAP.	PAGE
vi. 6-8,	249
vii. 4, 7,	57
vii. 8,	295
vii. 14,	197

NAHUM.

CHAP.	PAGE
iii. 4,	229

HABAKKUK.

CHAP.	PAGE
i.-iii.,	76
ii. 1 ff.,	57
ii. 6,	63

HAGGAI.

CHAP.	PAGE
i. 13,	56

ZECHARIAH.

CHAP.	PAGE
vii. f.,	98
ix.-xiv.,	415
ix. 6,	191
ix. 9-xi. 12,	64
x. 2,	228
x. 4,	191
xi. 4 ff.,	167
xiii. 2,	273
xiii. 2-6,	96
xiii. 4,	97
xiv. 16-19,	202

MALACHI.

CHAP.	PAGE
iii. 1,	56
iii. 5,	101
iii. 17,	284
iv. 4,	101
iv. 5,	101

MATTHEW.

CHAP.	PAGE
ii.,	231
iii. 3,	125
v. 13-16,	133
v. 19,	449
v. 21 ff.,	124, 252
v. 21-40,	255
v. 33-37,	127
v. 48,	109
vi. 7,	201, 250
vi. 22 f.,	138
vi. 26-28,	138
vi. 29,	138
vii. 21-23,	252
ix. 28,	232
ix. 36,	453
x.,	132
x. 16,	226
x. 26, 31,	32
x. 27,	133
x. 28,	30
xi. 9,	107
xii. 34-36,	138

MATTHEW—continued.

CHAP.	PAGE
xii. 36 f.,	118, 127
xii. 39,	282
xiii.,	132
xiii. 3 ff.,	138
xiii., 13-17,	133
xiii. 52,	127, 447
xiv. 5,	107
xiv. 27,	32
xvi. 4,	282
xvi. 17,	281
xvii. 7,	32
xviii. 6,	232
xviii. 17,	201, 250
xix. 5 f.,	453
xix. 8,	117
xx. 25-28,	109
xx. 28,	110
xxi. 26,	107
xxii. 21,	109
xxii. 41-45,	117
xxiii. 2-36,	255
xxiii. 16-22,	127
xxiii. 28 f.,	26
xxiii. 37 f.,	217
xxiv.,	132
xxiv. f.,	217
xxiv. 11, 24,	252
xxiv. 15,	132
xxiv. 36,	118
xxiv. 45-47,	86
xxv.,	132
xxv. 44 f.,	252
xxviii. 5, 10,	32

MARK.

CHAP.	PAGE
i. 11,	102
ii. 25,	138
iv. 41,	33
v. 36,	32, 232
vi. 15,	107
viii. 27-30,	108
viii. 28,	107
ix. 7,	102
ix. 23 f.,	232
ix. 42,	232
ix. 49 f.,	138
x. 28,	32
xi. 1-10,	108
xi. 22-25,	280
xv. 2,	108

LUKE.

CHAP.	PAGE
iv. 16-21,	451
v. 8-10,	33
xii. 13-15,	113
xii. 24-28,	138
xii. 42-44,	86
xii. 57,	138
xiii. 1-5,	138

INDEX OF SCRIPTURE REFERENCES. 481

LUKE—continued.
CHAP.	PAGE
xiii. 32,	109
xxiv. 13-32,	35

JOHN.
CHAP.	PAGE
i. 1-18,	118
i. 4 ff.,	143
i. 14, 17,	122
i. 14-18,	120
i. 17,	118, 122
i. 21-25,	107
i. 32,	113
i. 51,	113
ii. 18 f.,	282
iii. 1 ff.,	133
iii. 21,	122
iii. 34,	113
iv. 7 ff.,	133
iv. 19,	107
iv. 21,	217
iv. 23 f.,	122
iv. 24,	143
iv. 28,	282
v. 39,	450
v. 45-47,	117
vi. 14,	107
vi. 30 ff.,	282
vi. 47-xxi. 15,	232
vi. 66-70,	108
vii. 16-18,	282
vii. 17,	116
vii. 22,	117
vii. 23,	449
vii. 40,	107
viii. 5 ff.,	124
viii. 9,	9
viii. 12,	143, 145
viii. 32,	143, 145
viii. 39-58,	126
ix. 17,	107
x. 8,	124, 252, 255
x. 35,	449
xi. 25,	146
xi. 51,	269
xii. 12-36,	108
xii. 28-30,	103
xii. 37,	282
xiv. 6,	146
xiv. 11 f.,	116, 282
xiv. 12-14,	280
xvi. 23 f.,	280
xvii. 12,	118
xviii. 33-37,	108
xviii. 37 f.,	114

ACTS.
CHAP.	PAGE
ii.-v.,	36
ii. 2-6,	103
ii. 22-40,	256

ACTS—continued.
CHAP.	PAGE
ii. 34 f.,	256
ii. 38-40,	121
ii. 39,	256
ii. 43,	33
iii. 12-26,	121
iv. 8-12,	121
v. 5,	33
v. 11,	33
v. 32,	393
vii.,	126
viii. 9-24,	299
viii. 39,	393
ix. 1-19,	43
ix. 2,	144
ix. 4 ff.,	103
ix. 4-8,	66
x. 19,	393
xi. 12,	393
xiii. 2,	393
xiii. 6-12,	299
xv. 28,	393
xvi. 16,	227
xix. 9-23,	144
xix. 11-19,	299
xxi. 11,	393
xxii. 5 ff.,	43
xxii. 21,	256
xxvi. 12 ff.,	43

ROMANS.
CHAP.	PAGE
i. 19 f.,	204
i. 24-32,	260
ii. 17-24,	250
iii. 19,	450
xii. 6,	130
xv. 4,	450

1 CORINTHIANS.
CHAP.	PAGE
i. 22,	239
iii. 19,	449
iv. 6,	449
vi. 16,	453
vii. 40,	136, 137, 393
x. 11,	450
xii.	130
xiii. 12,	62
xiv.,	130
xiv. 27 f.,	70
xiv. 32,	130, 137

2 CORINTHIANS.
CHAP.	PAGE
iii. 6, 15,	450
iii. 7-15,	124
iii. 13-16,	126
vii. 15,	32
xii. 1-10,	134

GALATIANS.
CHAP.	PAGE
i. 15 f.,	43
ii. 14,	201
iii. 19 f.,	76, 124

EPHESIANS.
CHAP.	PAGE
i. 10,	111
ii. 12,	257
ii. 13, 17,	256
v. 31 f.,	453

PHILIPPIANS.
CHAP.	PAGE
ii. 12,	32
iii. 13,	136
iii. 15,	43, 393

1 THESSALONIANS.
CHAP.	PAGE
ii. 14-16,	260
iv. 15,	393
v. 1,	393

1 TIMOTHY.
CHAP.	PAGE
iii. 16,	395
iv. 8,	153
v. 11,	377

2 TIMOTHY.
CHAP.	PAGE
i. 7,	273
iii. 15-17,	396
iii. 16,	153, 451
iv. 17,	377

TITUS.
CHAP.	PAGE
i. 2,	111
iii. 8,	153

HEBREWS.
CHAP.	PAGE
xi. 24-28,	126

1 PETER.
CHAP.	PAGE
ii. 21-25,	125
ii. 25,	453
iv. 3,	260
iv. 11,	128

2 PETER.
CHAP.	PAGE
iii. 16,	452

1 JOHN.
CHAP.	PAGE
i. 5-7,	143
i. 6, 8,	122

EWALD I.   2 H

1 JOHN—continued.		2 JOHN.		REVELATION—continued.	
CHAP.	PAGE		PAGE	CHAP.	PAGE
ii. 8–10,	143	1–4,	122	i. 17,	66
ii. 21,	122			ii. 7,	123, 393
iii. 19,	122	3 JOHN.		ii. 17,	123
iv. 1,	273	1–4,	122	xiv. 13,	123
iv. 6,	122, 273			xviii. 2,	273
iv. 8,	143	REVELATION.		xix. 10,	129, 130, 393
iv. 16,	143			xxii. 9,	130
iv. 18,	32	i. 5,	292	xxii. 17,	123
v. 21,	261	i. 6,	287		

THE END.

www.ingramcontent.com/pod-product-compliance
Lightning Source LLC
Chambersburg PA
CBHW071432300426
44114CB00013B/1407